EYIEL Monographs is a subseries of the European Yearbook of International Economic Law (EYIEL). It contains scholarly works in the fields of European and international economic law, in particular WTO law, international investment law, international monetary law, law of regional economic integration, external trade law of the EU and EU internal market law. The series does not include edited volumes. EYIEL Monographs are peer-reviewed by the series editors and external reviewers.

More information about this subseries at http://www.springer.com/series/15744

European Yearbook of International
Economic Law

# EYIEL Monographs - Studies in European and International Economic Law

Volume 14

**Series Editors**
Marc Bungenberg, Saarbrücken, Germany
Christoph Herrmann, Passau, Germany
Markus Krajewski, Erlangen, Germany
Jörg Philipp Terhechte, Lüneburg, Germany
Andreas R. Ziegler, Lausanne, Switzerland

María José Luque Macías

# Re-Politicising International Investment Law in Latin America through the Duty to Regulate Paradigm

 Springer

María José Luque Macías
Landau in the Palatinate, Germany

ISSN 2364-8392          ISSN 2364-8406   (electronic)
European Yearbook of International Economic Law
ISSN 2524-6658          ISSN 2524-6666   (electronic)
EYIEL Monographs - Studies in European and International Economic Law
ISBN 978-3-030-73271-4          ISBN 978-3-030-73272-1   (eBook)
https://doi.org/10.1007/978-3-030-73272-1

This Springer imprint is published by the registered company Springer Nature Switzerland AG.
The registered company address is: Gewerbestrasse 11, 6330 Cham, Switzerland

# Preface

The development of the 'duty to regulate' paradigm in the present study is an attempt to revisit the long-standing critical stand of Latin American countries towards international legal instruments protecting foreign investment and steer it towards the contentious issues which, from a human rights law perspective, should be addressed.

By using Latin America as a case example, this monograph invites international investment law (IIL) scholars to integrate international human rights law (IHRL) in their analysis. These legal standards not only indisputably apply to states in the investment context, but also normatively inform foreign investors' responsbilities throughout the undertaking of their economic activities in these countries. Concerning human rights scholars, this work provides a normative tool to frame the issues of contention regarding the IIL regime's operation and to articulate their views in a way that IIL is familiar with while consistent with IHRL.

This monograph, which was originally submitted with the title 'International Investment Protection and the Duty of Latin American Host States to Regulate Private Foreign Investment in Furtherance of Human Rights', was the result of many years of research at the Law Faculty of the FAU Erlangen-Nürnberg.

This book owes much to the many persons and institutions that inspired and supported me throughout this path. I am most grateful to my doctoral supervisor, Professor Dr. Markus Krajewski, for his support and guidance during the years of this doctoral project. I also thank my second examiner, Professor Dr. Laura Clerico, for her comments and constant critical exchange. This project would have never been possible without the financial support of the doctoral scholarship provided by the German Academic Exchange Service (DAAD) and the grant of the STIBET-DAAD Program for supporting foreign doctoral candidates, provided by the FAU Erlangen-Nürnberg.

In addition, I want to thank all my friends and colleagues in Erlangen for their immense support. My gratitude also goes to Mxolisi and Martin for the proofreadings and to Diego and Darwin, for assisting me in resolving all the technicalities that were required to publish this monograph.

I dedicate this book to my parents, Nelly and Isidro.

Landau, Germany                                                    María José Luque Macías
January, 2021

# Contents

1 Introduction .......................................................... 1
   1.1 Setting the Scene .................................................. 1
       1.1.1 The Ways and Moments in Which IIL Frustrates States'
           Protection of Human Rights in Latin America .......... 1
       1.1.2 The Functional Underpinning of IIL as the Reason Behind
           the Limited Success of Human Rights Argumentation in
           States' Favour ..................................... 8
       1.1.3 The Need for Re-politicising IIL in View of Its Increasing
           Problematic Interplay with States' Protection of Human
           Rights ............................................ 11
   1.2 Hypothesis, Aims and Structure of This Study ............... 14
   1.3 Methodology and Significance .......................... 16
   References ........................................................ 18

2 The Politicisation of International Legal Instruments Protecting
   Foreign Investment in Latin America Through States' Articulation
   of Sovereign Rights ................................................ 23
   2.1 Politicisation Through States' Articulation of the Right to Freely
       Determine the Legal Scope of Foreign Property Rights' Protection
       (1830–1930) ...................................... 24
       2.1.1 Definition of States' Obligations vis-à-vis Foreign Nationals
           in Case of Pecuniary Damages ..................... 29
           2.1.1.1 Legal Doctrines and Domestic State Practice .... 29
           2.1.1.2 Regional State Practice .................... 32
       2.1.2 Establishment of Limitations Upon Inter-State Arbitration
           of Diplomatic Protection Claims ................... 36
           2.1.2.1 Denial of Justice and Local Remedies Rules .... 36
           2.1.2.2 By Means of the Calvo Clause in Investor-State
                Contracts ............................... 39
       2.1.3 Preliminary Conclusions .......................... 41

2.2   Politicisation Through States' Articulation of the Right to
      Expropriate Foreign Property (1930–1980) . . . . . . . . . . . . . . . . .   42
      2.2.1   Definition of States' Obligations Vis-à-vis Foreign
              Nationals
              in Case of Expropriation of Property Rights . . . . . . . . . . .   46
              2.2.1.1   Domestic State Practice . . . . . . . . . . . . . . . . .   46
              2.2.1.2   Regional State Practice . . . . . . . . . . . . . . . . .   50
      2.2.2   Establishment of Limitations Upon International Arbitration
              of Investor-State Contract-Based Disputes . . . . . . . . . . . .   53
              2.2.2.1   National and Regional Practice . . . . . . . . . . . . .   53
              2.2.2.2   Latin American Refusal to Adhere to the ICSID
                        Convention . . . . . . . . . . . . . . . . . . . . . . . . . .   56
      2.2.3   Preliminary Conclusions . . . . . . . . . . . . . . . . . . . . . . . .   58
2.3   De-Politicisation of International Legal Instruments Protecting
      Foreign Investment (1990–present)? . . . . . . . . . . . . . . . . . . . . . .   59
      2.3.1   Consolidation of the International Investment Treaty
              Regime . . . . . . . . . . . . . . . . . . . . . . . . . . . . . . . . . . .   62
              2.3.1.1   National Approach Towards Investment Treaty
                        Protection . . . . . . . . . . . . . . . . . . . . . . . . . . .   62
                        2.3.1.1.1   Ratification of Bilateral Investment
                                    Treaties (BITs) . . . . . . . . . . . . . . . .   62
                        2.3.1.1.2   Ratification of International Arbitration
                                    Rules . . . . . . . . . . . . . . . . . . . . . .   65
              2.3.1.2   Regional Approach Towards Investment Treaty
                        Protection . . . . . . . . . . . . . . . . . . . . . . . . . . .   67
                        2.3.1.2.1   South American Context . . . . . . . . . .   67
                        2.3.1.2.2   For the Americas? . . . . . . . . . . . . . .   69
              2.3.1.3   Preliminary Conclusions . . . . . . . . . . . . . . . . .   71
      2.3.2   Concerns About Investment Treaty-based Dispute
              Settlement . . . . . . . . . . . . . . . . . . . . . . . . . . . . . . . .   73
              2.3.2.1   The Interpretation and Application of States'
                        Obligation Under the FET Standard . . . . . . . . . .   73
              2.3.2.2   The Interpretation and Application of States'
                        Obligation in Cases of an Indirect Expropriation . .   78
              2.3.2.3   Preliminary Conclusions . . . . . . . . . . . . . . . . .   82
      2.3.3   Re-Politicisation of IIL Through States' Articulation of the
              Right to Regulate . . . . . . . . . . . . . . . . . . . . . . . . . . . .   83
              2.3.3.1   National Approaches . . . . . . . . . . . . . . . . . . . .   84
                        2.3.3.1.1   Reformed IIAs . . . . . . . . . . . . . . . .   84
                        2.3.3.1.2   Denunciation of BITs and the ICSID
                                    Convention . . . . . . . . . . . . . . . . . . .   89
                        2.3.3.1.3   The Adoption of CFIAs . . . . . . . . . . .   93
              2.3.3.2   (Sub)regional Approaches . . . . . . . . . . . . . . . . .   95
                        2.3.3.2.1   Along the Pacific . . . . . . . . . . . . . . .   95

2.3.3.2.2 The UNASUR Centre for the Settlement
of Investment Disputes . . . . . . . . . . . 97
2.3.3.3 Preliminary Conclusions . . . . . . . . . . . . . . . . . 98
2.4 Conclusion . . . . . . . . . . . . . . . . . . . . . . . . . . . . . . . . . 98
References . . . . . . . . . . . . . . . . . . . . . . . . . . . . . . . . . . . . 101

3 **The States' Duty to Regulate Foreign Investment Activities Under
IHRL As a Paradigm for Re-politicising IIL** . . . . . . . . . . . . . . . . . . 105
3.1 The Duty to Regulate in Universal Human Rights Law . . . . . . . . 108
3.1.1 The Duty to Regulate in General . . . . . . . . . . . . . . . . . . 108
3.1.1.1 The Duty to Regulate Under the UN Instruments . . 108
3.1.1.2 The Duty to Regulate Under the ICESCR . . . . . . 111
3.1.2 The Duty to Regulate in Furtherance of the Right to Water . 118
3.1.2.1 Legal Basis . . . . . . . . . . . . . . . . . . . . . . . . . 118
3.1.2.1.1 Universal Human Rights Treaties . . . . 118
3.1.2.1.2 Customary International Law . . . . . . . 121
3.1.2.2 Scope of Application . . . . . . . . . . . . . . . . . . . 129
3.1.2.2.1 In the Context of Foreign Investment
in Water Facilities and Services . . . . . 130
3.1.2.2.2 In the Context of Foreign Investment
Activities' Pollution or Depletion of
Water Resources . . . . . . . . . . . . . . 133
3.1.3 Interim Conclusion . . . . . . . . . . . . . . . . . . . . . . . . . . . 135
3.2 The Duty to Regulate Under Inter-American Human Rights Law . . 137
3.2.1 The Duty to Regulate in General . . . . . . . . . . . . . . . . . . 137
3.2.1.1 The Duty to Regulate Under Inter-American
Instruments . . . . . . . . . . . . . . . . . . . . . . . . . 137
3.2.1.2 The Duty to Regulate Under the ACHR . . . . . . . 140
3.2.2 The Duty to Regulate in Furtherance of Indigenous
People's Land Rights . . . . . . . . . . . . . . . . . . . . . . . . . 145
3.2.2.1 Legal Basis . . . . . . . . . . . . . . . . . . . . . . . . . 145
3.2.2.1.1 International Treaties and Non-binding
Instruments . . . . . . . . . . . . . . . . . . 145
3.2.2.1.2 Customary International Law . . . . . . . 150
3.2.2.2 Scope of Application . . . . . . . . . . . . . . . . . . . 154
3.2.2.2.1 In the Context of Foreign Property
Rights' Interference with Indigenous
People's Rights to Possess Traditional
Lands and Territories . . . . . . . . . . . . 157
3.2.2.2.2 In Cases Where Natural Resources'
Exploration and Exploitation Activities
May Pose a Real and Imminent Risk
upon Indigenous People's Survival . . . 158

3.2.3   Interim Conclusion . . . . . . . . . . . . . . . . . . . . . . . . . . . . . . 162

3.3   Conclusion . . . . . . . . . . . . . . . . . . . . . . . . . . . . . . . . . . . . . . . 165

References . . . . . . . . . . . . . . . . . . . . . . . . . . . . . . . . . . . . . . . . . . . . . . 169

**4  Re-politicisation of IIL by States Through an Articulation of Their
Duty to Regulate in IIAs** . . . . . . . . . . . . . . . . . . . . . . . . . . . . . . . . . . 171

4.1   Current Deployment of Human Rights Argumentation Before ISDS
Tribunals . . . . . . . . . . . . . . . . . . . . . . . . . . . . . . . . . . . . . . . . . . . . 173

    4.1.1   Invoking IHRL as Applicable Law in ISDS? . . . . . . . . . . . 173

        4.1.1.1   In Cases Arising in the Context of Investors'
Provision in the Drinking Water Services . . . . . . 173

        4.1.1.2   In Cases Arising Out of Investors' Exploration
and Exploitation Activities of Natural Resources . 179

    4.1.2   Articulation of the Duty to Regulate on Questions of
Substantive IIA Obligations . . . . . . . . . . . . . . . . . . . . . . 184

        4.1.2.1   On Questions of the FET Standard . . . . . . . . . . . 184

        4.1.2.2   On Questions of Indirect Expropriation . . . . . . . . 190

    4.1.3   Articulation of the Duty to Regulate on Questions of
Procedural IIA Rights . . . . . . . . . . . . . . . . . . . . . . . . . . . 193

        4.1.3.1   On Questions of States' Right to Challenge
Tribunals' Jurisdiction and/or the Admissibility
of Investors' Claims . . . . . . . . . . . . . . . . . . . . . 193

        4.1.3.2   On Questions of States' Right to Submit
Counterclaims . . . . . . . . . . . . . . . . . . . . . . . . . . 197

    4.1.4   Interim Conclusion . . . . . . . . . . . . . . . . . . . . . . . . . . . . . 203

4.2   Required IIAs Reforms to Strengthen States' Duty to Regulate
in IIL . . . . . . . . . . . . . . . . . . . . . . . . . . . . . . . . . . . . . . . . . . . . . . . 205

    4.2.1   Reformed IIAs Substantive Provisions . . . . . . . . . . . . . . . 205

        4.2.1.1   Explicit Reference to States' Duty to Regulate
Protected Investment . . . . . . . . . . . . . . . . . . . . . 205

        4.2.1.2   Imposing Investor Obligations . . . . . . . . . . . . . . 207

    4.2.2   Reformed IIAs Procedural Provisions . . . . . . . . . . . . . . . . 210

        4.2.2.1   Jurisdictional Clauses . . . . . . . . . . . . . . . . . . . . 210

        4.2.2.2   Counterclaims . . . . . . . . . . . . . . . . . . . . . . . . . . 212

    4.2.3   Interim Conclusion . . . . . . . . . . . . . . . . . . . . . . . . . . . . . 214

4.3   Legal Consequences Faced by States for Abstaining from
Articulating Their Duty to Regulate in IIAs . . . . . . . . . . . . . . . . 215

4.4   Conclusion . . . . . . . . . . . . . . . . . . . . . . . . . . . . . . . . . . . . . . . . 217

References . . . . . . . . . . . . . . . . . . . . . . . . . . . . . . . . . . . . . . . . . . . . . . 218

**5  Re-politicisation of IIL by a Regional ISDS Tribunal Through Its
Engagement with Inter-Regime Tensions** . . . . . . . . . . . . . . . . . . . . . 221

5.1   Hypothetical Scenarios Likely to Cause Inter-Regime Tensions
During the Conduct of Arbitration Proceedings . . . . . . . . . . . . . . 222

5.1.1  ISDS Tribunal's Review of States' Measure Adopted
in Compliance with a Human Rights Body's Interim
Measure . . . . . . . . . . . . . . . . . . . . . . . . . . . . . . . . . . . .  222
5.1.2  A Provisional Measure Issued by an Investor-State Tribunal
Encounters a Human Rights Body's Interim Measure . . . . .  223
5.2  Legal Strategies Available to a Regional ISDS Tribunal for
Settling Inter-Regime Tensions . . . . . . . . . . . . . . . . . . . . . . . . . .  226
5.2.1  Tribunal's Settlement of Inter-Regime Tensions *by Itself* . . .  226
5.2.2  Tribunal's Settlement of Inter-Regime Tensions with the
Assistance of Human Rights Bodies . . . . . . . . . . . . . . . . .  227
5.3  Additional Legal Strategies Conducive to Underpin Tribunal's
Engagement with Inter-Regime Tensions . . . . . . . . . . . . . . . . . . .  228
5.4  Conclusions . . . . . . . . . . . . . . . . . . . . . . . . . . . . . . . . . . . . . . .  229
References . . . . . . . . . . . . . . . . . . . . . . . . . . . . . . . . . . . . . . . . . . . .  230

6   **Conclusions and Outlook** . . . . . . . . . . . . . . . . . . . . . . . . . . . . . .  231

**Table of Cases** . . . . . . . . . . . . . . . . . . . . . . . . . . . . . . . . . . . . . . . . .  237

**Table of Legal Instruments** . . . . . . . . . . . . . . . . . . . . . . . . . . . . . . .  249

**Other Conventions, International Instruments, and Related Links** . . . .  263

**Table of State Practice** . . . . . . . . . . . . . . . . . . . . . . . . . . . . . . . . . .  267

**References** . . . . . . . . . . . . . . . . . . . . . . . . . . . . . . . . . . . . . . . . . . .  273

# Abbreviations/Acronyms

| | |
|---|---|
| 1899 Hague Convention | Convention adopted for the Settlement of International Disputes |
| ACHR | American Convention on Human Rights |
| ADRDM | American Declaration of the Rights and Duties of Man |
| ADRIP | American Declaration on the Rights of Indigenous Peoples |
| ALBA (Spanish acronym) | Bolivarian Alternative for the Americas |
| ANCOM | Andean Common Market |
| ARSIWA | Articles on Responsibility of States for Internationally Wrongful Acts |
| BITs | Bilateral Investment Treaties |
| CAITISA (Spanish acronym) | The Ecuadorian Citizens' Commission for a Comprehensive Audit of Investment Protection Treaties |
| CESCR | Committee on Economic, Social and Cultural Rights |
| CFIAs | Cooperation and Facilitation Investment Agreements |
| CIL | Customary International Law |
| CPTPP | Comprehensive and Progressive Agreement for Trans-Pacific Partnership |
| CSR | Corporate social responsibility |
| DPAIC | Draft-Pan African Investment Code |
| ECLAC | Economic Commission for Latin American and the Caribbean |
| ECOWAS | Economic Community of West African States |
| ECtHR | European Court of Human Rights |
| ESC rights | Economic, social and cultural rights |
| ESIA | Environmental and Social Impact Assessment |
| FCN treaties | Friendship, Commerce and Navigation Treaties |

| FET | Fair and equitable treatment |
| FPIC | Free, prior and informed consent |
| FTA | Free trade agreement |
| FTAA | Free Trade Agreement of the Americas |
| FTC (NAFTA) | Free Trade Commission (NAFTA) |
| GATS | General Agreement on Trade in Services |
| GATT | General Agreement on Tariffs and Trade |
| HRC | Human Rights Council |
| IACoHR | Inter-American Court of Human Rights |
| IACommHR | Inter-American Commission on Human Rights |
| IBRD | International Bank for Reconstruction and Development |
| ICCPR | International Covenant on Civil and Political Rights |
| ICESCR | International Covenant of Economic, Social and Cultural Rights |
| ICSID | International Centre for Settlement of Investment Disputes |
| ICSID Convention | Convention on the Settlement of Investment Disputes between States and Nationals of Other States |
| IHRL | International Human Rights Law |
| IIA | International Investment Agreement |
| IIL | International Investment Law |
| ILC Fragmentation Report | Report of the Study Group of the International Law Commission on the Fragmentation of International Law: Difficulties Arising from the Diversification and Expansion of International Law |
| ILC | International Law Commission |
| ILO | International Labour Organization |
| ILO Convention 169 | Convention concerning Indigenous and Tribal Peoples in Independent Countries |
| IMF | International Monetary Fund |
| ISDS | Investor-state dispute settlement |
| ISI policy | Import-Substitution Industrialization policy |
| LAFTA | Latin American Free Trade Association |
| MERCOSUR (Spanish acronym) | Southern Common Market |
| MFN | Most-favoured nation |
| MST | Minimum Standard of Treatment |
| NAFTA | North American Free Trade Agreement |
| NCP | National Contact Points |
| NIEO | New International Economic Order |
| OAS | Organization of American States |

| | |
|---|---|
| OECD | Organisation for Economic Co-operation and Development |
| OECD Guidelines | OECD Guidelines for Multinational Enterprises |
| OPIC | Overseas Private Investment Corporation |
| Pacific Alliance Protocol | Additional Protocol to the Framework Agreement of the Pacific Alliance |
| PAHO | Pan American Health Organization |
| PAU | Pan American Union |
| PCA | Permanent Court of Arbitration |
| Protect, Respect and Remedy Framework | Protect, Respect and Remedy: A Framework for Business and Human Rights |
| Report on Business and Human Rights | Report on Business and Human Rights: Inter-American Standards |
| *The Hague Conventions and Declarations of 1899 and 1907* | James Scott (ed), *The Hague Conventions and Declarations of 1899 and 1907* (OUP 1915) |
| *The International Conferences of American States 1889–1928, Scott Collection* | Scott JB (ed) (1931) *The International Conferences of American States 1889–1928; A Collection of the Conventions, Recommendations, Resolutions, Reports, and Motions Adopted by the First Six International Conferences of the American States, and Documents Relating to the Organization of the Conferences.* OUP, New York |
| TPP | Trans-Pacific Partnership |
| UDHR | Universal Declaration of Human Rights |
| UN | United Nations |
| UNASUR (Spanish acronym) | Union of South American Nations |
| UNASUR Centre | UNASUR Centre for the Settlement of Investment Disputes |
| UNCITRAL | United Nations Commission on International Trade Law |
| UNCTAD | United Nations Conference on Trade and Development |
| UNDRIP | United Nations Declaration on the Rights of Indigenous Peoples |
| UNGA | United Nations General Assembly |
| UNGP | UN Guiding Principles on Business and Human Rights |
| UNHRC | United Nations Commission on Human Rights |
| USMCA | United States–Mexico–Canada Agreement |
| VCLT | Vienna Convention on the Law of Treaties |
| WHO | World Health Organization |

# Chapter 1
# Introduction

## 1.1 Setting the Scene

### 1.1.1 The Ways and Moments in Which IIL Frustrates States' Protection of Human Rights in Latin America

International investment law (IIL) protects private foreign investors and their investment against any state action that may adversely impair the legal treatment to which they are entitled under international investment agreements (IIAs). This is usually done by means of investor-state arbitration, the most effective mechanism in investor-state dispute settlement (ISDS). On this basis, transnational corporations investing in the provision of drinking water services have continuously brought investment treaty claims against Argentina, for the executive measures conducive to protect users' right to water.[1] Similarly, an increasing number of Latin American

---

[1] *Compañía de Aguas del Aconquija, S.A. & Compagnie Générale des Eaux, Claimants v Argentine Republic*, ICSID Case No. ARB/97/3, Award (21 November 2000) (*Vivendi v Argentina I*); *Azurix Corp. v Argentine Republic* (I), ICSID Case No. ARB/01/12, Award (14 July 2006) (*Azurix v Argentina I*); *Aguas Cordobesas, S.A., Suez, and Sociedad General de Aguas de Barcelona, S.A. v Argentine Republic*, ICSID Case No. ARB/03/18, Order Taking Note of the Discontinuance of the Proceeding (24 January 2007) no public available (*Aguas Cordobesas and Suez v Argentina*); *Compañiá de Aguas del Aconquija S.A. and Vivendi Universal S.A. v Argentine Republic (formerly Compañía de Aguas del Aconquija, S.A. and Compagnie Générale des Eaux v Argentine Republic)* ICSID Case No. ARB/97/3, Award (20 August 2007) (*Vivendi v Argentina II*); *Impregilo S.p.A. v Argentine Republic*, ICSID Case No. ARB/07/17, Award (June 21, 2011) (*Impregilo v Argentina*); *SAUR International v Argentine Republic*, ICSID Case No. ARB/04/4, Award (22 May 2014) (Spanish version) (*SAUR v Argentina*); *AWG Group Limited v The Argentine Republic*, UNCITRAL (9 May 2015); *Suez, Sociedad General de Aguas de Barcelona, S.A. and Vivendi Universal, S.A. (formerly Aguas Argentinas, S.A., Suez, Sociedad General de Aguas de Barcelona, S.A. and Vivendi Universal, S.A.) v Argentine Republic*, ICSID Case No. ARB/03/19, Award (9 April 2015) (*Suez and Vivendi v Argentina II*); *Suez, Sociedad General de Aguas de Barcelona,*

© The Author(s), under exclusive license to Springer Nature Switzerland AG 2021
M. J. Luque Macías, *Re-Politicising International Investment Law in Latin America through the Duty to Regulate Paradigm*, European Yearbook of International Economic Law 14, https://doi.org/10.1007/978-3-030-73272-1_1

countries have had to respond to claims for regulatory measures taken in the wake of local[2] and indigenous communities' concerns[3] about the negative effect that foreign investment in mining,[4] oil,[5] and even tourism activities may have over their livelihood.[6] More recently, the judicial protection of high-altitude wetlands to safeguard natural sources of water supply has given rise to a growing number of investment treaty claims against Colombia,[7] while a judicial decision issued to preserve glaciers against the performance of nearby mining exploration and exploitation activities nearby could mean the submission of a new investment treaty claim for Argentina in the near future.[8]

On the other side of the spectrum are those in Latin America who are deprived from enjoying their human rights in the investment context, which constantly withstand the adverse human rights impacts of foreign investment activities that derive from states' omission to protect their enjoyment.[9] Within the United Nations (UN) human rights system, for instance, right-holders in Latin America have brought

---

*S.A. and Interagua Servicios Integrales de Agua, S.A. v Argentine Republic*, ICSID Case No. ARB/03/17, Decision on Liability (30 July 2010); *Urbaser S.A. and Consorcio de Aguas Bilbao Bizkaia, Bilbao Biskaia Ur Partzuergoa v The Argentine Republic*, ICSID Case No. ARB/07/26, Award (8 December 2016) (*Urbaser v Argentina*); *Azurix Corp. v Argentine Republic*, ICSID Case No. ARB/03/30 (*Azurix v Argentina II*) no pleadings are publicly available.

[2]See *Pac Rim Cayman LLC v Republic of El Salvador*, ICSID Case No. ARB/09/12 Award (14 October 2016) (*Pac Rim Cayman v El Salvador*).

[3]For investment treaty claims specifically interlinked with indigenous peoples' rights see *Copper Mesa Mining Corporation v Republic of Ecuador*, PCA No. 2012-2, Award (15 March 2016) (*Copper Mesa v Ecuador*); *Bear Creek Mining Corporation v Republic of Peru*, ICSID Case No. ARB/14/2, Award (30 November 2017) (*Bear Creek v Peru*); *South American Silver Limited (Bermuda) v The Plurinational State of Bolivia*, PCA Case No. 2013-15, Award (22 November 2018) (*South American Silver v Bolivia*); *Burlington Resources Inc. v Republic of Ecuador (formerly Burlington Resources Inc. and others v Republic of Ecuador and Empresa Estatal Petróleos del Ecuador (PetroEcuador)*, ICSID Case No. ARB/08/5, Decision on Reconsideration and Award (7 February 2017) (*Burlington v Ecuador*); *Álvarez y Marín Corporación S.A. and others v Republic of Panama*, ICSID Case No. ARB/15/14, Reasoning of the Decision on Respondent's Preliminary Objections pursuant to ICSID Arbitration Rule 41(5) (4 April 2016) (*Alvarez Marin v Panama*).

[4]*Pac Rim Cayman v El Salvador* (n 2); *Copper Mesa v Ecuador* (n 3); *Eco Oro Minerals Corp. v Republic of Colombia*, ICSID Case No. ARB/16/41, Request for Arbitration (8 December 2016) (*Eco Minerals Corp v Colombia*); *Bear Creek v Peru* (n 3); *South American Silver v Bolivia* (n 3).

[5]See *Burlington v Ecuador* (n 3).

[6]See *Alvarez Marin v Panama* (n 3).

[7]*Eco Oro Minerals Corp. v Colombia* (n 4); *Red Eagle Exploration Limited v Republic of Colombia*, ICSID Case No. ARB/18/12, Notice of Intent (14 September 2017); *Galway Gold Inc. v Republic of Colombia*, ICSID Case No. ARB/18/13, Request for Arbitration (Spanish) (21 March 2018). For an overview of the court's decision, see Hill (2016).

[8]See Centro de Informacion Judicial (2019).

[9]Adverse human rights impacts are commonly understood as the business entities' acts conducive to remove or reduce the ability of a third party to enjoy his or her human rights. See High Commissioner of Human Rights of the United Nations, The Corporate Responsibility to Respect Human Rights, An Interpretative Guide (2012) 5.

complaints before the UN Human Rights Council (HRC) to bring to the fore capital-exporting countries' breaches of their extraterritorial human rights obligations in recipient states of their nationals' investment.[10] More frequently, however, they have resorted to the Inter-American human rights systems, to challenge their own states' omission to protect their rights as laid down in the American Convention on Human Rights (ACHR).[11] To illustrate, those affected by foreign investment activities usually request the adoption of precautionary measures before the Inter-American Commission on Human Rights (IACommHR).[12] This is usually done to prevent the irreparable harms that the operation of foreign investment projects may have upon their rights.[13] Yet, if the state omits to follow these precautionary measures, the IACommHR may still request the Inter-American Court of Human Rights (IACoHR), in a case not yet submitted to its jurisdiction, to order the adoption of provisional measures to avoid irreparable harms if the situation at stake is of 'extreme gravity and urgency'.[14] Otherwise, rights holders traditionally seek legal

---

[10]To illustrate, a group of Latin American NGOs submitted a set of reports before the HRC, alleging China's violations of extraterritorial human rights obligations in investment projects within the context of the Universal Periodic Review (UPR) of China's human rights record, see Colectivo sobre Financiamiento e Inversiones Chinas.

[11]See American Convention on Human Rights (adopted 22 November 1969, entered into force 18 July 1978) 1144 UNTS 123 (ACHR).

[12]The IACommHR promotes and protects human rights in its capacity as OAs organ and as a treaty body of the American Convention on Human Rights (ACHR). For an overview of this double function within the Inter-American human rights system, see Sect. 3.2.1.2, Chap. 3.

[13]For illustrations of Commission's precautionary measures requesting to ensure the non-contamination of water sources of indigenous communities by a foreign corporation's minining activities, see *Communities of the Maya People (Sipakepense and Mam) of the Sipacapa and San Miguel Ixtahuacán Municipalities in the Department of San Marcos, Guatemala*, Precautionary Measures 260-07, IACommHR (Communities of the Maya People) (7 December 2017).

[14]ACHR (n 11) art 63 para 2.

remedies before the IACoHR to redress violations of their rights suffered in the context of land,[15] logging,[16] oil,[17] mining,[18] and touristic development projects.[19]

The above scenario shows that IIL and international human rights law (IHRL) promotes the values and objectives of their respective legal regimes through different institutional, procedural and substantive tools, to the point of turning themselves into self-contained regimes.[20] These opposite paths constitute the functional cause of the so-called 'fragmentation' of international law that aims to respond in a decentralised vein to the legal problems associated with globalisation.[21] Yet, although the fragmentation of international law has brought a number of benefits,[22] it has also posed considerable challenges. The overlapping investment and human rights treaty obligations of some Latin American countries clearly exemplifies the normative and institutional frictions that may arise between IIL and IHRL. The following cases illustrate ways and moments in which IIL has thwarted Latin American countries' regulation of foreign investment to hinder related human rights abuses.[23]

---

[15]*Yakye Axa Indigenous Community v Paraguay*, (Merits, Reparations and Costs) Judgement, IACoHR Series C no 125 (17 June 2005) (*Yakye Axa v Paraguay*); *Sawhoyamaxa Indigenous Community v Paraguay*, (Merits, Reparations and Costs) Judgement, IACoHR Series C No. 146 (29 March 2006) (*Sawhoyamaxa v Paraguay*); *Case of the Xákmok Kásek Indigenous Community v Paraguay*, (Merits, Reparations, and Costs) IACoHR Series 214 (24 August 2010) (*Xákmok Kásek v Paraguay*).

[16]*Case of the Mayagna (Sumo) Awas Tingni Community v Nicaragua*, (Merits, Reparations and Costs) Judgement, IACoHR Series C No. 79 (31 August 2001) (*Awas Tingni Community v Nicaragua*).

[17]*Kichwa Indigenous People of Sarayaku v Ecuador*, (Merits and Reparations) Judgement, IACoHR Series C No. 245 (27 June 2012) (*Sarayaku v Ecuador*).

[18]*Case of the Kaliña and Lokono Peoples v Suriname*, (Merits, Reparations and Costs) Judgement IACoHR, Series C No. 309 (25 November 2015) (*Kaliña and Lokono Peoples v Suriname*) para 224; *Caso Comunidad Garifuna de Punta Piedra v Honduras* (Excepciones Preliminares, Fondo, Reparaciones, y Costas) Sentencia, CIDH Serie C No. 304 (8 de Octubre 2015) (*Comunidad Garifuna de Punta Piedra v Honduras*); *Case of the Saramaka People v Suriname*, (Preliminary Objections, Merits, Reparations, and Costs) Judgement, IACoHR Series C No. 172 (28 November 2007) (*Saramaka v Suriname*).

[19]*Caso Comunidad Garifuna Triunfo de la Cruz y sus Miembros v Honduras* (Fondo, Reparaciones, Costas) Sentencia, CIDH Serie C No. 305 (8 de Octubre 2015) (*Comunidad Garifuna Triunfo de la Cruz v Honduras*).

[20]ILC, 'Report of the Study Group of the International Law Commission on the Fragmentation of International Law: Difficulties Arising from the Diversification and Expansion of International Law' (18 July 2006) UN Doc. A/CN.4/L.702 (ILC Fragmentation Report) paras 11–16.

[21]While Peters particularly highlights the institutional and ideational dimensions of international law's fragmentation, she also contends that the root causes of fragmentation lie on functional and political objectives. Peters (2017), pp. 674–678.

[22]Peters (2017), pp. 680–682.

[23]In this study, the term 'human rights' abuses' means the acts of these economic actors conducive to deprive third parties' enjoyment of the human rights codified in internationally recognised human rights instruments, and is used interchangeably with the term 'adverse human rights impacts'. See HRC, 'Report of the Special Representative of the Secretary-General on the issue of human rights and transnational corporations and other business enterprises, John Ruggie, Guiding Principles on

IIL may frustrate the objectives pursued by IHRL at the normative level in the shadow of a submission of an investment treaty-based claim. The host state may exercise self-restrain to regulate foreign investment activities, phenomenon commonly referred to as the 'regulatory chill' effect of ISDS.[24] Bounded rationality is adduced as one of the causes of this regulatory self-restraint of states, and with this, the impossibility of predicting legal outcomes in ISDS as a result of the vague nature of legal standards enshrined in IIAs and the jurisdictional powers of arbitrators to assess them in an expansive vein.[25] Another cause of regulatory chill is arguably the large sums of legal expenses in which respondent states must incur for their defence.[26] In fact, in some cases, the quantum of damages awarded in ISDS has considerably comprised respondent states' coffers.[27] In this context, although the discussion about the 'chilling effect' of ISDS has primarily taken place in connection with states' environmental measures,[28] the *Sawhoyamaxa v Paraguay* case clearly shows how IIL may considerably discourage states' protection of indigenous people's rights in benefit of foreign investment.[29] In this case, Paraguay sought to justify the non-recognition of Sawhoyamaxa people's land rights and the non-restitution of their ancestral lands in the hands of German nationals by invoking its obligation to protect German landowners' rights under the bilateral investment treaty (BIT) in force with Germany.[30] Accordingly, *Sawhoyamaxa v Paraguay* clearly illustrates that host states may prioritise their observance of investment treaty obligations over the protection of human rights considering the policy and monetary implications that are stake when responding to investment treaty claims.

---

Business and Human Rights: Implementing the United Nations "Protect, Respect and Remedy" Framework' (2011) UN Doc. A/HRC/17/31 (UNGP) para 12.

[24] See UNGA, Report of the Special Rapporteur of the Human Rights Council on the rights of indigenous peoples on the impact of international investment and free trade on the human rights of indigenous peoples, A/70/301 (7 August 2015) para 46. See also Bonnitcha (2014), p. 114. According to Tienhaara, ISDS only exerts an *indirect* chilling effect over state's regulatory autonomy that is contingent upon the implementation of *specific* policies. See Tienhaara (2011), p. 615.

[25] In this regard, Poulsen suggests that bounded rationality is also the underlying motive behind developing countries' decision to sign IIAs. See Poulsen (2015). See also, Tienhaara (2011), p. 615.

[26] For a detailed statistical overview of the legal fees incurred by disputing parties in ISDS (such as legal fees for counsels, experts, arbitrators, or remedies), see Gaukrodger and Gordon (2012).

[27] Recent examples of exorbitant quantum of damages in ISDS include two awards issued by arbitral tribunals constituted under the ICSID Convention: an award ordering Pakistan's payment of $5.75 billion in favour of Tethyan Copper Company for breaches of the Australia-Pakistan BIT and an award ordering Venezuela's payment of $8,7 billion in favour of ConocoPhillips companies for violations of the Netherlands-Venezuela BIT. See Hepburn (2019) and Peterson (2019), respectively. Yet, the most outrageous quantum of damages known so far is $ 50 billion in three investment arbitration proceedings commenced against Russia under the Energy Charter Treaty and administered by the Permanent Court of Arbitration (PCA). See Brauch (2014).

[28] To illustrate, see Tienhaara (2018) and Gross (2003).

[29] *Sawhoyamaxa v Paraguay* (n 15).

[30] *Sawhoyamaxa v Paraguay* (n 15) paras 115 lit. b and 137.

Beyond that, the same set of facts may trigger reaction among foreign investors and those facing adverse investment-related impacts leading to recourse in parallel to *ad-hoc* arbitral tribunals and international human rights bodies, respectively, producing an indirect interplay between IIL and IHRL without any direct inter-institutional encounter.[31] Examples of this indirect inter-institutional interplay include (a) the interaction between the provisional measures issued by the IACoHR in favour of Sarayaku indigenous communities[32] and the *Burlington v Ecuador* case, where the same facts provided the cause of action against Ecuador for its omission to guarantee full security and protection to their investment,[33] and (b) the interaction between the 2007 precautionary measure issued by the IACommHR in favour of La Oroya population[34] and the *Renco v Peru* case, submitted by the claimant investor in 2011, following refusal by domestic authorities' to grant reasonable extensions of the environmental management plan that prevented its subsidiary from securing funding to resume operations at the metallurgical complex at la Oroya.[35]

Yet throughout the conduct of investor-state arbitration proceedings, direct inter-institutional interactions might develop, having the potential effect of hindering host states' protection of human rights.[36] The interaction between the protective measures issued by the *Chevron v Ecuador II* tribunal and the precautionary measures almost issued by IACommHR in connection with this investment treaty case clearly portrays the likelihood of troublesome inter-institutional encounters. In *Chevron v Ecuador II*, for example, claimant investors successfully alleged that substantive parts of the domestic judgement issued in the environmental dispute between Lago Agrio plaintiffs and Chevron, where claimant investors were found liable and ordered to pay plaintiffs substantial damages, were corruptly 'ghostwritten' for the competent domestic judge by Lago Agrio plaintiffs' representatives in return for a promise of a bribe's payment resulting from the enforcement of that domestic

---

[31] See Hepburn (2012).

[32] The 2004 provisional measures issued by the IACoHR sought to counteract Ecuador's failure to adopt precautionary measures formerly required by the IACommHR to prevent the irreparable harms that the resumption of an Argentinian oil company's seismic exploration have over their lands and access to water sources. *Provisional Measures regarding Ecuador Matter of Pueblo Indígena Sarayaku*, IACoHR Order (6 July 2004).

[33] See Binder and Hofbauer (2016).

[34] This precautionary measure requested Peru to undertake and provide medical diagnosis and treatment for the health risks faced by La Oroya population resulting from metallurgical activities of the Doe Run Peru, subsidiary of the Renco Group Inc. IACommHR, Community of La Oroya, Peru, Precautionary measures (31 August 2007).

[35] Claimant's Notice of Arbitration and Statement of Claim from the Renco Group, Inc. and Doe Run Peru S.R.LTDA, to the Republic of Peru and Activos Mineros S.A.C (4 April 2011) (Claimant's Notice of Arbitration, Renco v Peru) para 53. Available via ITA Law. https://www.italaw.com/sites/default/files/case-documents/italaw3264.pdf. Accessed 10 December 2020.

[36] Emblematic cases in this context include *Chevron Corporation and Texaco Petroleum Company v The Republic of Ecuador (II)*, PCA Case No. 2009-23, Second Partial Award on Track II (30 August 2018) (*Chevron v Ecuador II*) and *The Renco Group, Inc. v The Republic of Peru*, ICSID Case No. UNCT/13/1, Final Award (9 November 2016) (*Renco v Peru*).

judgement.[37] The potential for institutional clashes arose when the *Chevron v Ecuador II* tribunal issued several interim measures against Ecuador, ordering the suspension of the enforcement of the domestic court's judgement within and outside its jurisdiction,[38] and the Lago Agrio plaintiffs requested, albeit later withdrawn, IACommHR's precautionary measures to have Ecuador abide by these tribunal's interim measures, alleging irreparable harms to their rights of judicial character and their right to life and health.[39] Had Lago Agrio plaintiffs continued with their request and the IACommHR thus issued precautionary measures in their favour, Ecuador would have been in the uncomfortable situation of choosing to meet one protective measure over the other with all the consequence that the choice of such a policy implies.[40]

Granted foreign investors not only seem to seek damages from respondent states as legal remedies, but also to block domestic proceedings for civil liability claims instituted against them by third parties by means of arbitral awards. In *Chevron v Ecuador II* and *Renco v Peru*, claimant investors sought, among others, tribunals' issuance of declaratory reliefs in which they were released from any civil liability for their subsidiaries' operation and the respondent states were held responsible and liable for any pending environmental remediation and payment of damages to third parties.[41] While claimant investors' pretensions in *Renco v Peru* were unsuccessful due to tribunal's dismissal of its claim on jurisdictional grounds,[42] the *Chevron v Ecuador II* tribunal partially conferred the legal remedies sought by the claimants since Ecuador was found liable for a denial of justice under the fair and equitable treatment (FET) standard and for the treatment required under customary international law (CIL) pursuant to the Ecuador-USA BIT since it 'maintain(ed) the

---

[37]*Chevron v Ecuador* II (n 36) Part X-1, para 10.4. For an overview of the claims and findings, see Desierto (2018).

[38]*Chevron Corporation and Texaco Petroleum Company v The Republic of Ecuador (II)*, PCA Case No. 2009-23, First Interim Award on Interim Measures (25 January 2012) para IV lit. (i. Failing Ecuador to comply with the former interim measure, the tribunal renewed its request. See *Chevron v Ecuador II* (n 36) Second Interim Award on Interim Measures (16 February 2012) para 3 lit. (i.

[39]'Letter from Pablo Fajardo, Julio Prieto and Juan Pablo Saenz (Plaintiffs' Legal Representatives Aguinda v Chevron Corp.) and Aaron Marr Page (Counsel) to Santiago Canton (Executive Secretary, Inter-American Commission on Human Rights)' (9 February 2012). Available via Slide Share Net. https://www.slideshare.net/EmbajadaUsaEcu/ex-114 accessed 10 December 2020.

[40]Presumably, the Lago Agrio plaintiffs withdrew their precautionary measures' request because of Ecuador's decision to not comply with any of these procedural measures to safeguard the legal interests of those affected by Texaco's activities domestically. *Chevron v Ecuador II* (n 36) para 10.18.

[41]As a form of reparation, the Renco Group requested a declaration that '[the respondent State] is required to (1) appear in and defend the Lawsuits and any similar lawsuits, (2) assume responsibility and liability for any damages that may be recovered and any judgments that may be issued in the Lawsuits and in any similar lawsuits, (3) indemnify, release, protect and hold Renco, DRP and their affiliates harmless from those third-party claims and (4) remediate the soil in and around the town of La Oroya'. See *Claimant's Notice of Arbitration, Renco v Peru* (n 35) para 84 lit. c.

[42]See *Renco v Peru* (n 36) Final Award.

enforceability and execute(ion of) the Lago Agrio judgement and knowingly facilitate(d) its enforcement outside Ecuador'.[43] As a result, the *Chevron v Ecuador II* tribunal not only granted the above-mentioned declaratory relief, but also an injunction ordering Ecuador's suspension of the domestic judgement where claimant investors are required to pay damages for their collective liability for environmental harms to the Lago Agrio population, and adoption of all measures to preclude its enforceability in third countries.[44] Therefore, the *Chevron v Ecuador II* case unambiguously illustrates how IIL may hinder states' protection of human rights through the domestic legal remedies' provision to those affected within the context of foreign investment activities even after the conclusion ISDS.

Faced with the far-reaching implications that investment treaty protection could have over host states' protection of human rights before, during, and after the conduct of investor-state arbitration proceedings, to what extent have Latin American countries deployed human rights arguments within ISDS? Does the relationship between IIL and IHRL human bear any relevance in ISDS? Such questions are answered in this study.

### 1.1.2 The Functional Underpinning of IIL as the Reason Behind the Limited Success of Human Rights Argumentation in States' Favour

Within the ISDS context, Latin American countries seem, at least, as an argumentative strategy, to call for a resolution of inter-regime tensions in favour of human rights. Some states have frequently invoked human rights as matter of applicable law,[45] and sought to justify their regulatory measures at the merits phase[46] and/or to challenge tribunals' jurisdiction and the admissibility of foreign investors' claims based on human rights arguments.[47] *Urbaser v Argentina*, for example, has been the first case, where a host state brings a separate cause of action, in terms of counter-claims, alleging claimant investors' breaches of users' enjoyment of their human right to water by failing to provide the necessary level of investment in the water service's concession.[48] Nevertheless, the deployment of human rights arguments by Latin American countries in ISDS has had so far marginal success,[49] and this trend

---

[43]*Chevron v Ecuador II* (n 36) part X-2, paras 10.5.

[44]*Chevron v Ecuador II* (n 36) Second Partial Award on Track II (30 August 2018), p. X-3-4, paras 10.12 (i) to 10.13 (viii).

[45]See Sect. 4.1.1, Chap. 4.

[46]See Sect. 4.1.2, Chap. 4.

[47]See Sect. 4.1.3.2, Chap. 4.

[48]*Urbaser v Argentina* (n 1). Guntrip (2018).

[49]For an extensive discussion, see Sect. 4.1.1, Chap. 4.

raises the general question of whether the relationship between IIL and human rights bears any relevance in current investment arbitration practice.

In most cases, IHRL has only played a prominent role in ISDS if it underpins the values and objectives pursued by IIL, namely the effective legal protection of foreign investment.[50] According to *Steininger*, claimant investors or respondent states' references to human rights have only bare relevance in tribunals' review of alleged breaches of claimant investors' rights to property and to fair trial, and the case law of the European Court of Human Rights (ECtHR) has great importance in the ISDS context since tribunals drew inspiration from this regional court's reasoning to determine breaches of the right to property.[51] Considering this arbitral tribunals' practice, some scholars have considered that, rather than competing, IIL and IHRL are gradually converging,[52] thereby posing no threat for the unity to international law.[53]

This understanding of the interaction between IIL and IHRL is based on a functional underpinning of IIL that past and current rationales have continuously reinforced. Traditionally, IIL has been regarded as an international legal instrument that contributes to the 'de-politicisation' of international investment dispute settlement,[54] understanding it as the process by which the legal resolution of these disputes is relocated from the diplomatic (inter-state) sphere to international and neutral *ad hoc* tribunals in accordance with a set of pre-established legal standards by means of IIAs.[55]

In addition, another attached advantage of IIL has been affording an additional layer of comprehensive protection to foreign investment in contexts where domestic recipient states' laws and regulations are likely to constrain its activities.[56] In fact, the Latin American region has usually featured as a case study in this historical account for portraying the considerable challenges faced by foreign investors in seeking effective legal protection of their property rights prior the consolidation of the investment treaty protection regime.[57] With the massive ratification of many treaties since the 1990s, IIL has been perceived as a set of almost widely-accepted set of neutral international legal rules and enforcement mechanisms,[58] which mitigates host states' political risk,[59] because investment treaty standards and their application by *ad hoc* arbitral tribunals subject states to the international rule of law, thereby

---

[50] See Steininger (2018), pp. 38–45; Petersmann and Kube (2016).

[51] See Steininger (2018), pp. 38–45.

[52] See Dupuy and Viñuales (2015) and Hirsch (2008).

[53] Binder (2015) cited from author's abstract in its English version.

[54] See, for instance, Kriebaum (2018a), pp. 14, 27–28. Also, Kriebaum (2009), p. 653.

[55] Kriebaum (2018a).

[56] See Taillant and Bonnitcha (2011), pp. 57, 61.

[57] To illustrate, see Salacuse (2015), pp. 75–77; Vandevelde (2005), p. 157.

[58] See Sornarajah (2010), p. 18.

[59] See Webb Yackee (2014), pp. 491–497.

promoting regulatory predictability by limiting their arbitrary behaviour.[60] Under this perspective, frictions between IIL and IHRL have been either denied as a result of the perception that human rights treaties only prescribe the attainment of a specific result, leaving at states parties' discretion the regulatory means by which they achieve that goal in conformity with IIAs,[61] or implicitly acknowledged under the premise that tribunals could satisfactorily resolved these frictions through the application of the systemic integration principle.[62]

In recent times, however, IHRL seems to have acquired, albeit to a minor degree, certain relevance in ISDS when it comes to the review of foreign investors' conduct in recipient states. The *Urbaser v Argentina* tribunal extensively engaged in reviewing whether claimant investors had an international obligation towards the human right to water.[63] In *Bear Creek v Peru*, relying upon the findings in the latter case, Professor Philippe Sands acknowledged in his separate opinion that although the Convention concerning Indigenous and Tribal Peoples in Independent Countries (ILO Convention 169) only obliges states parties, it had legal significance for claimant investors.[64] He contends that this non-investment treaty was applicable at the dispute before the tribunal, and that if the claimant investor had observed the international standards enshrined therein, it would have reduced its own losses.[65] Finally, the *Avec v Costa Rica* tribunal also addressed the issue of investors' obligations in connection with the concept of *erga omnes* norms within the framework of a counterclaim that arose from alleged investor's inobservance of environmental law of the respondent state in the development of a tourism project.[66] This tribunal held that investors could be considered subjects of international law when it came to 'rights and obligations that are the concern of all states, as it happens in the protection of the environment'.[67] With basis on this principle, it added that since the applicable treaty requires protected investors to abide and comply with the environmental measures of states parties, there is no justification to exempt the claimant

---

[60]See Guthrie (2013), pp. 1151, 1159–1160.

[61]See Fry (2007), p. 77.

[62]*Urbaser v Argentina* (n 1) para 1192. In relation to the application of the integration principle to cope with tensions between international investment and human rights, see Dupuy and Viñuales (2015), pp. 1739–1767. While endorsing the same view, Simma acknowledges that the challenges inherent to the normative tensions between IIL and IHRL cannot be solved by the current international dispute settlement system due to the availability of *ex post* remedies only. On this ground, he proposes to, inter alia, clarify the human rights' obligations of states from the outset in IIAs. Simma (2011), pp. 579–583.

[63]See Sect. 4.1.3.2, Chap. 4.

[64]*Bear Creek v Peru* (n 3) Separate Opinion of Philippe Sands para 10. See Convention concerning Indigenous and Tribal Peoples in Independent Countries (adopted 27 June 1989, entered into force 5 September 1991) 1650 UNTS 383 (ILO Convention 169).

[65]*Bear Creek v Peru* (n 3) Separate Opinion of Philippe Sands para 11.

[66]*David R Aven and Others v Republic of Costa Rica*, ICSID Case No. UNCT/15/3, Final Award (18 September 2018) (*Aven v Costa Rica*).

[67]*Aven v Costa Rica* (n 66) para 738.

from the application of that treaty norm.[68] Despite latter dismissed at the merits, the value of the *Urbaser* and *Aven* tribunals' approach to counterclaims and the reflections of Professor Sands resides in their explicit engagement with an exogenous legal regime to IIL, namely IHRL, in a way that departs from the functional values and objectives of IIL, giving space for the occurrence of -what some scholars have labelled as the 'moment of law'.[69]

Given the above-mentioned considerations, the following questions emerge: How true is the proposition under current universal and Inter-American human rights doctrine that states have a wide margin of discretion on how they protect human rights to achieve this end in a manner compatible with their investment treaty obligations? Which proposals have been put forward so far to align IIL with human rights that go beyond the application of the 'systemic integration' interpretive maxim? By which means have Latin American countries articulated their need for regulatory space outside the ISDS context?

### 1.1.3  The Need for Re-politicising IIL in View of Its Increasing Problematic Interplay with States' Protection of Human Rights

Parallel to the view that IIL and IHRL gradually come together on questions relating to investment treaty protection is also the belief that IIL and IHRL collide in the sense that IIL undermines states' protection of human rights by regulatory means.[70] In line with this perception, international human rights bodies and civil society have increasingly appealed to states to maintain an adequate policy space when observing their investment treaty obligations[71] or even called for the protection of investment treaty rights in conformity with human rights treaties owing to the multilateral

---

[68]*Aven v Costa Rica* (n 66) para 739.

[69]Crawford and Nevill define the 'moment of law' as 'the avoidance by tribunals of both conflict and zero-sum outcomes that would either deny or disregard the regimes or rules in conflict or fail to achieve the purpose of litigation, that of resolving disputes peacefully'. Crawford and Nevill (2012), p. 235.

[70]See Joseph (2013).

[71]Member States of the United Nations (UN) have been explicitly encouraged to 'maintain adequate policy space to meet their human rights obligations when pursuing business-related policy objectives (...) through investment treaties'. See UNGP (n 23) para 9. Also, they have been encouraged to implement novel policy tools to ensure that IIAs are consistent with their human rights obligations. See HRC, 'Report of the Special Rapporteur on the Right to Food, Olivier De Schutter, Guiding Principles on Human Rights Impact Assessments of Trade and Investment Agreements' (2011) Un Doc. A/HRC/19/59/Add.5. In the same direction, the IACoHR held in *Sawhoyamaxa v Paraguay* that the enforcement of foreign investor's treaty rights should be in conformity with the human rights obligations of the State concerned owing to the multilateral character of human rights treaties, which differs from the bilateral nature of IIAs. See *Sawhoyamaxa v Paraguay* (n 15) para 140.

character of human rights treaties that differs from the bilateral nature of IIAs.[72] Moreover, some scholars who endorse this view seek to accommodate both international legal regimes, but vary in their conceptualisation of how these legal regimes should interrelate with each other, thus leading to inter-regime tensions getting solved.[73]

Except in some instances,[74] this human rights-centred discussion has nevertheless overlooked the alleged *political* roots of IIL when developing options for its accommodation with human rights.[75] According to *Benvenisti* and *Downs*, the fragmentation of international law has been a deliberated-induced process by powerful states to restrict the negotiating capacity of weaker states and thus establishing an agenda that favours the creation of legal regimes aligned around their own interests.[76] This understanding of the cause of international law's fragmentation mirrors one conceptualisation of the relationship between politics and international law in international relations,[77] which has increasingly informed critical scholars' view about IIL.

In addition to the view that IIL continues to reflect the unsettled ideological tensions between North and South about the role that international legal instruments should play in protecting foreign capital[78] some contend that the emergence of IIL

---

[72]This was the opinion of the IACtHR in the *Sawhoyamaxa v Paraguay* case. See *Sawhoyamaxa v Paraguay* (n 15) para 140. As regard to the concerns of civil society in relation to the negotiation of investment treaties, see DPLF Staff (2018), p. 14.

[73]At the Inter-American level, Bustos and Bohoslavski, for instance, advocate for domestic courts' review of the conformity of arbitral tribunals' award with human rights standards if existing interpretative tools fail to achieve inter-regime harmonization, by giving an instrumental conceptualisation of IIL at the service of the realization of human rights. Justo and Bohoslavsky (2018). By recognising the importance of the two international legal regimes operating in the inter-American context, Urueña argues that the *ius constitutionale commune* could provide adequate normative and theoretical tools to allow arbitrators to establish when to give deference to states and when not. Urueña (2018). On the *ius constitutionale commune* project in the Latin American context, see von Bogdandy et al. (2017).

[74]Davitti (2019). In fact, Philip Alston, in his capacity as a Special Rapporteur contend that '[w]hile some proponents present privatization as just "a financing tool", others promote it as being more efficient, flexible, innovative and effective than public sector alternatives. In practice, however, privatization has also metamorphosed into an ideology of governance. As one advocate put it, "anything that strengthens the private sector [against] the State is protective of personal freedom". Freedom is thereby redefined as an emaciated public sector alongside a private sector dedicated to profiting from running key parts of the criminal justice system and prisons, determining educational priorities and approaches, deciding who will receive health interventions and social protection, and choosing what infrastructure will be built, where and for whom'. See UNGA, 'Report of the Special Rapporteur on extreme poverty and human rights' (26 September 2018) UN Doc A/73/396 para 2.

[75]According to Peters, the fragmentation of international law has also a political root because the existing relationships between legal regimes reflect the diverging perspectives that states have of their policy priorities. See Peters (2017), pp. 674–675; 700–701.

[76]See Benvenisti and Downs (2007), p. 615.

[77]Reus-Smit (2004).

[78]Kaushal (2009), pp. 491, 496; Sornarajah (2010), p. 18.

coincided with the European liberal ideological induced convergence between capital-exporting countries' interest with those of their nationals operating abroad.[79] Consistent with this view, other scholars further argue that IIL brought about a process of market deregulation in recipient states to facilitate and protect foreign investment activities through the sanctioning of their regulatory intervention by compensatory means, thus perceiving that IIL is not devoid of political ideology.[80] Based on this logic, others strongly challenge the alleged neutrality of IIL and view this latter argument as another way to 'de-politicise' the IIL regime.[81] It has been contended that historical rationales provided to justify the creation of the institutional machinery of IIL have contributed to the internalisation of the 'de-politicisation' narrative,[82] by intending to anchor the vision that IIL can provide legal technical solutions to disputes that actually have an inherent political character.[83]

Yet cases such as *Urbaser v Argentina* and *Aven v Costa Rica* might initially refute the argument that powerful economic actors, such as foreign investors, influence how IIL operates because these awards signalise IIL's potential to shape investors' behaviour and thus the inability of these stakeholders to evade the IIL regime. Notwithstanding the former, this study partially endorses the fact that the above-mentioned critical views are justified when it comes to the role of IIL in steering states' conduct. The predominant position in IIL has denied or averted it from sufficient engagement in critically discussing the potential for its normative overlapping with IHRL when states' obligation to protect human rights is at stake.[84] It is in this sense that the present study argues that the debate and reform about the IIL regime should be politicised, borrowing Peters' concept of 'politicisation', as 'a process through which certain issues become objects of public contention and debate',[85] and thus 'inevitably contestatory' due to the demands raised by stakeholders.[86]

---

[79]Miles (2013), pp. 39–40.

[80]See Tan (2015) and Sattorova (2018).

[81]See Davitti (2019), pp. 168, 172, 229. This study relies upon Fawcett, Flinders, Hay and Wood's definition of depoliticisation as the process 'that remove(s) or displace(s) the potential for choice, collective agency, and deliberation around a particular political issue. Fawcett et al. (2017), pp. 3, 5.

[82]According to Perrone and Schneiderman, the internalisation of the 'depoliticisation' narrative has its origin in the functional rationales provided by international financial institutions to remove investment dispute settlement from the state realm and to justify the creation of new institutions endowed with the competence of enforcing international rules in a way that it 'neutralize disagreement over market fundamentals'. See Perrone and Schneiderman (2019), pp. 449–451.

[83]See Davitti (2019); Radovi (2018), p. 143.

[84]This debate would be reflective of the so-called politics within law, another dimension of the interaction between politics and international law, according to which the interpretation of IIAs would correspond to one stage of governance where politics and IIL interact and where the meaning of IIAs provisions thus constitute one of the contested issues. See Reus-Smit (2004).

[85]Peters (2017), p. 701.

[86]Ibidem. Maxwell defines contestation as the actions by which 'political and theoretical claims to final, universal, or absolute to political dilemmas' is challenged. Maxwell (2014), p. 738.

Considering the critical place frequently allocated to the Latin American region in the competing histories of the origins of IIL, and in the current challenges made to the IIL regime in place, two sets of questions should be addressed. The first focuses on whether the Latin American critical approach towards these international instruments can be categorised as a politicisation process, and if so, which issues of contention and claims have characterised this process. Yet, faced with the fact that IIL may considerably inhibit states' protection of human rights in the investment context, but nevertheless abstain from dealing with inter-regime clashes, the second inquiry becomes whether current forms currently prevailing for framing the discussion and reform of IIL are adequate to frame these concerns from a human rights debate.[87] More specifically, this requires answering whether the so-called 'right to regulate' paradigm pervasively used in IIL to highlight the states' need of preserving regulatory autonomy is adequate to frame the shortcoming placed by the IIL upon states' protection of human rights in the investment context,[88] and if not, whether a new paradigm consistent with IHRL, yet independent from that legal field, can be developed and be applicable in IIL.

## 1.2   Hypothesis, Aims and Structure of This Study

Borrowing Peter's understanding of the 'politicisation' term, the present study argues that Latin American countries have engaged in a long-standing 'politicisation' of international legal instruments protecting foreign property rights and that this contestation has always been based on the articulation of sovereign rights. However, it further contends that maintaining this paradigm from a human rights perspective is inappropriate and that an adequate re-politicisation of IIL regime demands states' reconceptualization of how they articulate their need of regulatory space in the investment context. It proposes the 'duty to regulate' paradigm to articulate these claims since IHRL places legal obligations upon states that demand taking all appropriate preventative measures to ensure the protection of human rights vis-à-vis investors.

Informed by these hypotheses, the present study aims to develop the concept 'duty to regulate' as a practical and compatible concept with IIL and IHRL to facilitate the re-politicisation of the IIL and human rights debate as follows: As a critical tool, this concept enables to critically examine states' articulation and tribunals' understanding of the international rights, duties, and obligations of host states vis-à-vis foreign investment in current IIL. Analytically, the concept 'duty to regulate' not only facilitates to anchor this notion in IIL in conformity with international human rights law, but also to distinguish this international duty from the 'right

---

[87]Mouyal (2018).
[88]See, for instance, Hindelang and Krajewski (2016) and Titi (2014).

to regulate'. Finally, this concept provides a new normative paradigm to frame the discussion about and reform of IIL in Latin America and beyond.

The remaining chapters of this book are divided as follows:

The second chapter puts into historical perspective ways in which Latin American countries have channelled the articulation of sovereign rights to politicise international legal instruments protecting foreign investment since their independence up to the present time. To adequately handle this phase, the chapter is divided into three historical periods. categorised according to the political, legal, and economic framings of foreign investment protection put in place in Latin America. It employs the national and regional legal practices prevailed by these countries to legally protect foreign property rights in each epoch as the basis of this historical review. In addition, this chapter contextualises these practices considering the corresponding case law of international tribunals on the subject as well as international attempts by actors outside this region towards its institutionalization. This historical review shows that the articulation of this criticism has been traditionally made in terms of sovereign rights and that these forms still instruct how they 'politicise' current IIL regime. Faced with the normative challenges already highlighted in Sect. 1.1.1, this historical review thus makes evident the need for a new normative paradigm to frame the discussion and reform about IIL.

After this historical undertaking, the third chapter develops the concept 'duty to regulate', with its basis on IHRL, to elucidate how this normative paradigm should be understood and applied in IIL. To this end, this chapter initially discusses the legal basis and scope of this states' duty as defined by universal and Inter-American principles on business and human rights, on one hand, and on international human rights treaties binding upon these states, on the other. Subsequently, this chapter proceeds to elaborate the states' duty to regulate foreign investment activities arising from the right to water and indigenous people's right to lands and territories, since both rights have traditionally been at stake in investment treaty claims responded by Latin American countries. The chapter goes on to examine the legal basis that specifically allocates this international duty in relation to both rights and develops its scope of application accordingly. This analytical review demonstrates that universal and Inter-American human rights doctrine offers sufficient normative arguments to facilitate a theoretically convincing substantiation and/or review of Latin American countries' duty to regulate foreign investment activities and to differentiate it from the so-called 'right to regulate' paradigm pervasively used in IIL.

Drawing upon the concept 'duty to regulate' elaborated in Chap. 3, Chaps. 4 and 5 formulate reform proposals to anchor this normative paradigm in the interpretation and application of IIAs' provisions. To this end, this study focuses on IIAs and the idea of creating a regional ISDS forum, since both legal instruments have had so far a considerable amount of supporters within the broad array of legal instruments that have emerged in Latin America to redefine investor-state relations.[89]

---

[89]See Sect. 2.3.3, Chap. 2.

Based on a selected set of case studies where Latin American countries and human rights arguments have featured in investor-state arbitration proceedings, Chap. 4 begins to critically assess the extent to which Latin American countries currently advance their duty to regulate in ISDS and tribunals engage in the review of these human rights-based arguments. To this end, the argumentative strategies employed by states and tribunals' responses to substantiate human rights as the applicable law in ISDS are discussed. In the discussion, the articulation of these countries' regulatory duties under IHRL on questions of their investment obligations under the FET standard and expropriation are brought out, as well as their allegations of claimant investor's human rights abuses of human rights on jurisdictional/admissibility questions and by means of counterclaims. Each substantive and procedural aspect is accompanied by a discussion of tribunals' review of these submitted defence arguments and claims. This doctrinal analysis suggests that an articulation of states' duties under IHRL (and its recognition) may be on the rise, but that further reforms are required to achieve this end.

Based on these preliminary findings, the second part of this chapter sketches out several treaty reforms, first to improve states' articulation of regulatory duties in the interpretation and application of IIAs and, second, to use these international treaties as human rights-friendly regulatory devices of foreign investment activities. Concluding the chapter is a brief discussion of the legal consequences that Latin American countries may bear if they omit to articulate their human rights regulatory duties in IIAs.

Inspired by past sub-regional attempts to create a regional ISDS forum, Chap. 5 briefly outlines the existing legal mechanisms to which a *regional* ISDS centre could resort to underpin the re-politicisation of IIL in Latin America by engaging in the review of inter-regime tensions. To this end, this chapter initially recalls the legal situations involving host states' compliance with their duty to regulate foreign investment activities that may give rise to inter-regime collisions during the conduct and after the conclusion of investor-state arbitration proceedings. Against this background, this chapter proceeds to delineate the legal mechanisms already available to a regional ISDS forum to address these inter-regime tensions, both by itself, and with assistance of human rights bodies.

The sixth chapter concludes the study by presenting the summary of findings that emerged in the previous chapters and end by suggesting areas for future research.

## 1.3 Methodology and Significance

This research project considers international investment law and human rights law as disciplines of public international law and uses legal history as well as doctrinal analysis as legal methods to answer the critical, analytical, and normative research questions raised in all the chapters.

As an element of legal studies, legal history is used in this study for deconstructing the long-standing critical stand of Latin American countries against extra-regional attempts that have endeavoured their adherence to international legal instruments of foreign investment protection until present time. This implies dismantling Latin American countries' understanding and conception about the role of the state in the legal design of investor-state relations, the appropriate legal means to rule this interaction, as well as the corresponding justifications underlying prevailed preferences.[90] Hence, rather than tracing the evolution of IIL and Latin American countries' role in this process so as to justify the existence of international legal instruments of investment protection,[91] this historical account purposes to build awareness about the historical contingency of the forms favoured in Latin America to express dissatisfaction with these instruments, and to draw inspiration from this historical path to reframe the present discussion and reform of IIL in response to the great challenges of regulating foreign investment in furtherance of human rights' protection.

As far as the methodological approach to legal history is concerned, this study draws some inspiration from the so-called 'glocalization' methodology, understood as an approach that places local/regional legal historical perspectives in relation to global perspectives and examines the tensions between both dimensions by prioritising the former's views on a specific legal issue.[92] Thus, the present study puts into historical perspective the domestic and regional views in Latin American countries regarding the role that (international) legal instruments protecting foreign investment should attach to recipient states of foreign investment in investor-state relations, against the views put forwards by Western countries prior the ratification of IIAs and current IIL alike. For the historical contextualisation of the perspectives prevailed in IIL, this historical review incidentally employs an analytical and critical approach to how investment case law has understood the function of states' regulation when determining their obligations under the FET standards and expropriation provisions laid down in the so-called 'first generation' BITs.

Additionally, the book also follows an analytical, critical, and normative approach to legal doctrine to substantiate the re-politicisation of IIL by means of states' articulation of the IHRL-based duty to regulate foreign investment activities in ISDS. Consequently, this book examines human rights bodies' understanding and development of this international duty and draws up some principles from this human rights bodies' determination in relation to the right to water and indigenous people's right to land and territories. Based on this analytical review, the book critically assesses Latin American countries and arbitral tribunals' construction and understanding of host states' investment treaty substantive obligations and

---

[90]In discussing the space that Global Legal History has between history and law, Duve highlights that the disciplinary assignments of this legal field of research may range from being a special area of historical research to part of legal studies. The latter could serve to depict the evolution of the law under review, or to critically assess this legal construction over time. Duve (2017).

[91]Montt (2012).

[92]Duve borrows this methodological approach from national historiography to apply it on the study of global legal history concerning the processes of (re) production of law, more generally. See Duve (2017).

procedural rights, including their views about the role of states' regulation on both questions. Informed by the findings of the analytical and critical analysis, this book proposes different sets of treaty and institutional options to anchor the duty to regulate foreign investment activities as the normative paradigm that facilitates the re-politicisation of the IIL and human rights debate.

Like existing literature that develops human rights-friendly proposals to make IIL more consistent with IHRL, the present work also resorts to IHRL doctrine to substantiate reform of IIL and to the use of common concepts to foster a dialogue between both legal regimes, rather than a subordination of one under the other.[93] Yet, the special contribution of this study resides in reframing the discussion of states' obligations to protect human rights under IHRL in terms pervasively used in IIL such as 'states' regulation' to foster mutual recognition of both international legal regimes. Finally, ISDS has proved problematic for the enforcement of other human rights in other latitudes,[94] this research may assist states and scholars stemming therefrom to develop novel responses in a way that suits universal and even regional human rights standards alike.

## References

Benvenisti E, Downs G (2007) The empire's new clothes: political economy and the fragmentation of international law. Standford Law Rev 60:595–631

Binder C (2015) Einheit oder Fragmentierung des Völkerrechts am Beispiel der Rechtsprechung des Europäischen Menschenrechtsgerichtshofs und der Investitionsschiedsgerichte. ZöR 4:737–778

Binder C, Hofbauer J (2016) Case study: Burlington Resources Inc. v Ecuador/Kichwa Indigenous People of Sarayaku v Ecuador (July 15, 2016). Available at: https://doi.org/10.2139/ssrn. 2810062. Accessed 10 Dec 2020

Bonnitcha J (2014) Substantive protection under investment treaties: a legal and economic analysis. CUP, Cambridge

Brauch M. (2014) Yukos v. Russia: issues and legal reasoning behind US $50 billion awards. Investment Treaty News, September. Available at: https://www.iisd.org/itn/wp-content/uploads/2014/09/iisd_itn_yukos_sept_2014_1.pdf. Accessed 10 Dec 2020

---

[93]For instance, Davitti has called for an adaptation of the 'due dilligence' concept widely employed in IIL and IHRL to review states' conduct to achieve this aim. See Davitti (2012).

[94]For instance, Tanzania faced the submission an investment treaty claim out of the cancellation of a sugarcane plantation and ethanol production project of a Swedish Energy company after encountering resistance from local farmers for their displacement and absent consultation. See *EcoDevelopment in Europe AB & others v United Republic of Tanzania*, ICSID Case No. ARB/17/33 (documents are not public available). Similarly, India notified Ethiopia its intention to bring an investment treaty claim for its decision following the cancellation of its farm project. Davison (2016). Scholars have labelled this foreign investors' acquisition of extensive hectares of land for foodstuff's production and its transformation into renewable fuel as 'land grabbing'. They have expressed great concerns about its impact upon the right to food for the restrictions upon local farmers' access to land and the high food prices in host States, see Cotula et al. (2009).

Centro de Informacion Judicial (2019) La Corte Suprema convalidó la constitucionalidad de la ley de preservación de los glaciares rechazando el pedido de Barrick Gold, Minera Argentina Gold y provincia de San Juan, 4 June. Available at: https://www.cij.gov.ar/nota-34763-La-Corte-Suprema-convalid%2D%2Dla-constitucionalidad-de-la-ley-de-preservaci-n-de-los-glaciares-rechazando-el-pedido-de-Barrick-Gold%2D%2DMinera-Argentina-Gold-y-provincia-de-San-Juan.html. Accessed 10 Dec 2020

Colectivo sobre Financiamiento e Inversiones Chinas, Derechos Humanos y Ambiente (CICDHA). Evaluación de las Obligaciones Extraterritoriales de la República Popular de China desde Sociedad Civil: Casos de Argentina, Bolivia, Brasil, Ecuador y Perú. Available at: http://chinaambienteyderechos.lat/informe-regional/. Accessed 10 Dec 2020

Cotula L, Vermeulen S, Leonard R, Keeley J (2009) Land grab or development opportunity? Agricultural investment and international land deals in africa. IIED/ FAO/ IFAD, London/ Rome. http://www.fao.org/3/a-ak241e.pdf. Accessed 10 Dec 2020

Crawford J, Nevill P (2012) Relations between international courts and tribunals: the regime problem. In: Young MA (ed) Regime interaction in international law, facing fragmentation. CUP, Cambridge, pp 235–260

Davison W (2016) Karuturi Challenges Ethiopia Decision to Cancel Farm Project. Bloomberg (11 January). Available at: https://www.bloomberg.com/news/articles/2016-01-11/karuturi-challenges-ethiopian-decision-to-cancel-farming-project. Accessed 10 Dec 2020

Davitti D (2012) On the meanings of international investment law and international human rights law: the alternative narrative of due diligence. Human Rights Law Rev 12 (3):421–453

Davitti D (2019) Investment and human rights in armed conflict. charting an elusive intersection. Hart, Oxford

Desierto D (2018) 'From the Indigenous Peoples' Environmental Catastrophe in the Amazon to the Investors' Dispute on Denial of Justice: The Chevron v. Ecuador August 2018 PCA Arbitral Award and the Dearth of International Environmental Remedies for Private Victims' EJIL:Talk! (13 September). Available at: https://www.ejiltalk.org/from-indigenous-peoples-environmental-catastrophe-in-the-amazon-to-investors-dispute-on-denial-of-justice-the-chevron-v-ecuador-2018-pca-arbitral-award/. Accessed 10 Dec 2020

DPLF Staff (2018) IACHR – Inputs to the questionnaire for the thematic report on business and human rights: Inter-American standards. DPLF (8 August). Available at: http://www.dplf.org/en/resources/iachr-inputs-questionnaire-thematic-report-business-and-human-rights-inter-american. Accessed 10 Dec 2020

Dupuy P, Viñuales J (2015) Human rights and investment disciplines: integration in progress. In: Bungenberg M, Griebel J, Hobe S, Reinisch A (eds) International investment law: a handbook. C.H. Beck, Nomos and Hart, Baden-Baden/München/Oxford, pp 1739–1767

Duve T (2017) In: Global legal history: a methodological approach. Oxford Handbooks Online, History of Law. https://doi.org/10.1093/oxfordhb/9780199935352.013.25

Fawcett P, Flinders M, Hay C, Wood M (2017) Anti-politics, depoliticization, and governance. In: Fawcett P, Flinders M, Hay C, Wood M (eds) Anti-politics, depoliticization, and governance. OUP, Oxford, pp 3–27

Fry JD (2007) International human rights law in investment arbitration: evidence of international law's unity. Duke J Comp Int Law 18:77–150

Gaukrodger, D, Gordon K (2012) Investor-state dispute settlement: a scoping paper for the investment policy community. OECD Working Papers on International Investment. https://doi.org/10.1787/5k46b1r85j6f-en

Gross S (2003) Inordinate chill: BITS, Non-NAFTA MITS, and host-state regulatory freedom: an Indonesian case study. Mich J Int Law 24(3):893–960

Guntrip E (2018) Private actors, public goods and responsibility for the right to water in international investment law: an analysis of Urbaser v. Argentina. Brill Open Law 1(1):37–60

Guthrie BK (2013) Beyond investment protection: an examination of the potential influence of investment treaties on domestic rule of law. N Y Univ J Int Law Law Polit 45:1151–1200

Hepburn J (2012) Analysis: Interim Measures Granted by Inter-American Commission Have Featured in Several Recent Investment Controversies. IA Reporter (14 March). Available at: https://www.iareporter.com/articles/analysis-interim-measures-granted-by-inter-american-com mission-have-featured-in-several-recent-investment-controversies/. Accessed 10 Dec 2020

Hepburn J (2019) Pakistan faces hefty loss in newly-rendered ICSID award in Tethyan copper mining case; core damages exceed $4 billion, and pre-award interest adds another $1.75 billion. IA Reporter, 14 July. Available at: https://www.iareporter.com/articles/pakistan-faces-hefty-loss-in-newly-rendered-icsid-award-in-tethyan-copper-mining-case-core-damages-exceed-4-bil lion-and-pre-award-interest-adds-another-1-75-billion/. Accessed 10 Dec 2020

Hill D (2016) Colombian court bans oil, gas and mining operations in paramos. The Guardian, (21 February). Available at: https://www.theguardian.com/environment/andes-to-the-amazon/ 2016/feb/21/colombia-bans-oil-gas-mining-paramos. Accessed 10 Dec 2020

Hindelang S, Krajewski M (eds) (2016) Shifting paradigms in international investment law. More balanced, less isolated, increasingly diversified. OUP, Oxford

Hirsch M (2008) Interactions between investment and non-investment obligations. In: Muchlinski P, Ortino F, Schreuer C (eds) The Oxford handbook of international investment law. OUP, Oxford, pp 154–181

Joseph S (2013) Law and investment law: intersections with human rights issues (August 13, 2012). In: Shelton D (ed) The Oxford handbook of human rights law. OUP, Oxford, pp 841–870

Justo J, Bohoslavsky JP (2018) Control de convencionalidad y derecho económico internacional. Fines y medios. MPIL Research Papers 31. Available at: https://poseidon01.ssrn.com/delivery. php?ID=145065017119119025100114025074003027008078002074040050125080074031027025111067004099043027042032027032054069121017005014031118040087059200450890811030070670050900760190730800650700810191121231161200681251160181011240030881240971010821070190970080070868&EXT=pdf&INDEX=TRUE. Accessed 10 Dec 2020

Kaushal A (2009) Revisiting history: how the past matters for the present backlash against the foreign investment regime. Harv Int Law J 50(2):491–534

Kriebaum U (2009) Human rights and the population of the host state in international investment arbitration. JWIT 10:653–677

Kriebaum U (2018a) Evaluating social benefits and costs of investment treaties: depoliticization of investment disputes. ICSID Rev Foreign Invest Law J 33(1):14–28

Letter from Pablo Fajardo, Julio Prieto and Juan Pablo Saenz (Plaintiffs' Legal Representatives Aguinda v Chevron Corp.) and Aaron Marr Page (Counsel) to Santiago Canton (Executive Secretary, Inter-American Commission on Human Rights) (9 February 2012). Available via Slide Share Net. https://www.slideshare.net/EmbajadaUsaEcu/ex-114. Accessed 10 Dec 2020

Maxwell L (2014) Contestation. In: Gibbons M, Coole D, Ellis E, Ferguson K (eds) The encyclopedia of political thought. Wiley Online Library. https://doi.org/10.1002/9781118474396. wbept0207

Miles K (2013) The origins of international investment law: empire, environment and the safeguarding of capital. CUP, New York

Montt S (2012) State liability in investment treaty arbitration. Global constitutional and administrative law in the bit generation. Hart, Oxford

Mouyal L (2018) International investment law and the right to regulate. A human rights perspective. Routledge

Perrone N, Schneiderman D (2019) International economic law's wreckage: depoliticization, inequality, precarity. In: Christodoulidis E, Dukes R, Goldoni M (eds) Research handbook on critical legal theory. Edward Elgar Publishing, Cheltenham/Northhampton, pp 446–472

Peters A (2017) The refinement of international law: from fragmentation to regime interaction and politicization. I•CON 15(3):671–704

Petersmann E, Kube V (2016) Human rights law in international investment arbitration. Asian J WTO Int Health Law Policy 11(1):65–114

Peterson E (2019) Updated: Conoco is awarded over $8.3 billion plus interest in battle with venezuela. IA Reporter, 8 March. Available at: https://www.iareporter.com/articles/breaking-conoco-is-awarded-over-15-billion-inclusive-of-interest-for-venezuela-losses/. Accessed 10 Dec 2020

Poulsen L (2015) Bounded rationality and economic diplomacy: the politics of investment. CUP, Cambridge

Radovi Ć (2018) Inherently unneutral investment treaty arbitration: the formation of decisive arguments in jurisdictional determinations. J Disp Resol 1:143–183

Reus-Smit C (2004) The politics of international law. In: Reus-Smit C (ed) The politics of international law. CUP, Cambridge, pp 14–44

Salacuse J (2015) The law of investment treaties, 2nd edn. OUP, Oxford

Sattorova M (2018) The impact of investment treaty law on host states: enabling good governance? Hart, Oxford

Simma B (2011) Foreign investment arbitration: A place for human rights? Int Comp Law Q 60 (3):573–596

Sornarajah M (2010) The international law on foreign investment, 3rd edn. CUP, Cambridge

Steininger S (2018) What's human rights got to do with it? An empirical analysis of human rights references in investment arbitration. Leiden J Int Law 31(1):33–58

Taillant J, Bonnitcha J (2011) International investment law and human rights. In: Cordonier Segger M, Gehring M, Newcombe A (eds) Sustainable development in world investment law. Kluwer Law International, The Hague, pp 53–80

Tan C (2015) Reviving the emperor's old clothes: the good governance agenda, development and international investment law. In: Schill S, Tams C, Hofmann R (eds) International investment law and development: bridging the gap. Edward Elgar Publishing, Cheltenham/Northampton, pp 147–179

Tienhaara K (2011) Regulatory chill and the threat of arbitration: a view from political science. In: Brown C, Miles K (eds) Evolution in investment treaty law and arbitration. CUP, Cambridge, pp 606–628

Tienhaara K (2018) Regulatory chill in a warming world: the threat to climate policy posed by investor-state dispute settlement. Transnatl Environ Law 7(2):229–250

Titi C (2014) The right to regulate in international investment law. Nomos/Hart Publishing, Baden-Baden

Urueña R (2018) Después de la fragmentación: ICCAL, derechos humanos y arbitraje de inversiones (After Fragmentation: ICCAL, human rights and investment arbitration) Max Planck Institute for Comparative Public Law & International Law (MPIL) Research Paper 30. Available at: https://poseidon01.ssrn.com/delivery.php?ID=109064031101123074026013072068107076099057086000017035067090106103112017091107009100056057025002110121052124025109085083117019022073038044032007097030064072075005066084077054104022071024092071021110098028004112098079102087101007072127022076086073004110&EXT=pdf&INDEX=TRUE. Accessed 10 Dec 2020

Vandevelde KJ (2005) A brief history of international investment agreements. UC Davis J Int Law Policy 12(1):157–194

von Bogdandy A, Ferrer Mac Gregor E, Morales Antoniazzi M, Piovesan F, Soley X (2017) Ius constitutionale commune en América Latina: A regional approach to transformative constitutionalism. In: von Bogdandy A, Ferrer Mac Gregor E, Morales Antoniazzi M, Piovesan F (eds) Transformative constitutionalism in Latin America. OUP, New York, pp 3–23

Webb Yackee J (2014) Political risk and international investment law. Duke J Comp Int Law 24:477–500

# Chapter 2
# The Politicisation of International Legal Instruments Protecting Foreign Investment in Latin America Through States' Articulation of Sovereign Rights

This chapter departs from the premise that, although issues of contention regarding the international legal protection of foreign property rights have varied since the independence of Latin American countries until present time, the politicisation of these international instruments have always been based on the articulation of their sovereign rights.

To discuss this hypothesis, this chapter is divided into three historical periods: first, according to the political, legal, and economic framings of foreign investment protection put in place in Latin America and second, according to the different issues of contention that arise in relation with international legal instruments protecting foreign property as follows:

Following an overview of the issues of contention prevailing among Latin American countries from their independence until 1930, Sect. 2.1 explores the claims that these countries voiced in connection with their sovereign right to freely determine the scope of legal protection afforded to foreign property rights.

Section 2.1.1.1 discusses the domestic demands that these countries articulated on questions relating to the substantive and procedural legal protection afforded to foreign property rights. Section 2.1.1.2, which follows, addresses the sovereign acts under which Latin American countries were exclusively willing to agree to the settlement of diplomatic protection claims by means of both international arbitration—as expressed within the framework of the PAU conferences—and the codification attempts promoted by the League of Nations. Subsequently, Sect. 2.1.2.1 analyses the demands voiced by Latin American countries about the acts giving rise to their international legal responsibility in the context of pecuniary damages, together with an overview of the stand of Latin American countries towards arbitration as an international peaceful method of settling inter-state dispute. Section 2.1.2.2 then focuses on the domestic limitations placed by these countries upon the resolution of inter-state disputes for injuries inflicted to aliens by Mixed Claims Commissions.

© The Author(s), under exclusive license to Springer Nature Switzerland AG 2021    23
M. J. Luque Macías, *Re-Politicising International Investment Law in Latin America through the Duty to Regulate Paradigm*, European Yearbook of International Economic Law 14, https://doi.org/10.1007/978-3-030-73272-1_2

After exposing the issues of contention revolving around the legal conditions governing states' expropriation of foreign property rights and the international arbitration of investor-state contract-based disputes between 1930 and 1980, Sect. 2.2 explores the demands put forward by Latin American countries regarding the exercise of this sovereign right and the articulated consequences that it had for the substantive and procedural protection of foreign property rights.

Section 2.2.1 analyses the sovereign claims expressed by these countries on questions relating to the substantive protection afforded to foreign property in case of expropriation at the domestic and regional level. Incidentally, UN resolutions also form part of the material under review since Latin American countries also participated in the deliberation process for their adoption. Section 2.2.2 goes further to discuss the sovereign demands that these countries implicitly articulated on questions of the procedural rights granted to foreign property rights in different type of contracts.

Section 2.3.1 is an exposition on how investment treaty protection gradually consolidated in Latin America during the 1990s to determine the extent to which this shift in attitude towards the legal protection of foreign investment has entailed a de-politicisation of the IIL regime in the region. This entails to ascertain to what extent BITs and ISDS ceased to be no longer issues of contention and debate in Latin America. Since Chap. 1 already indicates this was not the case, and that the overly expansive interpretation and application of BITs by arbitral tribunals has become the issue of contention at the present time, Sect. 2.3.2 describes this controversial jurisprudential development on the basis of the FET standard and provisions governing the lawful exercise of states parties' right to expropriate. Section 2.3.3, on its part, discusses the so-called 'right to regulate' pervasively alluded to in IIL as the form prevailed to articulate sovereign demands at the national and regional level.

The examples of states' practice at the domestic, regional, and international level provided in each historical period does not intend to be comprehensive, but rather illustrative of the extent to which Latin American countries have engaged in a process of politicisation of international legal instruments protecting foreign investment.

## 2.1  Politicisation Through States' Articulation of the Right to Freely Determine the Legal Scope of Foreign Property Rights' Protection (1830–1930)

After gaining their independence from colonial powers, Latin American countries began to resort to different legal instruments to regulate their trade and commerce. In addition, these countries established friendly relations with capital-exporting countries and commercial relationships with foreign nationals by means of the so-called Friendship, Commerce and Navigation treaties (FCN treaties) and different type of contracts, respectively. Under FCN treaties, many countries committed to grant national treatment to the nationals of the other state party in relation to access to justice,[1] and in a few instances, this extended to the prevention of embargo or sequestration of foreign nationals' property.[2] To a lesser extent, other countries committed to grant the most-favoured-nation (MFN),[3] in connection to commerce,[4] payment of contributions,[5] and freedom of trade and movement.[6] Moreover, other countries celebrated loan agreements with foreign nationals for the financing of infrastructure projects,[7] and/or concession agreements for foreign financing, implementation or operation of infrastructure facilities.[8]

In case of international controversies arising from the contracts cited above, the contracting state has generally to agree with the home state of the affected alien to establish a Mixed Claim Commission to arbitrate its pecuniary claims.[9] This was an

---

[1]Treaty of Peace, Amity Navigation and Commerce between Colombia and the United States (signed 3 October 1824) (1824) 74 CTS 455 (Colombia-USA FCN treaty) art 10; Treaty of Friendship, commerce and Navigation between the Hanseatic Cities (Bremen, Hanover, Lubeck) and Venezuela (signed 31 March 1860) (1860) 122 CTS 53 (Hanseatic Cities-Venezuela FCN treaty) art III; Treaty of Peace, Friendship, Navigation and Commerce between the United States and Venezuela (signed 30 January 1826) (1826–1827) 77 CTS 1 art 13.

[2]Treaty of Friendship, Commerce and Navigation between Paraguay and the Zollverein (signed 1 August 1860) (1860) 122 CTS 283 art XIV.

[3]Hanseatic Cities-Venezuela FCN Treaty (n 1) art IV; Treaty of Amity and Commerce between Brazil and Great Britain (signed 17 August 1827) (1826–1827) 77 CTS 375 (Brazil-Great Britain FCN treaty) art V; Treaty of Friendship, Navigation and Commerce between Brazil and France (signed 8, January 1826) (1825–1826) 76 CTS 59 (Brazil-France FCN treaty) art VI.

[4]Treaty of Peace, Friendship, Commerce and Navigation between the Peru-Bolivian Confederation and the United States (signed 30 November 1836) (1776–1949) 7 Treaties and other international Agreements of the United States of America 257 art 2.

[5]Brazil-Great Britain FCN treaty (n 3) art V.

[6]Brazil-France FCN treaty (n 3) art X.

[7]For instance, British creditors signed loan agreements with Mexico, Colombia, Peru, Argentina, and Brazil. See, Dawson (1990), pp. 67–84.

[8]In relation to the concession agreement with North American Dredging Company of Texas, see *North American Dredging Company of Texas (USA) v United Mexican States* (31 March 1926) Decisions of Claims Commissions Mexico-United States, Reports of International Arbitral Awards (RIAA) IV (*North American Dredging Company v Mexico*) 26–27. In reference to article 11 of the contract celebrated with Mexican Union Railway (Limited), see *Mexican Union Railway (Limited) (Great Britain) v United Mexican States* (Decision No. 21, 21 February 1930), Decisions of Claims Commissions Great-Britain-Mexico, France-Mexico, and Germany-Mexico, Reports of International Arbitral Awards (RIAA) V (*Mexican Union Railway v Mexico*) footnote 1; *The Interoceanic Railway of Mexico (Acapulco to Veracruz) (Limited), and the Mexican Eastern Railway Company (Limited), and the Mexican Southern Railway (Limited) (Great Britain) v United Mexican States* (Decision No. 53, June 18, 1931), Decisions of Claims Commissions Great-Britain-Mexico, France-Mexico, and Germany-Mexico, Reports of International Arbitral Awards (RIAA) V (*Interoceanic Railway of Mexico and others v Mexico*); *Veracruz Railways (Mexico) Railways (limited) (Great Britain) v United Mexican States* (Decision No. 72, July 7, 1931), Decisions of Claims Commissions Great-Britain-Mexico, France-Mexico, and Germany-Mexico, Reports of International Arbitral Awards (RIAA) V (*Veracruz Railways v Mexico*) 221 para 4.

[9]Feller (1935).

instrument to attract foreign capital following their independence of colonial powers.[10] Few capital-exporting countries, in addition, resorted to use military intervention against capital-importing countries for the collection of their nationals' debts. Germany and Great Britain, for instance, invaded Venezuela in 1903 after the latter rejected settling of their differences diplomatically.[11] Germany condemned injuries inflicted on German nationals by Venezuela who, besides compelled them to provide loans, had also destroyed their agricultural land and instituted requisition of their personal property.[12]Great Britain, on its part, had deplored Venezuelan imprisonment of British nationals and pecuniary damages deriving from civil war, as well as default of payment of their loan debts.[13]

Considering the increasing use of military force in inter-state dispute settlement, several international efforts were devoted to the institutionalization of arbitration as a peaceful mechanism of inter-state dispute settlement.[14] The First Peace Conference convened at the Hague in 1899[15] discussed and adopted a set of International Conventions on disarmament, law of war and war crimes,[16] including the Convention adopted for the Settlement of International Disputes (1899 Hague Convention I).[17] Pursuant to this latter convention, arbitration constitutes one of the legal methods for the peaceful settlement of inter-state disputes[18] on questions exclusively of legal character, especially those relating to the interpretation or application of international treaties.[19] To this end, the 1899 Hague Convention I set up the

---

[10]Bértola and Ocampo (2012), pp. 48–80.

[11]Penfield (1903), p. 86.

[12]Ibidem.

[13]Penfield (1903), p. 89.

[14]These efforts dated back to 1898, when the Tsar Nicholas II of Russia convened an international conference to discuss issues relating to peace with States having diplomatic representation in St. Petersburg. To this end, the Russian government delivered a draft program addressing, among others, the acceptance of arbitration as means to prevent armed conflicts. See, respectively, 'Russian Circular Note Proposing the First Peace Conference of 24. Aug. 1898', and 'Russian Circular Note proposing the programme of the first conference of 30 December 1898' reprinted in *The Hague Conventions and Declarations of 1899 and 1907*, 1–4.

[15]The government of the Netherlands formally invited States having diplomatic representation in St. Petersburg to participate in this conference finally convened in May 1899. 'Circular Instruction of the Netherland Minister of Foreign Affairs to the diplomatic representatives of the Netherlands of 7 April 1899', reprinted in *The Hague Conventions and Declarations of 1899 and 1907*, 4–5.

[16]Convention regarding the Laws and Customs of War on Land and the Convention for the Adaptation to Maritime Warfare of the Principles of the Geneva Convention of the 22d August, 1864. Both Conventions were later complemented by other treaties adopted within the 1907 Second Hague Conference. See 'Final Acts of the First and Second Hague Peace Conferences', together with the 'Draft Convention on a Judicial Court', reprinted in *The Hague Conventions and Declarations of 1899 and 1907*, 25–26.

[17]Convention for the Pacific Settlement of International Disputes 1899 (signed 29 July 1899, entered into force 4 September 1900), reprinted in *The Hague Conventions and Declarations of 1899 and 1907* (The 1899 Hague Convention I) 41–81.

[18]The 1899 Hague Convention I (n 17) art 15.

[19]The 1899 Hague Convention I (n 17) art 16.

Permanent Court of Arbitration (PCA) to assist contracting states' recourse to international arbitration.[20]

Following concerns raised by some participant states regarding ceding their sovereignty permanently to an international tribunal,[21] the 1899 Hague Convention I subjects states' provision of consent to arbitrate to the conclusion of another agreement,[22] emphasising on the voluntary nature of states' submission of a claim before the PCA and states parties' freedom to appoint arbitrators.[23] Because the First Hague Conference was devoid of universal character,[24] the Second Hague Conference of 1907 was convened to enable newcomers to adhere to the 1899 Hague Convention I. Latin American countries featured among those new participants,[25] following the compromise previously achieved for their adherence to this Convention within the framework of the Pan American Union (PAU),[26] a space where Latin American countries regularly convened to discuss the legal protection afforded to foreign nationals and the denial of justice as the only ground under which they may assume international responsibility before international tribunals.[27]

Two objects of disagreement between capital-exporting and Latin American countries, however, began to be evident from the Second Hague Conference: the legal conditions under which capital-exporting countries could exercise diplomatic protection for the pecuniary injuries inflicted on their nationals abroad, and the acts giving rise to recipient states' responsibility under international law. A *separate* treaty proposal was put forward during this second conference to discuss several issues concerning the settlement of inter-state controversies arising out of the

---

[20]The 1899 Hague Convention I (n 17) arts 20 and 21.

[21]Myers (1914), p. 769.

[22]The 1899 Hague Convention I (n 17) art 19.

[23]The 1899 Hague Convention I (n 17) art 26.

[24]Limiting the Conference's invitation to those countries having diplomatic representation in St. Petersburg triggered, for instance, that only the United States of America (USA) and Mexico took part in its negotiation process and thus represented the American continent. Boyle (1999).

[25]Argentina, Brazil. Bolivia, Chile, Colombia, Cuba, Guatemala, Haiti, Nicaragua, Panama, Paraguay, Peru, Dominican Republic, Venezuela, Uruguay, Salvador, and Ecuador were the Latin American countries that adhered to the 1899 Hague Convention I See 'Procés-verbal of Adhesion' (signed 15 June 1907), reprinted in *The Hague Conventions and Declarations of 1899 and 1907*, xxx.

[26]At the Second PAU Conference, participant countries worked out a compromise for their adherence to the 1899 Hague Convention. 'Protocol on Adherence to the Convention of the Hague', reprinted in *The International Conferences of American States 1889–1928, Scott Collection*, 61–62.

[27]The PAU convened seven regional conferences: The First PAU Conference was celebrated in Washington (1889–1890); the Second, in Mexico City (1901–1902); the Third, in Rio de Janeiro (1906); the Fourth, in Buenos Aires (1910); the Fifth, in Santiago de Chile (1923); the Sixth, in The Habana (1928) and the Seventh, in Montevideo (1933). See *The International Conferences of American States 1889–1928, Scott Collection*.

collection of contract debts,[28] such as the legal guarantees laid down for home states to ensure that the infringing states go to arbitration and the legal conditions governing the exercise of the right to espouse diplomatic protection claims.[29] Years thereafter, codification attempts undertaken under the aegis of the League of Nations exhibited similar controversy on issues of states' responsibility for injuries inflicted on aliens under international law.[30] Having a large number of member states representing different parts of the world, the League of Nations promoted the codification of different topics of international law, among others, the responsibility of states for damage done within their territory to the person or property of foreigners.[31]

Having defined the issues of contention with capital-exporting countries and the international fora where these debates took place, Sect. 2.1 explores the demands that Latin American countries introduced in terms of sovereign rights in connection with the determination of their international legal responsibility and the resolution of diplomatic protection claims resulting from pecuniary damages. To this end, following a brief description of the legal doctrines prevailing in Latin America, Sect. 2.1.1 discusses the substantive and procedural legal protection afforded to foreign property rights at the domestic and regional level.

Section 2.1.2 centres on the sovereign acts under which Latin American countries were exclusively willing to agree to the settlement of diplomatic protection claims by means of international arbitration, as expressed within the framework of the PAU conferences and the codification attempts promoted by the League of Nations. Subsequently, Sect. 2.1.2.1 analyses the demands of Latin American countries in connection with the international settlement of diplomatic claims relating to pecuniary damages. Section 2.1.2.2 focuses on how these sovereign demands were expressed by states in investor-state contracts and Mixed Claims Commissions' stance thereon.

---

[28]See 'Convention Respecting the Limitation of the Employment of Force for the Recovery of Contract Debts' (signed 18 October 1907), reprinted in *The Hague Conventions and Declarations of 1899 and 1907*, 89–91.

[29]See Sect. 2.1.2.

[30]The League of Nations was established in 1919 and comprised 63 member States. For an overview see Pollock (1922). From this total, 20 member States of the League of Nations stemmed from Latin America.

[31]Nationality and territorial waters constituted the other topics of public international law that the Committee of Experts for the Progressive Codification of International Law determined as relevant for international codification. Work of the Committee of Experts for the Progressive Codification of International Law during its first Session (1925) League of Nations Official Journal (Annex, List of Subject of Study, adopted by the Committee on April 6th and 8th, 1925), Doc. C.275.1925.V, 843.

### 2.1.1  Definition of States' Obligations vis-à-vis Foreign Nationals in Case of Pecuniary Damages

#### 2.1.1.1  Legal Doctrines and Domestic State Practice

The Argentinians Carlos Calvo and Luis Drago developed legal doctrines that exerted a great influence on the domestic and regional legal practice of Latin American countries in their legal relations with foreign nationals and their home states, based on their understanding of the sovereign rights of states as subjects of international law.

Calvo concentrated on formulating key tenets of the legal principles he considered valid and applicable over the treatment of foreign nationals domestically. He advocated the validity of the equality principle under which a state shall deny more favourable substantive rights[32] and legal remedies to aliens than those granted to nationals at the domestic level.[33] Calvo categorically rejected the idea that states could bear international legal responsibility for diplomatic protection claims involving injuries deriving from contract breaches, civil war, or mob violence.[34] As a normative argument for justifying his views, Calvo claimed that the distinct manner in which European countries asserted their right to diplomatic protection against Latin American countries contradicted, among others, the principle of equality of states since the former did not resort to war for the settlement of conflicts arising among themselves.[35] Due to the access foreign nationals had to Latin American countries' domestic courts to bring claims deriving from contractual grievances,[36] Calvo qualified diplomatic coercive actions and the recourse to diplomatic protection as illegitimate home states' methods for enforcing their claims.[37]

On the contrary, Drago centred his views on the issue of diplomatic protection in the aftermath of the European military intervention in Venezuela.[38] Drago did not reject the institution of diplomatic protection claims; however, he only endorsed the view that home states' entitlement to exercise this right derived from a limited set of international acts by states that found states' international legal responsibility infringing. In his capacity as Foreign Affair Minister, Drago directed a note to the Argentine Minister in Washington to call upon the good offices of the USA to prevent the European military intervention in Venezuela that was motivated, inter

---

[32]Shea (1955), p. 18.

[33]Shea (1955), p. 19.

[34]Hershey (1907), p. 27.

[35]Shea (1955), p. 18. According to Shea, the diplomatic (military) actions of European countries against Latin American countries amounted for Calvo to the perpetuation of their semi-colonial relationship with these nations and thus a violation of the principle of territorial jurisdiction. Ibidem.

[36]Shea (1955), p. 19.

[37]Hershey (1907), pp. 26–27.

[38]Drago (1907), pp. 692–726.

alia, by the default of loan payment to European nationals.[39] He differentiated between aliens' pecuniary claims relating to breaches of contracts (categorised as acts *iure gestionis*) and those arising from the default of payment of public debt's bonds,[40] (classified as acts *iure imperi*).[41]

According to Drago, a state acted under contracts as another contracting party governed by domestic rules of private law,[42] which entitled the foreign national in case of non-compliance with its contractual obligations, to seek redress before domestic courts, without the consent of the infringing state, even in cases where it invoked its status as sovereign.[43] It was only in this scenario that Drago underpinned home states' recourse to diplomatic protection against Venezuela if foreign nationals suffered a denial of justice, understood as the lack of judicial instances to hear its claims, or unreasonable delay of its domestic courts.[44] However, Drago held inapplicable the customary rule of denial of justice upon diplomatic protection claims involving the default of loan payments against Venezuela.[45] In his view, Venezuela assumed loan obligations through legislation,[46] which amounted to an act *iure imperi* that enjoyed absolute immunity and, therefore, could not be challenged neither before other states' courts, nor before international tribunals,[47] informed by the principles of sovereign immunity, non-intervention and equality of states.[48] Similar to Calvo, Drago underpinned the validity of the local remedy rule upon foreign nationals, unless they suffered a denial of justice. That was the only host states' right entitling capital-exporting countries to espouse diplomatic protection claims on behalf of their nationals.

Against this background, domestic laws of Latin American countries reflected the main views of Calvo and Drago's doctrines in different forms. Many Constitutions

---

[39]Drago (1907), pp. 692–726.

[40]Drago (1907), pp. 693–695.

[41]Drago (1907), pp. 695–696.

[42]Drago (1907), pp. 693–694.

[43]Drago (1907), p. 694.

[44]Drago (1907), p. 696.

[45]Drago (1907), p. 697.

[46]Drago (1907), p. 695. In connection to this, Drago did not only emphasise on foreign bondholders' own acceptance of default of payment's risk, but also on their privileged position since the debtor state, unlike a company, do not disappear in case of insolvency. Drago (1907), p. 701. Concerning this later aspect, see Hershey (1907), pp. 28–29.

[47]Drago (1907), pp. 695–696.

[48]Drago perceived the military actions of Germany, Great Britain and Italy as a disguised attempt to conquest the Americas, and thus as a violation of the principle of non-intervention and equality of states. Hershey (1907), pp. 29–30 and Boyle (1999), p. 81. In addition, Drago also contested the legitimacy of European countries' military actions against Venezuela on the ground that they were demanding the payment of debts that did not compromise their own development. Also, he advanced hat Venezuela's public debts were in form of state bonds that could easily be transferred from one state to another, this making highly uncertain whether their intervention was likely to protect their own nationals. Drago (1907), pp. 701–702.

only recognised national treatment to aliens with respect to property,[49] or prescribed that domestic laws were the only instruments governing property, regardless of the nationality of its owner.[50] Additionally, some countries stipulated in their domestic legislation that foreign nationals, by deciding on their own to invest in the state concerned, subject themselves to its legal jurisdiction and renounce to claim a special status on the basis of their condition as foreigners with respect to the application of domestic laws or policies.[51]

Regarding legal remedies owed to foreign nationals, many constitutions at the time reaffirmed the exclusive jurisdiction of domestic courts to resolve disputes related to injuries inflicted on them, and explicitly compelled foreign nationals not to request diplomatic protection before their home states, usually known as the Calvo clause.[52] Additionally, other countries restated in their domestic laws that a denial of justice was the only exception to the application of the Calvo clause,[53] practice that led some scholars to understand it as a rule of international law.[54]

Outside the Latin American region, capital-exporting countries also recognised the validity of the local remedy rule with respect to pecuniary damages inflicted on aliens,[55] though attaching to the denial of justice, a broader scope of application than the one given in Latin American countries. In countries like the USA, for instance, a denial of justice occurred, if state's inobservance of its contractual obligations were confiscatory or discriminatory in nature and without compensation,[56] what implied a understanding of the rule that went beyond the mere absence of local remedies in contracting states.[57] Others understood this customary rule as containing a prohibition against discriminatory treatment, and as a protection against the insufficiency of legal remedies.[58]

These expansive views of the denial of justice rule were not free from criticism, since they departed from its main rationale, namely to ensure protection to foreign

---

[49]Fitzgibbon (1948), p. 670, citing article 35 of the Constitution of Bolivia.

[50]Fitzgibbon (1948) citing article 31 of the 1933 Constitution of Peru.

[51]Shea (1955) citing 32 AJIL Supp (1938) – 1938 Law of Ecuador art 26.

[52]Fitzgibbon (1948) citing art 31 of the 1933 Constitution of Peru; article 35 of the Constitution of Bolivia; and article 30 and 31 of the Constitution of Ecuador.

[53]Fitzgibbon (1948) citing article 35 of the Constitution of Bolivia; article 19 of the 1936 Constitution of Honduras; article 25 of the 1939 Constitution of Nicaragua.

[54]Bochard (1915).

[55]A majority acknowledged that while foreign nationals willing to remain in a country in an ongoing state of turmoil, accepted the risks and advantage of that place of residence, they were nevertheless entitled domestically to request protection for their life and property, and to have access to courts. Hershey (1907), p. 35.

[56]*International Fisheries Company Case (USA) v United Mexican States* (July 1931), Decision of Claims Commissions Mexican-United States, Report of International Arbitral Awards (RIAA), No. IV (Dissenting Opinion by American Commission) 691 (*International Fisheries Company v Mexico*).

[57]Lipstein (2014), p. 106.

[58]Hershey (1907), p. 32.

nationals against the absence of legal remedies in other states.[59] Moreover, while others justified home states' use of military force as the unique available means for protecting their nationals against injuring states' unwillingness to submit disputes concerning their loan agreements' obligations,[60] others contended that higher privileges had to be accorded to foreign nationals only if recipient states' acts were exclusively directed at them.[61]

In connection with those views, the idea about the existence of minimum standards of justice began to gain supporters among capital-exporting countries. According to this rule, every state had to observe in relation to foreign nationals' property rights and economic activities imply affording to them full protection under its legal system.[62]

### 2.1.1.2  Regional State Practice

Latin American countries firmly endorsed the validity of the equality principle and the denial of justice within the framework of the PAU Conferences, which provided a space for their discussion of issues of common concern, such as the equality between nationals and aliens regarding rights and legal remedies,[63] and the exclusive validity of their Constitution and domestic laws as the exclusive legal instruments to determine their obligations vis-à-vis foreign nationals.[64]

Guided by these principles, the Latin American states adopted the Convention relative to the Rights of Aliens at the Second PAU Conference,[65] later complemented by the Convention on the Status of Aliens,[66] following a study about aliens' rights under international law, admissible limitations and

---

[59]Lipstein (2014), p. 206.

[60]Hershey (1907), p. 33.

[61]Hershey (1907), p. 36. Some scholars endorsed Drago's views concerning that coercible actions underlying pecuniary claims were an exceptional practice in international law so that it had to be ruled in accordance with general international rules such as the non-intervention principle, which is corollary to the principle of sovereign equality among states. Hershey (1907), pp. 40–41.

[62]Bochard (1940).

[63]'Recommendation, Claims and Diplomatic Intervention' (adopted April 8, 1890), reprinted in *The International Conferences of American States 1889–1928, Scott Collection*, 45, first recital.

[64]Ibidem, second recital.

[65]'Convention Relative to the Rights of Aliens', reprinted in *The International Conferences of American States 1889–1928, Scott Collection*, 90–91. Signatories countries were Argentina, Bolivia, Chile, Colombia, Costa Rica, Dominican Republic, Ecuador, Guatemala, Honduras, Mexico, Nicaragua, Paraguay, Peru, El Salvador, Uruguay. From this group pf 15 countries, only 7 ratified it: Bolivia, Colombia, Ecuador, Guatemala, Honduras, Nicaragua, El Salvador (Convention Relative to the Rights of Aliens).

[66]'Convention on the Status of Aliens' (signed on 20 February 1928), reprinted in *The International Conferences of American States 1889–1928, Scott Collection* (Convention on the Status of Aliens) 415–416.

corresponding legal remedies.[67] Both Conventions restated the validity of the national treatment,[68] and the absolute jurisdiction of host states to rule, at their discretion, their legal relations with foreign nationals and their property rights.

The Convention relative to the Rights of Aliens proclaimed that states did not have any obligation to recognize other rights except those established within their domestic legal orders,[69] so that they did not bear any liability arising from injuries inflicted on aliens in case of *force majeure* or wars.[70] Under the Convention on the Status of Aliens, Latin American countries asserted their right to determine the conditions under which foreign nationals may enter and reside in its territory,[71] and emphasised on foreign nationals' obligation to subject themselves to host states' jurisdiction and laws, with due account to the exceptions established in treaties.[72] Differences were still evident among these Conventions in relation to the local remedy and denial of justice.

Pursuant to the Convention relative to the Rights of Aliens, foreign nationals were only entitled to seek legal remedies before competent domestic courts, and their respective home states, to assert their right to diplomatic protection, if there was a manifest denial of justice,[73] unusual delay or evident breaches of international law principles.[74] Contrarily, no reference to the Calvo clause was made in the Convention on the Status of Aliens, which arguably led to a minor adherence of Latin American countries to this instrument.[75] Hence, although these instruments were pursued to articulate alien's rights, they were defined in terms of the articulation of states' rights as traditional subjects of international law and the consequences attached to those legal entitlements.

The adoption of the Convention on the Status of Aliens within the framework of the PAU conferences coincided with the attempts taken by the League of Nations to codify relevant topics in international law that were susceptible of codification.[76] One of these topics was the issue of international legal responsibility of states for

---

[67] 'Resolution Consideration of the Rights of Aliens Resident within the Jurisdiction of Any of the American Republics' (adopted May 3, 1923), reprinted in *The International Conferences of American States 1889–1928, Scott Collection*, 282, recital one.

[68] Convention Relative to the Rights of Aliens (n 65) first recital; Convention of the Status of Aliens (n 66) art 5.

[69] Convention Relative to the Rights of Aliens (n 65) second recital para 1.

[70] Convention Relative to the Rights of Aliens (n 65) second recital para 2.

[71] Convention on the Status of Aliens (n 66) art 1.

[72] Convention on the Status of Aliens (n 66) art 2.

[73] Convention Relative to the Rights of Aliens (n 65) third recital.

[74] Ibidem.

[75] Only Brazil, Nicaragua, Panama, and the United States of America ratified the Convention on the Status of Aliens. Convention on the Status of Aliens (n 66) footnote 2. See Reinalda (2009), pp. 415–416.

[76] See Council Resolution (1924) LNOJ, Special Supplement No. 21 10.

injuries caused to aliens, with the aim of exploring the possibility to conclude an international convention thereon.[77]

After recognising that member states deemed to have a set of common international rules necessary,[78] the League of Nations' Assembly convened a codification conference and established an additional committee for its preparation.[79] To this end, a draft Convention on the Treatment of Foreigners was delivered for its discussion at the Conference for the Codification of International Law in 1930,[80] having as the theoretical underpinnings, the doctrines of reciprocal treatment, most-favoured nation treatment and equality between nationals and foreigners.[81]

Yet, the provision on national treatment, nevertheless, provoked strong disagreement between participant states. Although Latin American countries did not participate with a common approach because of the divergent views previously evidenced regarding the exclusivity of domestic courts to adjudicate pecuniary claims and the legal conditions that shall govern home states' exercise of diplomatic protection,[82] they jointly favoured the application of the national treatment standard in international law, whereas capital-exporting countries opposed it, basing their argument on the fact that the treatment accorded to nationals may be below the international minimum standards of justice. Consequently, these codification efforts did not lead to the adoption of an international multilateral treaty.[83]

---

[77]See Work of the Committee of Experts for the Progressive Codification of International Law during its First Session (n 31). To this end, the Sub-Committee sent a questionnaire to League of Nations' member States in 1926 to ascertain their views on whether this topic demanded a set of common international rules. See, 'Letter from the Chairman of the Committee of Experts for the Progressive Codification of International Law to the Secretary-General of the League of Nations, Communication to the Later, For Transmission to Governments, the Questionnaires and Reports adopted by the Committee at its Second Session Held in January 1926' (1926) 20 AJIL (Special Supplement) 18–20. Also, Committee of Experts for the Progressive Codification of International Law, Questionnaire No. 4 adopted by the Committee as its Second Session, held in January 1926 (Responsibility of States for Damage done in their Territories to the Person or Property of Foreigners)' (1926) 20 AJIL (Special Supplement) 176.

[78]Committee of Experts for the Progressive Codification of International Law, Report to the Council of the League of Nations on the Questions which Appear Ripe for International Regulation (1928) 22 AJIL (Special Supplement) 4–5, and Annex III, Analyses of Replies Received from Governments to Questionnaires Submitted by Members of the Committee (1928) 22 AJIL (Special Supplement) 15–21.

[79]League of Nations, Resolutions and Recommendations Adopted by the Assembly, September 27, 1927, (1928) 22 AJIL (Special Supplement) 231.

[80]Draft Convention on the Treatment of Foreigners, (1930) League of Nations Official Journal Doc. C. 97, M. 23, 13–22. In this Conference, Latin American countries' participation can be summarised as follows: Bolivia, Colombia, Cuba, Dominican Republic, Guatemala, Haiti, Panama, Paraguay, Peru, El Salvador, Uruguay, and Venezuela participated as League of Nations' member States. Additionally, Brazil and Mexico participated in their capacity of non-members. Ibidem.

[81]Ibidem.

[82]The Conference in mention was convened at the Hague from 13 March to 12 April 1930.

[83]League of Nations publication, V. Legal, 1930.V.17, document C.351(c) M.145(c).1930. V.

The futile codification attempts undertaken at the international level brought about the engagement of Latin American countries, once again, in the definition of their rights under international law and the consequences to be attached to their exercise for the treatment owed to aliens by means of the Convention on the Rights and Duties of States, the so-called 'Montevideo Convention', in force until the present day.[84]

The Montevideo Convention addresses issues involving statehood criteria[85] and the recognition of states[86] as a preliminary question for the enumeration of their fundamental rights and duties. The Montevideo Convention proclaims the states' right to equality in rights and legal capacity with respect to other sovereign countries,[87] and refers, to their corollary duty of non-intervention in the internal or external affairs of others.[88] At the time of its adoption, this was a clear reference to past experiences faced by some countries of the region in light of the military collection of debts by capital-exporting countries. Moreover, the Convention recognises states' right to exercise jurisdiction upon all the inhabitants located in their territory[89] and the corollary implication for foreign nationals as follows: 'Nationals and foreigners are under the same protection of the law and the national authorities and the foreigners may not claim rights other or more extensive than those of the nationals'.[90]

The Montevideo Convention clearly embodies the legal principles informing Latin American countries critical stand towards military intervention as a means for the international resolution of inter-state disputes and international legal instruments that protect foreign investment going beyond the national treatment. Moreover, the provision referring to aliens' treatment exhibited that the treatment of aliens was subsumed to states' exercise of their jurisdiction, despite the lack of consensus persisting among these states in relation to the recognition of higher privileges to foreign nationals and their property rights.[91]

---

[84]See 'Convention on the Rights and Duties of States' (signed 26 December 1933, entered into force 26 December 1934) (1934) 28 (2) AJIL (Supplement: Official Documents) (Montevideo Convention) 75–78. At the end, 16 American countries ratified the Convention.

[85]Montevideo Convention (n 84) art 1.

[86]Montevideo Convention (n 84) arts 3, 6 and 7.

[87]Montevideo Convention (n 84) art 4.

[88]Montevideo Convention (n 84) art 8.

[89]Montevideo Convention (n 84) art 9.

[90]Ibidem.

[91]In fact, no State made reservations to the validity of the principle of State's jurisdiction. Countries like the USA made reservations to the Montevideo Convention's provision regarding the non-intervention principle on account of the obscurity of this concept, while Brazil and Peru, to the Convention's provision on the non-recognition of State's acquisition of territory by means of force.

## 2.1.2   Establishment of Limitations Upon Inter-State Arbitration of Diplomatic Protection Claims

### 2.1.2.1   Denial of Justice and Local Remedies Rules

The two French military interventions in Mexico in the nineteenth century motivated the majority of (Latin) American countries, at the invitation of the US government, to convene from 1889 to 1890 to discuss and adopt a plan of arbitration for the settlement of inter-state disputes.[92] Yet, with the convening of the First Peace Conference in 1899, some Latin American countries worked out a compromise for their adherence to the 1899 Hague Convention I,[93] and adopted the Treaty on Compulsory Arbitration,[94] under which some (Latin) American countries reaffirmed their commitment to submit disputes among themselves before the PCA.[95] This preliminary consensus facilitated their massive participation at the Second Hague Conference convened in 1907, where they agreed to the 1899 Hague Convention I.

In the meantime, Germany, Italy and the United Kingdom invaded Venezuela in 1902 due to the material and pecuniary damages inflicted on their nationals' property. Other countries, however, abstained from employing coercive means, despite having similar claims.[96] Since these military actions were renewed efforts to settle these disputes following Venezuela's refusal to settle them diplomatically, Venezuela agreed to sign protocols with each invading European, recognising the merits of

---

[92]'Invitation to the (First) Conference of American States, Circular Instruction of the Secretary of State of the United States to the American Diplomatic Representations accredited to the Governments of Mexico, Central and South America, Haiti and Santo Domingo' (July 13, 1888), reprinted in *The International Conferences of American States 1889–1928, Scott Collection* 5–6.

[93]At the Second PAU Conference, participant countries worked out a compromise for their adherence to the 1899 Hague Convention. 'Protocol on Adherence to the Convention of the Hague', reprinted in *The International Conferences of American States 1889–1928, Scott Collection*, 61–62.

[94]'Treaty on Compulsory Arbitration' (signed 29 January 1902), reprinted in *The International Conferences of American States 1889–1928, Scott Collection* (Treaty on Compulsory Arbitration) 100–104.

[95]Treaty on Compulsory Arbitration (n 94) arts 1 and 3. Although ten American countries signed this treaty, only six countries ratified it. Signatory States were Argentina, Bolivia, Dominican Republic, Guatemala, Mexico, Paraguay, Peru, El Salvador, Uruguay. Only Dominican Republic, Guatemala, Mexico, Peru, El Salvador, and Uruguay became States parties.

[96]Belgium, France, Mexico, the Netherlands, Spain, Sweden, Norway and the USA were the countries that omitted to use military force against Venezuela. To settle the claims of their respective nationals, Venezuela agreed with them.

their claims[97] and committing itself to settle these claims through arbitration.[98] Additionally, these protocols explicitly stipulated the preferential treatment that allied powers to the PCA accorded to their claims.[99] Moreover, Venezuela also signed Protocols with non-invading states, but without making similar concessions in relation to the merits of their claims.[100] Against this backdrop, Venezuela and invading countries agreed to refer the settlement of these claims to an *ad hoc* tribunal constituted under the auspices of the PCA,[101] which in turn facilitated the submission of other states' claims against Venezuela.[102] After nine months of deliberations, the *Preferential Claims v Venezuela* tribunal rendered a unanimous award in 1904, upholding the preferential treatment of invading countries' claims.[103] However, it omitted addressing the question of the legality of their military intervention on the grounds of lack of competence,[104] thereby missing an opportunity to clarify whether, and under which conditions, states' use of military force may be valid for asserting protection on behalf of their nationals.

Given these circumstances, additional efforts were pursued towards the institutionalization of arbitration in connection with the collection of loan debts at the Second Hague Conference in 1907. At this juncture, participating states discussed a draft Convention to rule on legal controversies relating to treaty interpretation arising

---

[97]Protocol of February 13, 1903, Mixed Claims Commission (Germany-Venezuela) Reports of International Arbitral Awards (RIAA) X 359 (Germany-Venezuela Protocol) art I; Protocol of February 13, 1903, Mixed Claims Commission Great Britain-Venezuela, Reports of International Arbitral Awards (RIAA) IX 351 (Great Britain-Venezuela Protocol) art I; Protocol of February 13, 1903, Mixed Claims Commission (Italy-Venezuela), Reports of International Arbitral Awards (RIAA) X 479 (Italy-Venezuela Protocol) art I.

[98]Germany-Venezuela Protocol (n 97) art III; Great Britain-Venezuela Protocol (n 97) art III; Italy-Venezuela Protocol (n 97) art III.

[99]Germany-Venezuela Protocol (n 97) art V; Great Britain-Venezuela Protocol (n 97) art V; Italy-Venezuela Protocol (n 97) art V.

[100]For instance, see Protocol of an Agreement of 17 February 1903 between the Secretary of State of the United States of America and the Plenipotentiary of the Republic of Venezuela for Submission to Arbitration of All Unsettled Claims if Citizens of the United States of America against the Republic of Venezuela, Mixed Claims Commission United States-Venezuela, Reports of International Arbitral Awards (RIAA) IX 115.

[101]Protocol between Germany and Venezuela for the Reference of Certain Questions to the Permanent Court of Arbitration at the Hague, signed at Washington, May 7, 1903, The Venezuelan Preferential Case (Germany, Great Britain, Italy, Venezuela et al) Reports of International Arbitral Awards (RIAA) IX 105 (Protocol for the Reference of Certain Questions to the Permanent Court of Arbitration) art I. Venezuela signed identical protocols with Great Britain and Italy for the same purpose. See footnote 2.

[102]Protocol for the Reference of Certain Questions to the Permanent Court of Arbitration (n 101) art VI.

[103]*Award of the Tribunal of Arbitration Constituted in Virtue of the Protocols signed at Washington on 7 May 1903 between Germany, Great Britain, and Italy on the One Hand and Venezuela on the Other Hand*, done at the Hague, In the Permanent Court of Arbitration, 22 February 1904, Reports of International Arbitral Awards (RIAA) IX 107 (*Preferential Case against Venezuela Award*).

[104]*Preferential Case against Venezuela Award* (n 103).

between two or more contracting states, the so-called the Draft Convention on the Limitations of Employment of Force for Recovery of Contract Debts.[105] Conceived as a reference framework, rather than as a multilateral agreement on arbitration,[106] the purpose of this draft Convention was prevention of fraudulent or frivolous claims from creditor states.[107] Under this draft Convention, the PCA had jurisdiction upon the determination of the claim's validity, debt's amount and the time and mode of debt payment.[108] However, this draft Convention did not categorically prohibit coercive diplomatic actions, if the debtor state rejected an offer to arbitration, or after failure to implement arbitration result even after providing its consent to arbitration.[109] On these grounds, eight Latin American countries made reservations to this Convention, particularly when it did not include the denial of justice rule and exhaustion of local remedies as suggested by these states,[110] whereas others abstained from voting in favour of its adoption because its domestic framework already accorded legal protection to foreign nationals.[111]

Within the framework of the PAU Conferences, the recourse to inter-state arbitration for claims involving debt's collection was worth considering after the impossibility to achieve an international consensus on the legal conditions applicable to inter-state arbitration. In 1910, the PAU adopted the Convention on Pecuniary Claims,[112] to 'submit to arbitration all claims for pecuniary loss and damages' of their respective nationals.[113] The PCA was the competent body mandated to administer the conduct of arbitral proceedings pursuant to the 1899 Hague Convention,[114] unless disputing parties agreed otherwise under another treaty.[115]

Hence, the ratification of this convention by an important group of states signalised initial efforts to protect the property rights of other American nationals[116] arbitration.

---

[105]Convention Respecting the Limitation of the Employment of Force for the Recovery of Contract Debts (n 28) art 1.

[106]The draft Convention was designed to ease contracting states to agree to the PCA's jurisdiction by means of bilateral treaties See for instance, Giustini (1986).

[107]Boyle (1999).

[108]Convention Respecting the Limitation of the Employment of Force for the Recovery of Contract Debts (n 28) art 2.

[109]Convention Respecting the Limitation of the Employment of Force for the Recovery of Contract Debts (n 28) art 1.

[110]Scott (1908), pp. 78, 89.

[111]Ibidem.

[112]'Convention Pecuniary Claims' (adopted 11 August 1910), reprinted in *The International Conferences of American States 1889–1928, Scott Collection*, 183–185.

[113]Convention Pecuniary Claims (n 112) first recital.

[114]Convention Pecuniary Claims (n 112) art 2 paras 1 and 2.

[115]Convention Pecuniary Claims (n 112) art 2 para 1 and art 3.

[116]Signatory States of the Convention on Pecuniary claims were Argentina, Brazil, Chile, Colombia, Costa Rica, Cuba, Dominican Republic, Ecuador, Guatemala, Haiti, Honduras, Mexico, Nicaragua, Panama, Paraguay, Peru, El Salvador, United States of America, Uruguay, and

However, as a general inter-state mechanism of peaceful dispute settlement gradually displaced the discussion of arbitration as dispute settlement method in the context of pecuniary claims within the PAU.[117] Examples include promotion of the creation of a permanent court of arbitration in the Americas;[118] the approval of a Treaty to Avoid or Prevent Conflicts,[119] and the conclusion of the General Treaty on Inter-American Arbitration that explicitly ruled out controversies arising within the domestic jurisdiction of any disputing party and to which international law did not apply.[120] Hence, (Latin) American countries again safeguarded their jurisdiction to rule their internal affairs, including how they protected foreign property rights by particularly subjecting the Convention's application to the condition of denial of justice,[121] in addition to the exhaustion of local remedies[122] or that domestic court's judgement became *res judicata*.[123]

### 2.1.2.2  By Means of the Calvo Clause in Investor-State Contracts

Latin American countries not only articulated their exclusive jurisdiction to freely determine how they protected foreign property rights through the incorporation of the so-called 'Calvo clause' in domestic laws. They also included formulations of the

---

Venezuela. Ibidem 185. Ratifying countries were Brazil, Costa Rica, Dominican Republic, Ecuador, Guatemala, Honduras, Nicaragua, Panama, Paraguay, United States of America, and Uruguay. Convention Pecuniary Claims (n 112) footnote 1, 183.

[117]'Resolution Consideration of the Best Means to Give Wider Application to the Principle of the Judicial or Arbitral Settlement of Disputes that may arise between the Republics of the American Continent', reprinted in *The International Conferences of American States 1889–1928, Scott Collection*, recital one (Resolution Consideration of the Best Means to Give Wider Application to the Principle of the Judicial or Arbitral Settlement of Disputes).

[118]Resolution Consideration of the Best Means to Give Wider Application to the Principle of the Judicial or Arbitral Settlement of Disputes (n 117) recital three. The Costa Rican delegation introduced this proposal in the agenda of the Fifth PAU Conference and delivered a draft treaty to this end. For its content see 'Proposed Treaty Presented by the Delegation of Costa Rica Regarding the Creation of the Permanent Court of American Justice', reprinted in *The International Conferences of American States 1889–1928, Scott Collection*, 452–454.

[119]Treaty to Avoid or Prevent Conflicts Between the American States, reprinted in *The International Conferences of American States 1889–1928, Scott Collection*, 285–289. Ratifying States were Brazil, Chile, Cuba, Dominican Republic, Ecuador, Guatemala, Haiti, Panama, Paraguay, United States of America, Uruguay, and Venezuela. Adherent States were Costa Rica, Mexico, Peru, and El Salvador. See ibidem footnote one.

[120]General Treaty of Inter-American Arbitration, reprinted in *The International Conferences of American States 1889–1928, Scott Collection*, art 2 lit. a.

[121]For instance, see Reservations made by Uruguay, Colombia, El Salvador, General Treaty of Inter-American Arbitration [Translation of Reservations] (n 120) 460–461.

[122]For instance, see Reservation made by Venezuela, (n 120). In Ecuador, this Convention applied if the foreign national had previously exhausted domestic legal remedies. See Reservation made by Ecuador, (n 120).

[123]See for instance Reservation made by Mexico, (n 120).

Calvo clause in investor-state contracts by granting national status to foreign companies and thus. the legal treatment owned to nationals. Mexico clearly portrayed this later trend in contracts celebrated with US and British nationals and/or companies engaged in the provision of dredging services;[124] railways' operation;[125] services of the construction, maintenance, and acquisition of railways;[126] tramway services of animals, fodder, and passengers,[127] and the construction of food canning factories for the packing of sealed food.[128] As a result of the incorporation of the Calvo clauses, claims arising out of those contracts had to be exclusively resolved before domestic courts. In other words, foreign nationals were only entitled to seek legal remedies before domestic authorities and courts and were expected not to request the diplomatic protection before their home states, unless they faced a denial of justice.

The foreign contracting parties of the contract with Mexico mentioned above, however, suffered severe pecuniary injuries in Mexico, leading their home states to submit diplomatic protection claims on their behalf for the payment of damages through the establishment of Mixed Claims Commissions.[129] In the face of these diplomatic protection claims faced by Mexico, Mixed Claims Commissions upheld the validity of the Calvo clause and thereby provided important reflections on which acts constitute international wrongful acts, on one hand, and the scope of the denial of justice rule and its relationship with the local remedy rule, on the other.

In principle, Mixed Claims Commissions underpinned the Latin American countries' view that breaches of contractual obligations do not amount to international wrongful acts.[130] They, in fact, averted to hold Mexico internationally liable for breaches of its contractual obligations assumed in favour of foreign nationals, or for the pecuniary damages faced by foreign nationals out of international revolts and confiscation of their properties. Moreover, these Commissions confirmed the exhaustion of local remedies as an essential requirement for home states' diplomatic protection, and the denial of justice as the sovereign act, which might allocate international legal responsibility upon recipient states by failing to deliver proper justice, or undue delay to aliens when pursuing remedies for material and pecuniary

---

[124]In reference to the dredging services' contract signed with North American Dredging Company of Texas, see *North American Dredging Company v Mexico* (n 8) 26–27.

[125]In reference to article 11 of the contract celebrated with Mexican Union Railway (Limited), see *Mexican Union Railway v Mexico* (n 8) footnote 1.

[126]*Interoceanic Railway of Mexico and others v Mexico* (n 8); *Veracruz Railways v Mexico* (n 8) 221 para 4.

[127]*Douglas G. Collie Mac Neill (Great Britain) v United Mexican States* (Decision No. 27, April 10, 1931), Decisions of Claims Commissions Great-Britain-Mexico, France-Mexico, and Germany-Mexico Reports of International Arbitral Awards (RIAA) V (*Douglas G. Collie Mac Neill v Mexico*) 135.

[128]*International Fisheries Company v Mexico* (n 56) 691.

[129]See n 8.

[130]*Mexican Union Railway v Mexico* (n 8) paras 6–7; *Veracruz Railways v Mexico* (n 8) para 4; *International Fisheries Company v Mexico* (n 56) 701.

injuries.[131] However, it seems that there was no consensus among both Commissions on the relationship between the treaty waiver of exhaustion of local remedies requirement incorporated in international Conventions and alleged denial of justice.[132] The US-Mexican Mixed Claim Commission dealt with diplomatic protection claims, whose subject matter related to contractual grievances rather than allegations of denial of justice. Despite this fact, this Commission explicitly referred to the denial of justice and seemed to hold the view that the effect of the Calvo clause over this requirement was precluding the application of the local remedy rule with respect to claims of denial of justice.[133]

Contrarily, the Great Britain-Mexico Commission did settle claims, where the home state explicitly alleged denial of justice as the ground of its claim and the injured nationals had previously sought remedies before Mexican authorities. According to this Commission, this treaty waiver did not dispense home state's compliance with the requirement of exhaustion of local remedies for the submission of diplomatic protection claims.[134] The motivation behind this approach was that a denial of justice could only be established when all remedial instances of the host state had been exhausted.

## 2.1.3 Preliminary Conclusions

From the independence of Latin American countries until the 1930s, there was a noticeable politicisation of capital-exporting countries' recourse to military intervention for debts' collection and the submission of diplomatic protection claims on behalf of their nationals for pecuniary damages. Domestic legal instruments and regional conferences regularly held within the framework of PAU allowed Latin American countries to articulate their sovereign demands.

The first issue of contention was the alleged existence of international minimum standards and, even in few cases, the international denial of justice rule, as legal sources of international states' responsibility. This contestation was evidenced at international conferences aiming at the adoption of international treaties that defined

---

[131] *North American Dredging Company v Mexico* (n 8) para 22; *Mexican Union Railway v Mexico* (n 8) para 9; *Veracruz Railways v Mexico* (n 8) para 4; *Interoceanic Railway of Mexico and others v Mexico* (n 8) paras 11, 13.

[132] The US-Mexican Mixed Claim Commission held the view that states could waive the requirement of the exhaustion of local remedies rule in cases where a denial of justice occurred, while the Great Britain-Mexico Mixed Claim Commission endorsed the opposite view.

[133] *North American Dredging Company v Mexico* (n 8) paras 20–21.

[134] *Mexican Union Railway v Mexico* (n 8) para 115; *Veracruz Railways v Mexico* (n 8) para 221; *Interoceanic Railway of Mexico and others v Mexico* (n 8) para 115; *Douglas G. Collie Mac Neill v Mexico* (n 127) para 135; *El Oro Mining and Railway Company (Limited) (Great Britain) v United Mexican States* (Decision No. 55, June 18, 1931), Decisions of Claims Commissions Great-Britain-Mexico, France-Mexico, and Germany-Mexico, RIAA V 191.

their international obligations in cases related to inflicting pecuniary damages or at the resolution of diplomatic protection claims by Mixed-Claims Commissions.

In addition to demands of equality among states, Latin American countries articulated their jurisdictional power to freely define the substantive and procedural scope of protection granted to foreign nationals and their properties within their territories. This later demand was articulated in terms of the Calvo clause, which proclaimed the equality between nationals and foreigners before the law, or in other words, foreign nationals were entitled to exclusively seek legal remedies before domestic authorities and courts. Because of the above-mentioned demand, the second issue of contention was capital-exporting countries' attempt to submit diplomatic protection claims for the pecuniary injuries inflicted on their nationals. For Latin American countries, only denial of justice, understood as the lack of legal remedies within the infringing state, gave rise to home states' espousal of diplomatic protection claims on behalf of their nationals.

## 2.2  Politicisation Through States' Articulation of the Right to Expropriate Foreign Property (1930–1980)

Between 1930 and 1980, two regional developments triggered Latin American countries to devote great efforts in strengthening their sovereignty over their natural resources, and to delineate the legal conditions under which they exercised their right to expropriate foreign property. The first development was the diplomatic controversy between Mexico and the USA about the legal standard applicable to the payment of compensation after Mexico's expropriation of US citizen's agrarian properties in 1938. The USA argued that Mexico had the international obligation to exercise its right to expropriate foreign property in accordance with international law principles ordering the payment of an 'adequate, effective and prompt' compensation to aliens.[135] This principle is referred to as the 'Hull formula' standard, named after the US Secretary of state Cordell Hull, who upheld its validity in the case concerned.[136] In contrast, Mexico only recognised the payment of compensation to the US nationals being guided by its domestic laws,[137] alleging the

---

[135]'Mexico-United States: Expropriation by Mexico of Agrarian Properties Owned by American Citizens' (1938) 32 (4) AJIL (Supplement: Official Documents 193) 181.

[136]Ibidem.

[137]'Mexico-United States: Expropriation by Mexico of Agrarian Properties Owned by American Citizens' (n 135) 203.

implementation of its agrarian reform as its public purpose,[138] and the validity of the equality principle under which aliens had the same treatment as nationals.[139]

The second development was the publication of the Raul Prebrisch's study on 'The Economic Development of Latin America and its Principal Problems' under the aegis of the Economic Commission for Latin America and the Caribbean (ECLAC).[140] Prebrisch study looked at the Centre-periphery economic model prevailing in the region, under which developing countries—referred to as the 'periphery'—were usually in a position of dependency in relation to developed countries—referred as to the 'Centre'. Reason behind this phenomenon was that the Centre, by producing and manufacturing goods with the primary commodities stemming from the periphery, was in a better position to deal with the changes in the market than the periphery, and thus, able to steer the prices of the goods that the periphery imported from them.[141] Following Prebrisch study, the ECLAC staff founded the Latin American structuralist development school that devoted great efforts to distinguish structural features in developing countries' economies that may hinder their adjustment and responsiveness to development policies.[142]

To reduce developing countries' external economic dependency from the Centre, this school encouraged the adoption of the import-substitution industrialization policy (ISI policy) that consisted of inducing manufacturing imports' replacement with local production of industrialized goods through, among others, the nationalization of foreign property and foreign companies' rights.[143] ECLAC also recommended the promotion of regional integration through the creation of a common market,[144] where their members follow common economic and trade policies, and liberalised internal tariffs while setting a common external tariff.[145]

To materialise their aspirations of economic independence, Bolivia, Chile, Colombia, Ecuador, and Peru followed ECLAC recommendations and established

---

[138]'Mexico-United States: Expropriation by Mexico of Agrarian Properties Owned by American Citizens' (n 135) 202. In addition to the modernization of the agricultural sector, Mexico pursued the redistribution of land to counteract the limited agricultural diversification that compelled them to import agricultural commodities from developed countries. Another reason advanced by Mexico was to eliminate the latifundio and minifundio system, which favoured land concentration on few (foreign) owners and the corresponding limited use of lands by indigenous peoples, who were compelled to pay in exchange with their harvest or the adoption of landowners' instructions regarding their use, respectively. Ibidem.

[139]'Mexico-United States: Expropriation by Mexico of Agrarian Properties Owned by American Citizens' (n 135) 205.

[140]ECLAC (Department of Economic Affairs) 'The Economic Development of Latin America and its Principal Problems' (27 April 1950) E/CN.12/89/Rev.l.

[141]Ibidem.

[142]Kay (2009).

[143]Ibidem.

[144]ECLAC, 'A Contribution to the Economic Policy in Latin America' (3 June 1965) E/CN.12/728.

[145]ECLAC, 'The Latin American Common Market' (July 1959) E/CN.12/531.

the Andean Community (ANCOM) in 1969,[146] to achieve, inter alia, the promotion of a balanced and harmonious development among them by means of improvement of their position within international economic arena.[147] Although these countries previously joined the Latin American Free Trade Association (LAFTA),[148] they set up the ANCOM due to the economic and political challenges they faced in comparison with other Latin American countries having stronger economies.[149]

Latin American countries' aspirations of economic independence coincided with capital-exporting countries' post-war demands of access to raw materials[150] and former colonies' claims of self-determination.[151] Against these varied set of interests, the United Nations General Assembly (UNGA) especially underpinned the capital-importing countries' need of development by acknowledging states' right to dispose their natural resources freely,[152] and fostering the inclusion of the peoples' right to political and economic self-determination in the drafts of the two international covenants on human rights.[153] Informed by the preliminary work on these human rights instruments, the UNGA subsequently entrusted a Commission with the analysis of the principle of permanent sovereignty over natural resources as a 'constituent of the right to self-determination' and the adoption of recommendations for its reinforcement.[154]

---

[146]Thereafter, Venezuela joined the ANCOM in 1967, whereas Chile withdrew in 1976. Agreement on Andean Subregional Integration (signed 26 May 1969, entered into force 16 October 1969) (1969) 8 (5) ILM (Cartagena Agreement) 910.

[147]Cartagena Agreement (n 146) art 1 para 2.

[148]LAFTA was established in 1962 to create a free trade zone in the region among their members, and later replaced by the Latin American Integration Association in 1980. See Instrument Establishing the Latin American Integration Association (ALADI) (August 1980). Available via SICE: http://www.sice.oas.org/trade/Montev_tr/Montev1e.asp. Accessed 10 December 2020.

[149]Lopez Valdez (1972). The Commission and Junta were the principal organs of the ANCOM. The Commission adopt legislative acts in form of decisions, whereas the Junta propose legislative acts and supervise the implementation of the Cartagena Agreement. Cartagena Agreement (n 146) arts 6 and 14–17, respectively. For a detailed discussion on this point see O'Leary (1984).

[150]For instance, see Atlantic Charter (signed 14 August 1941) para 5. Other expressions of such aspirations can be found in the constitutive treaties of Bretton Woods institutions, see Agreement of the International Bank for Reconstruction and Development (signed 22 July 1944, entered into force 27 December 1945) 2 UNTS 134 art I, lit. iii, and Agreement of the International Monetary Fund (signed 22 July 1944, entered into force 27 December 1945) 2 UNTS 39 art I, lit. ii. In addition, see General Agreement on Tariffs and Trade of 1947 (signed 30 October 1947, entered into force 1 January 1948) 55 UNTS 187 preamble para 1.

[151]UNGA Res 1514 (XV) (14 December 1960) para 5.

[152]UNGA Res 523 (VI) (12 January 1952) GAOR 6th Session Supp. 20, 20 (on integrated economic development and commercial agreements). Also, UNGA Res 626 (VII) (21 December 1952) GAOR, 7th Session Supp. 20, 18.

[153]International Covenant on Civil and Political Rights (signed on 16 December 1966, entered into force on 23 March 1976) 999 UNTS (ICCPR) art 1 para 2. International Covenant on Economic, Social and Cultural Rights (signed on 16 December 1966, entered into force on 3 January 1976) 933 UNTS (ICESCR) art 1 para 2.

[154]UNGA Res 1314 (XIII) (12 December 1958), GAOR, 13th Session Supp. 18, 27.

Following these preliminary studies, the UNGA endorsed the Declaration on Permanent Sovereignty over Natural Resources aiming to address unsettled conflicts among capital-importing and capital-exporting countries regarding the legal conditions governing states' expropriation of foreign property.[155] Subsequently, the Group of 77 intended to legitimise the implementation of large-scale nationalization programs in some developing countries, and to rebuild the international economic relations among states in the benefit of developing countries by means of the Declaration on New International Economic Order (NIEO) (NIEO Declaration).[156] Subsequently, UNGA adopted the Charter of Economic Rights and Duties of states to implement this aspired economic order and articulate the scope of the permanent sovereignty over natural resources principle.[157]

In parallel to UN developments, capital-exporting countries and international financial institutions funding development projects in capital-importing countries developed their own strategies. First, European nations began the negotiation of BITs to stipulate the legal standards pursuant to which the other contracting states legally committed to treat their nationals and their investment. Germany was the first country to enter into a BIT,[158] followed by other European countries with a view to safeguarding the existing investment of their nationals in former colonies and other developing countries alike.[159] Second, countries like the USA, on the contrary, preferred to establish an investment insurance agency, the so-called Overseas Private Investment Corporation (OPIC), to protect their nationals' investment against the political risk they usually faced in capital-importing countries motivated by the latter's refusal to submit investment disputes to international arbitration because of their incompatibility with domestic laws.[160] Finally, the International Bank for Reconstruction and Development (IBRD) (hereafter called the 'World Bank'), together with the International Monetary Fund (IMF),[161] fostered the adoption in 1965 of the Convention on the Settlement of Investment Disputes between States

---

[155]UNGA Res 1803 (XVII) (14 December 1962) GAOR 17th Session Supp. 17, (Declaration on Permanent Sovereignty over Natural Resources) 15.

[156]UNGA Res 3201 (S-VI) (1 May 1974) UN Doc A/Res/S-6/3201 (NIEO Declaration). A group of 77 developing countries established this coalition in 1964 with the purpose of defining and promoting their collective economic interests as well as strengthened jointly their negotiating capacity within the UN system. See Joint Declaration of the Seventy-Seven Developing Countries Made at the Conclusion of the United Nations Conference on Trade and Development (15 June 1964).

[157]UNGA Res 3281 (XXIX) (12 December 1974) GAOR, 29th Session, Supp. 31 (1), 50 (Charter of Economic Rights and Duties of States) art 2 para 1.

[158]Treaty for the Promotion and Protection of Investments (with Protocol and exchange of notes) Germany-Pakistan (signed 25 November 1959, entered into force 26 March 1963) (Germany-Pakistan BIT) 457 UNTS 24.

[159]For instance, see Mann (1981).

[160]See 'U.S. Department of State Report on Nationalization, Expropriation, and Other Takings of U.S. and Certain Foreign Property since 1960', (1972) 11 (1) ILM (US Report on Nationalization, Expropriation, and other Takings) 84.

[161]Agreement of the International Bank for Reconstruction and Development (n 150).

and Nationals of Other States (ICSID Convention).[162] The ICSID Convention pursues to create an international arbitration facility that administers the settlement of investment disputes arising between a state party and the national of another state party to this instrument, the Centre for the Settlement of Investment Disputes (ICSID).[163] Latin American countries, however, were explicitly opposed to the adoption of this treaty that led to the creation of the ICSID.

Considering that the issues of contention during this epoch revolve around the legal conditions governing states' expropriation of foreign property rights and the international arbitration of investor-state contract-based disputes, Sect. 2.2 explores the demands put forward by Latin American countries and their corresponding articulation on questions relating to the substantive and procedural protection to be afforded to foreign property rights. To this end, Sect. 2.2.1 not only explores these demands but also considers the articulation of sovereign claims on questions relating to the substantive protection afforded to foreign property in case of expropriation at the domestic and regional level. Incidentally, UN resolutions also form part of the material under review since Latin American countries also participate in the deliberation process for their adoption. Section 2.2.2 then proceeds to discuss these demands on questions of the procedural rights granted to foreign property rights by these countries in different types of contracts.

## 2.2.1  Definition of States' Obligations Vis-à-vis Foreign Nationals in Case of Expropriation of Property Rights

### 2.2.1.1  Domestic State Practice

With the implementation of the ISI policy, Latin American countries explicitly articulated their right to expropriate any type of property, including those owned by foreign nationals.[164] Their domestic laws thus regulated in which forms, and under which conditions, they were entitled to exercise this right. Some countries did not restrict foreign nationals' rights to own and use property, but rather limited its exercise as follows:[165] some countries expressly prohibited foreign national's par-

---

[162]The Convention on the Settlement of Investment Disputes between States and Nationals of Other States (signed 18 March 1965, entered into force 14 October 1966) 575 UNTS 159 (ICSID Convention).

[163]Ibidem.

[164]For instance, see Avila Martel and Salvat Maguillot (1971), pp. 94–95.

[165]Seabra Fagundes (1971), p. 51; Treviño (1971), p. 115.

ticipation in exploration and exploitation activities in the oil,[166] mining[167] and other public services sectors,[168] while addressing secondarily substantive and procedural rights when defining the conditions governing their right to expropriate and in laws applicable to investor-state contracts.

Expropriation of foreign property rights was understood as the mandatory legal transfer of land and real state property's title owned by foreign nationals to the state itself or to one of its agencies,[169] and transfer of assets related to these properties.[170] In most cases, states adopted these measures with the intention to satisfy their aspirations of agrarian reforms.[171] On one hand, they expropriate foreign property by means of 'nationalization' of oil[172] and mining industries,[173] while to a lesser extent, the services sector.[174]

In addition to these forms of direct expropriation, Latin American countries also imposed exogenous corporate regulatory forms having a similar effect, the so-called 'creeping expropriation' or 'regulatory taking' on foreign companies, to induce the involvement of local activity in foreign companies' operations.[175] Illustrations of

---

[166]To illustrate, see Seabra Fagundes (1971) and Treviño (1971). Venezuela also featured as one of the Latin American countries that increased their control and ownership in the oil industry. UNGA, Report of the Economic and Social Council, Permanent Sovereignty over Natural Resources, Report of the Secretary General, Supplement to the report of the Secretary-General, Document A/9716 (20 September 1974), (ESCO Report) Table 1, p. 5.

[167]Pérez Olivares et al. (1971), pp. 215–216. Chile and Peru remarkably increased their control and ownership in the copper mining sector. See ESCO Report (n 166) 30–31.

[168]Mexico, for instance, precluded foreign companies from investing in the electricity and railroad sector. Treviño (1971), pp. 149–150.

[169]For instance, see Avendano Valdés and García Belaunde (1971), p. 181; Avila Martel and Salvat Maguillot (1971), pp. 106–107.

[170]Pérez Olivares et al. (1971), p. 229.

[171]For illustrations of US national's claims involving land expropriation in Bolivia and Peru see 'US Report on Nationalization, Expropriation, and other Takings' (n 160), 91 and 98, respectively.

[172]In relation the nationalization of the oil industry in Venezuela see UNGA, 'Report of the Economic and Social Council, Permanent Sovereignty over Natural Resources', Report of the Secretary General, Supplement to the report of the Secretary-General, Document A/9716 (20 September 1974), (ESCO Report) (n 166), Table 1, p. 5. This report was delivered by the Economic and Social Council and examined different developments concerning State's exercise over natural resources. For illustrations of US national's claims involving nationalization of oil industries in Argentina, Bolivia, Haiti and Peru see 'US Report on Nationalization, Expropriation, and other Takings' (n 160), 90, 91, 95 and 97, respectively.

[173]In relation to the nationalization of copper companies in Chile and Peru, see 'ESCO Report' (n 166) 30–31. For illustrations of US national's claims involving nationalization of zinc industries in Bolivia and Mexico see 'US Report on Nationalization, Expropriation, and other Takings' (n 160) 90 and 95, respectively.

[174]For illustrations of US national's claims involving nationalization of commercial banks in Chile and Peru see 'US Report on Nationalization, Expropriation, and other Takings' (n 160) 93 and 97, respectively. Concerning nationalization telephonic companies, see ibidem 95.

[175]For instance, foreign shareholders investing in Mexico had to obtain permission to acquire any share in Mexican companies. Treviño (1971), p. 151.

this form of indirect expropriation included the obligation of foreign companies to train nationals, use of domestic companies for importing or exporting materials, and transfer part of their production to national companies.[176] Other manifestations included transfer of foreign companies' control to nationals through the appointment of local managers responsible for its operation in conformity with host states' development strategies,[177] or states' acquisition of the majority of their shares.[178] Finally, the renegotiation of concession agreements with foreign companies was another regulatory measure to boost local production, particularly when these contracts were allegedly agreed in unequal terms by not anticipating future host states' concerns.[179]

Moreover, states generally laid down the conditions under which they shall exercise this sovereign right, namely by justifying a public purpose, following a due process and under the condition of compensation payment to the right-holder over the expropriated property. Regarding the public purpose, some countries referred to this requirement in their Constitutions,[180] or in laws that govern a specific economic sector.[181] Some countries broadly applied the concept 'public utility' by covering any type of property and activities,[182] while others qualified the conservation and exploitation of natural resources[183] or their distribution among nationals as the objective underlying their expropriatory actions.[184] An exception to this general rule was made in favour of those property holders who complied with labour rights,[185] pursued the conservation of natural resources,[186] or efficiently exploited

---

[176]Subhash (1983), p. 87, citing Vernon (1967), p. 87.

[177]Seabra Fagundes (1971), p. 57.

[178]Chile implemented several programs gearing towards acquiring most shares of foreign copper companies and appointing officials to their board of directors respectively. See 'US Report on Nationalization, Expropriation and other Takings' (n 160) 93. In addition, this country also obliged foreign companies providing public services (railroads, electricity, and telegraphs facilities) to transfer the majority of their shares to State agencies. Avila Martel and Salvat Maguillot (1971).

[179]In 1970, the Venezuelan government entered into contracts with oil foreign companies in which a bigger amount of ownership of oil was taken over by the state and the length of the corporate ownership was reduced to twenty years. Subhash (1983), p. 90.

[180]The Chilean government amended the Constitution for conferring property a social function and ensuring a distribution of natural resources among their nationals through the transformation of foreign industries into Chilean industries. Avila Martel and Salvat Maguillot (1971).

[181]Avendano Valdés and García Belaunde (1971), citing the Peruvian Organic Petroleum Law of 1952, 177.

[182]Gordillo (1971), pp. 11–48.

[183]To illustrate, Pérez Olivares et al. (1971), pp. 215–216.

[184]Avendano Valdés and García Belaunde (1971), citing the Peruvian Organic Petroleum Law of 1952, 177.

[185]To illustrate, see Avila Martel and Salvat Maguillot (1971), p. 106. Also, Avendano Valdés and García Belaunde (1971), p. 181; Pérez Olivares et al. (1971), p. 230.

[186]See Seabra Fagundes (1971), p. 57; Avila Martel and Salvat Maguillot (1971), p. 106; Pérez Olivares et al. (1971), p. 229.

the land and local factors of production.[187] Once the state declared the public utility of a particular property, the foreign national was entitled to all remedies available to nationals, including the payment of compensation in accordance with its domestic laws.[188]

In lack of the definition of legal standards, existing FCN treaties were another source for this determination and referred to states parties' obligation to pay compensation to aliens in case of property seizure. Some countries only guaranteed a 'sufficient' compensation to foreign nationals in cases of seizure of their property,[189] while others only a fair indemnification in case of the deprivation of their properties by their competent authorities.[190]

Furthermore, investor-state contracts also mirrored the validity of the national treatment of foreign nationals in connection with the context of natural resources. Many usually categorised concession agreements and other types of investor-state contracts as 'administrative contracts',[191] if the state or the state agency was one of the contracting parties, and their subject matter related to public services.[192] Host states' administrative law governed these contracts, while civil law were applied as secondary.[193] Being the contracting states' laws these were the only applicable laws; they often counteracted the privileged position of the contracting state by limiting their withdrawal of contracts to the exclusive grounds of public interest and national security.[194] Accordingly, the legal protection of foreign property rights was considerably contingent upon the states' conditions governing the exercise of their sovereign right to expropriate foreign property rights and their obligations under concession agreements.

---

[187]See Pérez Olivares et al. (1971), p. 229.

[188]See Avila Martel and Salvat Maguillot (1971), p. 107; Avendano Valdés and García Belaunde (1971), p. 183.

[189]Colombia-USA FCN treaty (n 1) art 5.

[190]Hanseatic Cities-Venezuela FCN treaty (n 1) art IV.

[191]Administrative contracts generally implied contracts relating to the construction of a public work, land lease, operation of public utility, concessions to perform a public service. See Cueto-Rua (1957).

[192]Cueto-Rua (1957), pp. 20–21. Public services in this context implied those relating to the construction of a public work, land lease, operation of public utility, concessions to perform a public service. Cueto-Rua (1957), p. 21.

[193]Cueto-Rua (1957), p. 21. Other States resorted to the incorporation of the so-called *Rebus Sic Stantibus* clause in contracts that embodied the doctrine of unforeseeable or changing circumstances under which a host State could invoke the unilateral termination of a contract in the event of changes in the circumstances of its operation. Sornarajah (1986), pp. 133–135. Advocating the use of this doctrine was made with basis on article 62 of the Vienna Convention on the Law of Treaties (hereinafter referred to as the 'VCLT'), on the assumption that if it applies to international treaties celebrated among States, it may also be applicable to investor-state contracts which indirectly serve to connect States' economy. Sornarajah (1986), p. 133.

[194]Cueto-Rua (1957), p. 22; Sornarajah (1986), pp. 130–133.

### 2.2.1.2   Regional State Practice

In this historical period, the focus of the discussion at the regional level shifted from issues relating to the legal treatment owed to foreign nationals to defining the role of the state in the design of investor-state relationship in the context of natural resources, as well as the consequences to be attached in case of inobservance of these international standards.

With the establishment of the Organization of American States (OAS), Latin American countries resumed the discussion about their international legal responsibility in relation to injuries inflicted on foreign property rights that previously took place within the framework of PAU Conferences. For instance, these countries reiterated the validity of the national treatment in relation to the legal remedies to aliens (again, the so-called Calvo clause).[195] Notably, reference to this principle was also made in connection with the acts and omissions, placing them as international responsibility. In their view, international law places upon them legal responsibility in favour of aliens under the same acts or omissions under which they assume liability for their nationals.[196] In principle, they reiterated that safeguarding judicial remedies to aliens is an international obligation, which a state fulfils through the provision of local remedies;[197] understanding a denial of justice as a situation where no legal remedies are available, or where courts do not render decisions upon an alien's claim. Beyond this regional instrument, however, the treatment owed to aliens became an incidental aspect of states' exercise of their sovereign rights (sub) regionally and internationally alike.

Within the framework of ANCOM, an investment code for the common treatment of foreign capital was introduced through Decision 24.[198] Beyond addressing diverse aspects relating to the registration of foreign capital,[199] this Decision encouraged foreign nationals to transform their companies into mixed enterprises. This was in exchange of duty relief programs for goods produced in collaboration with national companies,[200] and to give free disposal of their shares or participatory

---

[195]Ibidem art IV.

[196]ILC, First Report on State responsibility by Mr. Roberto Ago. Special Rapporteur—Review of previous work on codification of the topic of the international responsibility of States (7 May 1969 and 20 January 1970), Document A/CN.4/217 and Corr.1 and Add.1, citing Principles of international law that govern the responsibility of the State in the opinion of Latin American countries, prepared by the Inter-American Juridical Committee in 1962, Annex XIV (Principles of international law that govern the responsibility of the State in the opinion of Latin American countries) art III.

[197]Principles of international law that govern the responsibility of the State in the opinion of Latin American countries (n 196) art VIII.

[198]Andean Pact, Decision 24 'Andean Foreign Investment Code' (adopted 30 November 1976) (1977) 16 ILM 138 (Decision 24).

[199]Decision 24 (n 198) arts 2, 5–6.

[200]Decision 24 (n 198) art 27.

rights to domestic companies as a pre-condition for their establishment in a member state's territory.[201]

In addition, this instrument precluded foreign companies from making direct investment in some strategic state sectors such as mineral sector, public services, insurance, commercial and financial sector of member states.[202] In connection with this, Decision 24 also reflected South American countries' refusal to grant foreign nationals a more favourable treatment than the one accorded to their own nationals.[203] In fact, the Decision 24 categorically prohibited the incorporation of clauses in investor-state contracts enabling the resolution of related disputes outside the jurisdiction of the host state's domestic courts by the home state's subrogation of its nationals' rights.[204] While Decision 24 was considered an obstacle rather than an incentive for foreign investment,[205] its implementation was actually unsuccessful on different grounds, mainly because of the failure of the member states of the ANCOM to create favourable conditions for ensuring consistency with their own domestic policies.[206]

Within the framework of UNGA, different aspects relating to the permanent sovereignty over natural resources principle were addressed to complement domestic developments in the context of natural resources through a set of resolutions. Some resolutions dealt with issues that others excluded and exhibited an emerging consensus about the states' rights vis-a-vis foreign capital. The Natural Resources Declaration was the first instrument adopted under the aegis of UNGA in 1962 that explicitly engaged in the discussion of this principle by qualifying states and peoples as its right-holders.[207]

In this context, property expropriation was the central object of this Declaration, without-however, making any categorization of it as a right of sovereign states,[208] nor limiting these rules to property belonging to foreign nationals.[209] The Declaration begins emphasising the duty of foreign capital to comply with the rules and conditions that host states impose for the implementation of exploration, development and disposition of natural resources' activities.[210]

To this end, this Declaration refers to property-holders' right to legal treatment in accordance with national and international law.[211] Concerning states, the Declaration defines the legal standards governing the exercise of their right to expropriation

---

[201]Decision 24 (n 198) art 30.

[202]Decision 24 (n 198) arts 40–42.

[203]Decision 24 (n 198) art 50.

[204]Decision 24 (n 198) art 51.

[205]Preziosi (1989).

[206]O'Leary (1984), pp. 111–114.

[207]Declaration on Permanent Sovereignty over Natural Resources (n 155) para 1.

[208]Garcia-Amador (1980).

[209]Garcia-Amador (1980), p. 26.

[210]Declaration on Permanent Sovereignty over Natural Resources (n 155) para 2.

[211]Declaration on Permanent Sovereignty over Natural Resources (n 155) para 3.

foreign property as follows: public utility, security, or national interest are the only justifications of states' expropriation and the payment provided for compensation in an 'appropriate' manner.[212] To be entitled to payment, property holders shall seek remedies before the domestic courts of the expropriatory state, but they may bring their claims before international adjudicative bodies if the state consent thereto.[213] For some, this Declaration actually embodied certain international consensus since it reaffirmed the legal standards traditionally applicable to expropriation or nationalization of property, and the payment of compensation.[214]

Years after the Declaration on Permanent Sovereignty over Natural Resources, the NIEO Declaration and the Charter of Economic Rights and Duties of States were adopted, centring the debate on the determination of the rights and duties of states deriving from their permanent sovereignty over natural resources. However, in contrast to the former instrument, they reflected the opposite interests between capital-importing and capital-exporting countries.

Capital-importing countries called for the establishment of the NIEO in May 1974, despite divergences on the political and economic interests of these capital-importing countries.[215] Months thereafter, the Charter of Economic Rights and Duties of States came to complement the NIEO Declaration to provide a consensus on these issues that reflect the interests of capital-importing and capital-exporting countries alike. Both instruments conceived, albeit differently, the principle of permanent sovereignty over natural resources. Under the NIEO Declaration, this principle constitutes one of the pillars for the NIEO that it strives to propose;[216] whereas the Charter refers to it as an inalienable right and a duty of every sovereign state.[217] Moreover, both instruments recognised the states' right to nationalise or transfer of property ownership as a manifestation of this principle/right,[218] even though the Charter is the only one that broadly governs its exercise.

Aimed at regulating the exercise of this states' right with respect to foreign property only, the Charter stipulates that host states' domestic laws is the governing law of the payment of appropriate compensation and the settlement of related disputes in accordance therewith,[219] unless the states concerned have agreed on

---

[212]Declaration on Permanent Sovereignty over Natural Resources (n 155) para 4.

[213]Declaration on Permanent Sovereignty over Natural Resources (n 155) para 4.

[214]Garcia-Amador (1980), p. 23.

[215]Concerning political interests, while those countries attaining their independence claimed a right to development, Latin American countries only aimed at preventing a misuse of the right to diplomatic protection. Garcia-Amador (1980), p. 9. Regarding differences in economic interests, some capital-importing countries were exclusively raw material exporters, whereas others, oil-producers and exporters. In addition, some countries prevailed resorting to international public lending institutions to finance their development projects or balance of payment problems, while others preferred private financing of foreign commercial banks. Adede (1986), p. 1001.

[216]NIEO Declaration (n 156) para 4, lit. e.

[217]Charter of Economic Rights and Duties of States (n 157) art 2 para 1.

[218]NIEO Declaration (n 156) para 4, lit. e; Charter of Economic Rights and Duties of States (n 157) art 2 para 2, lit. c.

[219]Charter of Economic Rights and Duties of States (n 157) art 2 para 2, lit. c.

the employment of another international dispute settlement method.[220] Nevertheless, the Charter did not incorporate the public purpose ground for the expropriation of foreign property and to categorise the payment of compensation as a states' duty, thereby increasing the likelihood of arbitrary host states' acts.[221]

Finally, the NIEO Declaration and the Charter of Economic Rights and Duties of States to a *right to regulate* and supervise transnational corporations through measures serving to its national economic interest.[222] Pursuant to the Charter, states' right to regulate foreign investment activities shall be exercised in accordance with domestic laws and national objectives, but without being subject to an obligation to accord a preferential treatment to foreign nationals and their investment.[223] Moreover, the Charter also restates that this sovereign right also comprises the supervision of transnational corporations' activities within its jurisdiction and implementation of measures to ensure corporate activities' compliance with their regulations and economic and social policies.[224]

To sum up, this regional/universal discussion reflects to some extent the position of Latin American countries in advocating their design of investor-state relations, by centring on the articulation of their sovereign rights to expropriate and regulate, rather than on the international definition of the legal treatments and remedies of foreign nationals, since the latter aspect fell within the domain of their internal affairs.

## 2.2.2   Establishment of Limitations Upon International Arbitration of Investor-State Contract-Based Disputes

### 2.2.2.1   National and Regional Practice

Latin American countries not only endorsed arbitration as an alternative method for the resolution of international disputes among states, but they also began to employ this alternative method for the settlement of two type of disputes with foreign investors. One set of disputes comprised those arising out of breaches of loan agreements. Despite their floating interest rates determined by market forces, many Latin American countries prevailed to apply for short-term loans from commercial banks to finance their development projects and cope with balance of payment problems, than those granted by the IMF due to the strict credit conditions that this financial institution demanded from them.[225] Under these circumstances, loan

---

[220]Charter of Economic Rights and Duties of States (n 157) art 2 para 2, lit. c.

[221]Garcia-Amador (1980), pp. 27–28.

[222]NIEO Declaration (n 156) para 4, lit. g.

[223]Charter of Economic Rights and Duties of States (n 157) art 2 para 2 lit. a.

[224]Charter of Economic Rights and Duties of States (n 157) art 2 para 2 lit. b.

[225]Sarcevic (1987).

agreements usually incorporated choice of law clauses referring to the law of another country as its governing law, and arbitration clauses for the submission of disputes outside contracting states' domestic courts.[226] In turn, domestic laws of many Latin American countries explicitly permitted involving state agencies in the submission of disputes arising out of loan agreements to arbitration.[227] The other set of disputes were those arising out of trans-national commercial transactions, prior to the approval of the competent state authority.[228]

With the creation of the OPIC, the USA began to conclude agreements with Latin American countries hosting US investment,[229] to obtain the authorization for the insurer state's subrogation of its nationals' rights set forth in domestic laws of recipient states of their investment.[230] Through subrogation, US investment qualified, upon payment, for the investment insurance program offered by the OPIC against any political risk that they may face in the latter.[231] One relevant provision of these financial agreements was the arbitration clause, where Latin American countries committed to arbitrate disputes with the USA deriving from the claims of a US investor covered by the investment guarantee, such as for instance those arising out of an expropriation.[232] Notwithstanding the former, the *compromis* only covered disputes arising out of questions of public international law, subjecting the initiation of an arbitration proceeding to the prior exhaustion of local remedies by the US affected investor before host state's courts.[233] In addition, some countries even prohibited the submission of a dispute involving the exercise of its regulatory power to arbitration, and explicitly indicated that expropriation of foreign property only amounted to an issue of international law, only in case of denial of justice in seeking redress before its domestic courts.[234] Accordingly, one can observe that some Latin American countries maintained and reinforced the validity of the denial of justice as the only act giving rise to their legal responsibility in international law, in a context where states regularly articulated their sovereign rights over natural resources.

Nevertheless, Latin American countries made no concessions towards the settlement of contractual disputes by means of arbitration if the exercise of their sovereign power was at stake. They generally prohibited, in different ways, foreign national's recourse to arbitration to enable international tribunal's review of its regulatory

---

[226]For instance, see Delaume (1986).

[227]See Grigera Naón (1991), citing 1983 Colombian Decree 222 art 229 footnote 44; citing Brazilian Law No. 1518 and the Brazilian Law Decree 1312 footnote 45, and Argentinian Law 20548 art 7 footnote 46.

[228]In reference to Panama, see Grigera Naón (1991), pp. 215–216.

[229]Ocran (1988).

[230]Ocran (1988).

[231]Overseas Private Investment Corporation Act of 1985 (USA).

[232]Ocran (1988).

[233]In reference to arbitration clauses incorporated in financial agreements concluded between Brazil and the USA, and between Ecuador and the USA, see Steiner and Vagts (1986), p. 546.

[234]In reference to the Brazil-US agreement, see Steiner and Vagts (1986), pp. 546–547.

conduct.[235] They either reiterated domestic courts' exclusive jurisdiction to resolve disputes, where the state was the contracting party, or where the public interest was involved,[236] or specified the areas over which they foreclosed foreign courts or arbitral tribunals' review of their regulatory conduct.[237]

Within the framework of OAS, these countries strengthened the validity of the Calvo clause in relation to member states' exercise of diplomatic protection on behalf of their nationals. In addition, these countries endorsed the validity of this clause regarding the submission of disputes with foreign nationals before arbitral tribunals, if legal remedies were available within the jurisdiction of the state concerned.[238] Accordingly, foreign nationals were only entitled to seek remedies for their claims arising out of breaches of concession agreements or state's exercise of its right to expropriate before domestic courts.

Considering the rigid posture of Latin American countries towards arbitral tribunals' review of their regulatory conduct, foreign nationals engaged in economic activities in these countries brought cases before the domestic courts of their home states, albeit without success. For instance, German nationals challenged Chile's nationalizations of German copper companies before German courts.[239] However, German courts abstained from reviewing the legality of Chilean sovereign acts in deference of the act of state doctrine under which courts do not question the legality of foreign acts under foreign law, and recalled the exhaustion of local remedies and home states' espousal of diplomatic protection claims as appropriate alternatives to seek redress.[240] Given these major procedural limitations, foreign investors sought compensation through direct negotiations with the state concerned,[241] or by calling the offices of the World Bank to assist in the settlement of disputes.[242]

---

[235] An exception to this rule was made concerning issues relating to determination of the compensation's amount to be paid in connection with administrative contract's breaches. See Grigera Naón (1991), citing Argentinian Model Contract for the Exploration and subsequent Exploitation of Hydrocarbons art 18 para 3 footnote 30.

[236] See Grigera Naón (1991), citing 1978 Ecuadorian Constitution art 16 footnote No. 41 and 1961 Venezuelan Constitution art 127 footnote No. 39.

[237] See, Grigera Naón (1991), citing Mining Code of Uruguay art 19 footnote 52.

[238] Within the framework of the Ninth PAU Conference, American states also endorsed another treaty where they committed to strengthen peace and security among themselves by waiving their right to exercise diplomatic protection. Tratado Americano de Soluciones Pacíficas "Pacto de Bogotá" (signed 30 April 1948) preamble and art VII.

[239] Seidl-Hohenveldern (1975).

[240] Seidl-Hohenveldern (1975).

[241] For instance, see reference to the agreement achieved between Bolivian Gulf Oil Company and Bolivia, 'US Report on Nationalization, Expropriation and other Takings' (n 160) 90. Similarly, see reference to the agreements of American and Foreign Power Company, and of Companhia Telefonica Nacional with Brazil, 'US Report on Nationalization, Expropriation and other Takings' (n 160) 91. Also, see reference to the agreement achieved between Peruvian Telephone Company and Peru, 'US Report on Nationalization, Expropriation and other Takings' (n 160) 97.

[242] Address by World Bank President Eugene Black to the Annual Meeting of the Board of Governors (19 September 1961), *International Centre for the Settlement of Investment Disputes (ICSID), History of the ICSID Convention*, Vol. 2 (1) ICSID History 3.

### 2.2.2.2   Latin American Refusal to Adhere to the ICSID Convention

The elaboration and delivery of a draft convention to create the ICSID in 1962 among the members of the World Bank Board of Governors[243] was based on the presumption that the creation of this international arbitration facility would contribute to improve the investment climate of participant states and this, consequently, would increase foreign capital flows into their territories.[244] To this end, the World Bank Board of Governors adopted a resolution entrusting the Executive Directors with the finalisation of a final treaty draft proposal for the creation of this Centre at the Annual Meeting held in Tokyo in 1964.[245] This motion, however, encountered considerable opposition from Latin American countries, which jointly rejected its adoption by alleging inobservance of their domestic legal practice.[246] They alleged that foreign nationals were already entitled to constitutional and domestic legal protection in the same manner as their own nationals, particularly with regard to confiscation and the payment of unfair compensation in case of expropriation.[247] They also advanced that the ratification of such a treaty would considerably impair their own nationals since foreign nationals would have the right to file a claim before international adjudicative bodies without exhausting local remedies, as they are obliged to under the same circumstances.[248]

Notwithstanding the Latin American appeal to maintaining equality between nationals and foreigners by rejecting its adoption, the Convention on the Settlement of Investment Disputes (ICSID Convention) initially entered into force for 20 states in 1965,[249] including countries such as Jamaica and Trinidad and Tobago.[250] The

---

[243]'Resolution No. 174 Study of Settlement of Investment Disputes' (adopted 18 September 1962), *International Centre for the Settlement of Investment Disputes (ICSID), History of the ICSID Convention* (1968) II-1 2 para 11.

[244]'Paper Prepared by the General Counsel of the World Bank and Transmitted to the Members of the Committee of the Whole' SID/63-2 (18 February 1963) *International Centre for the Settlement of Investment Disputes (ICSID), History of the ICSID Convention* (1968) II-2, part I 73.

[245]'Resolution 214 "Settlement of Investment Disputes" of the Board of Governors' (adopted 10 September 1964), *International Centre for the Settlement of Investment Disputes (ICSID), History of the ICSID Convention* (1968) II-1 para 41.

[246]The countries which voted against the Resolution 214 'Settlement of Investment Disputes' were Argentina, Bolivia, Brazil, Chile, Colombia, Costa Rica, the Dominican Republic, Ecuador, El Salvador, Guatemala, Haiti, Honduras, Iraq, Mexico, Nicaragua, Panama, Paraguay, Peru, the Philippines, Uruguay, and Venezuela. See 'Resolution 214 'Settlement of Investment Disputes' of the Board of Governors' (adopted 10 September 1964), *International Centre for the Settlement of Investment Disputes (ICSID), History of the ICSID Convention* (1968) II-1 2 para 41 (footnote 2).

[247]'Press Release No. 57 (September 9, 1964, Tokyo), Excerpt from the statement by Felix Ruiz, Governor for Chile', *International Centre for the Settlement of Investment Disputes (ICSID), History of the ICSID Convention* (1968) II-1 2 para 39.

[248]Ibidem.

[249]ICSID Convention (n 162).

[250]Jamaica as well as Trinidad y Tobago signed the ICSID Convention on 23 June 1965 and 5 October 1966, respectively. The Convention entered into force for Jamaica and Trinidad y Tobago

ICSID Convention explicitly rules out states parties' recourse to diplomatic protection over investment disputes that are settled in accordance with its provisions[251] and reiterates the states parties' obligation to abide by and comply with the award,[252] and to recognise its binding force and enforce the pecuniary obligations laid down in it as it were a final judgement of its courts.[253] In fact, the Convention attaches a marginal role to the arbitration of diplomatic protection claims if the respondent state has failed to abide, or comply with, an award rendered in favour of the national of another contracting state.[254] This development generated that capital-exporting countries began to negotiate BITs that explicitly provide for investor-state arbitration by conferring covered investors direct access to arbitration under the ICSID Convention. By doing so, states parties to the ICSID waive their sovereign immunity to allow international *ad hoc* tribunals' review of their regulatory conduct vis-à-vis foreign investors and their investment.[255]

By avoiding the incorporation of arbitration clauses in concession agreements with foreign investors, Latin American countries minimised the adverse chances that a tribunal might consider the investment contract as internationalised for the presence of these clauses. The so-called internationalisation of investment contracts was a great subject of controversy within this period. Some tribunals were of the view that international law became the governing law of the contract for the mere presence of arbitration clauses.[256] In this respect, the ICSID Convention stipulates that it did not totally exclude the application of international law by providing that an arbitral tribunal shall decide in accordance with the law agreed by the disputing parties, and in absence of such agreement, it shall apply host state's laws and international law as it may be applicable.[257] Arbitral tribunals constituted thereafter under these

---

on 4 October 1966 and 2 February 1967, respectively. See ICSID, List of Contracting states and Other Signatories of the Convention, <https://icsid.worldbank.org/en/Documents/icsiddocs/List%20of%20Contracting%20States%20and%20Other%20Signatories%20of%20the%20Convention%20-%20Latest.pdf> accessed 10 December 2020.

[251]'Convention on the Settlement of Investment Disputes between States and Nationals of Other States, Documents Concerning the Origin and the Formulation of the Convention', *International Centre for the Settlement of Investment Disputes (ICSID), History of the ICSID Convention* Vol. II, Part 1, at 242, 273, 303, 372, 464. ICSID Convention (n 162) art 27.

[252]ICSID Convention (n 162) art 53.

[253]ICSID Convention (n 162) art 54. For a discussion, see Schreuer (2007), pp. 345–358.

[254]ICSID Convention (n 162) art 27.

[255]The Netherlands-Indonesia BIT was the first treaty incorporating an investor-state arbitration clause in accordance with the ICSID Convention. See Agreement between the Government of the Kingdom of the Netherlands and the Government of the Republic of Indonesia on Promotion and Protection of Investment (7 July 1968) 11386 UNTS 14 art 9 para 4. In contrast, the 1959 Germany-Pakistan BIT only allowed for the submission of disputes agreed by the states parties before the International Court of Justice (ICJ), or to an arbitral tribunal. See Germany-Pakistan BIT (n 158) art 11.

[256]*Texaco Overseas Petroleum Company and California Asiatic Oil Company v Government of the Libyan Arab Republic,* Award (19 January 1977) (1978) 17 ILM 1.

[257]ICSID Convention (n 162) art 42 para 1.

international arbitration rules seemed to have understood this provision as that the host states' law is the primary law governing the contract, whereas international law may play a complementary role.[258] This implied that the application of international law was not totally excluded in the settlement of contract-based investment disputes, a practice that was contrary to Latin American countries' approach in the regulation of their legal relationship.

## 2.2.3   Preliminary Conclusions

During the 1930s and 1980s, the politicisation of international instruments protecting foreign investment also took place in Latin America, albeit with a subtle tone, since there were neither inter-state disputes involving the international legal protection of foreign property rights before Mixed-Claims Commissions, nor a direct exchange with capital-exporting countries at international conferences where explicit disagreements were widely expressed.

The first issue of contention was the legal standards applicable to determine the payment of compensation in case of expropriation of foreign investment, which arose from Latin American countries' demand of preserving their sovereignty over their natural resources. The sovereign right to expropriate foreign property was the form employed by these countries to articulate these demands at the domestic and regional level. Explicit efforts were devoted to defining, inter alia, the legal conditions under which states could exercise this sovereign right; protection of strategic sectors in natural resources, and the validity of the Calvo clause in relation to foreign nationals. The historical analysis of this period also confirms the trend of Latin American countries to define their sovereign rights in the first place, and incidentally, the legal consequences for the protection of foreign property rights.

The second object of controversy in Latin American countries' relationship with international legal instruments protecting foreign investment was the submission of contract-based disputes with foreign nationals to international arbitration if this legal recourse implied a review of their regulatory acts. On one hand, this critical stand towards international arbitral underlied the demand of Latin American countries to protect the exercise of their jurisdiction to define the scope of legal protection of foreign property rights. On the other, this critical position reflected Latin American countries' understanding that only denial of justice due to of lack of domestic legal remedies give rise to international dispute settlement. This finding thus indicates that at least from this perspective issue of contention did not diverge from those of the previous historical period.

---

[258]These readings of article 42 of the ICSID Convention were given in annulment proceedings initiated against arbitral awards rendered under the Convention. See *Klöckner v Cameroon*, Decision (3 May 1985) 9 Foreign Investment Law Journal 89; *AMCO Asia Co. v Indonesia*, Decision (16 May 1986) (1986) 25 ILM 1441, 1445–1446. In the same vein see *Liberian Eastern Timber Co. (Letco) v Liberia*, Award (31 March 1986) (1987) 26 ILM 647, 658.

## 2.3   De-Politicisation of International Legal Instruments Protecting Foreign Investment (1990–present)?

To reduce the trade deficits following the implementation of ISI development policies, many Latin American countries in the 1970 had to look for private banks and public lenders' loans. Despite their floating interest rates determined by market forces, they preferred these credits over those provided by the International Monetary Fund (IMF) because they were granted on a short-term basis and without strict loan conditions by this international financial institution. However, the high interests of these loans created serious levels of indebtedness in this region, which caused concerns in Argentina, Brazil, Colombia and Mexico for the effect that this situation could have on the political dimension of inter-state relations.[259] In this context, these countries, in a joint declaration, rejected financial risk outcomes and called for a mutual solution between creditors and debtors.[260] These demands found echo in Venezuela, Ecuador and Peru, which together with the other countries, appealed for a shared responsibility of all involved actors and a mutual solution for their external indebtedness at a meeting held in London in 1984 with the respective creditors.[261]

Following these preliminary expressions of dissatisfaction with their external debt situation, a major group of Latin American countries provided an official statement, the so-called 'Consensus of Cartagena', in which they emphasised on the responsibility of both parties within their field of competence with respect to drastic changes in lending conditions.[262] They also reaffirmed their commitment to fulfil debt obligations and adjustments.[263] Addressees of this declaration were the developed nations[264] and the international banks.[265] Against this background, the US Secretary of Treasury, James Baker, brought forward a proposal (the so-called Plan Baker) before the IMF and World Bank in 1985 to assist Latin American countries in resolving their debt crisis.[266]

To explain the economic policy plan developed by the IMF, World Bank and the US Treasury Department to restructure their financial debt, Williamson developed a conceptual framework of prescriptions that he labelled as the

---

[259]Navarrete (1987), pp. 23–24.

[260]Navarrete (1987), citing 'Declaracion de los presidentes de México, Argentina, Brasil y Colombia sobre el problema de la deuda externa' (1987), pp. 36–37.

[261]Navarrete (1987), pp. 38–39.

[262]'Cartagena Communique on Foreign Debt and Economic Development' (adopted by Argentina, Bolivia, Brazil, Chile, Colombia, Dominican Republic, Ecuador, Mexico, Peru, Uruguay, and Venezuela) (1984) 23 (5) ILM (Cartagena Communique on Foreign Debt and Economic Development) para 7.

[263]Cartagena Communique on Foreign Debt and Economic Development (n 262).

[264]Cartagena Communique on Foreign Debt and Economic Development (n 262) para 18 A.

[265]Cartagena Communique on Foreign Debt and Economic Development (n 262) para 18 B.

[266]Navarrete (1987), pp. 23–24.

'Washington Consensus'.[267] According to his analysis, the provision of legal security for property rights did constitute one of the economic policies contained in the proposals of these institutions,[268] even though it explicitly recognised that achieving consensus on this policy was far from being reality due to its political nature.[269]

Leaving aside the fact that the connotation attached to the term 'Washington Consensus' (namely the implementation of the neoliberalism agenda in Latin America) arguably differs from what Williamson had originally intended in his seminal work,[270] it is undeniable that many Latin American countries waived their own sovereignty by entering into bilateral investment treaties (BITs).[271] This resulted in the redefinition of their traditional approach towards the legal protection of foreign national's property rights at the end of the 1980s,[272] which also began to be noticeable within the framework of the ANCOM. Decision 220 came to replace Decision 24 in an attempt to relax the conditions established in the former Decision,[273] such as the allowance of foreign investor's access to all economic sectors of member states, except those explicitly banned.[274] Additionally, while the Decision 220 maintained an explicit reference to the national treatment rule applicable to foreign nationals,[275] it excluded reference to the validity of this standard in the context of access to remedies by leaving it to member states' discretion how they rule

---

[267]See Williamson (1990).

[268]The other eight policies consisted in (1) fiscal discipline, (2) redirection of public expenditure, (3) tax reform, (4) financial liberalisation, (5) achieving a single competitive exchange rate, (6) trade liberalisation, (7) elimination of foreign direct investment's barrier, (8) deregulation of market entry and competition. Williamson (1990).

[269]In fact, Williamson acknowledged the existing controversy among economic experts on deregulation, as well as financial and trade liberalization. Notwithstanding the former, he presumed the attainment of a consensus on them in the near future on which he relied to coin this term in his analysis. See Williamson (1993).

[270]According to Naim, Williamson's term embodied a new set of ideas on how to organize economic and social policies following the fall of the Soviet Union, to which any stakeholder attached its own interpretation according to its academic, ideological, or political background. See Naim (2000).

[271]Meessen (1986), pp. 120–122.

[272]Notwithstanding this treaty practice became almost widespread only after the end of the 1980s, few Latin American countries signed BITs with capital-exporting countries even before the 'Washington Consensus' recommendations were in force put forward. Examples include the 1968 Ecuador- Switzerland BIT, or the BITs of Paraguay with South Africa, France and United Kingdom signed in 1974, 1978 and 1981, respectively. UNCTAD, Bilateral Investment Treaties 1959–1999, UNCTAD/ITE/IIA/2, internet edition only (Figure 4, Participation of countries in BITs, by region and decade, 1960–1999) <http://unctad.org/en/Docs/poiteiiad2.en.pdf> accessed 10 December 2020.

[273]Decision 220 Replacing Decision 24, The Common Foreign Investment and Technology Licensing Code (adopted 11 May 1987) (1988) 27 ILM 974 (Decision 220).

[274]Decision 220 (n 273) arts 25–26.

[275]Decision 220 (n 273) art 33.

the settlement of disputes arising out of foreign direct investment in accordance with their domestic laws.[276]

This new Latin American approach towards the legal protection of foreign capital meant departure from granting foreign nationals the same substantive and procedural rights that nationals were entitled to, observing a particular set of international norms designed to protect foreign investment and investors against any political risk that they may face within their territory. Moreover, international law became the principal law governing the resolution of investor-state disputes and international arbitration, the most appropriate method of ISDS.

By agreeing to submit themselves to the jurisdiction of arbitral tribunals under BITs, Latin American countries allowed *ad-hoc* tribunals to review their regulatory conduct in accordance with international legal standards laid down in these treaties. Yet, the unduly disproportionate restriction of host states' regulatory autonomy, through an overly expansive interpretation and application of these treaties began to raise great legitimacy concerns.[277]

Against this background, Sect. 2.3 investigates to what extent the consolidation of an investment treaty protection regime in Latin America led to de-politicise the regional stand towards international legal instruments protecting foreign investment. To this end, Sect. 2.3.1.1 initially outlines the substantive and procedural obligations Latin American countries committed to in favour of foreign investors and investment under BITs of first generation and international arbitration rules, while Sect. 2.3.1.2 explores whether a regional approach towards investment protection followed the same path as BITs. Subsequently, Sect. 2.3.2 examines how arbitral tribunals interpreted and applied states' treaty obligation to accord a fair and equitable treatment (FET) standard and to lawfully exercise their sovereign right to expropriate under the BIT, under BITs of first generation. In doing so, it not only centres on the criteria developed by arbitral tribunals to decide on claimant investor's claims, but also how they interpreted and applied these criteria when reviewing respondent states' acts. Following this brief doctrinal analysis, Sect. 2.3.3 discusses to what extent the expansive interpretation and application of IIAs have become an issue of concern and contention in Latin America. This not only entails exploring which forms Latin American countries have prevailed to articulate concerns and regulatory demands at the domestic and regional level, but also to what extent these expressions differ from claims advanced previously before the ratification of BITs.

---

[276]Decision 220 (n 273) art 34.

[277]Franck (2005), pp. 1521, 1523; Burke-White (2008).

## 2.3.1  Consolidation of the International Investment Treaty Regime

### 2.3.1.1  National Approach Towards Investment Treaty Protection

#### 2.3.1.1.1  Ratification of Bilateral Investment Treaties (BITs)

According to UNCTAD, Latin American countries had negotiated 205 BITs (out of a total of 366) with capital-exporting countries by the end of the 1990s.[278] Argentina and Chile stand out regionally as the countries with the highest number of BITs with 53 and 45 treaties, respectively,[279] whereas Brazil and Colombia signed few international treaties and did not ratify them in that decade.[280] With these treaties, the shortfalls of customary international law (CIL) for the protection of foreign investment came to an end as they became the exclusive legal source of states' international responsibility for injuries inflicted to foreign investor's rights abroad. In fact, these treaties clearly laid down the substantive and procedural obligations that one state party assumed in favour of the nationals of the other state party in pursuit of its economic development, which go beyond mere issues of denial of justice. Legal standards were the category of norms prevailed in BITs to articulate states parties' obligations. In contrast to rules, standards are flexible norms whose application is made case by case.[281] Accordingly, the adjudicative body entrusted with the enforcement of these international obligations is the one called to develop its scope of application *ex post*.[282] A broad description of the substantive and procedural standards codified in BITs of first generation is provided below.

The primary purpose of the first-generation BITs was the promotion and protection of foreign investment and investors in states parties' territories. To this end, BITs usually defined which type of assets and persons are covered by the treaty,[283] and which conditions apply for the entry of foreign investment. Furthermore, BITs codify a set of legal standards pursuant to which states parties shall treat covered investment and investors. BITs of Latin American countries granted national and

---

[278]In contrast, the negotiation of BITs was marginal intra-regionally and moderate, if compared with other capital-importing countries. UNCTAD, Bilateral Investment Treaties 1959–1999, UNCTAD/ITE/IIA/2, internet edition only, (UNCTAD, Bilateral Investment Treaties 1959–1999) 15–16.

[279]From the 53 BITs concluded by Argentina, only 43 were ratified up to 2000. In similar fashion, Chile only ratified 22 BITs from the 45 concluded. UNCTAD, Bilateral Investment Treaties 1959–1999 (n 278) 15–16, 26–27 and 38–39, respectively.

[280]UNCTAD, Bilateral Investment Treaties 1959–1999 (n 278) 34 and 41, respectively.

[281]Rules, on the contrary, define the content of legal obligations in advance. Wolfrum (2010).

[282]Ibidem. See also, Rosenfeld (2014), p. 191.

[283]To illustrate, Agreement between the Government of the United Kingdom of Great Britain and Northern Ireland and the Government of the Republic of Argentina for the Promotion and Protection of Investments (signed 11 December 1990, entered into force 19 February 1993) (Argentina-UK BIT) art 1.

most-favoured-nation treatment commitments to covered investment and investors,[284] which are standards of relative nature since they required a comparator for their application, namely the treatment accorded to other investment and investors.[285] In addition, BITs also contain absolute standards of protection that do not require additional elements to establish a breach of the obligation at stake. One of the absolute standards under BITs is the full security and protection standard, where the state party is expected to take all measures required to protect investment and investors from any (third party) acts that may affect them.[286]

Another absolute standard is the FET standard where states parties commit to treat foreign investment fairly and equitably and the BIT provision recognising states' right to expropriate, but such rights must be exercised in accordance with international law. Other treaty provisions seek to protect investment's entry and sojourn of personnel, senior management and/or boards, as well as covered investor's transfer of funds.[287] Finally, BITs usually incorporate umbrella clauses by which each contracting state commits to observe any obligation it may have assumed concerning investments of the nationals of the other state party.[288]

With the entry into force of BITs, international arbitration establishes itself as the main dispute settlement mechanism in two forms, namely investor-state arbitration, and inter-state arbitration. This situation led to the displacement of host states' courts and diplomatic protection as traditional methods for the settlement of investor-state disputes. On one hand, BITs maintain inter-state arbitration as a legal method for the resolution of any dispute relating to their interpretation or application.[289] On very few occasions, states have made use of this treaty clause. On the occasions that this has happened, all the claimant or respondent states have been Latin American countries, which instituted an inter-state arbitration in relation to legal questions

---

[284]For instance, Agreement between the Swiss Confederation and the Republic of Peru on the Promotion and Reciprocal Protection of Investment (signed 22 November 1991, entered into force 23 November 1993) (Peru-Switzerland BIT) art 3 para 2.

[285]Salacuse (2015).

[286]Tratado entre la Republica Federal de Alemania y la Republica del Paraguay sobre Fomento y Reciproca Proteccion de Inversiones de Capital (signed 11 August 1993, entered into force 3 July 1998) art 4 para 1 (Germany-Paraguay BIT).

[287]UNCTAD, *Bilateral Investment Treaties in 1995–2006: Trends in Investment Rulemaking* (2007).

[288]Argentina-UK BIT (n 283) art 2 para 2.

[289]Agreement between the Government of the Republic of Korea and the Government of the Republic of Bolivia on the Reciprocal Promotion and Protection of Investments (signed 1 April 1996, entered into force 4 June 1997) (Bolivia-Korea BIT) art 13.

that an investor-state tribunal also had to deal with.[290] On the other hand, BITs provide the settlement of disputes by means of investor-state arbitration.[291]

To facilitate covered investor's access to international arbitration, these countries consent in advance in jurisdictional clauses to submit any dispute arising with the investor of the other contracting state in relation to its investment and, additionally, left at investor's discretion the institution of its claim in accordance with the arbitration rules enumerated therein. They generally range from the ICSID Convention[292] and the United Nations Commission on International Trade Law (UNCITRAL) Arbitration Rules.[293] This was a major change for Latin American countries if one recalls their critical stance towards the arbitration of legal questions comprising their exercise of regulatory power under concession agreements and their explicit refusal to the creation of ICSID by means of the ICSID Convention between the 1930s and 1980s.[294]

Regarding the local remedies rule, BITs generally dispense with this requirement as a condition for the institution of arbitration proceedings.[295] Despite this fact, this rule has not declined in importance in IIL when investment treaty claims deal with contractual issues and the investor-state contract contains a domestic forum selection clause, or when the tribunal considers it as a question of review upon the merits of investor's claims under specific standards of treatment.[296]

---

[290]For a reference, see *Empresas Lucchetti, S.A. and Lucchetti Peru, S.A. v The Republic of Peru*, ICSID Case No. ARB/03/4, Award (7 February 2005); *Republic of Ecuador v United States of America*, PCA Case No. 2012-5) Award (29 September 2012). In this inter-state arbitration proceeding, Cuban was the respondent state. *Italian Republic v Republic of Cuba*, ad hoc state-state arbitration (Final Award) (1 January 2008). Peru tried to attain the suspension of an investor-state arbitration proceeding instituted by a Chilean investor. For a detailed discussion of these cases, see Luque Macías (2016a).

[291]Convenio entre el Gobierno de la Republica del Ecuador y el Gobierno de la Republica Popular de China para el Fomento y Protección Reciprocos de Inversiones (signed 21 March 1994, terminated) (China-Ecuador BIT) art 8.

[292]Agreement between the Government of the Republic of Chile and the Government of the Kingdom of Denmark concerning the Promotion and Reciprocal Protection of Investments (signed 28 May 1993, entered into force 3 November 1995) (Chile-Denmark BIT) art 9 para 2.

[293]Agreement between the Government of the Republic of Indonesia and the Government of the Republic of Cuba concerning the Promotion and Protection of Investment (signed 19 September 1997, entered into force 29 September 1999) (Cuba-Indonesia BIT) art VIII para 3, lit. ii.

[294]See Sect. 2.2.2.

[295]Some countries give priority to the local remedy rule, but after a period, entitles the covered investor to submit its investment claim. For instance, see Agreement between the Government of the United Kingdom of Great Britain and Nothern Ireland and the Government of the Oriental Republic of Uruguay (signed 21 October 1991, entered into force 1 August 1997) art 8 para 2, lit. a (i.

[296]Schreuer (2005).

### 2.3.1.1.2   Ratification of International Arbitration Rules

As mentioned above, the ICSID Convention and the UNCITRAL Arbitration Rules usually feature as the main arbitration rules pursuant to which a covered investor can institute arbitration proceedings for alleged breaches of its substantive rights under BITs. The moment of ratification of these arbitration rules however differed considerably because of the context and purpose underlying these arbitration rules since their origin. Prior the ratification of BITs, Latin American countries only adhered to the UNCITRAL Arbitration Rules since their initial purpose was to facilitate the settlement of *contractual* disputes by means of international arbitration, without limiting the disputing parties that could agree to use these rules. With the amendments of these arbitration rules in 2010, their purpose became the settlement of any legal dispute, whether of contractual nature, thereby expanding the jurisdiction of arbitral tribunals constituted in accordance with their rules.[297]

In contrast, the ICSID Convention encountered initial opposition from Latin American countries for a myriad of reasons. For one, this Convention creates an institution in charge of the administration of the conduct of arbitration proceedings, namely the ICSID.[298] Although the ICSID does not constitute an international court, it operates in accordance to the ICSID Convention to facilitate the conduct of arbitration proceedings under the auspices of the World Bank. Moreover, the type of disputes to be settled under this Convention is *investment* disputes and the disputing parties are the state party hosting the investment of the national of another contracting state, and the national fails to comply with its investment treaty obligations.[299] Despite their initial 'no' to this Convention in Tokyo, some Latin American countries reviewed their stance and signed the ICSID Convention in the early 1980s.[300] Other countries followed suit only after they began with the negotiation of BITs.[301] In the mid-2000s, Bolivia, Ecuador and Venezuela's discontent with how ICSID tribunals applied their BITs obligations motivated their denunciation. Except for Brazil, Mexico was the only country that was not party to this Convention, until July 2018 when it acceded to the Convention.[302]

---

[297] United Nations Commission on International Trade Law (UNCITRAL) Arbitration Rules (1976) (UNCITRAL Arbitration Rules) art 1 para 1, with UNCITRAL Arbitration rules (as revised in 2010) art 1 para 1 (UNCITRAL Arbitration Rules, as revised in 2010).

[298] ICSID Convention (n 162) art 1.

[299] ICSID Convention (n 162) art 2.

[300] Paraguay, El Salvador, and Ecuador signed the ICSID Convention in July 1981, June 1982 and January 1986, respectively.

[301] The ICSID Convention entered into force for Honduras, in March 1989; for Chile, in September 1991; for Costa Rica, in May 1993; for Peru, in August 1993; for Argentina, in October 1994; for Nicaragua, in April 1995; for Venezuela, in May 1995; for Bolivia, in June 1995; for Panama, in May 1996; for Colombia, in July 1997; for Uruguay, in August 2000; for Guatemala, in February 2003.

[302] 'Mexico Ratifies the ICSID Convention' (ICSID News Release, 27 July 2018) <https://icsid.worldbank.org/en/Pages/News.aspx?CID=285> accessed 10 December 2020.

To exercise jurisdiction under both arbitration rules, tribunals must ensure that both disputing parties have consented to their jurisdiction.[303] For the most part, host states agreed to arbitration in BITs jurisdictional clauses, while the foreign investors give their consent with the institution of arbitration proceedings following a particular set of arbitration rules. This BIT clause also establishes the subject matter of the dispute upon which tribunals are entitled to exercise jurisdiction. Under the ICSID Convention, this shall be 'any legal dispute arising directly out of an *investment*'.[304] To determine the fulfilment of this requirement in an investment treaty-based dispute, the ICSID tribunal shall resort to the BIT's definition of investment.

Different patterns are followed on how to define an investment to be protected under a particular treaty.[305] For the purpose of this research, it is relevant to highlight that many BITs protect only investment that are made in accordance with recipient states' laws.[306] Hence, tribunals must establish which laws were applicable to the investment at the moment of its admission, to establish its jurisdiction.[307] Furthermore, ICSID tribunals shall also determine how the BIT defines the investors protected under the treaty to establish whether the plaintiff is entitled to submit an investment claim before its jurisdiction.[308]

According to an UNCTAD report of 2010, 38% of disputes settled until 2009 were decided in favour of the respondent state whilst 29% were in favour of claimant.[309] Furthermore, it revealed that capital-importing countries, for the most part, are the responding party in comparison to capital-exporting countries.[310] More than 50% of investment treaty claims were resolved under the ICSID Convention.[311] If we compare these results with in the UNCTAD report of 2020, we note that although there has been an increase in the number of capital-exporting countries responding to investment treaty claims,[312] BITs remain an important tool for the

---

[303] ICSID Convention (n 162) art 25.

[304] ICSID Convention (n 162) art 25 (emphasis added).

[305] States follow an asset-based definition, or an enterprise-based definition. UNCTAD, Investment Policy Framework for Sustainable Development (2015).

[306] See n 90–91, Chap. 4.

[307] Ibidem.

[308] Some BITs may not define investors covered in an exhaustive manner. In relation to legal entities, these treaties may limit investment treaty protection to those that have a substantial business activity within the respondent state's jurisdiction or have ownership and control over the investment allegedly impair by host state's activities. UNCTAD, Investment Policy Framework for Sustainable Development (2015).

[309] UNCTAD, *Latest Developments in Investor–State Dispute Settlement* (2010) (1) IIA Issues Note.

[310] In 2009, 49 capital-importing countries have faced an investment treaty claim, whereas only 17 developed countries and 15 countries with economies in transition. UNCTAD, *Latest Developments in Investor–State Dispute Settlement* (2010) (n 309).

[311] UNCTAD, *Latest Developments in Investor–State Dispute Settlement* (2010) (n 309).

[312] In addition to Argentina and Venezuela, Spain and Canada have been capital-exporting countries involved in these disputes. UNCTAD, *Investor-State dispute Settlement: Review of Developments in 2019* (2020) 2 IIA Issues Note, 2.

protection of foreign investment stemming from capital-exporting countries.[313] If this is so, Latin American countries should redefine their approach towards foreign investment protection in light of the far-reaching implications that these legal instruments may have for their fiscal and social policies. Reforms of BITs and ISDS seem essential to achieve this end.

#### 2.3.1.2   Regional Approach Towards Investment Treaty Protection

##### 2.3.1.2.1   South American Context

Within South America, two sub-regional organizations introduced investment schemes to achieve certain degree of consistency with their national approach towards investment protection by means of BITs at the beginning of the 1990s. South American countries forming the ANCOM substituted Decision 220 with Decision 291 to align regional rules on investment with the national member states' policies towards investment liberalization.[314] Furthermore, Argentina, Brazil, Paraguay and Uruguay established the Southern Common Market (MERCOSUR) with the purpose of promoting trade and facilitating the free movement of goods, capital and people among their members.[315] To achieve these objectives, they adopted the Colonia Protocol on Reciprocal Promotion and Protection of Investments within MERCOSUR (Colonia Protocol) and the Protocol on the Promotion and Protection of Investments Coming from States Non Parties of MERCOSUR (Buenos Aires Protocol), with a view to attract and protect investment stemming from their member states and third-party countries, respectively.[316]

In all these investment schemes, one can observe that South American countries only committed to afford national treatment.[317] Otherwise, they present great

---

[313]UNCTAD, *Investor-State dispute Settlement: Review of Developments in 2019* (n 312) figure 2.

[314]Andean Group: Commission, 'Decision 291 – Common code for the Treatment of Foreign Capital and on Trademarks, Patents, Licenses and Royalties' (adopted 21 March 1991) (1991) 30 ILM 1283 (Decision 291) preamble. Hummel (2009), p. 561.

[315]Mercosur was established in 1991 by the Treaty of Asunción, which was later amended and updated by the 1994 Treaty of Ouro Preto. Treaty establishing a Common Market (signed 26 March 1991) 30 ILM (1991) 1041. Additional Protocol to the Treaty of Asuncion on the Institutional Structure of MERCOSUR ('Protocol of Ouro Preto') (signed 17 December 1994) (1995) 34 ILM 1244.

[316]Colonia Protocol on Reciprocal Promotion and Protection of Investments within MERCOSUR (signed 17 January 1994) (Colonia Protocol) and Protocol on the Promotion and Protection of Investments coming from states non-Parties of MERCOSUR (signed 5 August 1994) (Buenos Aires Protocol) <http://www.mercosur.int/t_ligaenmarco.jsp?contentid=4823&site=1& channel=secretaria> accessed 10 December 2020.

[317]Member states accord national treatment except as otherwise provided in the national legislation of Andean Pact members. Andean Group: Commission, Decision 291 (n 314) chapter II para 4 and 1, respectively. MERCOSUR, Colonia Protocol (n 316) art 3 para 2; Buenos Aires Protocol (n 316) Titel C paras 1 and 2.

variations in the scope of protection that they were willing to guarantee jointly to foreign investors. Member states of the ANCOM preserve great discretion under the Decision 291 to prescribe conditions under which those investment and investors covered therein are entitled to settle their claims since this instrument subject the resolution of these disputes to what their domestic laws provide.[318] Except for Colombia, all member states enacted investment codes during the 1990s.[319] Pursuant to these domestic instruments, some countries granted foreign investors and their investment the same treatment given to their own nationals,[320] while others merely granted them non-discrimination.[321] Certainly, all states restated their commitment to settle investment disputes in accordance with international arbitration rules.[322] Through these domestic provisions, these countries tacitly provided another offer to agree on investment disputes by means of international arbitration rather than the one given under BITs.

In contrast to Decision 291, MERCOSUR investment protocols were actually similar to BITs, even though they differed among themselves regarding the concessions that they were willing to afford to nationals of member states and to those stemming from non-member countries.[323] The Colonia Protocol granted fair and equitable,[324] as well as most-favoured nation, treatment to nationals of member states investing in the territory of another.[325] In case of member states' inobservance of these standards, they were entitled to bring their claims before arbitral tribunals constituted pursuant to the ICSID Convention or UNCITRAL Arbitration Rules.[326] However, investors stemming from non-member states were entitled to national treatment and to the payment of compensation in an 'adequate, effective and prompt' manner in case of expropriation.[327] Similarly, access to international arbitration was granted for the settlement of disputes arising out of Buenos Aires Protocol.[328]

---

[318] Andean Group: Commission, Decision 291 (n 314) chapter II para 10.

[319] Law 1182 (17 September 1990) (Bolivia) (Law 1182 Bolivia); Decreto Legislativo 662 for the Promotion of Foreign Investment (Ley de Promoción de las Inversión Extranjera, 29 August 1991) (Ley de Promoción de las inversiones Extranjeras Peru); Law No. 49 "Ley de Promoción y Garantía de Inversiones" (19 December 1997) (Ecuador) (Ley de Promoción y Garantía de Inversiones Ecuador); "Ley de Promoción y Protección de Inversiones" (3 October 1999) (Venezuela).

[320] Law 1182 Bolivia (n 319) art 2; Ley de Promoción de las inversiones Extranjeras Peru (n 319) art 2.

[321] Ley de Promoción de Inversiones Venezuela (n 319) art 8.

[322] Law 1182 Bolivia (n 319) art 10; Ley de Promoción y Garantía de Inversiones Ecuador (n 319) art 32; Ley de Promoción de las Inversiones Extranjeras Peru (n 319) art 16; Ley Marco para el Crecimiento de la Inversión Privada (Peru) art 48.

[323] For a detailed analysis of both investment schemes see Lerner (2010), p. 275.

[324] MERCOSUR, Colonia Protocol (n 316) art 3 para 1.

[325] MERCOSUR, Colonia Protocol (n 316) art 3 para 2.

[326] MERCOSUR, Colonia Protocol (n 316) art 9 para 4.

[327] MERCOSUR, Buenos Aires Protocol (n 316) Titel D para 1.

[328] MERCOSUR, Buenos Aires Protocol (n 316) Titel H.

Notwithstanding the former, neither protocols have hitherto entered into force as a result of the lack of willingness from Brazil to ratify these instruments.[329]

### 2.3.1.2.2   For the Americas?

In contrast to the investment schemes launched in South America, the North American Free Trade Agreement (NAFTA) was the first regional investment agreement that entered into force to rule comprehensively the investment disciplines among its member states, namely the USA, Canada and Mexico.[330] The investment chapter laid down within NAFTA adapted the structure of BITs to the specific needs of this treaty by affording covered investors and investment the same substantive and procedural protection.[331] With its entry into force, the USA promoted the discussion about the implementation of a Free Trade Agreement of the Americas (FTAA) with intention to reduce progressively the restrictions on trade and *investment* within the framework of the Summit of the Americas.[332] The latter is a non-institutional forum where American countries discussed the reorganization of inter-American relations outside the framework of the OAS, in particular the harmonization of reforms in a wide range of public policy areas.[333] To attain this end, the Ministers of Trade of American countries established working groups for the discussion of specific topics, such as investment,[334] and set the year 2005 as the deadline for the conclusion of the negotiations on this agreement.[335] The Working Group on Investment was entrusted

---

[329]See Lerner (2010), p. 275.

[330]North American Free Trade Agreement between the Government of the United States of America, the Government of Canada and the Government of the United Mexican States (signed 17 December 1992, entered into force 1 January 1994) 32 ILM 289 (1993) (NAFTA) chap 11.

[331]NAFTA's investment chapter granted to covered investors and investment, national and most-favoured-nation treatment, FET, and full protection and security under the title 'minimum standard of treatment'. NAFTA (n 330) chap 11 arts 1103 and 1105. In addition, it protected investor's investment from unlawful expropriation. NAFTA (n 330) chap 11 art 1110. The enforcement of these standards was available pursuant to the ICSID Convention, the Additional Facility Rules of ICSID, or UNCITRAL Arbitration Rules. NAFTA (n 330) chap 11 art 1120.

[332]See First Summit of the Americas, Miami, Florida, USA, December 9–11, 1994 (English version) <http://www.summit-americas.org/i_summit.html> accessed 10 December 2020.

[333]See Summits of the Americas, Secretariat, 'Introduction to the Summits of the Americas Process' <http://www.summit-americas.org/summit_process.html> accessed 10 December 2020.
  Fourth Summits of the Americas took place for the discussion of this initiative: The First Summit of the Americas was hold on 11 December 1994 in Miami; the Second, on 19 April 1998 in Chile; the Third, on 22 April 2001 in Québec; and the Fourth, on 05 November 2005 in Mar del Plata. For an overview of the declarations and plan of action of the Summits of the Americas above mentioned see, Summits of the Americas, Secretariat, Previous Summits <http://www.summit-americas.org/previous_summits.html> accessed 10 December 2020.

[334]Ibidem, para 5.

[335]Summit of the Americas, Trade Ministerial Joint Declaration, Denver, Colorado, June 30, 1995 para   1   <http://www.ftaa-alca.org/Ministerials/Denver/Denver_e.asp>   accessed 10 December 2020.

with the mandate of examining the domestic and regional treaty practice regarding investment protection for the elaboration of recommendations in this regard.[336] Based on this preliminary analysis, three drafts of the FTAA were prepared and made public in the first half of the 2000s.[337]

Draft proposals differed among themselves with respect to the exceptions introduced against the application of a particular standard of treatment, or the degree of detail by which they define these standards. Under drafts II and III, it was proposed to accord national and most-favoured-nation treatment to covered investors (and potentially to their investment).[338] Nevertheless, draft II suggested to exclude small and medium-size companies from the application of these provisions, while draft III, only applied to small companies.[339] Moreover, drafts II and III broadly granted fair and equitable treatment in accordance with international law and alternatively with CIL,[340] and placed the customary international minimum standard as a threshold to FET.[341] Only draft III of the FTAA agreement defined what is to be understood under the FET standard; it equated FET with the denial of justice principle.[342] With respect to expropriation, only draft II explicitly mentioned the 'Hull formula' as a criterion for assessing the lawfulness of an expropriation in all alternative provisions included for this purpose.[343] Moreover, both draft proposals did not refer to the exhaustion of local (judicial) remedies as pre-condition for the submission of an investment treaty claim before an arbitral tribunal. In relation to domestic courts, they featured as an alternative for the settlement of investment disputes.[344]

---

[336]Ibidem, Annex I, literal III.

[337]The first draft was delivered on 7 April 2001; the second draft, on 1 November 2002; and the third, on 21 November 2003. For an overview of the different versions of the draft text of the FTAA Agreement see Foreign Trade Information System, Trade Policy Developments, Free Trade Agreement of the Americas (FTAA), Draft texts of the FTAA Agreement. Available via SICE: http://www.sice.oas.org/tpd/ftaa/ftaa_e.asp#DraftTexts. Accessed 10 December 2020.

[338]FTAA, Second Draft Agreement, Chapter on Investment (Derestricted FTAA.TNC/w/133/Rev.2 (1 November 2002) (FTAA, Second Draft Agreement) art 5 para 1, and Third Draft Agreement, Chapter XVII Investment (Derestricted FTAA.TNC/w/133/Rev.3 (21 November 2003) (Third Draft Agreement) art 6 para 1.

[339]FTAA, Second Draft Agreement (n 338) art 5 para 2, and Third Draft Agreement (n 338) art 6 para 2.

[340]FTAA, Second Draft Agreement (n 338) art 6 para 1, and Third Draft Agreement, (n 338) art 9 para 1.

[341]FTAA, Second Draft Agreement, (n 338) art 6 para 2, and Third Draft Agreement (n 338) art 9 para 2.

[342]FTAA, Third Draft Agreement (n 338) art 9 para 2 lit. a stipulated that '"fair and equitable treatment" includes the obligation not to deny justice in criminal, civil, or administrative adjudicatory proceedings in accordance with the principle of due process embodied in the principal legal systems of the world'.

[343]FTAA, Second Draft Agreement, (n 338) art 10 para 1.

[344]FTAA, Second Draft Agreement (n 338) art 15 para 5, and Third Draft Agreement (n 338) art 29 paras 3 and 4.

The discussion of these draft proposals clearly revealed that there was a variety of approaches towards investment treaty protection among Latin American countries, which have arguably remained since the failure of this regional endeavour towards harmonization of investment rules. Some countries strongly endorsed the creation of a FTAA because all participating countries would be on equal footing,[345] whereas others raised serious questions about an agreement that impose broad common disciplines to countries unable to comply with them.[346]

In the specific context of investment protection, those questioning the comprehensive nature of these proposals called upon the adoption of complementary agreements on national treatment.[347] Faced with this dilemma, the deadline imposed by the Ministers of Trade for the conclusion of these negotiations was not met, leading to the non-approval of the FTAA due to lack of consensus among these countries.[348] In light of this outcome, some states prevailed to engage in bilateral negotiations of investment treaties. Others promoted the creation of sub-regional forum for a critical discussion about the implications of international investment law regime over their regulatory policy sovereignty, while the rest did not follow neither of these options.[349]

### 2.3.1.3   Preliminary Conclusions

With the ratification of BITs, many Latin American countries accepted to bear international legal responsibility if any regulatory acts and omissions impair the treaty obligations assumed in favour of investment and investors of the other contracting state, without confining this international legal protection exclusively to issues of denial of justice. These international treaties formulate states parties' obligations in terms of standards, a category of norms formulated in broader terms whose content the competent adjudicative body shall develop *ex post* and apply case by case.

These legal standards of treatment under BITs range from standards of relative nature for whose application the adjudicative requires a comparator such as national and most-favoured nation treatment, to absolute standards whose application is not contingent upon external factors such as the full security and protection and FET

---

[345]FTAA - Trade Negotiations Committee Costa Rica, El Salvador, Guatemala, Honduras, Nicaragua, Canada, Mexico, Chile, Dominican Republic, Panama, Colombia, Peru and Bolivia, Vision of the FTAA, Public FTAA.TNC/w/219 October 4, 2003 (Original: Spanish, Translation: FTAA Secretaria).

[346]FTAA - Trade Negotiations Committee, Uruguay, Vision of the FTAA, Public FTAA.TNC/w/221October 4, 2003 (Original: Spanish Translation: FTAA Secretaria).

[347]Ibidem, lit. k.

[348]Fourth Summit of the Americas, Declaration of Mar del Plata "Creating Jobs to Fight Poverty and Strengthen Democratic Governance", Mar del Plata, Argentina, 5 November 2005, para 19 <http://www.summit-americas.org/iv_summit.html> accessed 10 December 2020.

[349]For a brief overview of subsequent developments, see Luque Macías (2014).

standards. In addition, BITs explicitly codify one of the sovereign economic rights that the Charter of Economic Rights and Duties of states refers to as derivative from their permanent sovereignty over their natural resources, namely states' right to expropriate foreign property.

The novelty in the BITs is that they enumerate the conditions pursuant to which states parties' exercise of this sovereign right, either directly or indirectly, is lawful under international law. Mostly, the submission of investment treaty disputes has been based on the FET standard and BITs provisions on expropriation, which is why this research study discusses them in detail in Chaps. 1 and 3. BITs also incorporate an umbrella clause intending to ensure that states observe all commitments assumed in favour of covered investors and investments.

Another major development was that international arbitration became the main dispute settlement method for the resolution of foreign investors' claims under BITs. Although these treaties also provide for the settlement of disputes arising therefrom by means of inter-state arbitration, investor-state arbitration has prevailed since as the main dispute settlement method. By means of jurisdictional clauses, states parties thus agreed in advance to the submission of any dispute arising out of the treaty to arbitration, mostly without subjecting investors' access to the exhaustion of local remedies before respondent states' courts. This type of treaty clauses brought about significant changes for Latin American countries if one recalls the widespread use of the Calvo clause in their laws and contracts with foreign nationals, and their refusal to allow other forums than their domestic courts to review their regulatory exercise vis-à-vis foreign investment activities. Concurrently, these countries also ratified the ICSID Convention, which is one of the arbitration rules generally referred to in BITs pursuant to which covered investors are entitled to submit their investment claims. Under this Convention, arbitral tribunals constituted under their rules shall fulfil a set of requirements, which the BITs already provide, such as the consent of the respondent state to arbitration or further define, to establish their jurisdiction such as its provisions on investment and those defining the legal ties of covered investors with its respective home state. Notwithstanding these major developments, the critical stand of Latin American countries towards international instruments of investment protection did not completely disappear with the ratifications of BITs. South American countries as member states of the ANCOM and MERCOSUR devoted preliminary efforts to ensure certain degree of uniformity in their investment disciplines.

Investment schemes adopted under these inter-governmental institutions partially reflected the content of BITs and guarantee access to covered investors to international arbitration. Yet, MERCOSUR investment schemes never entered into force, while Decision 291 of the ANCOM ensures limited scope of protection than BITs. Outside these sub-regional institutions, there was an attempt to create a free trade area among all American countries, following the NAFTA model. The creation of common rules on investment protection was one of the purposes of this initiative, which (Latin) American countries discussed for almost a decade and revealed different views about the scope of protection that they were willing to guarantee to nationals of other (American) countries. Lack of consensus was the main reason for the abandonment of this effort, which reflected in turn their negative view to cede more space for definition of its investment policy disciplines.

## 2.3.2   Concerns About Investment Treaty-based Dispute Settlement

### 2.3.2.1   The Interpretation and Application of States' Obligation Under the FET Standard

The FET standard constitutes one of the absolute general standards of treatment embedded in all BITs. It generally stands as an autonomous standard in BITs,[350] or in combination with the full security and protection standard.[351] In other cases, states parties confer FET standard to covered investment and investment related activities in connection with relative standards of treatment, such as most-favoured-nation treatment,[352] national treatment,[353] or in combination with both relative standards.[354] Due to its vague formulation, covered investors have been entitled to challenge any host states' act deemed as unfair and unequitable, thereby making it the legal basis of every investment treaty claim.[355] Under these circumstances, arbitral tribunals are the ones competent to determine what fair and equitable means in light of the criteria that they develop to establish host states' breaches of their corresponding obligation under this standard.

Arbitral tribunals have generally relied on a set of benchmarks that, despite their overlapping nature and at times codified autonomously in BITs, form in their view the content of the FET standard. The first is the element of transparency, which refers to the idea that host states shall act transparently in relation to the laws in force and applicable thereto.[356] The second element constitutes a prohibition of discrimination to covered investment or its activities on arbitrary grounds or the provision of an arbitrary treatment in general.[357]

---

[350]For instance, see Argentina-UK BIT (n 283) art 2 para 2; Peru-Switzerland BIT (n 284) art 3 para 2; Germany-Paraguay BIT (n 286) 2 para 1.

[351]Bolivia-Korea BIT (n 289) art 3 para 1.

[352]For instance, see China-Ecuador BIT (n 291) art 3 para 2; Cuba-Indonesia BIT (n 293) art 3 para 2.

[353]Convenio entre la Republica de Panama y Ucrania sobre la Promoción y Protección Reciproca de Inversiones (signed 4 November 2003) art 3 para 1.

[354]China-Ecuador BIT (n 291) art 3 para 2; Chile-Denmark BIT (n 292) art 3 para 2.

[355]Dolzer referred to the widespread use of FET by claimant investors as its 'almost ubiquitous presence' in ISDS. Dolzer (2005).

[356]*Metalclad Corporation v The United Mexican States*, ICSID Case No. ARB(AF)/97/1, Award (30 August 2000) (*Metalclad v Mexico*) para 99.

[357]On one hand, factors usually relied on to establish an *arbitrary* host state's conduct include wilful disregard of due process of law, or an extreme insufficiency of action. See *Alex Genin,*

In light of the factors relied upon to determine arbitrariness,[358] a denial of reasonable request of information, or threats to investor's business have amounted to arbitrary actions giving rise to a breach of the FET standard.[359] On the other hand, to identify the existence of a discriminatory treatment, tribunals have usually focused on whether the measure was intentionally discriminatory, in benefit of a national and against a foreign investor, and that is not taken under similar circumstances against another national.[360]

The third element relates to the guarantee of procedural fairness that presupposes host states' governmental and judicial authorities' obligation to avert a denial of justice. Under this element, a host state may breach the FET standard if its administrative or judicial authorities omitted to deliver formal and appropriate notice of hearing in an administrative or judicial process,[361] or denied investor's appearance before administrative instances or domestic courts,[362] and if they acted with bias or prejudice against it.

Considered from a historical perspective, one may recall that this was the only international wrongful act under which Latin American countries waived their sovereignty to be judged by international tribunals prior the ratification of BITs, and that current arbitral tribunals attached the same meaning to this rule as the one given by these countries. Finally, the protection of investor's legitimate expectations has also figured out in arbitral practice as an essential element in the determination of host states' breaches of the FET standard. Nevertheless, this section discusses separately its scope of application since arbitral tribunals' interpretation and application of this criterion clearly illustrates why ISDS has given cause of concern for its effect on states' regulatory autonomy.

Investors' legitimate expectations have been generally understood as the expectancy of investment returns deriving from host states' actions and legal and policy

---

*Eastern Credit Limited, Inc. and AS Baltoil (US) v Estonia*, ICSID Case No. ARB/99/2, Award (25 June 2001) (*Genin v Estonia*) para 371. Arbitrary actions may include denial of reasonable request of information, threats to investor's business. See *Pope & Talbot Inc. v The Government of Canada*, UNCITRAL (NAFTA), Award in Respect of Damages (31 May 2002) (*Pope & Talbot v Canada*) paras 177–179. On the other, to identify a discriminatory treatment, tribunals usually focus on whether the measure was intentionally discriminatory, in benefit of a national and against a foreign investor, and that is not taken under similar circumstances against another national. *ADF Group Inc. v United States of America*, ICSID Case No. ARB (AF)/00/1, Award (9 January 2003) (*ADF Group v USA*) para 191.

[358] Willful disregard of due process of law, or an extreme insufficiency of action feature as the factors resorted to determine arbitrariness in a host state's action. See *Genin v Estonia* (n 357) para 371.

[359] *Pope & Talbot v Canada* (n 357) paras 177–179.

[360] *ADF Group v USA* (n 357) para 191.

[361] *Middle East Cement shipping and Handling Co SA v Arab Republic of Egypt*, ICSID Case No. ARB/99/6, Award (12 April 2002) para 147.

[362] *Metalclad v Mexico* (n 356) para 91.

framework that were conducive to invest in the territory.[363] Unlike the other elements forming the content of FET standard, host states' regulatory policies and legal instruments pursuing the fulfilment of non-investment objectives have played a key role in tribunal's assessment of this criterion, in addition to the review of the alleged host states' action breaching this standard of treatment.[364] As a result, the arbitral tribunals' understanding and application of this standard may have broader implications upon host states' general policy, than those arising out of a specific investment claim. For instance, the function of investors' legitimate expectations under the FET standard has increasingly become a source of concern in IIL scholarship, because it clearly illustrates the inconsistent implementation of interpretative methodologies to review host states' exercise of its regulatory power.[365]

Some tribunals have made investors' legitimate expectation an object of protection under this standard,[366] while others have employed this concept as a rule or principle for determining violations of the FET standard. In doing so, tribunals have generally drawn analogies with the application of the legitimate expectation's concept in domestic law; however, they have departed considerably from the domestic understanding of the scope of application of this states' obligation by conferring a broader scope of protection to investors' legitimate expectations under BITs.

A more relevant issue of contention has been how arbitral tribunals dealt with the host states' legal and policy framework as an act creating investors' legitimate expectations. In principle, host states' actions creating investors' legitimate expectations have ranged from specific commitments assumed in favour of the claimant investor[367] to stabilization clauses in contracts or similar guarantees to ensure domestic laws' stability.[368]

---

[363] See *Saluka Investments B.V. v The Czech Republic*, UNCITRAL, Partial Award (17 March 2006) (*Saluka v Czech Republic*) para 301; *El Paso Energy International Company v The Argentine Republic*, ICSID Case No. ARB/03/15, Award (31 October 2011) (*El Paso Energy v Argentina*) para 348.

[364] *Saluka v Czech Republic* (n 363) para 301; *El Paso Energy v Argentina* (n 363) para 348.

[365] Potesta (2013), p. 88.

[366] See *Enron Corporation and Ponderosa Assets, L.P. v Argentine Republic (also known as: Enron Creditors Recovery Corp. and Ponderosa Assets, L.P. v The Argentine Republic)*, ICSID Case No. ARB/01/3, Award (22 May 207) (*Enron v Argentina*) para 262.

[367] *Methanex Corporation v United States of America*, UNCITRAL (NAFTA), Final Award (3 August 2005) (*Methanex v USA*) para 7; *Waste Management Inc. v United Mexican States*, ICSID Case No. ARB(AF)/00/3, Award (30 April 2004) para 98; *Duke Energy Electroquil Partners & Electroquil SA v Ecuador*, ICSID Case No. ARB/04/19, Award (18 August 2008) (*Duke Energy v Ecuador*) paras 351–352; *Jan de Nul NV and Dredging International N.V. v Arab Republic of Egypt*, ICSID Case No. ARB/04/13, Award (6 November 2008) para 26; *El Paso Energy v Argentina* (n 363) paras 375–378.

[368] *Glamis Gold, Ltd v The United States of America*, UNCITRAL (NAFTA), Award (8 June 2009) para 267 (*Glamis Gold v USA*); *Enron v Argentina* (n 366) paras 130 and 133.

Other sources of investors' legitimate expectations include licences or authorizations to perform its activities,[369] as well as representations made by the host state when attracting its investment[370] or those made after its admission.[371] In this context, arbitral tribunals have regularly assessed one type of governmental act in light of another, and considered respondent states' legal and policy framework in place at the time of the investment on the grounds that it is what investors had anticipated as applicable to their investment when investing therein.[372]

Yet, the question arising is whether any subsequent change of that legal and policy framework may amount to a frustration of investors' legitimate expectations that leads to a breach of the FET standard, even though it is not directed to any specific addressee as contracts and unilateral declarations do. Arbitral tribunals constituted under the first generation of BITs answered this question in the affirmative by favouring an interpretation of the FET standard in light of the general purpose of the BIT, which explicitly refers to the stability of legal framework as one of its main purposes.[373] In light of this teleological interpretative approach, states' failure to ensure stability and a consistent application of its laws and policies amounts to an omission to protect claimant investors' legitimate expectations, which results in a violation of its obligation under the FET standard.[374]

The clearest expression of host states' obligation to avert any reform of its laws and policies upon which the investor had relied to invest in its territory can be found in the *Tecmed v Mexico* case. According to this tribunal, the '[g]ood faith principle established by international law, requires the Contracting Parties to provide to international investments treatment that does not affect the basic expectations that were considered by the foreign investor to make the investment. The foreign investor expects that the host state acts in consistent manner, free from ambiguity and totally

---

[369] *Metalpar S.A. and Buen Aire S.A. v The Argentine Republic*, ICSID Case No. ARB/03/5, Award on the Merits (6 June 2008) para 186.

[370] See *Duke Energy v Ecuador* (n 367) para 340; *AES Corporation v The Argentine Republic*, ICSID Case ARB/02/17, Award (23 September 2010) paras 9.3.8–9.3.12.

[371] *Ioannis Kardassopoulos v The Republic of Georgia*, ICSID Case ARB/05/18, Award (10 March 2010) (*Kardassopoulos v Georgia*) paras 434–441.

[372] See *Gami Investments, Inc. v The Government of the United Mexican States*, UNCITRAL (NAFTA), Final Award (15 November 2004) para 100; *Sergei Paushok, CJSG Golden East Company and CJSC Vostokneftegaz Company v The Government of Mongolia*, UNCITRAL, Award on Jurisdiction and Liability (28 April 2011) (*Paushok v Mongolia*) paras 301–302; *LG &E Energy Corp., LG&E Capital Corp., LG&E International Inc. v Argentina*, ICSID Case No. ARB/02/1, Decision on Liability (3 October 2006) para 133; *Impregilo v Argentina* (n 1, Chap. 1) paras 290–291, 299.

[373] See *Occidental Exploration and Production Co v Ecuador, LCIA Case No UN3467*, Award (1 July 2004) (*Occidental v Ecuador*) para 183; *CMS Gas Transmission Company v The Republic of Argentina*, ICSID Case No. ARB/01/8, Award (12 May 2005) *(CMS v Argentina)* para 74; *Enron v Argentina* (n 366) paras 264–268.

[374] See *CMS v Argentina* (n 373) para 74; *PSEG Global et al. v Republic of Turkey*, ICSID Case No. ARB/02/5, Award (19 January 2007) paras 252–253; *Enron v Argentina* (n 366) paras 264–268.

transparent, in its relations with the foreign investor so that it may know beforehand any and all rules and regulations that will govern its investments, as well as the goals of the relevant policies and administrative practices or directives, in order to be able to plan its investment and comply with such regulations'.[375]

Understanding the host states' obligation to protect foreign investors' legitimate expectations in this way does undermine its regulatory capacity to meet non-investment objectives in the context of foreign investment activities. In fact, subsequent tribunals uncritically recognised this finding as authoritative and followed it in their review of alleged violations of the FET standard.[376] This development in case of investor-state arbitral tribunals reinforced the impression that the FET standard demands from a host state to refrain from adopting any law or policy that may impair investors' expectations at the moment of investing. Despite this fact, other *ad-hoc* tribunals took opposite views on the same legal question by finding that the protection of investors' legitimate expectations does not implicate an obligation of legal stability and good governance for a host state,[377] unless it had expressly waived its right to pass laws by means of stabilization clauses.[378] For some tribunals, the motivation behind this approach has been that laws are of general application and do not target specific individuals so as to be considered a source of expectations of a particular investor.[379] Others have showed certain deference towards host states' regulatory powers, and assessed the legitimacy of investors' expectations against objective criteria.[380]

---

[375]See *Técnicas Medioambientales Tecmed, S.A. v The United Mexican States*, ICSID Case No. ARB (AF)/00/2, Award (29 May 2003) (*Tecmed v Mexico*) para 154.

[376]See *Toto Construzioni Generali S.p.A v The Republic of Lebanon*, ICSID Case No. ARB/02/8, Award (7 June 2012) para 152; *Siemens A.g. v The Republic Argentine Republic*, ICSID Case No. ARB/02/08, Award (17 January 2007) paras 298–299.

[377]*CMS v Argentina* (n 373) para 85; *MTD Equity Sdn. Bhd. and MTD Chile S.A. v Republic of Chile*, ICSID Case No. ARB/01/7, Decision on Annulment (21 March 2007) para 67.

[378]In *Total v Argentina*, the Tribunal acknowledged that stabilisation clauses have the 'intended effect of freezing a specific host State's legal framework at certain date, such that the adoption of any changes in the legal regulatory of the investment concerned (. . .) would be illegal'. *Total S.A. v The Argentine Republic*, ICSID Case No. ARB/04/01, Decision on Liability (27 December 2011) (*Total v Argentina*) para 101. Considering this effect, these clauses have been widely recognised as the only act that would protect investor's expectations under the host State's legal and business framework valid at the time of the investment. See *Paushok v Mongolia* (n 372) para 302; *Parkerings-Compagniet AS v Lithuania*, ICSID Case No. ARB/05/8, Award (11 September 2007) para 332.

[379]*Total v Argentina* (n 378) paras 121–124.

[380]*EDF (Services) Limited v Romania*, ICSID Case No. ARB/05/13, Award (8 October 2009) para 217; *El Paso Energy v Argentina* (n 363) paras 364 and 368.

### 2.3.2.2  The Interpretation and Application of States' Obligation in Cases of an Indirect Expropriation

States' right to expropriate foreign property has been the only sovereign economic right that found explicit recognition in BITs. States parties to these treaties generally commit not to expropriate the investment of covered investors, either directly or indirectly, through measures tantamount to expropriation or nationalization except under the conditions established therein.[381] Therefore, BITs do not deny states' sovereign right per se, but limit its exercise to the fulfilment of a set of requirements under which its exercise is considered lawful. In this context, there was certain degree of consistency among BITs on the criteria established to determine the lawfulness of a direct or indirect expropriation.[382] Broadly speaking, states parties were entitled to exercise this economic right for a public purpose, without discrimination, following a due process and upon the payment of compensation.[383] Regarding compliance with the latter requirement, however, divergence was the rule because BITs apply different standards to the payment of compensation.[384] As a result, arbitral tribunals were confronted with the question of how to differentiate an indirect expropriation from a non-compensable regulatory measure that a host state undertook to protect the public interest. Given these circumstances, arbitral tribunals began to develop a set of criteria and methodologies to make this distinction.

To draw the line between host states' action 'having effects similar to' expropriation and those non-compensable regulatory measures, arbitral tribunals have usually focused on the *economic impact* of the challenged states' measure, its *degree* of interference with investors' property rights as well as its *duration*. The emphasis given by tribunals to these elements is what has defined the outcome of disputes. If the state's measure brought about a claimant investor a *substantial* economic deprivation,[385] for a prolonged period,[386] the likelihood that arbitral tribunals establish an indirect expropriation is certainly high, particularly when it considerably

---

[381] Convenio para la Promocion y la Proteccion Reciproca de las Inversiones suscrito con la Union Economica Belgo-Luxemburguesa (signed 28 June 1990, entered into force 20 May 1994) art 5.

[382] Salacuse (2015), pp. 323–328.

[383] For an overview see UNCTAD, *Bilateral Investment Treaties in 1995–2006: Trends in Investment Rulemaking* (2007) 47.

[384] Salacuse (2015).

[385] To illustrate, *Metalclad v Mexico* (n 356) para 103; *CMS v Argentina* (n 373) para 262; *Vivendi v Argentina II* (n 1, Chap. 1) para 7.5.11, 7.5.17, 7.5.24–7.5.30; *Suez and Interagua v Argentina* (n 1, Chap. 1) Decision on Liability (30 July 2010) para 123; *Burlington v Ecuador* (n 3, Chap. 1) Decision on Liability (14 December 2012) paras 397 and 456. For an enumeration of different arbitral tribunals' references to the *substantial* character of investor's deprivation element see Kriebaum (2015), pp. 984–985.

[386] For instance, the *S.D. Meyers v Canada* tribunal rejected to qualify the Canadian export ban of polychlorinated biphenyl (PCB) waste to the United States on account of its *temporary* character. *SD Meyers Inc v The Government of Canada*, UNCITRAL, Partial Award (*Meyers v Canada*) para 287.

impaired investors' capacity to enjoy make use of its own investment,[387] or its capacity to control.[388] However, a mere loss in value of the claimant's investment allegedly affected does not amount to an indirect expropriation.[389]

With respect to the *duration* of states' interference, no consensus exists about how to measure its permanent character. While some tribunals argued that this interference with investors' rights up to a period of 18 months lead to an indirect expropriation,[390] it is certainly true that when it lasts for a period of several years, its permanent character is undeniable.[391] Once tribunals have examined the state measure at stake against these preliminary criteria, tribunals have preferred methodologies that have either led to a disproportionate limitation of host states' regulatory autonomy, or caused further confusion in what is already a murky legal question.

The so-called 'sole effect' doctrine is one interpretative methodology under which regulatory measures may amount to an indirect expropriation if the claimant investor bore a significant economic deprivation despite the public and legitimate character of the measure concerned.[392] Two cases illustrated the application of this methodology and the implication for the respondent state concerned, particularly when they had invoked their international obligations under non-investment treaties as a defence. In *Santa Elena v Costa Rica*, the issue at stake was whether regulatory measures conducive to enlarge a national park for the protection of rare species amounted to an indirect expropriation, where the respondent state justified, inter alia, compliance with its international obligations under environmental treaties as the purpose of its measure in its defence. On the grounds that '[t]he international source of the obligation to protect the environment makes no difference', the tribunal abstained from reviewing this argument to review the purpose of the challenged measure, by emphasising that states shall always comply with their obligation to pay compensation, regardless of the domestic or international obligatory nature of states' environmental measure.[393]

---

[387]*ADC Affiliate Limited and ADC & ADMC Management Limited v Hungary*, ICSID Case No. ARB/03/16, Award (2 October 2006) paras 423–444. Kriebaum (2007), p. 717.

[388]See *Archer Daniels Midland Company and Tate & Lyle Ingredients Americas, Inc v The United Mexican States*, ICSID Case No. ARB(AF)/04/5, Award (21 November 2007) paras 240–246; *El Paso Energy v Argentina* (n 363) paras 245–249.

[389]Kriebaum (2007).

[390]For instance, the *Wena v Egypt* tribunal deemed the deprivation of license related rights for a period of four months and the local entity's seizure and illegal possession of claimant investor's hotels for nearly a year as an interference with their ability to enjoy its benefits, respectively. *Wena Hotels Limited v Arab Republic of Egypt*, ICSID Case No. ARB/98/4, Award (8 December 2000) para 99.

[391]*Phelps Dodge International Corp v Islamic Republic of Iran*, Award No. 217-99-2 (19 March 1986) 10 Iran-US CTR 121.

[392]*Metalclad v Mexico* (n 356); *Compañía del Desarrollo de Santa Elena, S.A v Republic of Costa Rica*, ICSID Case No. ARB/96/1, Award (17 February 2000) 5 ICSID Rep. 153 (*Compañía del Desarrollo de Santa Elena v Costa Rica*) para 71.

[393]See *Compañía del Desarrollo de Santa Elena v Costa Rica* (n 392) para 72.

In *Vivendi v Argentina II*, the respondent states' interference in the tariff regime applicable to the drinking water supply services' concession constituted an indirect expropriation, despite pursuing to guarantee population's access to drinking water, owing to its effect of rendering useless claimant investors' economic use and enjoyment of its investment.[394] This conception of host states' obligation to exercise its sovereign right under BITs considerably limits its capacity to respond to any event despite being obliged under domestic and international law, and in turn reflect the strong paradigm on the protection of foreign investors' rights in IIL.

The 'police powers' doctrine is another methodology prevailed by some tribunals to assess the legitimacy of states' actions allegedly tantamount to an expropriation against the criteria laid down in BIT to establish the lawfulness of an expropriation.[395] In *Methanex v USA*, the tribunal had to determine, whether local authorities' executive order and regulations prohibiting the use of a fuel additive on the grounds of the high presence of this component in drinking water supplies and the corresponding significant threats on health, safety and the environment constituted an indirect expropriation.[396]

The tribunal asserted that 'as a matter of general international law, a non-discriminatory regulation for a public purpose, which is enacted in accordance with due process (...) is not deemed expropriatory and compensable unless specific commitments had been given'. Due to lack of the respondent state's specific commitments assuring regulatory predictability[397] and claimant investor's retention of management control of its investment, the tribunal ruled in favour of the respondent state.[398]

In *Saluka v Czech Republic*, the question was whether the forced administration and transfer of claimant investor's controlling block of shares imposed by the Czech National Bank amounted to an indirect expropriation of claimant investor's investment.[399] The tribunal ruled in favour of the respondent state by underscoring the legality of the financial entity's actions pursuant to domestic laws;[400] its reasonable consideration of the facts in the exercise of its regulatory discretion as well as the reasonable application of domestic laws upon the facts,[401] and domestic courts' upholding of the legality of financial entity's decision.[402] This interpretative approach shows certain instrumentalization of existing benchmarks for the application of this BIT provision, even though they are intended to perform a different

---

[394] *Vivendi v Argentina II* (n 1, Chap. 1) para 7.5.34.

[395] *Marvin Roy Feldman Karpa v The United Mexican States*, ICSID Case No. ARB(AF)/99/1, Award (16 December 2002) 7 ICSID Report 341 para 103.

[396] *Methanex v USA* (n 367) para 7.

[397] *Methanex v USA* (n 367) paras 8–10.

[398] *Methanex v USA* (n 367) paras 16–17.

[399] See *Saluka v Czech Republic* (n 363) paras 253–265.

[400] See *Saluka v Czech Republic* (n 363) para 271.

[401] See *Saluka v Czech Republic* (n 363) para 272.

[402] See *Saluka v Czech Republic* (n 363) para 274.

function. In doing so, these tribunals failed to answer the question how to distinguish a legitimate non-compensable regulatory act from an indirect expropriation by applying criteria that presuppose the existence of an expropriatory act.[403]

To conclude, one should point out that some tribunals have employed the proportionally test to weigh the substantial economic deprivation that a state measure may exert upon claimant investors' investment and the public interest to draw a line between a non-compensable regulation and an indirect expropriation. Followed thereafter by other tribunals,[404] the *Tecmed v Mexico* tribunal employed a three-step process[405] to establish whether this measure was proportional to the legitimate aim pursued,[406] and proportional in relation to the legal protection ensured to investment under the Mexico-Spain BIT.[407] First, the tribunal focused on whether the challenged measure is in fact capable of achieving the allegedly pursued states' objective. Second, if the measure had served to achieve this goal, the tribunal then explored whether other less restrictive options that could have been used to achieve the same goal existed.[408] If the answer is positive in these preliminary stages, the tribunal will proceed to balance the two competing interests in the third stage of the inquiry.

The *Tecmed v Mexico* tribunal found that an indirect expropriation occurred by the governmental agency's refusal to renew claimant investors' license to operate the landfill of hazardous industrial waste, located near the town Hermosillo.[409] The reason for this was that the tribunal, at the second stage of its analysis, recognised that the challenged measure did not respond to an emergency or serious situation as alleged by the respondent state, but rather to social-political circumstances such as the social protest of those living near the landfill's operation.[410]

The relevance of this approach lies on the fact that some tribunals have showed a willingness to examine the purpose behind a state measure when reviewing its obligations under BIT provision on expropriation, which may inspire others to follow suit. Nevertheless, having a large margin of discretion in deciding whether other alternatives were better suitable to achieve a particular regulatory aim, may have great policy implications in how states parties to these treaties weigh up their varying interests vis-à-vis foreign investors and other societal goals.

Investors' legitimate expectations have also become an important element in the context of regulatory measures tantamount to an indirect expropriation, beyond alleged breaches of FET. However, its scope of application is narrower than the

---

[403]See Kriebaum (2007); Weiler (2005), p. 903.

[404]*Azurix v Argentina I* (n 1, Chap. 1) para 311; *LG&E v Argentina*, Decision on Liability (3 October 2006) (2007) 46 ILM 36 paras 189 and 195.

[405]*Tecmed v Mexico* (n 375) para 122.

[406]*Tecmed v Mexico* (n 375).

[407]*Tecmed v Mexico* (n 375).

[408]*Azurix v Argentina I* (n 1, Chap. 1) para 312.

[409]*Tecmed v Mexico* (n 375) para 122.

[410]*Tecmed v Mexico* (n 375) paras 123–147.

one attached under the FET standard because explicit or implicit assurances or representations in force at the moment of making its investment are generally considered as the only set of regulatory acts founding investors' expectations.[411]

### 2.3.2.3   Preliminary Conclusions

The way arbitral tribunals have understood host states' investment treaty obligations has been the main source of Latin American countries' dissatisfaction with ISDS. Taking the FET standard and BIT provision on expropriation as case studies, one may identify that tribunals have developed basic criteria to determine whether the respondent state had treated the claimant investor unfairly and inequitable, and whether its regulatory actions had tantamounted to an indirect expropriation. However, the inconsistent application of methodologies to make this determination among cases has been a problem, which at times conveys the impression that host states should refrain from taking any regulatory measure that is likely to impair investors' treaty rights.

Concerning the FET standard, its content consists in acting transparently, ensuring a non-discriminatory treatment to covered investment and its activities on arbitrary reasons, and providing guarantees of due process and protecting covered investors' legitimate expectations. Methodological inconsistencies become particularly evident in relation to this standard when it comes to the analysis of the investors' legitimate expectation criterion. In investment treaty claims, some tribunals have dealt with investors' legitimate expectations as an object worthy of protection, while others have treated it as another legal principle that assist in determination of breaches of the FET standard. In this connection, tribunals have drawn analogies from domestic laws about the protection of legitimate expectations but elaborating further this concept in accordance with their judgement on this matter. Added to this, other tribunals have followed these arguments uncritically. But the most critical point here is that some tribunals, when considering host states' legal and policy framework as an act creating legitimate expectations, have understood the corresponding obligation as an obligation to guarantee its stability and consistent application, which may lead to a severe regulatory self-restriction and thus non-fulfilment of societal objectives.

---

[411] According to the *Tecmed v Mexico* tribunal, local authorities' declaration regarding the long-term duration of the landfill concerned, authorization for the landfill operation and related permits built upon this declaration were considered the basis of claimant investor's expectation. *Tecmed v Mexico* (n 375) paras 149–150. In *Gran River v USA*, the tribunal did not only confirm that specific State's actions in form of representations or assurances create legitimate expectations on investors, but also deny that host State's domestic laws and treaty obligations amount to a conduct valid generating such expectations. *Grand River Enterprises Six Nations Ltd. Et al. v USA*, UNCITRAL (NAFTA), Award (12 January 2011) (*Grand River v USA*) paras 140–141. See also, *Copper Mesa v Ecuador* (n 3, Chap. 1) para 6.60. In *Azurix v Argentina*, the tribunal seem to suggest that a contract could found legitimate expectations on foreign investors. *Azurix v Argentina I* (n 1, Chap. 1) paras 320–322.

Similarly, one may arrive to a similar policy implication concerning BITs on provisions on expropriation if the explicit purpose of the BIT exclusively guides tribunal's interpretation and application of this provision. All arbitral tribunals rely on the economic impact of host states' measure, its degree of interference with investors' investment, as well as its duration over time, to draw the line between a non-compensable regulatory measure and indirect expropriation. For some tribunals, an indirect expropriation solely exists if the regulatory measure under review significantly impairs investors' investment over a relevant period, without any further consideration to the legal character of the measure. Notwithstanding the former, the flexibility of BITs norms in terms of standards have also allowed other tribunals to decide in a more deferential vein towards host states' regulatory needs by developing more elaborated interpretative methodologies.

### 2.3.3   Re-Politicisation of IIL Through States' Articulation of the Right to Regulate

In addition to the major concerns about the expansive interpretation and application of BITs by tribunals, the unsuccessful negotiation of the FTAA shaped, in two different ways, the investment policy scenario in Latin America from 2005 onwards. First, the failure of the FTAA speeded the adoption of national and regional investment agendas that underpin the negotiation of bilateral negotiations of IIAs among its supporters by including a reformed version of substantive and procedural IIA provisions. Second, the negotiation of the FTAA led to the creation of the Bolivarian Alternative for the Americas (ALBA) among several Latin American countries that were highly critical of comprehensive trade and investment liberalisation agenda pursued under that treaty.[412] Thus, following the unsuccessful adoption of the FTAA, some member states of the ALBA agreed to withdraw from the ICSID Convention driven by the need to safeguard—what they called—their sovereign right to regulate foreign investment.[413]

Beyond these opposite investment policy trends, novel approaches began to emerge at the national and regional level during the second half of the twenty-first century. While some countries engaged in (trans)regional negotiations of IIAs, others began to formally discuss the establishment of a *regional* forum for the

---

[412]The ALBA was founded on Venezuela and Cuba's initiative in 2004 and comprised eight left-oriented Latin American and Caribbean countries by 2009. In addition to Venezuela and Cuba, they included Bolivia, Nicaragua, the Commonwealth of Dominica, Antigua and Barbuda, Ecuador and San Vincent and the Grenadines. In 2013, Saint Lucia joined the ALBA. With the primary objective to counteract the FTAA, ALBA member states existing at that time adopted the People's Trade Agreement (ALBA-TCP) in 2006 with the aim of consolidating a regional platform for their economic integration based on economic complementarity and the non-competition among members, without conceiving trade and investment as ends in themselves.

[413]Luque Macías (2014), p. 290.

settlement of investment disputes under the auspices of the South American Union of Nations (UNASUR), a regional intergovernmental organisation that pursued building a regional integration and a union among South American countries on the grounds of the progress achieved by MERCOSUR and the Andean Community.[414] Finally, countries like Brazil that kept BITs at bay during the 1900s and the 2000s commenced to negotiate the so-called Cooperation and Facilitation Investment Agreements (CFIAs) to facilitate, rather than to protect, foreign investment from nationals of the other contracting party.

Against the wide range of national and regional approaches towards the legal protection of foreign investment, this section explores the re-politicisation of IIL in Latin America. It addresses the extent to which and by which forms these countries articulate their demands for preserving regulatory autonomy in the investment context, on one hand, and to what extent these demands differ from Latin American countries' claims made in previous historical periods.

### 2.3.3.1   National Approaches

#### 2.3.3.1.1   Reformed IIAs

In face of the considerable policy implications that may derive from an expansive tribunals' application of IIAs, a considerable number of Latin American countries have explicitly articulated their need for preserving regulatory autonomy through treaty provisions referring to their *right to regulate*, when entering new IIAs.[415] References to the right to regulate of states parties is observable in IIAs preamble[416] or in autonomous provision.[417] Other IIAs, instead, provide that their provisions

---

[414]The idea was discussed within the auspices of the Union of South American Nations (UNASUR) in 2009, which sought to consolidate this forum as an alternative to existing international institutions administering the conduct of investor-state arbitration proceedings. See Luque Macías (2016b), p. 291.

[415]A review of the investment treaty making approach of Latin American countries begins as of 2014, based on the findings of the following publications: Luque Macías (2014) and Ononaiwu (2016).

[416]The Colombia-France BIT pursues to strengthening States parties' economic cooperation and creating favourable conditions for investment, without affecting their regulatory power. See Acuerdo entre el Gobierno de la Republica de Colombia y el Gobierno de la Republica Francesa Sobre El Fomento y Proteccion Reciprocos de Inversiones (signed 10 July 2014) (Colombia-France BIT) preamble. The Mexico-Panama FTA alludes to the preservation of contracting parties' capacity to safeguard the public well-being. Tratado de Libre Comercio entre los Estados Unidos Mexicanos y la República de Panamá (signed 3 April 2014) (Mexico-Panama FTA) preamble; Bilateral Agreement for the Promotion and Protection of Investments between the Government of the Republic of Colombia and the Government of the United Arab Emirates (signed 13 November 2017) (Colombia-United Arab Emirates BIT) preamble.

[417]Investment Agreement between the Government of the Hong Kong Special Administrative Region of the People's Republic of China and the Government of the Republic of Chile (signed 18 November 2016) (Chile-Hong Kong China SAR BIT) art 15 para 1.

shall not affect the right to regulate, if its exercise pursues the achievement of policy objectives qualified as 'legitimate',[418] or explicitly establish which regulatory objective should be observed in ISDS.[419]

In addition, some IIAs limit the type of regulatory measures that may not be considered as breaches of IIAs upon compliance with one benchmark such as proportionality,[420] non-arbitrariness or unjustifiable non-discrimination,[421] or with all these standards as a whole, in terms of the so-called general exceptions, modelled after the general exceptions codified in articles XX of the General Agreement on Tariffs and Trade (GATT) and XIV of the General Agreement on Trade in Services (GATS).[422]

The formulation of above-mentioned treaty provisions suggests that Latin American countries indeed articulate their regulatory demands in the investment context by means of IIAs. That said, IIAs remain the only legal basis according to which tribunals will review the regulatory conduct of states parties[423] and the latter do not underpin to ease an unrestricted integration of *any* domestic regulatory objective in tribunals' determination of their compliance with IIAs. In fact, general exceptions laid down in IIAs only exempt states parties from compliance with their treaty obligations, if the implementation of the regulatory measure is non-arbitrary and non-discriminatory towards the investor, or without the intention of constraining international trade and investment.[424]

Further, many Latin American countries have opted for the refinement of the content of the FET standard to safeguard regulatory space, reflecting to some extent the different existing approaches in ISDS. Yet not all treaty formulations of the FET

---

[418]This is usually accompanied by an illustrative enumeration of the objectives considered legitimate. The Reciprocal Promotion and Protection of Investment between the Argentine Republic and the State of Qatar (signed 6 November 2016) art 10.

[419]Pursuant to the Mexico-Panama FTA, nothing shall be understood as affecting State' right to adopt or induce investor to comply with environmental laws. Mexico–Panama FTA (n 416) art 10.9 para 2. See also, Agreement between the Republic of Guatemala and the Republic of Trinidad and Tobago on the Reciprocal Promotion and Protection of Investments (signed 13 August 2013) (Guatemala-Trinidad and Tobago BIT) art 16.

[420]See Agreement between the Government of the Republic of Colombia and the Government of the Republic of Turkey Concerning the Reciprocal Promotion and Protection of Investment (signed 28 July 2014) (Colombia-Turkey BIT) art 11 para 1; Tratado de Libre Comercio entre Argentina y Chile (signed 2 November 2017) (Argentina-Chile FTA) art 8.4.

[421]Moreover, pursuant to the Colombia-United Arab BIT, measures shall be non-arbitrary or unjustifiable non-discriminatory in relation to investment and investors, construed to prevent States from adopting, maintaining, or enforcing any measure to ensure that investment fulfil environmental and labour laws. See Colombia-United Arab Emirates BIT (n 416) art 10 para 1.

[422]Under these treaty provisions, states are only entitled, upon compliance with these requirements, to disregard their IIAs obligation if their regulatory measures seek to protect human life or health, the conservation of living or non-living exhaustible natural resources. For a detailed analysis of these treaty provisions, see Newcombe (2011).

[423]Titi (2014), p. 275.

[424]*CMS v Argentina* (n 373) Decision on Annulment (25 September 2007) para 146.

standard may lead to the attainment of this result. On the one hand, the IIAs negotiated during the first decade during the twenty-first century in Latin America considerably resemble the NAFTA member states' approach towards the FET standard by stipulating that states parties shall guarantee a treatment in accordance with international law, including the FET standard, and incorporating a definition of what this provision should mean.[425] This implies considering CIL as the minimum standard of treatment (MST) and understanding that FET does not require a treatment in addition to, or beyond, what the customary rule requires in relation to the MST of aliens.[426] Consistent with the former approach, IIAs perspective concluded during the last decade, even reflects a formulation of the FET standard as developed in NAFTA-based case law to some extent.[427] Some IIAs accord a treatment to the investment of investors covered by the treaty in accordance with the minimum standard of treatment (MST) as a rule of international law,[428] or as a rule of CIL, including FET.[429] Therefore, some treaties mirrored the FTC understanding of its content by placing the MST as a threshold,[430] whereas other treaties place the MST

---

[425]This was certainly the case since many IIAs were signed with NAFTA countries during that decade. For an overview of the investment treaty-making practice of South American countries until 2013, see Luque Macías (2014), pp. 292–294.

[426]Ibidem. This formulation of the FET standard resembles the interpretation of article 1105 (1 of the NAFTA provided by the NAFTA Free Trade Commission, and that trigger that some NAFTA member states engaged in a review process of international investment policies in NAFTA countries in the first half of the twenty-first century, to align them with this interpretation. See also Gantz (2003), p. 679; Lévesque (2007), p. 249.

[427]In the resolution of investment disputes under NAFTA, some tribunals did attach the meaning given by the FTC to this provision. *Genin v Estonia* (n 357) para 367; *Occidental v Ecuador* (n 373) paras 188–190. Others, instead, clearly abstained from endorsing the interpretation given by FTC and held that FET standard guarantees an additional level of protection to what is already guaranteed under the MST. See *SD Meyers v Canada* (n 386) para 64; *Pope & Talbot v Canada* (n 357) Award on the Merits of Phase 2 (10 April 2001) paras 105–18; *Mondev International Ltd v United States of America*, ICSID Case No. ARB(AF)/99/2, Award (11 October 2002); *United Parcel Service of America Inc. v Canada*, ICSID Case No. UNCT/02/1, Award on the Merits (24 May 2007); *ADF Group v USA* (n 357); Loewen Group, Inc. and Raymond L. Loewen v United States of America, ICSID Case No. ARB(AF)/98/3, Award (26 June 2003).

[428]Colombia-Turkey BIT (n 420) art 4 para 1.

[429]Chile-Hong Kong BIT China SAR BIT (n 417) art 6 para 1. Other states prescribe that they accord a treatment in accordance with CIL. See Guatemala-Trinidad and Tobago BIT (n 419) art 4 para 1.

[430]Chile-Hong Kong China SAR BIT (n 417) art 6 para 2; Agreement between Japan and the Oriental Republic of Uruguay for the Liberalization, Promotion and Protection of Investment (signed 26 January 2015; entered into force 14 April 2017) (Japan-Uruguay BIT) para 1 and para 2. When IIAs establish (customary) international law as a minimum or threshold of FET scope of protection, they usually provide that the scope of protection of FET is 'no less favourable than' or 'not beyond that which is required to' these sources of international law, respectively. Under this type of formulation of the FET standard, tribunals might assess state's conduct considering the benchmarks developed in the *Neer* case. According to these criteria, the claimant investor has the burden of proving that the state's action denoted either 'bad faith', a 'wilful neglect of duty', or an 'insufficiency of governmental action to the extent that international standards that every reasonable

as a minimum of the legal protection intended by the parties to be accorded pursuant to this provision.[431] On the other hand, other IIAs reflect a different line of reasoning developed in arbitral tribunals' case law as to the content of FET by codifying some of its constitutive elements.[432]

Granted, tribunals have generally relied on whether the respondent state's measure at stake was transparent, non-discriminatory, guarantee procedural fairness and did not impair investors' legitimate expectation.[433] In IIAs under review, the legal protection against denial of justice features as the most prominent and common element among all these benchmarks.[434] In summary, there is an observable trend in recent IIAs of some Latin American countries to articulate the FET standard as a rule of IIL. Nevertheless, the language employed in these formulations of FET is still highly undetermined to prescribe in advance how the tribunals shall understand FET under these criteria. Thus, these formulations will not substantially change how tribunals may address the regulatory needs of states parties on questions of their obligations under the FET standard. These legal norms remain highly flexible and hence allow tribunals to reject and/or incorporate the regulatory needs of states under certain circumstances.

Finally, few IIAs greatly depart from the above-mentioned approaches by restricting considerably how tribunals shall understand their obligations under the FET standard in two different ways. The Chile-Hong Kong China SAR BIT, for instance, entitles covered investment as a treatment in accordance with CIL MST, including FET,[435] but provides that states parties' actions or omissions inconsistent with investors' expectations do not constitute a breach of the MST.[436] By doing so, these states avoid that the frustration of the so-called investors' expectations by potential changes in legislation or policies in place at the time of the admission of its investment becomes a critical element in tribunals' review of their liability under this standard.[437]

---

and impartial man would readily recognise its sufficiency'. *LFH Neer and Pauline Neer v Mexico (US v Mexico)* (1926) 4 RIAA 60, pp. 61–62.

[431]Mexico-Panama FTA (n 416) art 10.5 para 1. In this respect, other IIAs additionally make it clear that these minimum standards comprise all legal principles protecting the economic rights and interests of aliens. See Acuerdo entre el Gobierno de la Republica del Peru y el Gobierno de la Republica de Colombia sobre Promocion y Proteccion Reciproca de Inversiones (signed 11 December 2007, entered into force 30 December 2010) Annex A; Tratado de Libre Comercio entre Panama y Peru (signed 25 May 2011, entered into force 1 May 2012) ch 12 Annex 12.4; Chile-Hong Kong China SAR BIT (n 417) art 6 para 1, footnote 1.

[432]See Mexico-Panama FTA (n 416) art 10.5 para 2 lit. a; Japan-Uruguay BIT (n 430) art 5 para 2 lit a.

[433]See Sect. 2.3.2.1.

[434]Ibidem. See also, Colombia-United Arab Emirates BIT (n 416) art 5 para 2.

[435]See Chile-Hong Kong China SAR BIT (n 417) art 6 para 1.

[436]See Chile-Hong Kong China SAR BIT (n 417) art 6 para 4.

[437]Other acts creating investor's legitimate expectations include specific commitments made in favour of investors, stabilization clauses, licenses, or authorization to perform their activities, as well as representations. For a discussion, see Sect. 2.3.2.1.

Moreover, the Colombia-United Arab Emirates BIT grants FET to covered investment in accordance with the laws and regulations of the recipient state[438] and defines the type of measures against which the FET standard intends to protect: measures or series of measures that amount to a denial of justice, fundamental breaches of due process or manifest arbitrariness.[439] Under the latter approach, these states displace international law as the legal basis of tribunals' determination of breaches of the FET standard. In addition, the limitation of the types of measures against which the FET shall protect indirectly leads to ruling out tribunals' consideration of investors' legitimate expectations as a relevant element of protection.

Furthermore, all IIAs of the Latin American countries surveyed in this section explicitly foreclose the adoption of the 'sole effect" approach applied by arbitral tribunals to determine whether a regulatory measure is tantamount to an indirect expropriation,[440] and what constitutes a clear effort to preserve regulatory space in the investment context. Despite these commonalities, IIAs provisions ruling an indirect expropriation differ as follows: Some IIAs establish the reasonable and distinguishable investors' expectations as the criteria to be relied upon by tribunals to avoid equating the significant impairments suffered by a foreign investment with an indirect expropriation.[441] If consistent with existing case law, this treaty-making approach would thus mean that only assurances provided by the executive or legislative power of states parties should feature as the only source of legitimate expectations in tribunals' determination of an alleged existing indirect expropriation.

Other IIAs require, in addition, that the scope and/or the character of challenged measure designed and implemented to protect legitimate regulatory objectives is observed,[442] implying that tribunals should examine all circumstances underlying the adoption of the regulatory measure allegedly tantamount to an indirect expropriation. An opposite investment treaty making approach consists in providing that there is no indirect expropriation through a regulatory measure taken in favour of legitimate objectives of public policy that are proportional and necessary considering these objectives and its application effectively respond to these objectives.[443] Under this type of provision, states parties usually give the protection of the environment, human health, and security as an example of legitimate objectives, which may not lead in principle to the exclusion of the protection of human rights in the investment

---

[438]See Colombia-United Arab Emirates BIT (n 416) art 5 para 1.

[439]See Colombia-United Arab Emirates BIT (n 416) art 5 para 2.

[440]Colombia-Turkey BIT (n 420) art 7 para 2, lit. b (iv; Mexico-Panama FTA (n 416) Anexo 10.11 lit. c (I; Chile-Hong Kong China SAR BIT (n 417) Annex I para 3 lit. a (i; Argentina-Chile FTA (n 420) art 8.8 para 2, lit. c (ii.

[441]Colombia-Turkey BIT (n 420) art 7 para 2, lit. b (ii; Chile-Hong Kong China SAR BIT (n 417) Annex I para 3 lit. a (ii; Colombia-United Arab Emirates BIT (n 416) art 7 para 2 lit. b (iii.

[442]See Colombia-Turkey BIT (n 420) art 7 para 2, lit. b (i and (iv; Argentina-Chile FTA (n 420) art 8.8 para 2, lit. c (iii; Chile-Hong Kong China SAR BIT (n 417) Annex I para 3 lit. a (ii and (iii; Colombia-United Arab Emirates BIT (n 416) art 7 para 2 lit. b (i.

[443]See Colombia-France BIT (n 416) art 6 para 2.

context.[444] This type of provision however places a considerable number of requirements upon states parties to be met in order to be successful in their defence arguments, which considerably reduces the type of regulatory measures for which they may not be held liable under this provision.

In contrast, a small number of IIAs only require that regulatory measures are non-discriminatory and conducive to protect public purpose or social interest to not be categorised as an indirect expropriation.[445] Under this type of treaty provision, states parties may satisfy more easily the non-discrimination requirement than benchmarks such as proportionality or necessity as implicit in the former treaty approach, for instance, by proving that their measures also intended to address nationals. Moreover, since this type of provision foresees to exclude from its scope of application measures aiming at protecting the social interest, they are likely to cover a broader set of regulatory objectives than those implicit under the public purpose.

To sum up, Latin American countries entering IIAs during the first two decades of the twenty-first century have articulated their need for preserving regulatory autonomy through explicit references to their right to regulate, and through the refinement of the FET standard and provisions ruling how states lawfully expropriate foreign investment. Moreover, there exist different investment treaty-making approaches echoing the divergent existing case laws developed by arbitral tribunals. However, not all investment treaty-making approaches deviate from the predominant functional underpinning of IIL, namely, to ensure an effective legal protection to foreign investors and investments. While some IIAs clearly restrict the scope of protection afforded to covered investors and investment by relaxing the legal requirements to be met by states to be relieved from international responsibility, other treaties adopt the opposite approach by subjecting states parties' regulatory conduct to a considerable scrutiny in conformity with a set of vaguely drafted standards of review.

### 2.3.3.1.2   Denunciation of BITs and the ICSID Convention

Like the above-mentioned Latin American countries, Bolivia, Ecuador, and Venezuela articulated their demands to safeguard regulatory autonomy in terms of the so-called 'right to regulate'. Yet rather than staying in the IIL regime, these three countries gradually abandoned it. In conformity with the critical views expressed within the ALBA against the legal instruments forming the IIL regime, these three countries denounced the ICSID Convention and began to consider the termination of BITs in force by the late 2000s.[446] This is not surprising in light of the high-profile cases or amount of investment treaty claims that they had to respond to before ICSID

---

[444]Ibidem.

[445]See Colombia-Turkey BIT (n 420) art 7 para 2, lit. (c; Guatemala-Trinidad and Tobago BIT (n 419) art 8 para 4; Mexico-Panama FTA (n 416) Anexo 10.11 lit. d.

[446]See ICSID Staff (2007, 2009, 2012).

tribunals. On one hand, Bolivia, together with Argentina, was one of the first Latin American countries facing a high-profile investment case that exposed how ISDS could have severe implications over users' enjoyment of the right to water in the context of investors' provision of water services.[447] On the other hand, Ecuador and Venezuela belonged by 2010 to the group of countries responding to the highest amount of investment treaty cases worldwide.[448]

Yet, although the overly expansive interpretation and application of BIT provisions by arbitral tribunals motivated the adoption of this controversial approach at that time, a closer look to their claims reveals that main reasons behind the denunciation of the ICSID Convention include the broad tribunals' reading of jurisdictional treaty clauses and recently adopted domestic laws forbidding the submission of investment disputes to international arbitration alike. As to the first reason, the broad definition of investors to be covered under BITs became the major cause of concern because such treaty clauses facilitated the treaty shopping by investors from third countries, which intend to benefit from the protection a BIT through the establishment of a shell company in the territory of one state party, even though the control of their business activities were located elsewhere.[449]

In investment cases involving Bolivia and Venezuela, tribunals uphold their jurisdiction to hear these claims since claimant investors are nationals of one of the contracting parties to the BIT through its incorporation in the territory of the latter, and as such they are entitled to treaty protection. Concerning the domestic driven motivation to denounce the ICSID Convention, Bolivia invoked its constitutional provision, pursuant to which companies established within its territory for exploitation (of natural resources), utilisation or business are considered nationals and thereby subject to its sovereignty, law and regulations.[450] In fact, the Bolivian constitution prohibits foreign companies engaged in extractive activities in the oil and gas sector to bring international claims before arbitral tribunals.[451] Ecuador, on the contrary, followed a different approach. It originally withdrew its consent in December 2007 to settle investment disputes arising out of the utilisation of natural resources in accordance with ICSID arbitration rules. However, following the enactment of the 2008 Constitution prohibiting the resolution of investment disputes before international arbitral tribunals, Ecuador finally withdrew from the ICSID Convention in July 2009.

The reasons behind the denunciation of the ICSID Convention also motivated the termination of BITs in Bolivia, Ecuador, and Venezuela at the late 2000s, even

---

[447]*Aguas del Tunari S.A. v Bolivia*, ICSID Case No. ARB/02/3, Decision on Respondent's Objections to Jurisdiction (21 October 2005) (*Aguas del Tunari v Bolivia*).

[448]UNCTAD (n 309).

[449]*Aguas del Tunari v Bolivia* (n 447). See *The Mobil Corporation Venezuela Holdings B.N, Mobil Cerro Negro Holding, Ltd, Mobil Venezolana de Petroleos Holdings, Inc., Mobil Cerro Negro Ltd., and Mobil Venezolana de Petroleos Inc. v Bolivarian Republic of Venezuela*, ICSID Case No. ARB/07/27, Decision on Jurisdiction (10 June 2010).

[450]Luque Macías (2014), p. 290.

[451]Constitution of the Plurinational State of Bolivia (2009) article 366.

though these countries adopted this investment policy at a varying pace, and not all countries maintained a policy of reviewing and terminating BITs over time. At first, Bolivia and Venezuela terminated their respective BITs with the Netherlands because of the use of the broadly drafted substantive and procedural clauses that US companies made to bring their claims before ICSID tribunals.[452]

In contrast to Venezuela, Bolivia's withdrawal was a foreseeable step after it announced its decision to review BITs in parallel to its 2007 withdrawal from the ICSID Convention. Like Bolivia, Ecuador's termination of BITs directly related to its denunciation of the ICSID Convention and responded to the reforms in its constitution, which prohibit ceding national jurisdiction to international arbitration in disputes of contractual or commercial character between the state and natural or legal persons.[453] Moreover, the participation of the adjudicative and legislative attached a particular legitimacy to the Ecuadorian review process. The Constitutional court declared the unconstitutionality of dispute settlement clauses allowing investor-state arbitration in BITs for being contrary to constitutional provisions. Based on this judgement, the legislative to authorise the termination of BITs with several Western European states began in 2010.[454] Yet, previous to this legislative's authorisation, the Ecuadorian government had already commenced termination of nine BITs with Latin American countries[455] and one with an East European country.[456] Moreover, the BIT with Finland was the only treaty that, after this legislative authorisation, was formally no longer in force,[457] based on normative considerations of domestic legal nature. Constitutional reforms redefined the international responsibilities of Ecuador,[458] so that BITs shall be consistent with the Constitution,[459]

---

[452]Venezuela terminated its BIT with the Netherlands in May 2008, while Bolivia, on 1 November 2009.

[453]Pursuant to article 422 of the Ecuadorian constitution, no international treaties could be signed in which the Ecuadorian state cedes jurisdiction to international arbitration tribunals, in contractual or commercial disputes that arise with natural or legal persons.

[454]By 2011, the National Assembly authorized the termination of BITs with Germany and the United Kingdom in September 2010; the BIT with Finland, in November 2010; and BITs with Sweden and France in March 2011.

[455]On the 18th January 2008, Ecuador terminated its BITs with Cuba, Dominican Republic, El Salvador, Guatemala, Honduras, Nicaragua, Paraguay, Uruguay.

[456]Ecuador terminated its BIT with Romania, on 18 January 2008.

[457]Justifications provided by the Assembly to terminate the BIT with Finland include absent direct investment by Finnish nationals, and the function of BITs in reinforcing the position of extractive foreign companies while hindering the recipient state to introduce tax reforms and domestic regulations. Asamblea Nacional de la Republica del Ecuador, Comisión Especializada Permanente No. 5 de Soberanía, Integración, Relaciones Internacionales y Seguridad Integral, Informe de la Comisión sobre el "Convenio entre el Gobierno de la Republica del Ecuador y el Gobierno de la Republica de Finlandia sobre la promoción y Protección de las Inversiones", DM (18 October 2010) (Commission's report to Ecuador-Finland BIT) para 3.3.

[458]Commission's report to Ecuador-Finland BIT (n 457) para 3.6.

[459]Commission's report to Ecuador-Finland BIT (n 457) para 4.1.2. Pursuant to article 417 of the 2008 Ecuadorian constitution, international treaties ratified by the Ecuadorian state shall be subject to what is established in the Constitution.

implying termination of international treaties, such as BITs, that cede national jurisdiction to international arbitration in disputes of contractual or commercial character between the state and natural or legal persons.[460] Yet, despite these initial steps, only Bolivia and Ecuador remained engaged in a long-term process of BIT revision, while Venezuela kept negotiating BITs without denouncing further BITs.[461]

In the case of Bolivia, the termination of BITs has been a gradual process from 2012 onwards.[462] In the case of Ecuador, however, this revision was postponed since the executive began an auditing process of its BITs in force in 2013, through the establishment of The Ecuadorian Citizens' Commission for a Comprehensive Audit of Investment Protection Treaties (the so-called CAITISA), with basis on political economy and legal considerations.[463] CAITISA's audit of BITs concluded with an extensive report delivered in May 2017. Considering the findings that BITs were not necessarily drivers of foreign investment and thus not contributed to Ecuador's development, CAITISA recommended the termination of BITs still in force.[464] Yet, it did not discourage the negotiation of new instruments, either in form of IIAs or investment contracts if these investment instruments do not contain broadly drafted formulations of substantive standards and explicitly define state's rights and investor's obligations. At the procedural level, CAITISA additionally proposed opting out investor-state arbitration in new instruments and to establish instead domestic courts' adjudication as an option for investment dispute settlement, together with a set of strategies for easing this transition. Based on these findings, Ecuador resumed its revision of BITs and since then terminated one BIT in 2017 and 2020, and 12 BITs in 2018.[465]

To sum up, arbitral tribunals' understanding of the scope of jurisdictional clauses in ISDS has been one of the main reasons behind the denunciation of the ICSID Convention and termination of BITs in Bolivia, Ecuador, and Venezuela. This has facilitated treaty shopping by foreign companies, which intend to benefit from the

---

[460]Commission's report to Ecuador-Finland BIT (n 457) para 4.13.

[461]Venezuela negotiated BITs with Belarus, Iran, Russia, and Vietnam.

[462]To date, Bolivia has terminated 14 BITs, following the termination of the BIT with the Netherlands in 2009. These comprise BITs with Spain, USA, and Italy, in 2012; with Austria, Sweden and France, in 2013; with Denmark, Argentina, the Belgium-Luxemburg Economic Union, United Kingdom and Germany, in 2014; with Ecuador, in 2018; with Switzerland, in 2019; and with Chile, in 2020.

[463]The Ecuadorian executive set up, by decree, the Comisión para la Auditoria Ciudadana de los Tratados de Protección Recíproca de Inversiones y del Sistema de Arbitraje Internacional en Materia de Inversiones (known by its Spanish acronym CAITISA) in 2013. Presidencia de la Republica, Decreto 1506, Registro Official No. 958 (21 May 2013) art 2.

[464]Fach Gómez (2019).

[465]Ecuador unilaterally denounced its BIT with Peru in 2017. In 2018, Ecuador unilaterally denounced 12 BITs. On 18 May 2018, Ecuador terminated the BIT with Argentina, Germany, Sweden, and the United Kingdom. On 19 May 2018, BITs denounced included Bolivia, Canada, Chile, China, and Venezuela. On 11 September 2018, Ecuador terminated its BIT with Switzerland, and on 1 February 2020, its BIT with Italy.

protection of a specific treaty despite not having substantial business activities in their alleged home state and contracting party to the treaty they invoked. Arguably, this development in investor-state arbitration practice indirectly underpinned the wave of constitutional reforms in Bolivia and Ecuador that redefine state's responsibilities at the international level.

Despite being a consequence of this tribunals' practice, these South American countries used these domestic reforms as another justification to shift the course of their investment policy at that time. This initially reveals that although these states re-politicise IIL in terms of the 'right to regulate', past ideas of states' jurisdiction, rather than the preservation of regulatory autonomy, informed their current demands. In other words, ceding jurisdiction to arbitral tribunals' review of their regulatory conduct, other than the review itself, has been normative value informing their claims. This is not to say that the idea of preserving regulatory autonomy is totally irrelevant in these developments. The Ecuadorian legislative, for instance, recognise the chill effect that BITs may have over state's regulation and invoked it as a reason to terminate the Ecuador-Finland BIT. In addition, the review process of BITs, after the denunciation of the ICSID Convention, reveals the clear determination of these states to rethink by which legal instruments regulate their legal relations with foreign investors and provoke a general debate over these issues internationally.

### 2.3.3.1.3   The Adoption of CFIAs

Traditionally, Brazil has been reluctant to adhere to the international investment regime for the same reasons advanced by the above-mentioned South American countries to gradually abandon it. In addition to the doubts about the role of BITs in attracting foreign investment, Brazilian lawmakers were of the view in the early 2000s that ISDS clauses prevail foreign over national investors, and provisions relating to indirect expropriation could considerably limit state's exercise of its regulatory powers.[466] These ideas once again confirm that the need to safeguard state's jurisdiction and preserve regulatory autonomy were the values informing its criticism.

Yet, since 2015, this South American country has developed and proposed a novel type of investment treaty to African,[467] Latin American[468] and Asian states,[469] and even to the MERCOSUR,[470] which focuses on facilitation, rather than on

---

[466]Maggeti and Choer Moraes (2018).

[467]In 2015, Brazil signed a CFIA with Mozambique, Angola, and Malawi. From this group of treaties, only the Angola-Brazil CFIA has entered into force on 28 July 2017. Subsequently, Brazil concluded CFIAs with Ethiopia and Morocco in 2018 and 2019, respectively.

[468]In 2015, Brazil also signed CFIAs with Mexico, Colombia, and Chile. In 2018, this country concluded CFIAs with Suriname and Guyana, and a year thereafter, with Ecuador.

[469]Brazil signed CFIAs with United Arab Emirates and India in 2019 and 2020, respectively.

[470]Protocolo de Cooperación y Facilitación de Inversiones Intra-Mercosur (signed 7 April 2017) (Protocolo Intra-Mercosur) Available at: https://www.mercosur.int/documento/protocolo-de-

protection, of foreign investment. Although the above-mentioned concerns considerably instructed the Brazilian approach, the increasing need of protecting Brazilian capital abroad has also played a decisive role in the design of the recent Brazilian investment initiative.[471]

To address investor and state's needs, CFIAs combine a set of investment facilitation rules with provisions that recognise the regulatory powers of contracting states and encourage the prevention of investment disputes, through the establishment of a clear institutional framework that oversees their operationalization. In favour of investors, CFIAs only afford protection against direct expropriation and nationalization,[472] and only in a few occasions, treatment no less favourably than domestic investors and investors of other states concerning a specific set of economic activities.[473] In fact, CFIAs explicitly foreclose covering substantive standards traditionally laid down in IIAs[474] and granting *locus standi* to investors before arbitral tribunals, which exhibits states parties' intention to hinder that arbitrators rely upon these standards in the inter-state resolution of investment disputes that may arise in the CFIAs context.[475] In return for this limited protection, CFIAs support and facilitate investor's interaction with local authorities by means of national focal points,[476] established in recipient states for, inter alia, evaluating investor's complaints and recommending actions conducive to improve the investment environment, and seeking the prevention of investment controversies in collaboration with public and private entities. Hence, through the optimization of the domestic regulatory framework in which foreign investment operates, CFIAs aim at correcting in advance any regulatory deficiency in recipient states, without the need of securing further protective means to remedy future regulatory shortcomings.[477]

---

cooperacion-y-facilitacion-de-inversiones-intra-mercosur/. Accessed 10 December 2020. See, Damien and Peterson (2017).

[471]Ratton Sanchez and Morosini (2017), pp. 218, 248.

[472]Acordo de Cooperação e Facilitação de Investimentos entre o Governo da República Federativa do Brasil e o Governo da República de Moçambique (signed 30 March 2015) art 9; Acuerdo de Cooperación y Facilitación de Inversiones entre la República Federativa del Brasil y la República de Chile (signed 24 November 2015) (Brazil-Chile CFIA) art 7; Acordo de Cooperação e Facilitação de Investimentos entre a República Federativa do Brasil e a República do Colômbia (signed 9 October 2015) (Brazil-Colombia CFIA) art 6; Acuerdo de Cooperación y de Facilitación de las Inversiones entre la República Federativa del Brasil y los Estados Unidos Mexicanos (signed 26 May 2015) (Brazil-Mexico CFIA) art 6.

[473]Investment Cooperation and Facilitation Agreement between the Federative Republic of Brazil and the Republic of Malawi (signed 26 June 2015) art 10; Brazil-Chile CFIA (n 473) arts 5 and 6.

[474]To achieve greater certainty in the application of its clause labelled 'treatment', the MERCOSUR CFIA clearly provides that it does not cover standards relating to fair and equitable treatment, full protection and security and those relating to the pre-establishment of investors' investment. Protocolo Intra-MERCOSUR (n 471) art 4 para 3.

[475]Maggeti and Choer Moraes (2018).

[476]Brazil-Chile CFIA (n 473) art 19; Brazil-Colombia CFIA (n 473) art 17; Brazil-Mexico CFIA (n 473) art 15; Protocolo Intra-Mercosur (n 471) art 18.

[477]Maggeti and Choer Moraes (2018).

Concerning states, CFIAs clearly articulate states' right to regulate health, labour and environmental matters[478] and reaffirm investors' obligation to comply with domestic laws, regulations and investment policies of the recipient state,[479] and mandate host state (in some cases) to raise investors' inobservance, if the home state brings a claim alleging CFIA's breaches by the former.[480] Accordingly, beyond the exclusion of ISDS, CFIAs place foreign investors and recipient states on equal footing with regards to their treaty and domestic rights and obligations, and ensure their corresponding offsetting in the settlement of disputes by states parties to the CFIAs.

To conclude, CFIAs offer limited substantive investment protection and strengthen states' sovereign rights to freely determine the legal protection to be accorded to foreign nationals and to regulate, while turning back to inter-state dispute settlement. For advocates of this type of treaty, this renewed form of politicization of investment disputes is not necessarily a disadvantage if compared with investment treaty arbitration since it does not greatly differ from the political and diplomatic considerations already involving current ISDS.[481] Furthermore, CFIAs' focus on investment facilitation attracts the participation of states that not necessarily coincide with the Brazilian approach towards investment protection. CFIAs bilaterally signed in the Latin American context clearly exemplify this development since countries reforming and abandoning the investment protection regime currently in place gradually endorse the Brazilian treaty model.

### 2.3.3.2  (Sub)regional Approaches

#### 2.3.3.2.1  Along the Pacific

In the Latin American region, two regional approaches endorsing foreign investment promotion and protection emerged during the second decade of the twenty-first century. One investment policy approach that favours the creation of an institutional platform for underpinning the consolidation of a free trade zone and adopts further additional legal instruments for its reinforcement, and another, prevailing the direct conclusion of trade agreements. In both cases, provisions directed to achieve the above-mentioned investment objectives are integral part of their scope.

The first regional approach refers to the one prevalent by the Pacific Alliance, a platform of regional integration created to promote the consolidation of a free trade

---

[478]Brazil-Chile CFIA (n 473) arts 15–17; Brazil-Colombia (n 472) arts 13–15; Brazil-Mexico CFIA (n 473) art 13.

[479]Protocolo Intra-Mercosur (n 471) art 13.

[480]Protocolo Intra-Mercosur (n 471) art 23 para 3 (c.

[481]Gertz et al. (2018).

area among Chile, Colombia, Peru, and Mexico in 2011,[482] which fortify the idea of free trade as an appropriate means to achieve economic regional integration within the Americas, in a period where the ALBA and the UNASUR promoted an opposite agenda.[483] To strengthen the actions conducive to achieve the objectives of the Pacific Alliance, its member states adopted the Additional Protocol to the Framework Agreement of the Pacific Alliance in 2014, codifying an investment chapter.[484] The Protocol provides, among others, that this investment chapter applies to any state enterprise or any person exercising regulatory authority to expropriate, license, approve or impose charges.[485] Yet, it also stipulates that nothing in the chapter shall be constructed as preventing states parties to adopt, maintain and enforce any measure, otherwise compatible with this chapter, that is considered appropriate to ensure that investment activities are made considering health, environmental or other regulatory objectives.

In doing so, member states of the Pacific Alliance articulate their need of preserving regulatory autonomy, even though its exercise is subject to be consistent with the Protocol. In this connection, this Protocol resonates with some of investment treaty practice of its member states as described in Sect. 2.3.3.1.1. To illustrate, the Protocol defines the constitutive elements of the FET standard,[486] while ruling out explicitly the application of the 'sole effect" doctrine in the determination of the existence of a regulatory measure tantamount to an indirect expropriation.[487]

The second regional approach can be observed within the Comprehensive and Progressive Agreement for Trans-Pacific Partnership (CPTPP), which was negotiated between Australia, Brunei, Canada, Chile, Japan, Malaysia, Mexico, New Zealand, Peru, Singapore, and Vietnam, after the entry into force of the Trans-Pacific Partnership (TPP) failed due to USA's withdrawal.[488] To date, only Mexico is state party to this treaty. In addition, the USA–Mexico–Canada Agreement (USMCA) that came to replace the NAFTA also reflects this approach.[489]

---

[482]Acuerdo Marco de la Alianza del Pacifico (signed 6 June 2012, entered into force 20 July 2015) Art 3(2.a) https://alianzapacifico.net/download/acuerdo-marco-de-la-alianza-del-pacifico/ (accessed 10 December 2020).

[483]Luque Macías (2020). In: Framework Agreement of the Pacific Alliance, 6th June 2012, OXIO 496: Oxford International Organizations (OXIO). Available at: https://opil.ouplaw.com/view/10. 1093/law-oxio/e496.013.1/law-oxio-e496?rskey=rICTWl&result=1&prd=OXIO     (accessed 10 December 2020).

[484]Procolo Adicional al Acuerdo Marco de la Alianza del Pacifico (signed 10 February 2014, entered into force 1 May 2016) https://alianzapacifico.net/download/protocolo-adicional-al-acuerdo-marco-de-la-alianza-del-pacifico/ (accessed 10 December 2020) (Protocolo Alianza del Pacifico).

[485]Protocolo Alianza del Pacifico (n 485) art 10.3 para 4.

[486]Protocolo Alianza del Pacifico (n 485) art 10.6 para 2 lit. a.

[487]Protocolo Alianza del Pacifico (n 485) Anexo 10.12 para 3 (i.

[488]Comprehensive and Progressive Agreement for Trans-Pacific Partnership (CPTPP) (signed 8 August 2018).

[489]United States–Mexico–Canada Agreement (signed 30 November 2018, entered into force 1 July 2020) (USMCA) ch 14.

The CPTPP and the USMCA refer to the regulatory need of states parties by providing that these investment chapters shall not be understood as hindering appropriate regulatory measures in benefit of the environment, health, or any regulatory objective if they are in conformity with chapter's provisions.[490] Hence, while the regulatory objectives of states parties are relevant, their implementation shall conform investment chapters, leaving tribunals wide discretion as to the scope of IIAs' provisions. Moreover, both investment chapters define the FET standard, subjecting its protection to rules of international law, while defining its constitutive elements.[491] Again, these formulations of the FET standard provide more elements for tribunals' determination of breaches, but in doing so, they do not guarantee more regulatory space to states parties.

### 2.3.3.2.2  The UNASUR Centre for the Settlement of Investment Disputes

The UNASUR Centre for the Settlement of Investment Disputes (UNASUR Centre) was conceived as an alternative to ICSID and PCA because of the great concerns about the failure of *ad hoc* tribunals administered by these arbitration facilities to observe their regulatory demands in the settlement of investment disputes.[492] The Ecuadorian government was entrusted in 2009 with the development of a draft constitutive treaty serving as the basis for deliberations among UNASUR member states,[493] and a working group of experts was established to conduct this process.[494] This working group held twelve working meetings and achieved to update the 2012 draft by 2014.[495]

From the scarce information available regarding the provisions laid down in the draft treaty for the establishment of the UNASUR Centre, however, one may argue that the only difference with existing international arbitration facilities was its regional character. The draft treaty addressed similar issues, inter alia, the structure and operation of the Centre, requirements to become states parties, and references to existing international legal mechanisms of dispute settlement.[496] Nevertheless, many of these issues already caused disagreement among UNASUR members,[497] and the gradual withdrawal of membership of UNASUR seem to indicate that its establishment is an extinct idea.[498]

---

[490]CPTPP (n 489) art 9.1; USMCA (n 490) art 14.16.

[491]CPTPP (n 489) art 9.16; USMCA (n 490) art 16.6.

[492]Luque Macías (2016a).

[493]Ibidem.

[494]Fach Gómez and Titi (2016b).

[495]Sarmiento (2016).

[496]Fach Gómez and Titi (2016a).

[497]Ibidem.

[498]Mijares and Nolte (2018).

### 2.3.3.3  Preliminary Conclusions

Section 2.3.3 shows that the re-politicisation of IIL has taken place in Latin America, albeit in varying degrees, depending upon the investment policy approach prevailed by states at the domestic and regional level.

The review undertaken in Sects. 2.3.3.1.1 and 2.3.3.2.1 suggests that many Latin American countries indeed acknowledge the concerns that could pose an expansive tribunals' interpretation and application of legal provisions by introducing a more-detailed formulation of the FET standard and provisions ruling the lawful exercise of states' right to expropriate foreign investment, when entering into IIAs and regional treaties such as Additional Protocol to the Pacific Alliance, CPTPP and USMCA alike. Most IIAs have thus intended to define the content of the FET standard by enumerating its constitutive elements and to prevent that the 'sole effect' of a regulatory measure is tantamount to an 'indirect expropriation'.

In addition to this, states' articulation of their need to preserve regulatory autonomy has taken place in form of explicit reference to the so-called 'right to regulate' or in terms of the environmental, health or other regulatory measures that states parties to IIA may consider appropriate for their protection. That said, all IIAs under analysis subject the exercise of this regulatory autonomy to compliance with their substantive legal standards. This implies that the articulation of the 'right to regulate' to safeguard regulatory space merely performs a rhetorical, rather than an assertive function in IIL. Accordingly, some Latin American countries entering IIAs are not willing to politicise the IIL regime, despite the severe constraints that investment treaty protection may have upon their regulatory autonomy.

The analysis undertaken in Sects. 2.3.3.1.2, 2.3.3.1.3 and 2.3.3.2.2 demonstrate that a process of re-politicisation of IIL in the twenty-first century did take place in Latin America, by abandoning the IIL regime through the denunciation of the ICSID Convention and withdrawals of BITs, and more recently, by adopting alternative instruments to IIAs such as CFIAs. However, although the contestation of IIL has been articulated in terms of the 'right to regulate', ideas of states' jurisdiction, rather than the preservation of regulatory autonomy, inform the demands raised at the domestic and regional level. This suggests that past forms for the articulation of states demand prevailed in the former two periods of study still instruct how they politicise international legal instruments protecting foreign investment.

## 2.4  Conclusion

The review undertaken in this chapter confirms that Latin American countries have traditionally politicised international legal instruments protecting foreign investment through the articulation of sovereign rights since their independence until to date. However, the paradigms prevailed to articulate demands have varied in each period of study, contingent upon the issues of contention and the values informing these claims.

Between the independence of Latin American countries and 1930, the issues of contention were as first, capital-exporting countries' attempts to ensure stricter legal protection for their national's capital abroad, which arose from asserting the existence of minimum standards governing the international responsibility for the injuries inflicted to foreign property rights abroad, and second, the request of waiver from the application of the local remedies rule as a condition for home states' espousal of diplomatic protection claims on their behalf. The paradigm prevailed by Latin American countries to introduce their demand was the articulation of their sovereign right to rule in their best interest the legal protection granted to foreign property rights based on the principle of states' jurisdiction. Denial of justice by domestic courts was the only sovereign act that Latin American countries were willing to arbitrate through Mixed-Claim Commissions. Issues relating to the substantive and procedural legal protection to be afforded to foreign nationals were only to be resolved by domestic courts and the Calvo clause embodied such stance. The military interventions of some European nations in Latin American countries for the default of loan debt's payment also lead to the non-intervention principle indirectly being served as a normative basis to justify the limited scope of protection afforded to aliens.

From 1930 until the 1980s, the issues of contention were mainly focused on the legal standard applicable to pay compensation for the expropriation for foreign property rights and attempts by international financial institutions to establish arbitration as an alternative method for the settlement of disputes arising between foreign investors and states. The paradigm prevailed by Latin American countries to raise their demands was through the articulation of their economic sovereign right to expropriate foreign property based on the principle of permanent sovereignty over their natural resources, by which the host state could deprive (in)directly foreign property for reasons of public utility or interest. Informed by this principle and the principle of states' jurisdiction, states thus ruled the legal conditions governing the exercise of this sovereign right and reaffirmed the validity of the Calvo doctrine with respect to the substantive and procedural legal guarantees granted to foreign nationals in case of expropriation of their property rights. Indirectly, other principles such as their right to regulate and control corporate activities in accordance with their domestic laws and policies also inform the politicisation during this period but did not feature prominently as a normative ground.

The historical analysis undertaken in the first two periods also reveals the trend of Latin American countries to articulate their sovereign rights and to define correspondingly the legal consequences that their exercise had over the substantive and procedural protection they afforded to foreign property rights.

During the first decade of the 1990s, a consolidation of investment treaty protection took place in Latin America, raising the question of whether this shift in investment legal policy implicated a de-politicisation of BITs and ISDS. However, Chap. 1 already suggests that this was not the case and Chap. 2 shows that, in addition to the *ad hoc* nature of investment dispute settlement, another cause of the overly expansive interpretation and application of BITs resides on the type of legal norms to which they have consented as applicable for the review of their regulatory conduct. BITs define their legal obligations in terms of standards, which are a category of norms so broadly defined that the competent adjudicator is called to develop *ex post* and apply case by case. Hence, to determine the scope of application of BITs' provisions, arbitral tribunals establish criteria and follow a methodology to review states' conduct on a case-by-case basis.

The brief analysis of investment case law regarding alleged breaches of the FET standard and IIAs on expropriation under BITs of first generation demonstrates that, although some degree of convergence among tribunals exists concerning the interpretative benchmarks to review states' conduct under both provisions, their application varied depending on the facts of the case and mostly served the purpose of granting an effective legal protection to claimant investors. Under the FET standard, concern arises when tribunals treat host states' legal and policy framework as an act creating legitimate expectations whose frustration to ensure its stability and consistent application leads to a breach of the FET standard, while on provisions ruling the expropriation of protected investment, if the significant deprivation that a regulatory conduct has over the investment is the only criterion considered to determine breaches of these provisions.

Chapter 2 shows that since the 2000s onwards, the politicisation of international legal instruments protecting foreign investment remains persistent in Latin America and that an articulation of the 'right to regulate' has been the paradigm prevailed by all states to convey issues of concerns. However, this articulation has not always entailed a departure of the IIL regime. On the contrary, the prevalent trend remains the negotiation IIAs, albeit with some references to this sovereign right in a bilateral or regional setting in order to preserve regulatory autonomy. This reference of the 'right to regulate,' however, does not entail a politicisation of the IIL in terms of subjecting the scope of investment treaty protection to questioning. On the contrary, some states still favour broad formulations of IIAs' standards so that they may implicitly endorse the fact that arbitral tribunals may review their regulatory conduct in broader terms.

A clear politicisation of the IIL regime is mirrored by the practice of few South American states that have abandoned the IIL regime or endorsed new type of investment treaties that are not designed to afford protection to foreign investors. Moreover, although they have also prevailed the 'right to regulate' paradigm, the normative values that seem informing the articulation of demands are ideas of states' jurisdiction, rather than the preservation of regulatory autonomy. This suggests that normative values that inform the articulation of states' demands in the former two periods still instruct how they currently politicise the IIL regime.

Against the background of these findings, and the new issues of contention that should arise regarding the IIL regime in Latin America because of its overlapping with states' protection of human rights in the investment context, the need of adopting a new paradigm consistent with IHRL is essential to not only highlight the potential of inter-regime tensions but also to express the need to preserve regulator autonomy to prevent investors' abuses of human rights within the framework of their economic activities.

# References

Adede AO (1986) The minimum standards in a world of disparities. In: Macdonald R St J, Johnston DM (eds) The structure and process of international law: essays in legal philosophy doctrine and theory. The Hague, Martinus Nijhoff, p 1001

Avendano Valdés J, García Belaunde D (1971) Perù. In: Lowenfeld A F (ed) Expropriation in the Americas, A comparative law study. Dunellen, New York

Avila Martel A, Salvat Maguillot M (1971) Chile. In: Lowenfeld AF (ed) Expropriation in the Americas, A comparative law study. Dunellen, New York

Bértola L, Ocampo JA (2012) The economic development of Latin America since independence. OUP

Bochard EM (1915) The diplomatic protection of citizens abroad: or the law of international claims. The Banks Law Publishing, New York

Bochard E (1940) The "minimum standards" of the treatment of aliens. Mich Law Rev 38(40):445–461

Boyle FA (1999) Foundations of world order. The legalist approach to international relations, 1898–1922. Duke University Press, Durham

Burke-White W (2008) The Argentine financial crisis: state liability under BITs and the legitimacy of the ICSID system. Univ Pa Law School Inst Law Econ 8(1):199–234

Cueto-Rua J (1957) Administrative, civil and commercial contracts in Latin-American law. Fordham Law Rev 26(1):15–49

Damien C, Peterson L (2017) Analysis: In new Mercosur investment protocol, Brazil, Uruguay, Paraguay and Argentina radically pare back protections, and exclude investor-state arbitration. IIA Reporter, 4 May. Available at: https://www.iareporter.com/articles/analysis-in-new-mercosur-investment-pro-tocol-brazil-uruguay-paraguay-and-argentina-radically-pare-back-protections-and-exclude-investor-sta-te-arbitration/. Accessed 10 Dec 2020

Dawson FG (1990) The first Latin American debt crisis: the city of London and the 1822-25 Loan Bubble. Yale University Press, New Haven

Delaume GR (1986) ICSID and the transnational financial community. ICSID Rev Foreign Invest Law J 1(2):237–256

Dolzer R (2005) Fair and equitable treatment: a key standard in investment treaties. Int Lawyer 39 (1):87–106

Drago LM (1907) State loans in their relation to international policy. AJIL 1(3):692–726

Fach Gómez K (2019) Latin America. In: Krajewski M, Hoffmann R (eds) Research handbook on foreign direct investment. Edward Elgar Publishing, Cheltenham/Northampton, pp 494–522

Fach Gómez K, Titi C (2016a) UNASUR centre for the settlement of investment disputes: comments on the draft constitutive agreement. Investment Treaty News (10 August). Available at: https://www.iisd.org/itn/2016/08/10/unasur-centre-for-the-settlement-of-investment-dis putes-comments-on-the-draft-constitutive-agreement-katia-fach-gomez-catharine-titi/. Accessed 10 Dec 2020

Fach Gómez K, Titi C (eds) (2016b) Special Issue: the Latin American challenge to the current system of investor-state dispute settlement. JWIT 17(4):511–699

Feller AH (1935) The Mexican claims commissions, 1823-34: a study in the law and procedure of international tribunals. The MacMillan Company, New York

Fitzgibbon R (1948) The constitutions of the Americas. University of Chicago Press, Chicago

Franck SD (2005) The legitimacy crisis in investment treaty arbitration: privatizing public international law through inconsistent decisions. Fordham Law Rev 73(4):1521–1625

Gantz DA (2003) The evolution of FTA investment provisions: from NAFTA to the United States – Chile Free Trade Agreement. Am Univ Int Law Rev 19(4):679–767

Garcia-Amador FV (1980) The proposed new international economic order: a new approach to the law governing nationalization and compensation. Univ Miami Inter-Am Law Rev 12(1):1–58

Gertz G, Janddhyala S, Poulsen L (2018) Legalization, diplomacy, and development: do investment treaties de-politicize investment disputes? World Dev 107:239–252

Giustini A (1986) Compulsory adjudication in international law: the past, the present, and prospects for the future. Fordham Int Law J 9(2):213–256

Gordillo AA (1971) Argentina. In: Lowenfeld AF (ed) Expropriation in the Americas: a comparative law study. Dunellen, New York

Grigera Naón HA (1991) Arbitration in Latin America: overcoming traditional hostility (an update). Univ Miami Int Am Law Rev 22(2/3):203–257

Hershey A (1907) The Calvo and Drago doctrines. AJIL 26(1):26–45

Hummel W (2009) Investment rules in regional integration agreements in Latin America: the case of the Andean pact/Andean community. In: Binder C, Kriebaum U, Reinisch A, Wittich S (eds) International investment law for the 21st century: essays in honour of Christoph Schreuer. OUP, Oxford, pp 561–592

ICSID Staff (2007) Bolivia Submits a Notice under Article 71 of the ICSID Convention. ICSID Press Releases (16 May). Available at: http://icsidfiles.worldbank.org/icsid/icsid/staticfiles/Announcement3.html. Accessed 10 Dec 2020

ICSID Staff (2009) Denunciation of the ICSID Convention by Ecuador. ICSID Press Releases (9 July). Available at: https://icsid.worldbank.org/news-and-events/news-releases/denunciation-icsid-convention-ecuador. Accessed 10 Dec 2020

ICSID Staff (2012) Venezuela Submits a Notice under Article 71 of the ICSID Convention. ICSID Press Release (26 January). Available at: https://icsid.worldbank.org/news-and-events/news-releases/venezuela-submits-notice-under-article-71-icsid-convention. Accessed 10 Dec 2020

Kay C (2009) Latin American structuralist school. In: Kitchin R, Thrift N (eds) International encyclopedia of human geography, vol 6. Elsevier, Amsterdam, pp 159–164

Kriebaum U (2007) Regulatory takings: balancing the interests of the investor and the state. JWIT 8 (5):717–744

Kriebaum U (2015) Expropriation. In: Bungenberg M, Griebel J, Hobe S, Reinisch A (eds) International investment law: a handbook. C.H. Beck, Nomos and Hart, Baden-Baden/München/Oxford, pp 959–1030

Lerner F (2010) The protection of foreign investment in MERCOSUR. In: Franca Filho MT, Lixinski L, Olmos Giupponi MB (eds) The law of Mercosur. Hart, Portland, pp 277–290

Lévesque C (2007) Influences on the Canadian FIPA model and the US model BIT: NAFTA chapter 11 and beyond. Canadian Yearb Int Law/Annuaire canadien de droit international 44:249–298

Lipstein K (2014) The place of the calvo clause in international law. In: Feuerstein P, Heinz-Peter M (eds) Collection of essays by K Lipstein. Mohr Siebeck, Tübingen

Lopez Valdez A (1972) The Andean foreign investment code: an analysis. Georgia J Int Comp Law 7:656–668

Luque Macías MJ (2014) Current approaches to the international investment law regime in South America. Eur Yearb Int Econ Law 5:285–308

Luque Macías MJ (2016a) Inter-State investment dispute settlement in Latin America: is there space for transparency? JWIT 17:634–657

Luque Macías MJ (2016b) Reliance on alternative methods for investment protection through national laws, investment contracts, and regional institutions in Latin America. In: Hindelang S, Krajewski M (eds) Shifting paradigms in international investment law, more balanced, less isolated, increasingly diversified. OUP, Oxford, pp 291–315

Luque Macías MJ (2020) In: Framework Agreement of the Pacific Alliance, 6th June 2012, OXIO 496: Oxford International Organizations (OXIO). Available at: https://opil.ouplaw.com/view/10.1093/law-oxio/e496.013.1/law-oxio-e496?rskey=rICTWl&result=1&prd=OXIO. Accessed 10 Dec 2020

Maggeti M, Choer Moraes H (2018) The policy-making of investment treaties in Brazil: policy learning in the context of late adoption. Learn Public Policy, 295–316

Mann FA (1981) British treaties for the promotion and protection of investments. Br Yearb Int Law 52(1):241–254

Meessen KM (1986) IMF Conditionality and state sovereignty. In: Dicke DD (ed) Foreign debts in the present and a new international economic order, in cooperation with the International Law

Association's Committee on legal aspects of a new International Economic Order. Fribourg University Press, Fribourg, pp 117–129

Mijares V, Nolte D (2018) Regionalismo posthegemónico en crisis. ¿Por qué la Unasur se desintegra? Foreign Affairs Latinoamérica 18(3):105–112

Myers DP (1914) The origin of the Hague arbitral courts. Am J Int Law 8(4):769–801

Naim M (2000) Fads and fashion in economic reforms: Washington consensus or Washington confusion? Third World Quart 21(3):505–528

Navarrete JE (1987) La deuda externa. Una perspectiva Latinoamericana. Biblioteca Joven, Fondo de Cultura Economica.

Newcombe A (2011) General exceptions in international investment agreements. In: Cordonier Segger MC, Gehring M, Newcombe A (eds) Sustainable development in world investment law. Kluwer Law International, Alphen aan den Rijn, pp 351–370

O'Leary T (1984) The Andean common market and the importance of effective dispute resolution procedures. Int Tax Bus Lawyer 2:101–128

Ocran TM (1988) International investment guarantee agreements and related administrative schemes. Univ Pa J Int Law 10(3):341–370

Ononaiwu C (2016) Regional investment treaty arrangements in the Caribbean: developments and implications. In: Tanzi A, Asteriti A, Polanco Lazo R, Turrini P (eds) International investment law in Latin America/Derecho internacional de las inversiones en América Latina. Problems and prospects/Problemas y perspectivas. Brill Nijhoff, Leiden/Boston, pp 468–496

Penfield WL (1903) The Anglo-German intervention in Venezuela. N Am Law Rev 177:86–96

Pérez Olivares E, Brewer-Carias AR, Rondón de Sansó H, Polanco Martínez T (1971) Venezuela. In: Lowenfeld AF (ed) Expropriation in the Americas. A comparative law study. Dunellen, New York, pp 199–240

Pollock F (1922) The league of nations, 2nd edn. Stevens & Sons, London

Potesta M (2013) Legitimate expectations in investment treaty law: understanding the roots and limits of a controversial concept. ICSID Rev 28(1):88–122

Preziosi A (1989) The Andean pact's foreign investment code decision 220: an agreement to disagree. Univ Miami Int-Am Law Rev 20(3):649–677

Ratton Sanchez M, Morosini F (2017) Navigating between resistance and conformity with the international investment regime: The Brazilian agreements on cooperation and facilitation of investments (acfis). In: Morosini F, Ratton Sanchez M (eds) Reconceptualizing international investment law from the global south. CUP, New York, pp 1–46

Reinalda B (2009) Routledge history of international organizations. From 1815 to the present day. Routledge, Abingdon

Rosenfeld F (2014) The trend from standards to rules in international investment law and its impact upon the interpretive power of arbitral tribunals. Proc ASIL Annual Meeting 108:191–193. https://doi.org/10.5305/procannmeetasil.108.0191

Salacuse J (2015) The law of investment treaties, 2nd edn. OUP, Oxford

Sarcevic P (1987) Two approaches of the debt problem: (a) Adjustment of loan agreements (De Lege Lata) (b) Strengthening of international monetary soft law (De Lege Ferenda). In: Dicke DD (ed) Foreign debts in the present and a new international economic order. Fribourg University Press, Fribourg, pp 130–156

Sarmiento MG (2016) The UNASUR centre for the settlement of investment disputes and Venezuela: will both ever see the light at the end of the tunnel? JWIT 17(4):658–680

Schreuer C (2005) Calvo's grandchildren: the return of local remedies in investment arbitration. Law Pract Int Courts Tribunals 4:1–17

Schreuer C (2007) Investment protection and international relations. In: Reinisch A, Kriebaum U (eds) The law of international relations – Liber Amicorum Hanspeter Neuhold. Eleven International Publisher, Utrecht, pp 345–358

Scott GW (1908) Hague convention restricting the use of force to recover on contract claims. Am J Int Law 2(1):78–94

Seabra Fagundes M (1971) Brazil. In: Lowenfeld AF (ed) Expropriation in the Americas. A comparative law study. Dunellen, New York

Seidl-Hohenveldern I (1975) Chilean nationalization cases before German courts. Am J Int Lax 69:110–119

Shea DR (1955) The Calvo clause: a problem of inter-american and international law and diplomacy. University of Minnesota, Minneapolis

Sornarajah M (1986) The pursuit of nationalized property. Martinus Nijhoff, Dordrecht

Steiner HJ, Vagts DF (1986) Transnational legal problems: materials and text, 3rd edn. Foundation Press, Mineola/New York

Subhash CJ (1983) Nationalization of foreign property: a study in North-South dialogue. Deep & Deep Publications, New Delhi

Titi C (2014) The right to regulate in international investment law. Nomos/Hart Publishing, Baden-Baden

Treviño JC (1971) Mexico. In: Lowenfeld AF (ed) Expropriation in the Americas. A comparative law study. Dunellen, New York

Vernon R (1967) Long-run trends in concession contracts. In: Proceedings of the American Society of International Law at its annual meeting (1921–1969) 61:81–89

Weiler T (2005) Methanex Corp. v. U.S.A: turning the page on NAFTA chapter eleven? JWIT 6:903–921

Williamson J (1990) Latin American adjustment. How much has happened? Institute for International Economics, Washington, DC

Williamson J (1993) Democracy and the "Washington consensus". World Dev 21(8):1329–1336

Wolfrum R (2010) General international law (Principles, Rules and Standards). In: Max Planck Encyclopedia of Public International Law (MPEPIL). Available at: https://opil.ouplaw.com/view/10.1093/law:epil/9780199231690/law-9780199231690-e1408?rskey=NWovJq&result=20&prd=MPIL

# Chapter 3
# The States' Duty to Regulate Foreign Investment Activities Under IHRL As a Paradigm for Re-politicising IIL

The negative impact of corporate activities over human rights has become a subject of a wide-ranging discussion within the UN and OAS human rights systems alike. Increasing efforts have been made to delineate business entities' responsibilities towards human rights,[1] and to underscore the role of states in preventing and addressing corporate abuses of human rights beyond the confines of the adjudication of human rights claims.[2] However, despite the growing recognition of the great potential of human rights abuses within the context of corporate activities,[3] states

---

[1]The UNGP has been so far the major effort towards the articulation of corporate responsibilities to respect human rights by preventing their interference with third party rights and address negative impacts which they have caused or contributed to. See UNGP (n 23, ch 1). The other initiative that is relevant at the moment is the negotiation of a treaty that rules the activities of transnational corporations and other economic entities in conformity with human rights standards. To this end, the HRC established an open-ended intergovernmental working group in 2014. See HRC, Res. 26/9 Elaboration of an international legally binding instrument on transnational corporations and other business enterprises with respect to human rights (2014), UN Doc A/HRC/RES/26/9. This working group has engaged in negotiations since 2015 to define the content and scope of corporate obligations. See Lopez (2017). Based on the discussion and review of two preliminary drafts, this working group currently discusses the second revised draft issued on 6 August 2020. See Open-ended Intergovernmental Working Group on transnational corporations and other business enterprises with respect to human rights, OEIGWG Chairmanship Second Revised Draft 06.08.2020, Legally Binding Instrument to Regulate, in International Human Rights Law, the Activities of Transnational Corporations and Other Business Enterprises. Available at: https://www.ohchr.org/Documents/HRBodies/HRCouncil/WGTransCorp/Session6/OEIGWG_Chair-Rapporteur_second_revised_draft_LBI_on_TNCs_and_OBEs_with_respect_to_Human_Rights.pdf. Accessed 10 December 2020.

[2]See Sects. 3.1.1.1 and 3.2.1.1 below.

[3]Prior the UN developments to be discussed in Sect. 3.1.1.1, the CESCR already highlighted the major impact of corporate activities over the enjoyment of ESC rights. See CESCR, General Comment No. 18: The Right to Work (Art. 6) (6 February 2006) UN Doc. E/C.12/GC/18 para 52 (General Comment No. 18); General Comment No. 14: The Right to the Highest Attainable Standard of Health (Art. 12) (11 August 2000) UN Doc. E/C.12/2000/4, paras 26 and 35 (General

© The Author(s), under exclusive license to Springer Nature Switzerland AG 2021
M. J. Luque Macías, *Re-Politicising International Investment Law in Latin America through the Duty to Regulate Paradigm*, European Yearbook of International Economic Law 14, https://doi.org/10.1007/978-3-030-73272-1_3

remain their 'principal guarantor' and, thus, the only legal subject bearing international legal responsibility for their omission to advert foreign investment activities' adverse impact over their enjoyment.[4] In light of this legal fact, this chapter initially argues that certain universal and Inter-American human rights obligations impose a duty to regulate private foreign investment upon Latin American countries, and that this duty greatly differs from the content and legal implications of their sovereign right to regulate foreign investment activities under international law. In addition, it contends that universal and Inter-American human rights doctrine provides sufficient normative tools to articulate and review states' fulfilment of this duty with respect to the right to water and indigenous people's right to lands and territories in IIL.

To discuss the first hypothesis, Sects. 3.1 and 3.2 initially explore extent to which universal and Inter-American human rights law allocates a duty to regulate upon Latin American countries. Section 3.1.1 investigates the legal obligation that inform this duty by looking into the states' obligations that specifically arise in the business context as defined in the UN Guiding Principles on Business and Human Rights (UNGP) and the International Covenant of Economic, Social and Cultural Rights (ICESCR). Section 3.2.1 puts forward the same question through a review of the states' human rights obligations as understood under the recently enacted Thematic Report on 'Business and Human Rights: Inter-American Standards' and the ACHR. In addition, both sections broadly refer to the human rights bodies in charge of the implementation of these instruments and their practice in determining the scope of states' legal obligations. This initial part of the analysis will show that states' obligation to ensure the enjoyment of human rights founds the duty to regulate under universal and Inter-American human rights instruments, and that this duty not only differs from content and legal implications from the right to regulate, but it also differs from the human rights obligation informing such duty alike.

To analyse the second hypothesis, Sects. 3.1.2 and 3.2.2 examine the duty of Latin American countries to regulate foreign investment activities in furtherance of the right to water and indigenous people's right to lands and territories, respectively. Sections 3.1.2.1 and 3.2.2.1 discuss the legal basis of such duty. Section 3.1.2.1.1, on its part, explores the legal basis of the duty to regulate foreign investment activities regarding the right to water under universal human rights treaties, while Sect. 3.2.2.1.1 focuses on indigenous people's right to land and territories under universal and Inter-American human rights instruments. The study of universal and Inter-American instruments in this latter section intends to highlight the well-established *pro persona* approach favoured by Inter-American human rights bodies

---

Comment No. 14); General Comment No. 12 on the Right to Adequate Food (Art. 11) (12 May 1999) UN Doc. E/C.12/1999/5 paras 19 and 20 (General Comment No. 12).

[4]According to the IACoHR, the implementation of the American Convention on Human Rights (ACHR) exclusively deals with 'the international responsibility of the states and not of that of individuals'. See *International Responsibility for the Promulgation and Enforcement of Laws in Violation of the Convention (Arts. 1 and 2 of the American Convention on Human Rights*, Advisory Opinion OC-14/94, IACoHR Series A No. 14 (9 December 1994) paras 52–53, 56.

to interpret Inter-American instruments in the most favourable vein to the victim and in conformity with universal human rights standards.[5] Sections 3.1.2.1.2 and 3.2.2.1.2 then look into whether CIL might also provide a legal basis for this duty regarding both rights. Although the majority of Latin American countries are states parties to the ICESCR and the ACHR,[6] it is still necessary to provide answers to the latter question, since these treaties do not have binding force for all the states in the region.[7] Hence, both sub-sections initially determine whether states share a consistent and uniform,[8] as well as a widespread practice by endorsing a specific conduct (action or omission) for a reasonable length of time,[9] and then whether there is evidence of states' belief that this conduct is legally mandatory.[10] In doing so, they deal with domestic laws and judgements addressing selected rights as evidence of state practice, whereas states' belief regarding the legally binding nature of both rights[11] is derived from the content and the conditions involving the adoption of UNGA resolutions addressing selected rights.[12] The 193 UN member states serve as a reference point to determine the degree of states' adherence towards a particular norm.[13]

Finally, Sects. 3.1.2.2 and 3.2.2.2 develop the scope of application of states' duty to regulate foreign investment activities as elaborated by the competent human rights bodies. Section 3.1.2.2 defines the content and legal implications of the states' duty to regulate these activities in relation to the right to water in accordance with the case law of the Committee on Economic, Social and Cultural Rights (CESCR), while Sect. 3.2.2.2 does the same but with respect to indigenous people's right to lands and territories pursuant to the jurisprudence of the Inter-American human rights bodies. Both sections reveal, on one hand, that the ICESCR and the ACHR unequivocally place a duty to regulate foreign investment activities in benefit of the right to water

---

[5]Medellin Urquiaga (2019) and Rodiles (2016). The widespread use of the *pro persona* doctrine within the Inter-American human rights system has been considered as a normative instrument that guarantees the unity of international law. See Hennebel (2011) and Lixinski (2010).

[6]The Statute of the International Court of Justice (ICJ Statute) defines this source of international law as an 'evidence of a general practice accepted as law'. Statute of the International Court of Justice UKTS 67 (1946) [United Kingdom Treaty Series] art 38 para 1 lit. b.

[7]Regarding the ICESCR, Cuba is the only Latin American country that is not state party. In addition, the ACHR has not entered into force for Belize and Cuba. Moreover, Trinidad and Tobago and Venezuela were States parties to the ACHR, but they denounced in 1998 and 2012, respectively.

[8]See *Asylum case (Colombia v Peru)* Judgement [1950] ICJ Rep 266 para 276.

[9]See *North Sea Continental Shelf cases (Federal Republic of Germany v Denmark and the Netherlands)* (Judgement) [1969] ICJ Rep 3 para 73 (*North Sea Continental Shelf cases*).

[10]See *North Sea Continental Shelf cases* (n 9) para 77.

[11]*Military and Paramilitary Activities in and against Nicaragua (Nicaragua v United States of America)* (Merits) [1986] ICJ Rep 14 (referring to the use of force) para 188.

[12]*Legality of the Threat or Use of Nuclear Weapons* (Advisory Opinion) (1996) ICJ Rep 226 para 70.

[13]United Nations, General Assembly, Member States (List) http://www.un.org/en/member-states/index.html accessed 10 December 2020.

and indigenous communities' rights, respectively. On the other hand, the two sections show that universal and Inter-American human rights doctrine offers sufficient normative elements that allow a review and integration of states' duty to regulate foreign investment in IIL.

The doctrinal analysis of universal and Inter-American human rights case law only intends to fulfil an analytical purpose, meaning that its objective is to determine concepts and general principles that can be derived from this jurisprudence and, partially, their corresponding construction by international bodies to develop the 'duty to regulate' paradigm. The review enhances establishing which states' claims can and should be raised to IIL regime, on one hand, and underscoring the impact of IIL to discharge this regulatory duty imposed by IHRL, on the other. As such, this chapter does not engage in determining the soundness of universal and Inter-American case law on the rights under analysis, nor does it address the shortcomings detected in this doctrinal analysis.

## 3.1   The Duty to Regulate in Universal Human Rights Law

### 3.1.1   The Duty to Regulate in General

#### 3.1.1.1   The Duty to Regulate Under the UN Instruments

Within the UN human rights system, member states are committed to take action in conjunction with the UN to promote universal respect for, and observance of, human rights and fundamental freedoms.[14] In light of this pledge, there has been certain support for the proposition that UN member states have assumed certain international obligations relating to human rights.[15] To facilitate a common understanding of the human rights referred to in the UN Charter,[16] the UN General Assembly (UNGA) adopted the Universal Declaration of Human Rights ('UDHR') in 1948 as a 'common standard of achievement for all peoples and nations'.[17] Notwithstanding its lacking a binding force, the UDHR nevertheless remains an important human rights instrument since it provides an authoritative interpretation of the term 'human rights' in the UN Charter and the normative foundation of all human rights activities within the UN alike.

---

[14]United Nations, Charter of the United Nations (24 October 1945) 1 UNTS XVI (UN Charter) arts 55 and 56.

[15]*Case concerning the Barcelona Traction, Light and Power Co Ltd* [New Application: 1962] (*Belgium v Spain*) (Second Phase) ICJ Rep X paras 33-34; *Legal Consequences for States of Continued Presence of South Africa in Namibia (South West Africa) notwithstanding Security Council Resolution 276* (1970) (Advisory Opinion) ICJ Rep X para 131.

[16]Universal Declaration of Human Rights (adopted 10 December 1948) UNGA Resolution Res 217 A (III) (UDHR) preamble.

[17]UDHR (n 16) preamble recital 8.

Together with the UNGA, the HRC has played a key role in advancing diverse strategies to anchor the protection of human rights enshrined in the UDHR within the business context.[18] One of the most important undertakings in this regard has been the adoption of the UNGP, following the UN General Secretary's appointment of John Ruggie, as a Special Representative in 2005. Ruggie is credited with the initial development of the 'Protect, Respect and Remedy' Framework in 2008.[19] Based on this framework, the HRC extended the mandate of the Special Representative until 2011 with the responsibility of developing recommendations for its operationalisation.[20] Widely endorsed by the HRC, the result of this process was the UNGP,[21] which touch upon states' preventative and remedial measures against the adverse impacts of business enterprises' activities over human rights,[22] in addition to corporations' responsibility to respect human rights.[23]

As to the question to what extent UN instruments (the UNGP and the Protect, Respect and Remedy: A Framework for Business and Human Rights (Protect, Respect and Remedy Framework)) allocate a duty to regulate upon UN member states in the investment context, states' duty to protect human rights against abuses by corporate actors sets the starting point of this inquiry because it provides the main cornerstone of both UN initiatives.[24] The states' duty to protect is understood as an obligation of conduct and as such states are not considered responsible for the abuses committed by corporations themselves.[25] On the contrary, their international responsibility under IHRL only arises for their omission to *prevent*, investigate, punish and redress abuse by private economic actors.[26] Both instruments recognise regulation, in addition to legislation and internal policies as some of the steps of preventative nature[27] conducive to induce the establishment of a corporate culture where their responsibility is mainly to respect human rights.[28]

---

[18] Since 2006, this UN organ has assisted the UNGA in reinforcing the promotion and protection of human rights worldwide, after succeeding and replacing the UN Commission on Human Rights (UNHRC) established by Economic and Social Council (ECOSOC) in 1946.

[19] See Report of the Special Representative of the Secretary-General on the issue of human rights and transnational corporations and other business enterprises, John Ruggie, 'Protect, Respect and Remedy: A Framework for Business and Human Rights' (2008) UN Doc. A/HRC/8/5 (Protect, Respect and Remedy Framework).

[20] See HRC, 'Mandate of the Special Representative of the Secretary General on the issue of human rights and transnational corporations and other business enterprises' (2008) UN Doc. A/HRC/8/7.

[21] See HRC, 'Human rights and transnational corporations and other business enterprises' (2011) UN Doc. A/HRC/17/4 para 1.

[22] UNGP (n 23, ch. 1) paras 1–10 and 25–31, respectively.

[23] UNGP (n 23, ch. 1) paras 22–24.

[24] Protect, Respect and Remedy Framework (n 19) 9.

[25] UNGP (n 23, ch 1) para 1, commentary.

[26] Ibidem (emphasis added).

[27] Ibidem.

[28] Protect, Respect and Remedy Framework (n 19) 29.

Among the states' actions through which UN member states would discharge this duty to protect feature the enforcement of laws requiring states to respect human rights and inducing that corporate law enables, rather than constrain corporate respect for human rights.[29] In doing so, the UNGP acknowledge the failure to enforce existing laws as a major gap in state practice and encourage states to address the causes behind the lack of effective enforcement.[30] They also underscore states' duty to oversight corporate provisions of services that may interfere in the enjoyment of human rights to ensure that companies operate in conformity with their international obligations and encourage UN member states to articulate their regulatory expectations in the applicable contracts and legislations[31] As far as the IIAs of member states are concerned, the UNGP strongly commend preservation of adequate policy space when assuming these international obligations.[32] Consistent with the view of other international human rights bodies,[33] the UNGP acknowledge that IIAs can affect the domestic regulatory space required to protect human rights in the business context.[34] Notwithstanding the former, the UNGP commend maintenance of regulatory space, while affording the necessary investment protection.

Considering the above, one may conclude that the UNGP clearly delineate the duty to protect as the normative basis of UN member states' duty to regulate foreign investment activities. Understood in this way, states would discharge this duty, inter alia, by requiring regulation, oversighting contractual obligations to be discharged by corporate actors to avoid their interference with human rights, and maintaining regulatory space when entering into IIAs. However, since the UNGP do not lay down new international obligations other than those already in existence for UN member states,[35] they can only conceptualise this obligation to only involving host states' requirement to adopt preventative measures, rather than the home states of these corporations engaging in cross-border economic activities.[36] While as a consequence of this gap the UNGP has received much criticism,[37] these principles have certainly contributed to informing the scope of the existing states' obligations and the actions likely to prevent and address business entities' abuses of human rights. Moreover, they indirectly outline some normative standards that states could borrow to steer investors' conduct in the IIL regime context.

---

[29]UNGP (n 23, ch 1) para 3 lit. a and b.

[30]UNGP (n 23, ch 1) para 3, commentary.

[31]UNGP (n 23, ch 1) para 5, commentary.

[32]UNGP (n 23, ch 1) para 9.

[33]See n 24, 71, 72 ch 1.

[34]UNGP (n 23, ch 1) para 9, commentary.

[35]UNGP (n 23, ch 1) preamble.

[36]UNGP (n 23, ch 1) para 2, commentary.

[37]This normative gap has been considered the major shortcoming of the UNGP. See De Schutter (2016), Bernaz (2013) and McCorquodale and Simons (2007).

### 3.1.1.2 The Duty to Regulate Under the ICESCR

Adopted in 1966, the ICESCR constitutes one of the four instruments forming the so-called International Bill of Rights,[38] and one of the core treaties of the UN human rights system.[39] Through the ratification of the ICESCR, 29 Latin American states have committed, on one hand, to take steps, individually and through international economic and technical assistance and co-operation, to attain progressively the full realization of Covenant's rights by employing all appropriate means.[40] On the other hand, they assume to guarantee right-holders' exercise of these rights without discrimination.[41]

The CESCR is the treaty body responsible for monitoring states' implementation of Covenant's rights by means of the concluding observations it provides to the reports submitted by states parties, and more recently, by means of individual communications,[42] allowing everyone subject to the jurisdiction of states parties to this optional protocol to forward communication for alleged violations of Covenant's rights.[43] In addition, the statements provided by the CESCR in the above-mentioned instruments provide an authoritative interpretation of the content and

---

[38]The other instruments include the UDHR, the International Covenant on Civil and Political Rights (ICCPR) and its two additional protocols.

[39]To illustrate, Convention on the Elimination of All Forms of Discrimination against Women (adopted 18 December 1979, entered into force 3 September 1981) 1249 UNTS 13 (CEDAW); Convention on the Rights of the Child (adopted 20 November 1989, entered into force 2 September 1990) 1577 UNTS 3 (CRC); Convention on the Rights of Persons with Disabilities (adopted 13 December 2006, entered into force 3 May 2008) 2515 UNTS 3 (CRPD).

[40]ICESCR (n 153, ch 2) art 2 para 1. The following Latin American countries are parties to the ICESCR: Argentina, Bahamas, Barbados, Belize, Bolivia, Brazil, Chile, Colombia, Costa Rica, Dominica, Dominican Republic, Ecuador, El Salvador, Grenada, Guatemala, Guyana, Haiti, Honduras, Jamaica, Mexico, Nicaragua, Panama, Paraguay, Peru, Saint Vincent and the Grenadines, Suriname, Trinidad and Tobago, Uruguay, Venezuela. Office of the High Commissioner on Human Rights (OHCHR), Status of Ratification Interactive Dashboard, International Covenant on Economic, Social and Cultural Rights, Countries http://indicators.ohchr.org/ accessed 10 December 2020. Cuba is only signatory State of the ICESCR, while Antigua and Barbuda, Saint Kitts and Nevis, as well as Saint Lucia have taken no action in this regard.

[41]ICESCR (n 153, ch 2) art 2 para 2.

[42]Other complaint procedures laid down in this protocol include state-to-state complaints and inquiries. Optional Protocol to the International Covenant on Economic. Social and Cultural Rights (adopted on 10 December 2008 UNGA Res A/RES/63/117) (Optional Protocol to the ICESCR) arts 1 and 2.

[43]Hitherto, eight Latin American countries have ratified this optional protocol. The following Latin American countries are States parties to the Optional Protocol to the ICESCR: Argentina ratified the Protocol on 24 October 2011; Bolivia, on 13 January 2012; Costa Rica, on 23 September 2014; Ecuador, on 11 June 2010; El Salvador, on 20 September 2011; Honduras, on 16 January 2018; Uruguay, on 5 February 2013, and Venezuela, on 10 October 2018. Chile and Guatemala signed the Protocol on 24 September 2009, while Paraguay on 6 October 2009, respectively.

scope of ESC rights,[44] thereby assisting states parties in understanding how to implement their obligations.[45]

In performing this mandate, the CESCR contributed to putting an end on the doctrinal controversies surrounding the justiciability of ESC rights that arose following its adoption in 1966, from the differences it exhibited with the International Covenant on Civil and Political Rights (ICCPR).[46] To recall, the main issue of contention was that ESC rights were not legal rights in a strict legal sense, but rather were political and ethical standards particularly due to the different language used in both human rights treaties to define states parties' obligations.[47]

While the ICCPR clearly refers to rights and defines individuals as their addressees,[48] the ICESCR formulates ESC rights in terms of states' obligations, subjecting their realisation to resource allocation by its states parties. This view was reinforced by the widespread use of positive/negative categories to distinguish the different legal nature of states parties' obligations under both Covenants. It was argued that states parties to the ICCPR fulfilled their obligations by merely abstaining from actions conducive to breach civil and political rights, what conveyed, in turn, the idea that this set of rights were, among others, capable of immediate implementation, while compliance with ICESCR, required taking actions that guaranteed the enjoyment of ESC rights to the maximum of their available resources, and thus subject to progressive realization.[49] These arguments, however, encountered strong criticism for their underlying misconception of human rights.[50] Detractors of the application of positive/negative dichotomy generally pointed out that this conceptual framework failed to consider that the realisation of some civil and political rights also require the adoption of positive actions and their realisation

---

[44]Indeed, regional human rights bodies and scholars have resorted to the CESCR's findings to delineate State's obligations in the business context beyond the UN framework. To illustrate, see African Commission on Human and Peoples' Rights, The Social and Economic Rights Action Center, and the Center for Economic and Social Rights v Nigeria, Comm. No. 155/96 (2001) A.H. R.L.R. 60 (ACHPR 2001) (15th Annual Activity Report) paras 44-69, and Maastricht Guidelines on Violations of Economic, Social and Cultural Rights (1997) (adopted by a group of academic experts meeting in Maastricht 22-26 January 1997, later reissued as UN Doc. E/C.12/2000/13) para 6, respectively.

[45]CESCR, 'General Comment No. 3: The Nature of States Parties' Obligations (Art. 2, par.1 of the Covenant)' (14 December 1990) UN Doc. E/1991/23 (General Comment No. 3).

[46]International Covenant on Civil and Political Rights (adopted 16 December 1966, entered into force 23 March 1976) 999 UNTS 171.

[47]Vierdag (1978).

[48]Pursuant to the ICCPR, states parties undertake 'to respect and to ensure to *all individuals* within its territory and subject to its jurisdiction the rights recognized in the present Covenant (...)', whereas the ICESCR provides that states parties commit 'to take steps, individually and through international assistance and co-operation, especially economic and technical, to the maximum of its available resources, with a view to achieving progressively the full realization of [Covenant's] right (s). ICCPR (n 153, ch 2) art 2 para 1 (emphasis added) and ICESCR (n 153, ch 2) art 2 para 1.

[49]Eabre (1998), p. 263.

[50]Arambulo (1999).

may not always be of immediate effect. At the same time, ESC rights may entail elements of negative character enabling states parties their immediate implementation.[51]

With the adoption of the General Comment No. 3 in 1990, the CESCR gradually departed from the generalised use of the 'positive and negative' categories prevailing in the doctrinal discussion at that time,[52] and since then, served as the reference point for its monitoring of contracting parties' compliance with their obligations regarding specific Covenant's rights.[53] Yet, in virtue of the increasing expressed concerns about the negative impact of corporate activities over the enjoyment of ESC rights and the determination of the corresponding states' obligations,[54] the Committee adopted General Comment No. 24 in 2017 to enlighten how states should discharge their Covenant's obligations within the business context.[55]

As to the question which Covenant's obligation allocates a duty to regulate foreign investment activities upon states parties to the Covenant, a closer look should be provided to the obligations of conduct laid down by the treaty. To attain progressively the full realization of ESC rights, the ICESCR provides that states parties shall undertake to take steps in accordance with the maximum of its available resources, and resort to all appropriate means towards the achievement of this aim.[56] The first was conceived as an obligation of result, while the latter two were seen as obligations of conduct with immediate effect.[57] To explain, the obligation to 'take steps' is a treaty obligation that states parties shall satisfy first and foremost within the limits of their own jurisdiction.[58] It implies moving expeditiously and effectively, by taking deliberate, concrete and targeted steps, towards the full realization

---

[51] Arambulo (1999). See also Sepúlveda (2003).

[52] CESCR, 'General Comment No. 3 (n 45) paras 1 and 2.

[53] For instance, see CESCR, 'Concluding observations on the second to fourth periodic reports of Viet Nam' (15 December 2014) UN Doc. E/C.12/VNM/CO/2–4 paras 22 and 29; 'Concluding observations on the sixth periodic report of Canada' (23 March 2016) UN Doc. E/C.12/CAN/CO/6 paras 15 and 16.

[54] CESCR, General Comment No. 18 (n 3) para 52; General Comment No. 14 (n 3) paras 26 and 35; General Comment No. 12 (n 3) paras 19 and 20.

[55] CESCR, 'General Comment No. 24 on State obligations under the International Covenant on Economic, Social and Cultural Rights in the context of business activities' (10 August 2017) (General Comment No. 24) para 1.

[56] See ICESCR (n 153, ch 2) art 2 para 1. The other major obligation of states parties to the Covenant is guaranteeing the exercise of ESC rights without discrimination. ICESCR (n 153, ch 2) art 2 para 2.

[57] CESCR, General Comment No. 3 (n 45) para 1. This meant that the Covenant contains obligations demanding the achievement of a particular result by leaving contracting parties to attain this goal by the means at their discretion, and obligations requiring the employment of specific means to attain its implementation. For an extensive discussion on the differences of these obligations, see Wolfrum (2011).

[58] States parties to the Covenant are also called to meet this obligation through assistance and international cooperation. However, this aspect is deliberately excluded from this analysis. See Saul et al. (2014), pp. 137–138.

of Covenant's rights to be achieved progressively.[59] Moreover, the obligation to employ appropriate means relates to the use of all adequate and available means at states parties' disposal to attain the progressive realization of ESC rights.[60] These may not only comprise the adoption of legislative measures,[61] in terms of giving constitutional recognition to ESC rights or incorporating the Covenant in domestic laws,[62] but also the provision of effective legal remedies[63] as well as any kind of appropriate measure of the executive.[64] Lastly, since the *raison d'être* of the ICESCR is establishing clear obligations,[65] states parties are also demanded to satisfy minimum core obligations that entail to guarantee the fulfilment of at least minimum levels of each ESC right by employing the maximum of their available resources.[66]

Since the conceptualisation of Covenant's obligations of conduct towards the achievement of the obligation of result still remained vague, the CESCR gradually incorporated Eide's tripartite terminology of respect, protect and fulfil in its determination of the scope of Covenant's obligations[67] and their relation with respect to every Covenant's right.[68] In doing so, the CESCR aimed at overriding the use of the positive/negative categories prevailing at that time and elucidating the complexities

---

[59]CESCR, General Comment No. 3 (n 45) para 2.

[60]See Saul et al. (2014), p. 157.

[61]Ibidem. The CESCR certainly highlights that legislation is not the exclusive policy tool that is appropriate to discharge Covenant's obligations of result CESCR, General Comment No. 3 (n 45) para 4.

[62]CESCR, General Comment No. 3 (n 45) para 6.

[63]CESCR, General Comment No. 3 (n 45) para 5.

[64]CESCR, General Comment No. 3 (n 45) para 6.

[65]CESCR, General Comment No. 3 (n 45) para 10. Although the Covenant provides for states parties' realisation of ESC rights over time, this does not implicate to permit deliberately retrogressive measures without full consideration and justification. CESCR, General Comment No. 3 (n 45) para 9.

[66]CESCR, General Comment No. 3 (n 45) para.

[67]In his capacity as the Special Rapporteur to the UN Sub-Commission, Eide employed a tripartite terminology respect, protect, and fulfil to explain the responsibility of States parties to the ICESCR in more detail. Eide (1989), 35. In fact, the origin of this framework dates back to Shue and Eide's attempts to depart from using the categories of positive and negative obligations prevailing in the human rights scholarship in the 1980s. Shue applied an analytical framework of duties, whereas Eide resort to a scheme of layers to explain State's obligations in relation to Covenant's rights. See Shue (1980), p. 52, and UN-Sub-Commission on Prevention of Discrimination and Protection of Minorities 'Study on the right to adequate food as a human right: preliminary report/by Asbjorn Eide, Special Rapporteur' (1983) UN Doc. E/CN.4/Sub.2/1983/25, and 'Study on the right to adequate food as a human right: report prepared by Asbjorn Eide' (1987) UN Doc E/CN.4/Sub.2/1987/23. For additional analytical schema, see Sepúlveda (2003), pp. 157–173.

[68]See CESCR, General Comment No. 12 (n 3) para 15; General Comment No. 13: The Right to Education (Art. 13)' (8 December 1999) UN Doc. E/C.12/1999/10 (General Comment No. 13) para 46; General Comment No. 14 (n 3) para 33; General Comment No. 24 (n 55) para 10.

involved in the realization of Covenant's rights.[69] Notwithstanding its detractors,[70] the use of the duty to respect, protect and fulfil framework has certainly facilitated to envision different situations where these levels or dimensions of states parties' obligations may operate with respect to each ESC right. This development is especially obvious in the General Comment No. 24, where the Committee delineates potential scenarios where these states' duties may apply, following previous attempts to draw states' attention of their obligations in the business context.[71]

According to the CESCR, the duty to respect Covenant's rights requires states parties to abstain from undertaking any action that may lead to violations of ESC rights.[72] In the investment context, this states' duty would consist in ensuring that ESC rights are protected over foreign investors' interests,[73] and avoiding benefitting business entities' operation through actions that may lead to the impairment of such rights.[74] Hence, states parties to the Covenant shall particularly observe this duty when promoting themselves as an attractive destiny of foreign capital.

Moreover, states parties to the ICESCR have a duty to protect which demands from them prevention from and prosecution of third parties' interference with the enjoyment of ESC rights,[75] as well as provision of effective access to remedies to those aggrieved by corporate behaviour.[76] This states' duty has been considered the most relevant obligation under the ICESCR[77] because it involves the responsibility of states parties to regulate corporate behaviour and intervene in cases of business

---

[69]Koch (2005), pp. 87–88.

[70]Koch argues that the tripartite typology fails to fully explain the actual complexities involved in the realization of ESC rights because it falls short in encompassing all type of State's actions required to ensure the full realisation of ESC rights. In her opinion, this is reflected in the degree of inconsistency in CESCR's allocation of the type of measures belonging to each level or dimension of State's obligation towards every right in the Covenant. For this reason, she calls for the adoption of further layers in CESCR's determination of States parties' obligations under the ICESCR. See Koch (2005), pp. 87–93.

[71]The CESCR issued a statement in 2011 explicitly recalling states parties to ensure the respect and protection of ESC rights. See CESCR, 'Statement on the Obligations of States Parties regarding the Corporate Sector and Economic. Social and Cultural Rights', (2011) UN Doc E/C.12/2011/1, para 1.

[72]To illustrate, CESCR, General Comment No. 12 (n 3) para 19; General Comment No. 13 (n 68) para 59; General Comment No. 14 (n 3) para 50.

[73]CESCR, General Comment No. 24 (n 55) para 12.

[74]Ibidem.

[75]In this context, third parties should be understood as those having no legal ties with the State concerned; otherwise, abuses of ESC rights committed by a State-owned business entity may be attributed to the State concerned and thus give rise to international legal responsibility for breaches of its Covenant's obligation to respect ESC rights. De Schutter (2014), pp. 428–440.

[76]In relation to the right to health, the CESCR argued that a breach of Covenant's right may arise out of State's failure 'to regulate the activities of individuals, groups or corporations so as to prevent them from violating the [ESC right] of others', including 'the failure to enact or enforce laws to prevent the pollution of water, air and soil by extractive and manufacturing industries'. CESCR, General Comment No. 14 (n 3) para 51.

[77]CESCR, General Comment No. 24 (n 55) para 10.

entities' abuses of ESC rights by resorting to all appropriate means.[78] In light of this understanding, this treaty obligation unequivocally provides the normative foundation of states' duty to regulate foreign investment activities, even though it additionally encompasses the obligation to prosecute business entities for their abuses of ESC rights[79] and to grant effective (legal) remedies to those aggrieved by corporate misconduct.[80] In the present study, both concepts are not equivalent terms in the strict sense. Rather, the duty to regulate foreign investment activities only covers preventative measures conducive to avert investors' abuses of human rights, while the duty to protect includes additional remedial measures once the state fails to exercise its duty to regulate these activities.

Lastly, there is also a duty to fulfil deriving from the Covenant that mandates states parties to ensure the facilitation, promotion, and provision of ESC rights.[81] In the investment context this duty would implicate to facilitate the provision of goods and services essential for the enjoyment of Covenant's rights, inter alia, through private foreign investors' involvement to underpinning their realization.[82] States' concession of the water supply service to foreign corporations provides a clear example of their compliance with this duty: corporations facilitate the provision of drinking water services by delivering it in suitable conditions for human consumption and thereby the host state enables users' enjoyment of the right to water.

The above-mentioned description of states' duties in the investment context already indicates that their performance should not be conceived in isolation, but rather in a complementary fashion. Only in this way, would states progressively achieve the full realization of ESC rights. For instance, when attracting foreign investment without lowering human rights standards, states meet their duty to respect, and when concluding a concession agreement to provide a public service with foreign investors, states discharge their duty to fulfil. On the other hand, states discharge their duty to regulate, when introducing any legislative or executive action against foreign investors' activities conducive to impair ESC rights.

---

[78]CESCR, General Comment No. 24 (n 55) paras 14 and 38. For previous examples of CESCR's reference to State's duty to protect see, CESCR, General Comment No. 12 (n 3) para 33; CESCR, General Comment No. 15: The Right to Water (Arts. 11 and 12 of the Covenant) (20 January 2003) UN Doc. E/C.12/2002/11 (General Comment No. 15) para 57.

[79]CESCR, General Comment No. 24 (n 55) para 49.

[80]The CESCR explicitly focused on the issue of access to remedies for the first time in its General Comment No. 9. See, CESCR 'General Comment No. 9: The domestic application of the Covenant' (3 December 1996) UN Doc. E/C.12/1998/24 para 2. In relation to remedial State's measures in the business context, see UNGP (n 23, ch 1) paras 25–31; CESCR, General Comment No. 24 (n 55) paras 38–57.

[81]States enable or assist the enjoyment of ESC rights by explicitly recognising them in their domestic legal system. See, CESCR, General Comment No. 14 (n 3) para 33; General Comment No. 13 (n 68) para 37. Also, the obligation to provide ESC rights requires undertaking national policies, monitoring as well as allocating public resources for their realization. See, CESCR, General Comment No. 14 (n 3) para 52.

[82]CESCR, General Comment No. 24 (n 55) para 23.

Additionally, in performing their duty to regulate foreign investment, states parties to the Covenant also request the employment of all appropriate means. According to the Committee, the mandatory features of goods and services to which right-holders are particularly entitled under an ESC right is what establishes their appropriateness.[83] These features relate to the availability, accessibility, acceptability and affordability of these goods or services implicit in every ESC right (the so-called AAAA scheme).[84]

According to the CESCR, the appropriate means to discharge the duty to regulate foreign investment activities include legislative measures, ranging from the enactment of laws typifying criminal and administrative sanctions for corporations investing in its territory and entitling those aggrieved to bring civil claims against corporations,[85] to the enactment of laws compelling private foreign investors to adopt a due diligence conduct to detect, avert and lessen the risk of breaches of ESC rights.[86] Executive means may include the implementation of stricter regulations upon public services' providers, including the so-called public services obligations,[87] even, in some cases, the revocation of licenses or any privilege awarded to business entities if they fail to observe ESC rights when developing their economic activities.[88] In fact, direct regulation and intervention in the economic sector where the foreign investor concerned perform its investment activities may also be essential, in some cases, to avert their interference with ESC rights.[89] Following Committee's view that 'the scope of Covenant's provisions extends to the relation of individuals',[90] legislative and executive means are, therefore, appropriate if they induce foreign investment activities' observance of these features in the provision of goods or services facilitating the enjoyment of an ESC right, or in their performance of their economic activities, more broadly.

To sum up, although the ICESCR does not contain expressed references to obligations to ensure human rights from which a duty to regulate may directly

---

[83]De Schutter (2014), p. 294.

[84]Regarding the right to adequate housing, see CESCR, CESCR, General Comment No. 4: The Right to Adequate Housing (Art. 11 (1) of the Covenant' (13 December 1991), UN Doc. E/1992/23 (General Comment No. 4) para 8. Also, the use of this framework can be identified in the Preliminary Report of the Special Rapporteur on the Right to Education. See UNCHR, 'Preliminary Report of the Special Rapporteur on the Right to Education, Ms Katarina Tomasevski, submitted in accordance with Commission on Human Rights Resolution 1998/33' (1999), UN Doc. E/CN/.4/1999/49 paras 42–74.

[85]Ibidem.

[86]CESCR, General Comment No. 24 (n 55) para 16.

[87]CESCR, General Comment No. 24 (n 55) para 21.

[88]Ibidem.

[89]CESCR, General Comment No. 24 (n 55) para 18. For instance, against real estate investors' abuses of the right to adequate housing in urban areas by introducing high prices in the private housing market, see CESCR, General Comment No. 4 (n 84) para 8 lit. c.

[90]*Mohamed Ben Djazia and Naouel Bellili v Spain* (20 June 2017) Communication No. 5/2015, CESCR/E/C.12/61/D/5/2015 para 14.2.

derive,[91] Covenant's determination of states' obligations of conduct (namely to take step and to employ all appropriate means to achieve progressively the full realization of Covenant's rights) through the 'duties' typologies has permitted to ascertain better their scope of application in the business context.

From the obligation to undertake to take steps derives the duty to respect, to protect and to fulfil Covenant's rights. Yet, the duty to protect is the Covenant's obligation that allocates a duty to regulate foreign investment activities upon states parties because compliance with this duty requires implementing all appropriate preventive and remedial measures that are appropriate to avert and address third parties' interference (such as that from investors) in the enjoyment of Covenant's rights. Yet, although the duty to protect is the normative basis of the duty to regulate foreign investment, the latter differs from the former to the extent that it only covers all preventative legislative and executive measures that are essential to avert foreign investors' abuses of human rights. Thus, by default, the duty to regulate is not understood in this study as including remedial measures once the state failed to exercise its duty to regulate. Which preventative measure is appropriate is determined on a case-by-case basis contingent upon the mandatory features implicit in ESC rights.

That said, states' compliance with their duty to regulate foreign investment activities does not suffice to meet their Covenant's obligation to attain progressively the full realization of Covenant's rights in the investment context. States are also required to refrain from breaching ESC rights in which they would incur if they attract foreign investment by relaxing domestic laws conducive to guarantee ESC rights (namely their duty to respect), and to facilitate, promote, or provide goods and services that may guarantee their enjoyment such as entering into a water concession agreement with a foreign corporation to ensure the provision of drinking water services (namely, their duty to fulfil).

### 3.1.2   The Duty to Regulate in Furtherance of the Right to Water

#### 3.1.2.1   Legal Basis

3.1.2.1.1   Universal Human Rights Treaties

Under the ICESCR, there is no explicit reference to the right to water, whose protection may assign a duty to regulate upon host states of foreign private investment. However, several UN institutions have upheld the right to an adequate

---

[91]McBeth (2010), pp. 15–16.

standard of living as the legal basis of this ESC right.[92] Article 11 of the ICESCR provides for states parties' recognition of the right to an adequate standard of living for everyone, including adequate food, clothing and housing, and to the continuous improvement of living conditions.[93] According to the CESCR, the rationale behind the word 'including' used in this article in connection with other rights was to avoid excluding any guarantee vital for securing an adequate standard of living.[94] It is in this context that the CESCR attaches vital importance to the right to water as one of the implicit guarantees for the realization of everyone's right to an adequate standard of living[95] and other ESC rights alike.[96] Likewise, the right to water has an inextricable relation with other guarantees essential for the realization of the right to life (such as the right to the highest attainable standard of health, and to the rights to an adequate housing and food), in addition to its link with the right to life and human dignity enshrined in the UDHR.[97]

Moreover, the ICESCR does not define the material and personal scope of application of ESC rights. It is in this regard that other universal human rights treaties further enlighten some of the legal entitlements inherent to the right to water owed to the right-holders specifically protected under these treaties. To illustrate, the Convention on the Elimination of All Forms of Discrimination against Women protects this group of society against any distinction, exclusion or restriction made on the grounds of sex leading to affect or nullify the recognition, enjoyment or exercise of human rights.[98] In recognising women in rural areas as one of the subjects of legal protection against discrimination, this Convention emphasises on states' obligation to ensure the right 'to enjoy adequate living conditions, particularly in relation to (. . .) water supply'.[99] In a similar way, the Convention on the Rights of Child protects a specific group of society, namely every human being below the age

---

[92]In addition to the CESCR, the UNGA and the HRC have endorsed the view in some of their resolutions that the right to water derives from the right to an adequate standard of living laid down in article 11 (1 of the ICESCR). See Sect. 3.1.2.1.2 below.

[93]See ICESCR (n 153, ch 2) art 11 para 1. The other sentence of this provision underscores the relevance of states'cooperation based on free consent to underpin states' commitment to take appropriate steps to ensure the realization of the right to an adequate standard of living.

[94]See CESCR, General Comment No. 15 (n 78) para 3.

[95]In the General Comment No. 15, the Committee defines the right to water as an essential guarantee for securing an adequate standard of living codified in article 11 of the Covenant. CESCR, General Comment No. 15 (n 78) para 3.

[96]The CESCR has emphasised on the inextricable relation of the right to water with Covenant right to the highest attainable standard of health. See, CESCR, General Comment No. 14 (n 3) paras 11, 12 (a, (b, (c, 15, 34, 36, 40, 43, and 51. The Committee also links the right to water to other Covenant's rights to adequate housing and adequate food. See General Comment No. 4 (n 84) para 8, lit. (b.

[97]See CESCR, General Comment No. 15 (n 78) para 3.

[98]See CEDAW (n 39), art 1.

[99]See CEDAW (n 39) art 14 para 2 lit h.

of 18 years.[100] In doing so, this Convention emphasises on the states' obligation to undertake all appropriate measures for the implementation of the rights codified in the Convention, and, in particular, on states parties' duty to undertake such measure to the maximum of their available resources as far as the ESC rights are concerned.[101] The Convention on the Rights of Child explicitly alludes to the right to water, when recognising the right of every child to the enjoyment of the highest attainable standard of health. It provides for states' obligation to pursue the full implementation of this right, and in particular, to undertake any appropriate measure to combat disease and malnutrition through, inter alia, the 'provision of clean drinking-water', by taking into account the dangers and risks of environmental pollution.[102] Lastly, the Convention on the Rights of Persons with Disabilities aims to promote, protect and ensure the full and equal enjoyment of all human rights.[103] It recognises the right of persons with disabilities to social protection and the right to enjoy this right, without discrimination based on disability, by requiring states to safeguard and promote its realization by introducing measures conducive to guarantee their equal access to clean water and appropriate and affordable services.[104]

Regional human rights treaties, for their part, explicitly codify the right to water in connection with specific groups of society, or implicitly allude to this right when addressing the services required to states parties to secure the enjoyment of ESC rights. Within the Africa continent, the African Charter on the Rights and Welfare of the Child deals with the right to water as an entitlement arising from the right to health,[105] whereas the African Charter on Human and Peoples' Rights on the Rights of Women derives the right to water from the right to food.[106] In the Americas, however, there is no explicit reference to the right to water in existing human rights instruments. Notwithstanding the former, the San Salvador Protocol may afford protection to the right to water within the right to have access to basic public services.[107] Furthermore, despite the absent codification of the right to water by

---

[100]The temporal scope of application of this Convention may be inapplicable if the laws applicable to the child stipulates that he or she reach full age earlier. See CRC (n 39) art 1.

[101]See CRC (n 39) art 4.

[102]See CRC (n 39) art 24 para 2 lit. c.

[103]To this end, this Convention understands the term 'persons with disabilities' as including 'those who have long-term physical, mental, intellectual, or sensory impairments which in interaction with various barriers may hinder their full and effective participation in society on an equal basis with others'. See CRPD (n 39) art 1 paras 1 and 2, respectively.

[104]See CRPD (n 39) art 28 para 2 lit. a.

[105]See African Charter on the Rights and Welfare of the Child (adopted 1 July 1990, entered into force 29 November 1999) art 14 para 2.

[106]See African Charter on Human and Peoples' Rights on the Rights of Women in Africa (signed 11 June 2003, entered into force 25 November 2005) art XV (a.

[107]The Additional Protocol to the American Convention on Human Rights in the Area of Economic, Social and Cultural Rights stipulates that '[e]veryone shall have the right to live in a healthy environment and to have access to basic public services'. Additional Protocol to the American

the ACHR, Inter-American human rights treaty bodies have upheld breaches of the right to water in light of states parties' obligation correlative to the right to life enshrined in the ACHR. In its country report on the *Situation of Human Rights of the Inhabitants of the Interior of Ecuador Affected by Development Activities,* the IACommHR indirectly alluded to the right to water by drawing attention to the negative impact of oil companies' discharging of gallons of untreated toxic wastes and oil into the waterways of the Oriente river.[108] On the other hand, the IACoHR has recognised the right to water as a condition for the realization of children's right to life.[109]

Accordingly, article 11 of the ICESCR provides the legal basis of states parties' duty to regulate corporate abuses of the right to water, as one of the basic guarantees to secure everyone's enjoyment of the right to adequate standard of living. The only limitation to the enjoyment of the right to water is the one generally applicable under article 4 of the ICESCR, by which states may introduce limitations to ESC rights in accordance with domestic laws and provided that these restrictions exclusively intend to promote the public welfare. Moreover, since the ICESCR does not outline the legal entitlements deriving from the right to water, the general comments and jurisprudence of the CESCR play a fundamental role in the determination of the material scope of application of the right to water. Universal and regional human rights instruments may certainly guide this Committee's task. Most of these treaties do not only define specific groups of society as right-holders of ESC rights, but also do not envisage, to some extent, elements of the right to water, as entitlements of different ESC rights.

### 3.1.2.1.2   Customary International Law

*State Practice*

The recognition of the right to water has been widespread within the domestic legal orders of states worldwide. Explicit references to this right can be found at the

---

Convention on Human Rights in the Area of Economic, Social and Cultural Rights "Protocol of San Salvador" (signed on 17 November 1988, entered into force on 16 November 1999) (1989) 28 ILM 156 (San Salvador Protocol) art 11 para 1.

[108]IACommHR, 'Report on the Situation of Human Rights in Ecuador' OAS/Serv/V/II.96 Doc. Rev 1 (24 April 1997) ch VIII.

[109]*Juridical Condition and Human Rights of the Child*, Advisory Opinion OC-17/02, IACoHR (28 August 2002) para 80; *Case of the "Juvenile Re-education Institute" v Paraguay* (Preliminary Objections, Merits, Reparations and Costs) IACoHR Case (Sr. C) No. 63 (2 September 2004).

constitutional level[110] or within domestic laws of lower rank.[111] In other cases, this recognition has been implicit within the scope of another right,[112] showing the instrumental function that the right to water fulfils for the realization of other rights.[113] Moreover, some constitutions and domestic laws proclaim the right to water in generic terms,[114] while the majority guarantees specific entitlements of this right. Many domestic legal instruments broadly guarantee a right to drinking/potable water,[115] or specifically protects a right to clean and safe water in adequate quantities,[116] what entails that water shall be acceptable for human consumption. Moreover, many domestic legal instruments considerably emphasise on the accessibility to drinking water in connection with different water services or goods and on different mandatory features that shall be fulfilled. First, access to drinking water supply services or facilities is one of the legal entitlements massively codified in domestic laws,[117] which, to some extent, allude to the affordability[118] and/or the quality of drinking water provided as mandatory characteristics of this service.[119] Second, access to water sources is the other legal entitlement extensively protected

---

[110]See Constitution of the Plurinational State of Bolivia (2009) arts 16, 20 para 1, 373; Constitution of the Republic of Ecuador (2008) art 12; Constitution of the Republic of Nicaragua (1987, as of September 2010) art 105; Constitution of the Oriental Republic of Uruguay (1967, as last amended 31 October 2004) art 47; Constitution of the Democratic Republic of the Congo (2006) art 48; Constitution of Kenya (2010) art 43; Constitution of the Seventh Republic of Niger (2010) art 12; Constitution of Angola (2010) art 85; Constitution of Afghanistan (2003) art 9; Constitution of the Kyrgyz Republic (2010) art 6; 2011 Fundamental Law of Hungary (as last amended 11 March 2013) lit. P; Fiji Constitution (2013) art 36 para 1.

[111]See Water Supply and Sanitation Act (2009) (Tanzania) arts 4 and 22; Water Resources Management Act (2009) (Tanzania) sections 4 and 7; Law on Water Resources Management of the Kingdom of Cambodia (2007) art 11; Water Act 2013 (Bangladesh) art 3; Water Services Industry Act (Act 655) (2006) (Malaysia) art 33; Drinking Water Law (2009) (Netherlands) art 8; Flood and Water Management Act (2010) (United Kingdom) art 44; Environment Canterbury (Temporary Commissioners and Improved Water Management) Act 2010 (New Zealand) Schedule 1, Part 1–7.

[112]Constitution of Colombia (of 1991 as amended on 1 April 2005), arts 365 and 366; Constitution of the Bolivarian Republic of Venezuela (1999), arts 82 and 83; Constitution of Angola (2010) art 85; Constitution of Afghanistan (2003) art 9.

[113]In connection to the right to health, see Constitution of Colombia (1991 as last amended 1 April 2005) art 49; Constitution of the Bolivarian Republic of Venezuela (1999) art 83; Constitution of the Dominican Republic (2010) art 61. In connection to the right to adequate housing, see Constitution of the Bolivarian Republic of Venezuela (1999) art 82.

[114]To illustrate, see Constitution of the Democratic Republic of the Congo (2006) art 48.

[115]Constitution of the Seventh Republic of Niger (2010) art 12; Water Act 2013 (Bangladesh) art 3.

[116]Constitution of Kenya (2010) art 43; Fiji Constitution (2013) art 36 para 1; Quebec—Bill 27: An Act to Affirm the Collective Nature of Water Resources and Provide for Increased Water Resource Protection (Canada) (2009) Division I (2).

[117]To illustrate, see Water Supply and Sanitation Act (2009) (Tanzania) art 4.

[118]For instance, see Water Supply and Sanitation Act (2009) (Tanzania) art 22; Organic Law on the Provision of Potable Water (2001) (Venezuela) art 95.

[119]To illustrate, see Water Resources Act No. 29338 (2009) (Peru) art 40.

in domestic laws. In contrast to the access to drinking water facilities and services, the right to access to water sources mainly comprises access to safe drinking water and/or the availability of this natural resource for domestic uses by preventing its pollution or unstainable extraction.[120] In this connection, some laws in fact prioritise the protection of the domestic use of water resources over its economic use.[121] Furthermore, a non-discriminatory exercise of the access to water services and facilities[122] and the access to water resources features as another relevant entitlement codified in the majority of domestic laws.[123] Other entitlements explicitly protected in connection with this right is users' right to access to information of water provision services,[124] and their right to participate in the use or administration of this public service.[125]

In addition to the actions of the legislative, the conduct of the adjudicative constitutes another important element to establish the existence, or at least the formation, of a customary rule in relation to the right to water. While the adjudicative provides the most relevant indication in this regard, actions of the executive are not less important. To illustrate, some domestic courts have upheld the instrumental nature of the right to water for the realization of other rights.[126] Similar to domestic laws, courts have afforded legal protection to the right to water services and facilities

---

[120]For instance, see Water Resources Management Act (2009) (Tanzania) sections 4 and 7; Law on Water Resources Management of the Kingdom of Cambodia (2007) art 11; Water Act 2013 (Bangladesh) art 26; Law on Water Resources (2012) (Vietnam) art 3 para 4; 2011 Fundamental Law of Hungary (as last amended 11 March 2013) section P; Constitution of the Dominican Republic (2010) art 15; Quebec - Bill 27: An Act to Affirm the Collective Nature of Water Resources and Provide for Increased Water Resource Protection (2009) (Canada), division I (2; Water Resources Act No. 29338 (2009) (Peru) arts 36 and 38.

[121]To illustrate, see Water Law (2009) (Afghanistan) art 6; Water Resources Act No. 29338 (2009) (Peru) art 35.

[122]For instance, see Water Supply and Sanitation Act (2009) (Tanzania) art 22; Flood and Water Management Act (2010) (United Kingdom) art 44; Indigenous Law, Law No. 19.253 (1993) (Chile) art 64.

[123]Constitution of the Republic of Nicaragua (1987, as of September 2010) art 89 para 3.

[124]See Constitution of the Argentine Nation (1994), art 42; Constitution of the Republic of Panamá (1972, as last amended on 15 November 2004) art 43. In addition to constitutional provisions, domestic laws specifically address this right. Law 142 establishing the regime for the public household services (1994) (Colombia) art 9 para 4; Decree No. 118-2003, Framework Law for the Drinking Water and Sanitation Sector (Honduras) art 25 para 2; General law 1614 governing the regulatory and tariff framework for the public drinking water and sanitation services for the Republic of Paraguay (2000) art 35 lit. d and e.

[125]See Constitution of the Argentine Nation (1994), art 42; Constitution of the Republic of Ecuador (2008), art 57 para 6; Constitution of the Bolivarian Republic of Venezuela (1999), art 184 para 2.

[126]For instance, South African and Kenyan courts have considered the access to water as vital for the realization of the right to human dignity. See, *Beja and Others v Premier of the Western Cape and Others* (2011) (South Africa) and *Ibrahim Sangor Osman v Minister of State for Provincial Administration & Internal Security eKLR* (2011) (Kenya). In connection to the right to education, see *Environment & Consumer Protection Foundation v Delhi Administration and Others* (2012) Supreme Court WP (Civil) no 631 (India).

and to the right to water resources and defined the scope of states' protection owed to this right. First, users' right to access to water supply services and water facilities has been one of the legal entitlements usually guaranteed by domestic courts. Some courts have underscored states' duty to provide users at least with 'minimum essential amounts of water', even in those cases where private economic actors are responsible for the delivery of this service.[127] Other courts have also protected, in addition, the economic dimension of users' access to this service by emphasising on its affordability, and even prohibiting its disconnection for users' inability to pay high tariffs.[128]

Certainly, the quality of the drinking water supplied has also stood out as another important feature in relation to users' access to this service[129] as well as information about the quality of these services.[130] Second, albeit in a minor degree, the right to access to water resources for domestic uses has also found legal protection before domestic courts in cases relating to forcible eviction[131] or unstainable corporate extraction of ground water.[132] Third, the non-discriminatory exercise of the right to

---

[127]In this case, the Court emphasised on the State's responsibility to guarantee the supply of 'minimum essential amounts of water', even in cases where private actors are responsible for the delivery of this services. *Quevedo, Miguel Ángel y Otros c/Aguas Cordobesas SA*, Juez Sustituta de Primera Instancia Civil y Comercial *(Ciudad de Córdoba)* considerando séptimo (8 de Abril 2002) (Argentina) http://www.cedha.org.ar/docs/doc220-spa.doc accessed 10 December 2020.

[128]*Asociación Civil por la Igualdad y la Justicia c/ Gobierno de la Ciudad de Buenos Aires*, Cámara de Apelaciones en lo Contencioso Administrativo y Tributario (Ciudad Autónoma de Buenos Aires) (18 July 2007) (Argentina) 70-72 www.acij.org.ar/blog/2011/12/13/sentencia-por-aguaen-la-villa-31-bis/ accessed 10 December 2020; *Hernán Galeano Díaz c/ Empresas Públicas de Medellín ESP, y Marco Gómez Otero y Otros c/ Hidropacífico SA ESP y Otros*, Corte Constitucional T-616/10, Quinta Camara de Revision (5 August 2010) (Colombia) 107-111 http://www.corteconstitucional.gov.co/relatoria/2010/T-616-10.htm accessed 10 December 2020; *Carolina Murcia Otálora c/ Empresas Públicas de Neiva ESP*, Corte Constitucional T-546/09 (6 August 2009) (Colombia) 112-114 http://www.corteconstitucional.gov.co/relatoria/2009/t-546-09.htm accessed 10 December 2020. In similar vein, South African domestic courts have argued that the right to water includes restoring the supply of drinking water and guaranteeing the temporary provision in case of supply shortage; as well as preventing disconnection of water supplies. See, *Federation for Sustainable Environment and Others v Minister of Water Affairs and Others* (2012), High Court (North Gauteng, Pretoria) 35672/12, (2012) ZAGPPHC 128 (South Africa); *City of Cape Town v Strümpher* (2012) Supreme Court of Appeal 104/2011, (2012) ZASCA 54 (South Africa); *Highveldridge Residents Concerned Party v Highveldridge Transitional Local Council and Others* (2002) High Court (Transvaal Provincial Division) 28521, (2002) (6) SA 66.

[129]*Jorge Hernán Gómez Ángel c/ Alcalde Municipal de Versalle— Valle del Cauca y el Gerente de la Empresa de Servicios Públicos de Versalles, Corte Constitucional, Cuarta Camara de Revision*, T-410/03 (22 May 2003) (Colombia) http://www.corteconstitucional.gov.co/relatoria/2003/T-410-03.htm accessed 10 December 2020.

[130]*Red de Vigilancia y Exigibilidad de los Derechos Económicos, Sociales y Culturales Región Junín c/ Municipalidad Provincial de Huancayo*, Corte Superior de Justicia 1230-2005 (Junín, Peru) (2 September 2005), 146-148.

[131]*Matsipane Mosetlhanyane and Gakenyatsiwe Matsipane v The Attorney General* (2011) (Botswana).

[132]*Halalt First Nation v British Columbia* (2011) (Canada).

access to drinking water supply and/or to facilities has been recognised in favour of elderly people,[133] children,[134] or indigenous groups,[135] whereas the right to access water resources, mostly in benefit of the later social group.[136] With respect to the practice of domestic courts, it is noteworthy to point out that many adjudicative organs have invoked international[137] and regional human rights treaties to afford protection to these rights,[138] and, correspondingly, applied the normative criteria developed by human rights treaty bodies to ascertain the scope of states' obligations under domestic laws.[139] Additionally, as far as the executive function of states is concerned, one can observe efforts towards the development of policy principles to rule the access to safe drinking water,[140] and the adoption of measures conducive to involve civil society in water service delivery.[141]

The overview just provided shows that although states' domestic protection of the right to water is widespread, this practice is neither consistent nor uniform because

---

[133] *Beja and Others v Premier of the Western Cape and Others* (n 126).

[134] *Environment & Consumer Protection Foundation v Delhi Administration and Others* (n 126).

[135] For references of this right in favour of Colombian indigenous communities and Israeli Bedouins, see *Dagoberto Bohórquez Forero c/ EAAB Empresa de Acueducto y Alcantarillado de Bogotá y Otros, Tribunal Administrativo (Cundinamarca)* (3 May 2012) 11001-33-31-003-2007-00186-01, and *Abadallah Abu Massad and others v Water Commissioner and Israel Lands Administration* (2011) (Israel).

[136] *Halalt First Nation v British Columbia* (n 132).

[137] For examples of Latin American domestic courts referring to the ICESCR, see *Defensor del Pueblo de la Nación c/ Estado Nacional y Provincia del Chaco* (2007) Suprema Corte D.587.XLIII (Argentina); *Carolina Murcia Otálora c/ Empresas Públicas de Neiva ESP* (2009) Corte Constitucional T-546/09 (Colombia). Similarly, South African domestic courts have referred to the ICESCR: *Mazibuko and Others v City of Johannesburg and Others (Centre on Housing Rights and Evictions, Amicus Curiae)*, Constitutional Court of South Africa (CCT 39/09) (2009). Also, *Government of the Republic of South Africa and Others v Grootboom and Others*, Constitutional Court, 4 October 2009 (South Africa). *Government of the Republic of South Africa and Others v Grootboom and Others* (2000) Constitutional Court CCT11/00, (2000) ZACC 19 (South Africa). When indigenous peoples were the claimants in a particular case, some domestic courts do resort to the ILO Convention No. 169, see *Alejandro Papic Domínguez con Comunidad Indígena Aimara Chusmiza y Usmagama* (2009) Corte Suprema 2.840-2008 (Chile).

[138] For examples of Latin American domestic courts referring to the American Convention on Human Rights, and San Salvador Protocol, see *Habeas Corpus Colectivo presentado por Víctor Atencio c/ el Ministerio de Gobierno y Justicia, Director General del Sistema Penitenciario* (2011) Corte Suprema de Justicia 928-09 (Panama); *Comité Pro-No Construcción de la Urbanización Linda Vista, San Juan Sur de Poás c/ Ministerio de Ambiente y Energía y Otros*, Corte Suprema de Justicia (2004) Corte Suprema de Justicia 2004-01923 (Costa Rica).

[139] For examples of domestic courts invoking general comments of the CESCR, see *Ileana Vives Luque c/ Empresa de Servicios Públicos de Heredia* (2003) Corte Suprema de Justicia 2003-04654 (Costa Rica); *Caso no 0006-10-EE* (2010) Corte Constitucional 0010-10-SEE-CC (Ecuador).

[140] 'Executive Decree No. 30480-MINAE Principles governing the national policy in the field of water resources management' (2002) (Costa Rica) arts 1.1 and 1.2.

[141] Centre on Housing Rights and Evictions, "The Significance of Human Rights in MDG-based Policy Making on Water and Sanitation: An Application to Kenya, South Africa, Ghana, Sri Lanka and Laos" (Geneva, 2009), 5-7.

not all states protect the same entitlement in connection to this right. Many laws and courts recognise a right to access drinking water, which usually relates to a right to access safe and affordable water facilities and services, and/or a right to access water resources enabling satisfaction of domestic needs. Furthermore, although the laws and case law cited mostly protect a non-discriminatory exercise of one of these rights, they differ in relation to the individuals recognised as rights-holders in a particular case. Further, some states guarantee a right to access to information about the provision of water services, and, even in some cases, recognise a right to participate in the administration of water services. Despite this lack of consistent and uniform state practice in every detail, states endorse this set of legal entitlements in relation to the right to water, which the CESCR qualifies as the core of the right to water protected under the ICESCR.

*Opinio Juris*

The review made above about the states' domestic protection of the right to water point to the fact that the legal entitlements of this right include a right to access affordable and safe drinking water services and facilities, a right to access safe water resources to satisfy domestic needs, and a right to a non-discriminatory exercise of the former two rights. Whether states accept these rights as legally binding norms may depend on the content and conditions involving their political declarations on this right. To illustrate this, there has been plenty of international summits and conferences addressing the right to water, in which states adopted concrete plan of actions for its implementation.[142] In some of them, states recognised access to water as a right,[143] and strengthened its inherent relation with the right to an adequate standard of life, regardless of whether or not these summits took place under the auspices of the UN.[144] Nevertheless, since these conferences have not dealt with the

---

[142]See 'Report of the United Nations Water Conference, Mar del Plata Action Plan' (14-25 March 1977) UN Doc. E/Conf.70/29 numeral II a) and b) 66-67; 'Report of the United Nations Conference on Environment and Development 'Agenda 21'' (3-14 June 1992) UN Doc. A/CONF.151/26, Vol. II chap 18.47; 'Programme of Action of the International Conference on Population and Development, Cairo' (5-13 September 1994) UN Doc. A/CONF.171/13 principle 2. The adoption of this programme of action was made by consensus of the 177 States represented at the Conference. See also, 'Report of the United Nations Conference on Human Settlements (Habitat II), Istanbul, 3–14 June 1996, UN. Doc. A/CONF.165/14 principle 11; See Economic and Social Council 'Guiding Principles on Internal Displacement' E/CN.4/1998/53/Add.2 (11 February 1998) Annex, principle 18; UNGA 'The Right to Development', Res. 54/175 (15 February 2000) art 12; UNCHR (Commission), Resolution (2005/15) on Adverse effects of the illicit movement and dumping of toxic and dangerous products and wastes on the enjoyment of human rights (14 April 2005) UN Doc. E/CN.4/RES/2005/15.

[143]See Final Document of the 14th Summit Conference of Heads of State or Government of the Non-Aligned Movement, Havana, Cuba, 11-16 September 2006 para 226. Also, Report of the United Nations Water Conference, Mar del Plata Action Plan (n 142) numeral II lit. a); Dublin Statement on Water and Sustainable Development, 1992, principle 4.

[144]Habitat II (n 142) principle 11.

right to water in its human right dimension, they do not constitute political instruments providing evidence of what states believe as legally mandatory regarding the right to water. Hence, this section focuses on the content and conditions involving the adoption of UNGA resolutions as embodying *opinio juris*.

The UNGA has adopted several resolutions that address the right to water as a human right and broadly mention the entitlements deriving from it. The UNGA resolution 64/292 clearly refers to a right to safe and drinking water as a human right, and underscores its relevance for the full enjoyment of all human rights.[145] Furthermore, this resolution demands that states take different actions conducive to increase efforts towards the provision of safe, clean, accessible and affordable drinking water for all.[146] Therefore, the resolution was adopted with the favourable vote of 122 out of 193 UN member states, implying that a two-third majority of UN members did not reject the general idea of an existing human right norm that requires from them to guarantee a right to water acceptable for human consumption and accessible in its physical and economic dimension.[147] Nevertheless, even those countries which approved the resolution explicitly pointed out that, despite their vote in favour of the recognition of this right,[148] the resolution does not constitute any intention to assume international obligations with respect to this right.[149] Subsequently, two UNGA resolutions further elaborate on the legal nature of the right to water and allude to some of the entitlements already guaranteed at the domestic level. To illustrate this, UNGA resolutions unequivocally establish that the right to safe drinking water derives from the right to an adequate standard of living and this, thus, constitutes a human right.[150] When calling upon states' undertaking of specific actions towards the realisation of the right to water, these UNGA resolutions implicitly allude to other entitlements of this right, other than those already referred to by the UNGA resolution 64/292. These entitlements range from a right to a non-discriminatory exercise of the right to safe drinking water (including sustainable access to this right),[151] to a right to information about water services providers which may imply a recognition to a right to drinking water services.[152] However,

---

[145]UNGA 'The human right to water and sanitation' (2010) UN Doc. A/RES/64/292 para 1.

[146]UNGA 'The human right to water and sanitation' (2010) UN Doc. A/RES/64/292, para 2.

[147]UNGA 'The human right to water and sanitation' (2010) UN Doc. A/RES/64/292, para 1.

[148]See UNGA, 'Summary of the 18th plenary meeting of the 64th General Assembly' UN Doc. A/64/PV.108, (2010) (Statement by the Bolivian representative, or Statement of the Colombian representative) 4-6 and 6-7, respectively.

[149]See ibidem (Statement by the Guatemalan representative) 5.

[150]UNGA, 'The human right to safe drinking water and sanitation' (18 December 2013) UN Doc. A/RES/68/1567 preamble and para 1 (The human right to safe drinking water and sanitation I); UNGA, 'The human rights to safe drinking water and sanitation' (17 December 2015) UN Doc. A/RES/70/169 para 1 (The human rights to safe drinking water and sanitation II).

[151]The human right to safe drinking water and sanitation I (n 150) preamble and para 6, lits. d and e; The human rights to safe drinking water and sanitation II (n 150) paras 2 and 5 lits. a, d, h.

[152]The human right to safe drinking water and sanitation I (n 150) preamble and para 6, lit. f; The human rights to safe drinking water and sanitation II (n 150) para 5. Lit. i.

notwithstanding these notable remarks concerning the right to safe drinking water, the UNGA adopted the two latter resolutions without a vote of UN member states so that they do not provide, in a strict sense, any evidence of whether states consider the protection of the right to safe drinking water as legally mandatory.

Last but by no means the least, the resolutions of the HRC have been other international instruments deemed relevant in the promotion and protection of the right to water. Through these instruments, the HRC has appointed Special Rapporteurs to investigate the human rights obligations related to access to safe drinking water, and to outline, among others, practical solutions for its implementation.[153] Moreover, the HRC has further outlined the legal nature of the right to water[154] as well as its corresponding legal entitlements such as the right to drinking water, especially the right to enjoy this right without discrimination.[155]

The HRC has also emphasised on states' obligation to ensure the realization of this right even in the case of delegation of drinking water supply service to third parties, which may implicitly denote Council's endorsement of the right to drinking water services and facilities.[156] Yet, despite the significant relevance of Council's work in anchoring the notion of an existing right to water, the composition of the HRC by only 47 UN member states speaks up against considering its resolutions as reference point for the determination of what states believe to be law with respect to the right to water.

To sum up, the outlook provided above on states' political commitments regarding the right to water reveals that the state community is not yet ready to accept the idea of human right to water as a binding norm. Notwithstanding the former, the UNGA resolution 64/292 may reflect certain consensus among states of the legal entitlements worthy of protection under an international right to water. To recall, they include the rights to safe and drinking water and the right to enjoy the former right without discrimination. Since both rights are broadly conceived in this UNGA resolution, states' protection of this international human right may cover situations where the provision of drinking water services and facilities, and access to water resources facilitate its enjoyment. In fact, the domestic practice of states addressed

---

[153]Catarina de Albuquerque was the first Special Rapporteur appointed by the HRC. UNHRC, 'Resolution 7/22 on human rights and access to safe drinking water and sanitation' (28 March 2008) UN Doc. A/HRC/RES/7/22. In November 2014, the HRC appointed Léo Heller as the second Special Rapporteur and extended his mandate for a second period in 2016. See, UNHRC, 'Resolution 33/10 on the human rights to safe drinking water and sanitation' (29 September 2016) UN Doc. A/HRC/RES/33/10 para 11 (Resolution 33/10).

[154]See, UNHRC, 'Resolution 15/9 on human rights and access to safe drinking water and sanitation' UN Doc. A/HRC/15/9 (6 October 2010) (Resolution 15/9) paras 2 and 3, and 'Resolution 16/2 on the human right to safe drinking water and sanitation' (8 April 2011) UN Doc. A/HRC/RES/16/2 paras 1, 3 and 7.

[155]See UNHRC, 'Resolution 21/2 on the human right to safe drinking water and sanitation' (9 October 2012) UN Doc. A/HRC/RES/21/2 para 7; UNHRC, 'Resolution 27/7 on the human right to safe drinking water and sanitation' (2 October 2014) UN Doc. A/HRC/RES/27/7 para 11 lit. b; Resolution 33/10 (n 153) para 2.

[156]UNHRC, Resolution 15/9 (n 154) para 6.

above on the right to water already exhibits that states endorse these rights, even though their practice is not entirely consistent and uniform. Accordingly, although there are no customary legal basis for the right to water, there is certain consensus among states about the legal entitlements composing this right.

### 3.1.2.2 Scope of Application

According to the CESCR, the right to water entitles everyone to 'sufficient, safe, acceptable, physically accessible and affordable water for personal and domestic uses'.[157] They constitute mandatory features of the goods or services (the so-called AAAA scheme) to which protected right-holders are entitled under the right to water and which states parties are mandated to observe in all circumstances. The first benchmark is *availability* that implies sufficiency and continuity of water supplies necessary for satisfying personal and domestic needs, in quantities that preferably corresponds to those established by the World Health Organization (WHO),[158] while *acceptability* (referred also as quality) involves the idea of having safe water for personal or domestic consumption; water that does not constitute a threat to human health, and is of acceptable physical conditions.[159] Moreover, *accessibility* to water is a feature[160] that denotes a non-discriminatory access of right-holders to water facilities and services,[161] and comprises further overlapping dimensions, namely physical[162] and economic accessibility.[163] Lastly, information concerning water issues demands states parties to facilitate and provide water when requested.[164]

---

[157]CESCR, General Comment No. 15 (n 78) para 2.

[158]CESCR, General Comment No. 15 (n 78) para 12, lit. a. For instance, the IACoHR has made explicit reference to the normative criteria employed to define the scope of protection of the right to water in cases dealing with the right to life of indigenous peoples. In *Sawhoyamaxa Indigenous Community* and *Yakye Axa Indigenous Community* cases, the IACoHR strengthened the status of the availability and non-discriminatory access to drinking water as attributes of the right to life. See *Sawhoyamaxa v Paraguay* (n 15, ch 1) paras 159, 166 and 168. *Yakye Axa v Paraguay* (n 15, ch 1) paras 165 and 162.

[159]CESCR, General Comment No. 15 (n 78) para 12, lit. b. In *Yakye Axa v Paraguay*, the IACoHR alluded to the acceptability criterion associated with the right to adequate water by reinforcing the importance of 'clean water' in the living environment of this Community. See *Yakye Axa v Paraguay* (n 15, ch 1) para 164.

[160]In *Xákmok Kásek v Paraguay*, the IACoHR deemed the provision of sufficient amounts of water for meeting basic needs, as well as the access to safe water whose quality does not exceed tolerable levels of risk (quality) as constitutive elements of the right to the right to life. See *Xákmok Kásek v Paraguay* (n 15, ch 1) para 195.

[161]CESCR, General Comment No. 15 (n 78) para 12, lit. c.

[162]CESCR, General Comment No. 15 (n 78) para 12 lit. c (i).

[163]CESCR, General Comment No. 15 (n 78) para 12 lit. c (ii).

[164]CESCR, General Comment No. 15 (n 78) para 12 lit. c (iv).

Moreover, states parties are accordingly expected to satisfy the minimum core of the right to water by meeting a set of core obligations despite resource constraints.[165] They reflect the normative benchmarks described above and range from ensuring access to sufficient and safe amount of water for personal and domestic uses, thus preventing diseases;[166] the right of access to water and water facilities and services on a non-discriminatory basis,[167] and lastly, physical access to water facilities and services.[168]

Against this background, the question becomes how states parties to the Covenant discharge their duty to regulate foreign investment activities to protect the right to water. According to the CESCR, states parties' obligation to protect the right to water entails ensuring that corporations controlling or operating water services do not 'compromis[e] equal, affordable, and physical access to sufficient, safe and acceptable water',[169] and '(...) to restrain (...) third parties from polluting and inequitably extracting it from water resources'.[170] Departing from this understanding, the following section elaborates means by which Latin American countries may appropriately discharge this duty in the investment context, and then explores whether these countries do exercise their duty to regulate with respect this ESC right.

### 3.1.2.2.1  In the Context of Foreign Investment in Water Facilities and Services

The ICESCR does not prohibit that states parties resort to foreign business entities' involvement in the provision of public goods and services. In fact, the CESCR has held that corporate participation may enable them to meet their obligation under the ICESCR. At the same time, states parties shall discharge their *duty to regulate* against these economic actors in order to fulfil their Covenant's obligation to protect water resources and the indigenous communities from foreign investment activities that may lead to infringement of rights. The provision of drinking water services clearly exemplifies this scenario in the Latin American region. States usually involve foreign corporations in the operation of water facilities or delivery of water services to provide drinking water and thus meet their obligation to fulfil the right to water, while at the same time regulation of their economic activities is required to avert direct interferences with users' enjoyment of this Covenant's right. Taking into account the CESCR's case law, there are several elements inherent to states' protection of the right to water that form the scope of their duty to regulate in the

---

[165]CESCR, General Comment No. 15 (n 78) para 37.

[166]CESCR, General Comment No. 15 (n 78) para 37 lit. a.

[167]CESCR, General Comment No. 15 (n 78) para 37 lit. b.

[168]CESCR, General Comment No. 15 (n 78) para 37 lit. d.

[169]CESCR, General Comment No. 15 (n 78) para 24; General Comment No. 24 (n 55) para 21.

[170]CESCR, General Comment No. 15 (n 78) para 23.

context of corporate operation and control of water facilities and services.[171] According to CESCR law, states shall avert that transnational water companies deprive right-holders from the affordability,[172] as well as physical access to water facilities and services[173] and information about their provision.[174] In addition, states shall ensure that business entities adequately deliver water related goods or services,[175] by guaranteeing that the delivery of drinking water is sufficient and uninterrupted,[176] as well as being suitable for human consumption.

To discharge the regulatory duties deriving from Covenant's obligation to protect the right to water against transnational water corporations engaged in the provision of drinking water services, Latin American countries have resorted to domestic laws, concession agreements and the creation of independent regulatory agencies in charge of supervising the implementation of these domestic laws and contracts.[177] As already described in Sect. 3.1.2.1.2, domestic laws of Latin American countries explicitly protect the affordability of drinking water services and the suitability of drinking water for human consumption. In addition, states induce concessionaires' compliance with these normative features that drinking water services shall meet to achieve the full realisation of the right to water when granting concessions for the provision of this service.

Concession agreements define providers' contractual obligations and may even restate their applicable obligations under domestic laws.[178] In addition, these contracts may include safeguards to guarantee providers' delivery of sufficient and continuous drinking water supply in conditions suitable for users' consumption,[179] and even link these safeguards with concessionaires' obligation to undertake all necessary operative arrangements on external networks connected to users' properties located in the area of their operation.[180]

---

[171]CESCR, General Comment No. 15 (n 78) para 24; General Comment No. 24 (n 55) para 21.

[172]CESCR, General Comment No. 15 (n 78) para 12 lit. c (ii).

[173]CESCR, General Comment No. 15 (n 78) paras 12 lit. c (i and 37, lit. c.

[174]CESCR, General Comment No. 15 (n 78) para 12 lit. c (iv).

[175]The CESCR clearly refers to States parties' obligation to 'prevent [third parties] from compromising equal, affordable, and physical access to *sufficient, safe* and *acceptable* water'. CESCR, General Comment No. 15 (n 78) para 24 (emphasis added).

[176]In connection to this, those quantities established by the World Health Organization are considered as adequate amount of water. CESCR, General Comment No. 15 (n 78) para 12 lit. a.

[177]For an overview of the institutional setting governing the economic regulation of water services in some Latin American countries see Akhmouch (2002).

[178]CESCR, General Comment No. 24 (n 55) para 21.

[179]Under domestic laws, concessionaire's obligation may consist, for instance, of supplying drinking water 'on conditions that ensure its continuity, regularity, quality and widespread nature'. See *Urbaser v Argentina* (n 1, ch 1) paras 79 citing *Law No. 11820* (adopted 17 July 1996) as amended by Law No. 12292 (adopted 21 April 1999), Exhibit I (entitled 'Regulatory Framework for the Provision of Drinking Water and Wastewater Public Services') Sec. 4-II.

[180]See *Urbaser v Argentina* (n 1, ch 1) paras 79 citing *Law No. 11820*, Sec. 7-II.

Certainly, states may prevent that concessionaires deprive users from their economic access to drinking water services by introducing contractual clauses regulating extraordinary revisions or modifications of drinking water services' tariffs,[181] and a regime of sanctions and penalties in case of concessionaires' non-compliance with their obligations.[182] In this regard, the unilateral termination of contracts features in some of them as one of the penalties for concessionaires' inobservance of contractual obligations laws and unjustified delays of investments.[183]

As far as the regulatory agencies are concerned, some countries have established these entities at the central governmental level,[184] while others, such as Argentina, have decentralised the economic regulation of water concession agreements by transferring this function to the provinces.[185] Generally, these regulatory agencies enforce domestic laws applicable to water concessions[186] and supervise concessionaires' provision of water services in accordance with the terms enshrined in concession agreements.[187] Vested with this authority, regulatory agencies protect users' enjoyment of the right to water by prohibiting concessionaires to increase their water bills if corporate measures are inconsistent with applicable domestic laws.[188] In addition, they shall implement sanctions and penalties for inadequate concessionaires' provision of drinking water services,[189] and introduce any regulatory measure

---

[181]See *SAUR v Argentina* (n 1, ch 1). Decision on Jurisdiction and Liability (6 June 2012) para 47.

[182]For instance, see *SAUR v Argentina* (n 1, ch 1) para 38 citing *Contrato de concesión entre la Provincia y Obras Sanitarias de Mendoza S.A.* (adopted 9 June 1998, entered into force 22 September 1998) art 12 para 2.

[183]For instance, see *SAUR v Argentina* (n 1, ch 1) para 38 citing *Contrato de concesión entre la Provincia y Obras Sanitarias de Mendoza S.A.* art 13 para 3.

[184]Examples include the Bolivian Superintendencia de Saneamiento Basico (SISAB), the Chilean Superintendencia de Servicios Sanitarios (SISS), the Costa Rican Autoridad Reguladora de Servicios Publicos (ARESEP), or the Venezuelan C.A. Hidrológica de Venezuela (HIDROVEN).

[185]Pursuant to the Argentine Constitution, the provinces preserve the competences not delegated to the Federal Government and maintain the original dominion of the natural resources available in their territories. See Constitution of the Argentine Nation (1994) arts 121 and 124. Illustrations of regulatory agencies of water services in Argentina include the Organismo Regulador Bonaerense de Aguas y Saneamiento (ORBAS) from the Province of Great Buenos Aires; the Ente Provincial del Agua y de Saneamiento (EPAS) from the Province of Mendoza, or the Ente Tripartito de Obras y Servicios Sanitarios (ETOSS), from the Province of Buenos Aires. For references to these regulatory agencies see, *Urbaser v Argentina* (n 1, ch 1) para 53; *SAUR v Argentina* (n 1, ch 1) para 35; and *Suez and Vivendi v Argentina II* (n 1, ch 1), Decision on Liability (30 July 2010) para 75, respectively.

[186]*Urbaser v Argentina* (n 1, ch 1) paras 76-77 citing *Law No. 11820* (adopted 17 July 1996) as amended by Law No. 12292 (adopted 21 April 1999), Exhibit I (entitled 'Regulatory Framework for the Provision of Drinking Water and Wastewater Public Services') Sec. 2 and 3-I.

[187]See, *Urbaser v Argentina* (n 1, ch 1) para 53 and *SAUR v Argentina* (n 1, ch 1) para 38.

[188]In reference to the regulatory agency's resolution precluding the concessionaire to bill higher amounts for water services, see *Azurix v Argentina I* (n 1, ch 1) paras 83–84.

[189]For instance, see *SAUR v Argentina* (n 1, ch 1) para 38 citing *Contrato de concesión otorgado entre la Provincia y Obras Sanitarias de Mendoza S.A.* (adopted 9 June 1998, entered into force 22 September 1998) art 12 para 2.

conducive to ensure the acceptability of drinking water services, and the protection of users' interest.[190]

Having described the means by which Latin American countries appropriately exercise their duty to regulate foreign investment activities in accordance with the ICESCR, one may recall that the adoption of preventative measures has led to the submission of investment treaty claims faced by Argentina[191] and that this country has resorted to different argumentative strategies to advance these regulatory duties.[192] Albeit not in all cases, tribunals have considered these arguments and at times not held Argentina liable.[193] It is for this reason that understanding states' regulation as an international duty in conformity with IHRL-based doctrine is vital to point out the potential for inter-regime tensions and thus re-politicise IIL.

### 3.1.2.2.2   In the Context of Foreign Investment Activities' Pollution or Depletion of Water Resources

States parties to the ICESCR discharge their duty to protect the right to water by averting business entities' pollution or abusive use of water sources,[194] including natural resources, wells and other type of water distribution systems.[195] Although preventing their contamination, however, does not represent a core obligation that states shall discharge with respect to the right to water despite resource constraints,[196] its inobservance constitute a breach of the right to water under the Covenant.[197] Viewed this way, the states' duty to regulate thus implies preventing that corporations' deposit chemical substances into rivers or wells, to avoid compromising basic food and health needs of communities inhabiting near these water supplies.[198] Moreover, counteracting corporations' unsustainable extraction of water sources becomes another regulatory duty regarding the protection of the right to water, particularly if these water supplies facilitate drinking water to these communities.[199] Discharging these regulatory duties should specifically be directed to protect the participation of women in decision-making about the allocation of water sources[200] and indigenous people's access thereto.[201]

---

[190]In reference to ORBAS' powers see *Urbaser v Argentina* (n 1, ch 1) para 81 citing *Law No. 11820*, Sec. 13-II.

[191]See n 1, ch 1.

[192]See Sect. 4.1.1.1, ch 4.

[193]Ibidem.

[194]CESCR, General Comment No. 15 (n 78) para 23.

[195]CESCR, General Comment No. 15 (n 78) para 23.

[196]CESCR, General Comment No. 15 (n 78) paras 37 and 38.

[197]CESCR, General Comment No. 15 (n 78) para 6.

[198]CESCR, General Comment No. 15 (n 78) para 37 lit. b and para 12, lit. c (iii.

[199]CESCR, General Comment No. 15 (n 78) para 23.

[200]CESCR, General Comment No. 15 (n 78) para 16 lit. a.

[201]CESCR, General Comment No. 15 (n 78) para 16 lit. d.

If one broadly examines the legislative practice of Latin American countries, one may argue that some states indirectly articulate this regulatory duty against investors' pollution of water sources. In their Constitutions, some countries formally recognise their duty to plan, control or regulate the sustainable management of water sources,[202] while others' exercise of this regulatory duty is particularly oriented to protect the access to water.[203] Furthermore, states have a duty to adopt laws that impose obligations on business entities to exercise human rights due diligence under the Covenant.[204] In this context, one can observe that beyond investors' compliance with domestic environmental laws,[205] recent investment codes in some Latin American countries also impose a duty to behave socially responsible upon business actors by emphasising on the public character of goods and services they supply to their population.[206] Accordingly, some Latin American countries do articulate their duty to regulate against the unsustainable corporate abuse of water sources conducive to breaches of the right to water. At the executive level, states meet this duty by conditioning the authorization of exploitation concessions upon compliance with strict requirements such as written permission of landowners of the area concerned and environmental local authorities,[207] or by requesting corporations' compliance with these requirements thus constituting a concrete exercise of host states' duty to regulate their activities.[208]

Even though it is yet to constitute an overall cause of action, states' fulfilment of their duty to regulate foreign investment activities may be prominent in ISDS in the near future. In *Pac Rim Cayman v El Salvador*, this Latin American state faced an investment claim under CAFTA and Salvadoran mining laws,[209] for San Salvadoran legislature's rejection of amendment proposals of mining laws from executive

---

[202]Constitution of the Plurinational State of Bolivia (2009) art 374; Constitution of the Republic of Ecuador (2008) art 318; Constitution of the Oriental Republic of Uruguay (1967, as last amended 31 October 2004) art 47.

[203]Law governing the suspension of concession for the use of water, Law 440 (Nicaragua) (11 August 2003) art 1; Paraguay, Law on Water Resources Law 3239 (10 July 2007) art 3 lit. b; Peru, Water Resources Act (June 2009) art III para 2; Venezuela, Water Law (January 2007) art 5.

[204]CESCR, General Comment No. 24 (n 55) para 16.

[205]Republica Bolivariana de Venezuela, Ley Constitucional de Inversion Extranjera Productiva (2017) art 35 para 10. Pursuant to the 1997 Ecuadorian investment code, foreign investors shall conserve, preserve and restitute any damage caused to the environment and natural resources. Ecuador, Ley de Promocion y Garantia de Inversiones (1997) art 29.

[206]Republica Bolivariana de Venezuela, Ley Constitucional de Inversion Extranjera Productiva (2017) art 32.

[207]*Pac Rim Cayman v El Salvador* (n 2, ch 1) para 2.35 citing *Ley de Mineria*, Decreto Legislativo No. 544 (14 de diciembre de 1995), modificada por el Decreto Legislativo No. 475 (11 de julio de 2001) art 37 para 2 lit. b and c.

[208]*Pac Rim Cayman v El Salvador* (n 2, ch 1) paras 6.24 and 6.25.

[209]This dispute was nevertheless decided in favour of the respondent state. *Pac Rim Cayman v El Salvador* (n 2, ch 1) Award. Certainly, it is important to recall that the legal basis of investor's claim was domestic rather than international law, so that the central question for the tribunal was whether the mining law entitled the claimant investor to a gold exploitation concession.

entities seeking to reduce the amount of requirements for the delivery of mining exploitation concessions,[210] and the suspension of the process granting new mining concessions.[211] The case was decided in favour of San Salvador because the legal basis of claimant's rights and state's obligations were domestic, rather than, international law so that the state had a broader space for regulatory manoeuvre to redefine its legal relationship with the investor.[212] Following this positive outcome, the Salvadoran legislative enacted thereafter a domestic law permanently banning any development project pursuing the exploration, exploitation and processing of metal mining.[213] Through this latter action, this country unequivocally prevented the unsustainable use of water sources stemming from the operation of gold mining activities and safeguarding the availability and acceptability of water to satisfy personal and domestic needs.

That said, it is important to recall that domestic courts' provision of judicial remedies is another way to protect sources of water supply and thereby the right to water. While this states' action is not addressed in this study as a manifestation of states' duty to regulate,[214] one may not overlook the fact that foreign investors have begun to target this specific states' action in the Latin American region and that further research may be required in the near future.[215]

### 3.1.3   Interim Conclusion

In addition to obligations of the result of progressive realization, article 2 (1) of the ICESCR charges two obligations of conduct upon states parties that are of immediate effect. First is an obligation to undertake to take steps and to employ all appropriate means necessary to address the situation. Pursuant to the ICESCR, discharging the obligation to take steps implies that states parties shall protect ESC rights through preventative and remedial measures. In the investment context, this would imply, through all regulatory means, prevention of investors' abuse of ESC rights and in the case of violations, provision of legal remedies to the victims. It is the states' obligation to prevent third parties' abuses of ESC rights that allocates a duty to regulate upon Latin American countries, as states parties to the Covenant. That said, to ensure the full realization of ESC rights in the investment context, states

---

[210]*Pac Rim Cayman v El Salvador* (n 2, ch 1) paras 6.114 citing, 6.118 and 6.124.

[211]*Pac Rim Cayman v El Salvador* (n 2, ch 1) paras 6.125 and 6.129.

[212]For a discussion, see Hepburn (2016).

[213]Ley de Prohibicion de la Mineria Metalica, Decreto No. 639 (29 March 2017) arts 1 and 2 www.asamblea.gob.sv accessed 10 December 2020. See also Reuters Staff (2017).

[214]See n 63, 76, 80 above.

[215]As already mentioned in the introduction, Colombia is facing several investment treaty-based claims because of the 2016 Constitutional court's decision declaring the unconstitutionality of a domestic law's loophole allowing the operation of mining, oil and gas activities in the high-altitude wetlands. See n 7, ch 1.

are also to comply with an obligation to respect in terms of avoiding favouring investment treaty protection over the protection of ESC rights with the aim of attracting foreign investment, and with an obligation to fulfil, consisting in facilitating and/or promoting foreign investors' provision of good or services if they guarantee the enjoyment of ESC rights. Yet, to establish which legislative and executive means are appropriate to discharge this regulatory duty, and thus attain the Covenant's obligation of result, states shall adopt all regulatory measures that conform the good or services' features to which right-holders are entitled under a specific ESC right.

In the specific case of the right to water, a duty to regulate arises for Latin American countries from the right to an adequate standard of living codified in article 11 (1) of the ICESCR, rather than from CIL. While many domestic laws and courts recognise a clear set of legal entitlements forming this ESC right and the corresponding normative features of the goods and services essential for its effective enjoyment, states seem to avoid endorsing the right to water as legally mandatory norms within the framework of UNGA resolutions. Notwithstanding the former, the UNGA continues to foster the idea that the rights to safe and drinking water and to enjoy it without discrimination are legal entitlements worthy of international legal protection as a right to water, and state practice explicitly endorse them so that one may assume that some of the entitlements protected under the right to water may be indicative of a customary rule under formation.

According to the case law of the CESCR, states parties to the Covenant would particularly meet their duty to regulate in furtherance of the right to water in a context where foreign investors provide drinking water facilities and services and they have to prevent that the provision of these services compromise the sufficiency and continuity of drinking water's supply essential for satisfying personal and domestic needs, limit users' access to water services and facilities through disproportionate water tariffs' increase or deliver water unfit for human consumption.

The other scenario where states parties to the Covenant are encouraged to discharge these regulatory duties are in those cases where business actors' activities may lead to the pollution or depletion of sources of water supply. In this latter scenario, states are to regulate, in particular, the business entities' deposit of chemical substances or their unsustainable extraction since this may compromise the availability and quality of water sources.

In addition to the enactment of domestic laws protecting the right to water, appropriate regulatory means to carry out this duty include states' review of laws and policies' adequacy, suspension of licenses and even their intervention if the circumstances so required. As to the question of whether Latin American host states of foreign investment meet this duty, one may answer it in the affirmative. States have discharged their duty by actions that go beyond the mere adoption of protective legislation. These regulatory actions have ranged from host states' modification or termination of contracts to their suspension of investors' licenses for water services' provision or those allowing them to extract and exploit mineral resources.

However, host states' exercise of this duty in accordance with these normative standards has triggered the submission of investment treaty claims since these measures inevitably affect investors' venture. Argentina is a typical example where regulation of foreign investment in the drinking water sector in compliance with the Covenant becomes a cause of action in ISDS. Moreover, except for the *Pac Rim Cayman v El Salvador*, states' regulation conducive to prevent water sources' depletion or pollution has not yet prominently featured in ISDS. Additionally, judicial protection of the right to water by domestic courts in the latter scenario may not undergo the same fate as the cases recently faced by Colombia suggest. For these reasons, it is the submission of this study that IIL regime should not overlook the regulatory duties states must fulfil to protect the right to water in the investment context.

## 3.2 The Duty to Regulate Under Inter-American Human Rights Law

### 3.2.1 *The Duty to Regulate in General*

#### 3.2.1.1 The Duty to Regulate Under Inter-American Instruments

Within the Inter-American human rights system, OAS member states have committed to observe the fundamental rights of the individual,[216] as defined by the Declaration on the Rights and Duties of Man (ADRDM).[217] Considered as the source of legal obligation for those OAS member states that are not contracting parties of the ACHR,[218] the IACommHR is mandated to promote the observance and protection of the rights laid down in the ADRDM.[219] The IACommHR is bestowed with some powers upon all OAS member states, regardless of their status *vis-à-vis* the ACHR. In addition, it has differentiated functions in relation to the ADRDM and the ACHR, when it comes to affording protection to human rights.[220]

In performing its twofold mandate under both Inter-American human rights instruments, the IACommHR has strongly underscored states' duty to protect

---

[216]Charter of the Organization of American States (adopted 30 April 1948, entered into force 13 December 1951) (OAS Charter) art 3 recital (l.

[217]American Declaration of the Rights and Duties of Man (adopted 2 May 2008) OAS Res XXX adopted by the Ninth International Conference of American States (1948), AJIL Vol. 43 Supp. 133; see also *Interpretation of the American Declaration of the Rights and Duties of Man with the Framework of Article 64 of the American Convention on Human Rights*, Advisory Opinion OC-10/89, IACoHR Series A, No. 10 (14 July 1989) (Interpretation of American Declaration) para 43.

[218]Interpretation of American Declaration (n 217) para 45.

[219]Statute of the Inter-American Commission on Human Rights, Res. No. 447 adopted by the OAS General Assembly during its ninth period of sessions (1979) (Statute of the Inter-American Commission on Human Rights), art 2. Available at: http://www.oas.org/xxxiiga/english/docs_en/cidh_statute_files/basic15.htm. Accessed 10 December 2020.

[220]See n 246 below.

human rights in the investment context by upholding that states have a duty to respect and guarantee human rights that are implicit in the ADRDM,[221] or condemning, by means of public hearings, states' failure to promote and protect these human rights against corporate abuses of indigenous communities' rights arising in the extractive sector.[222] It has pointed out that OAS member states have a duty to abstain from underpinning or tolerating any act leading to interferences with indigenous people's rights in particular.[223] Though not binding upon OAS member states in a strict doctrinal sense, the determinations of the IACommHR in relation to the right laid down in the ADRDM have a great normative value and provide a mechanism for those affected by investment activities to make public the failure of states, not bound by the ACHR, thus compelling them to take measures against investors' impairments.

Following the great reception of the UNGP within the OAS[224] and the increasing concerns expressed by the IACoHR against corporate misbehaviour in the Americas,[225] the IACommHR adopted its Report on Business and Human Rights: Inter-American Standards (Report on Business and Human Rights) in November 2019 to elucidate, inter alia, the normative regional principles that should guide this debate,[226] as well as the states' obligations that inextricably arise in the regional

---

[221]The IACommHR has strongly endorsed such proposition in its capacity of OAS organ. See IACommHR, 'Maya Indigenous Communities of the Toledo District v Belize', Report No. 40/04, Case 12.053 (12 October 2004) paras 136–156 (Maya Indigenous v Belize); 'Jessica Lenahan (Gonzales) and others (United States)' Report 80/11, Case No, 12.626 (21 July 2011) para 117; 'Murdered and Missing Indigenous Women in British Columbia, Canada' OEA/Ser. L/V/II, Doc. 30/14 (21 December 2014) para 107.

[222]IACommHR, 160 Extraordinary Period of Sessions 'Human Rights Situation of Indigenous Persons in the Context of Projects and Extractive Industries in the United States', (9 December 2016); 159 Period of Sessions 'Human Rights Situation in the Context of the Implementation of the Trans-Pacific Partnership (TPP) in the Americas', (7 December 2016); 158 Extraordinary Period of Sessions 'States, Corporations, and Human Rights in South America' (7 June 2016).

[223]IACommHR, 'Indigenous Peoples, Afro-Descendent Communities, and Natural Resources: Human Rights Protection in the Context of Extraction, Exploitation, and Development Activities', OEA/Ser. I/V/II Doc. 47/15 (31 December 2015) (Indigenous People and Extractive Industries), 44.

[224]See OAS, 'Promotion and Protection of Human Rights in Business' General Assembly Res AG/Res 2840 (XLIV-O/14) (Washington DC 4 June 2014) para 1. In 2016, the OAS General Assembly renewed its commitment towards the promotion of the UNGP's application in the region. OAS, 'Promotion and Protection of Human Rights' General Assembly Res AG/Res 2887 (XLVI-O/ 16) (Washington DC 14 June 2016) paras 1 lit. (ii and 3.

[225]In *Sarayaku v Ecuador*, the IACoHR considered corporate misconduct the loading of indigenous peoples' territories with explosives, cave's destruction, pollution of water sources and underground rivers, and removal and destruction of plants used by the Sarayaku people for their subsistence. *Sarayaku v Ecuador* (n 17, ch 1) paras 101 and 105. In *Kaliña and Lokono Peoples v Suriname*, the IACoHR stated that corporations have a responsibility 'to respect (. . .) human rights, as well as to prevent, mitigate, and accept responsibility for the adverse human rights impacts linked to their activities'. *Kaliña and Lokono Peoples v Suriname* (n 18, ch 1) paras 223-224.

[226]IACommHR, Special Rapporteurship on Economic, Social, Cultural an Environmental Rights, 'Informe sobre Empresas y Derechos Humanos: Estándares Interamericanos' (1 November 2019) OEA/Ser.L/V/II) (Report on Business and Human Rights) paras 42-43.

business and human rights context,[227] and the common situations where these obligations should be particularly observed.[228] Although this report strongly 'inter-americanise' the UNGP's pillar on the duty to protect in relation to the remedial measures that states shall provide to victims of corporate abuses,[229] the report explicitly refer to OAS member states' duty to regulate foreign investment activities, indistinctly of which is the Inter-American human rights instrument that allocates this regulatory duty upon them.

According to this report, the duty to regulate foreign investment activities is as follows: Concerning legislative measures, the duty to regulate implies constant reviewing of the laws applicable to the business sector,[230] ensuring consistency between constitutional and domestic laws and Inter-American human rights instruments,[231] and introducing all substantive and procedural measures that necessary prevent weakening of corporate laws or denying rights in the investment context.[232] Regarding executive measures, the Report specifically underscores the duty to regulate all activities that could cause harms on the environment, ensuring consistency with the recent approach of the IACoHR towards the protection of a right to a healthy environment.[233] Under this report, OAS member states are to regulate economic activities through oversight of concession agreements, particularly in those cases where economic actors provide a public service.[234] Otherwise, if the state fails to regulate foreign investment activities, it will incur international responsibility under the Inter-American Human Rights instruments.[235] Understanding the duty to regulate in conformity with Inter-American standards thus exhibit the great potential for overlapping with IIL regime.

To sum up, OAS member states have a duty to regulate foreign investment activities under Inter-American instruments, understanding the latter as those relating to the ADRDM and other instruments that the IACommHR adopted to assist OAS member in observing human rights. The Report on Business and Human Rights is one important regional milestone in promoting the observance of human rights in the business context. One of the reasons is that it clearly establishes the existence of a duty to regulate foreign investment activities through legislative and executive measures by systematising the existing case law involving the

---

[227]Report on Business and Human Rights (n 226) paras 54–146.

[228]Report on Business and Human Rights (n 226) paras 199–407.

[229]Herencia-Carrasco (2020).

[230]Report on Business and Human Rights (n 226) para 104.

[231]Report on Business and Human Rights (n 226) para 105.

[232]Report on Business and Human Rights (n 226) para 106.

[233]*Obligaciones Estatales en Relación con el Medio Ambiente en el Marco de la Protección y Garantía de los Derechos a la Vida y a la Integridad Personal - Interpretación y Alcance de los Artículos 4.1 y 5.1, En Relación con los Artículos 1.1 Y 2 de la Convención Americana Sobre Derechos Humanos Solicitada por la República de Colombia*, Opinión Consultiva OC-23/17 Serie A No. 23 (15 November 2017).

[234]Report on Business and Human Rights (n 226) paras 114–115.

[235]Report on Business and Human Rights (n 226) para 117.

interpretation and application of the ADRDM and the ACHR. Moreover, the Report has been also praised for expanding the scope of economic activities and right-holders that OAS member states shall protect through regulatory measures because it goes beyond the extractive industries sector and indigenous communities as rights-holders.[236] Additionally, the Report has also been considered a frontrunner in criticising the 'voluntary' approach towards the business and human rights debate,[237] since it condemns it as insufficient to meet IHRL standards.[238]

### 3.2.1.2 The Duty to Regulate Under the ACHR

Together with the ADRDM, the ACHR constitutes the second pillar of Inter-American human rights system.[239] Through their ratification, the 23 Latin American states have committed to respect all rights enshrined in the ACHR and ensure that all persons subject to their jurisdiction exercise their freedom fully without discrimination,[240] as well as to adopt the necessary measures that may be required to give these rights effect if not already guaranteed in their domestic laws.[241] The ACHR codifies 23 civil and political rights.[242] Concerning ESC rights, the ACHR mandates states parties to achieve progressively the full realization of the 'rights implicit in the economic, social, educational, scientific and cultural standards set forth' in the OAS Charter,[243] further expanded by the Protocol to the ACHR in the Area of Economic, Social and Cultural Rights (the 'San Salvador Protocol').[244]

---

[236]Herencia-Carrasco (2020).

[237]Carrillo-Santarelli (2020).

[238]Report on Business and Human Rights (n 226) para 408.

[239]The OAS mandated the Inter-American Council of Jurist in 1959 to formulate a draft treaty on human rights, modelled after the European Convention for the Protection of Human Rights and early versions of the UN Covenants' drafts. Once the Inter-American Commission on Human Rights (IACommHR) modified this initial version, the Inter-American Specialized Conference on Human Rights was convened in San Jose, Costa Rica in 1969, and after reviewing IACommHR's observations, the Conference adopted the American Convention on Human Rights. For an overview see OAS, 'Conferencia Especializada InterAmericana sobre Derechos Humanos', reprinted in Thomas Buergenthal and Robert E. Norris (eds), Human Rights: The Inter-American System, Ocean Publication (1984).

[240]ACHR (n 11, ch 1) art 1. The following 23 OAS member States are currently States parties of the ACHR: Argentina, Barbados, Bolivia, Brazil, Chile, Colombia, Costa Rica, Dominica, Dominican Republic, Ecuador, El Salvador, Grenada, Guatemala, Haiti, Honduras, Jamaica, Mexico, Nicaragua, Panama, Paraguay, Peru, Suriname, and Uruguay. Trinidad and Tobago and Venezuela also ratified the ACHR, but they denounced in 1998 and 2012, respectively.

[241]ACHR (n 11, ch 1) art 2.

[242]They comprise, inter alia, the rights to life, freedom of thought and expression, to assembly, to property, and to judicial protection. ACHR (n 11, ch 1) arts 4, 13, 15, 21, 25.

[243]ACHR (n 11, ch 1) art 26.

[244]San Salvador Protocol (n 107).

The IACommHR and the IACoHR are the competent treaty bodies mandated to supervise and enforce states parties' compliance with the ACHR and the San Salvador Protocol where applicable.[245] As a treaty body of the ACHR, the IACommHR has the function of receiving individual petitions alleging breaches of these rights,[246] and hearing them once all admissibility requirements have been fulfilled.[247] On the other hand, the IACoHR finds violations of the ACHR's rights under its contentious jurisdiction,[248] and provides advisory opinions about the interpretation of ACHR and other Inter-American human rights treaties.[249]

Yet, in addition to the above-mentioned *ex post* protection of ACHR's rights, both Inter-American human rights bodies may protect right-holders *ex ante*. The IAcommHR, for instance may issue precautionary measures in 'cases of serious and urgent situations to request states' prevention of irreparable harms to persons'.[250] It derives the power to do so from its appointed mandate of promoting the observance and protection of human rights under the OAS Charter and its Statute, by applying the criteria developed by IACoHR when dealing with Commission's request of provisional measures.[251]

Despite challenges to their legally binding nature,[252] precautionary measures have a great normative relevance regarding the scope of states' obligations under the Inter-American human rights system that is comparable to its reports under

---

[245] ACHR (n 11, ch 1) art 33. This refers to the rights to organize or join trade unions, and the right to education. See San Salvador Protocol (n 107) art 19 para 6.

[246] With the ratification or adherence to the ACHR, States parties automatically recognise the Commission's competence to receive and examine individual petitions. See ACHR (n 11, ch 1) art 45. Petitioners may be any person, group of persons or any non-governmental entity legally recognized in the jurisdiction of one or more OAS member State party. See ACHR (n 11, ch 1) art 44 and Statute of the Inter-American Commission on Human Rights (n 219) art 19 lit. a.

[247] Petitioners shall fulfil the following cumulative conditions: (a) exhaustion of local remedies; (b) submission of the communication's petitions within a period of 6 months from the date of aggrieved individuals' reception of the final judgement; (c) that the petition is not pending before the jurisdiction of other international tribunal and d) contact details of petitioners. See ACHR (n 11, ch 1) art 46.

[248] ACHR (n 11, ch 1) art 63 para 1.

[249] ACHR (n 11, ch 1) art 64 para 1. The Commission is bestowed with the power to request an advisory opinion on Inter-American human rights treaties pursuant to article 19 lit. d of its Statute. In addition, States parties to the ACHR may request an advisory opinion concerning the compatibility of one of its domestic laws with the ACHR or another human rights treaty. See ACHR (n 11, ch 1) art 64 para 2.

[250] See Rules of Procedure of the Inter-American Commission on Human Rights, art 25 paras 1 and 2. Available at: http://www.oas.org/en/iachr/mandate/basics/rulesiachr.asp. Accessed 10 December 2020.

[251] IACommHR, 'Garza v United States', Case 12.243, IACommHR, Report No. 1255, OEA/ser.L/V/II/111, doc. 20 rev (2001) para 117.

[252] The Commission, however, is of the view that OAS member States have a duty to comply with its precautionary measures, thereby implying their legally binding nature. See IACommHR, Resolution No. 1/05 (8 March 2005) resolving para 1.

individual cases.[253] It is in this context where the IHRL and IIL have coincided with each other that the IACommHR issues a precautionary measures against a state for failing to observe their human rights obligations in the investment context,[254] or in indirect connection with an investment treaty claim.[255] Moreover, the IACoHR, for its part, has also indirectly participated in this indirect inter-regime encounter following states' failure to respond to the Commission's precautionary measure in favour of Sarayaku people that were in extreme gravity and urgency of irreparable damage and the lack of effectiveness of state's measures as a result of the oil exploration activities of Burlington's subsidiary.[256]

As to the question of which ACHR's obligation allocates a duty to regulate foreign investment activities upon states parties, one should recall that in addition to an obligation to respect the civil and political rights laid down in the ACHR,[257] states parties to the ACHR shall discharge an obligation to ensure the free and full enjoyment of Convention's rights without discrimination, to all persons, subject to their jurisdiction.[258] The latter obligation has been understood as demanding from state parties to organise their legislative, executive and adjudicative functions in a way that they are able to satisfy the free and full enjoyment of Convention's rights to all persons,[259] and guarantee the prevention, investigation and prosecution of any breach of the ACHR, as well as the provision of legal remedies.[260] In addition to ensuring that the ACHR exerts full effect in its own jurisdiction by means of the direct incorporation or as provided within their respective Constitutions,[261] states parties to the ACHR also comply with the obligation to the expected assurance of ACHR rights by discharging further obligations of conduct.[262] Accordingly, it is safe to assume a this point that the obligation to this assurance under the ACHR provides, in generic terms, the legal foundation of states parties' duty to regulate foreign investment activities within the Inter-American human rights system.

Yet not all obligations of conduct required to satisfy the obligation to ensure ACHR's rights allocates this regulatory duty upon states parties in the investment context. Only those obligations of conduct that would require the adoption of preventative measures in the investment context may provide the foundation of this

---

[253]See Rodríguez-Pinzón (2013).

[254]See n 13, ch 1.

[255]See n 35, 39, 40, ch 1.

[256]See n 32, 33.

[257]ACHR (n 11, ch 1) art 1 para 1. States parties discharge their obligation to respect ACHR's rights by abstaining from undertaking actions that may directly or indirectly lead to breaches of Convention's rights. See *Case of Velásquez-Rodríguez v Honduras* (Merits) Judgement, IACoHR Serie C No. 4(29 July 1980) (*Velásquez-Rodríguez v Honduras*) para 165.

[258]ACHR (n 11, ch 1) art 1 para 1.

[259]*Velásquez-Rodríguez v Honduras* (n 257) para 166.

[260]*Velásquez-Rodríguez v Honduras* (n 257) para 167.

[261]For a detailed discussion of each obligation, see Ferrer Mac-Gregor and Pelayo Möller (2019b), pp. 77–78.

[262]*Velásquez-Rodríguez v Honduras* (n 257) para 167.

states' duty. Therefore, the obligation to investigate, prosecute, and punish all agents of foreign investors' subsidiary responsible for human rights abuses,[263] and to guarantee full restitution to those affected by foreign investor's abuses of human rights through different types of remedies would not constitute the normative basis of this regulatory duty because it requires the adoption of remedial measures once human rights violations cannot be prevented.[264]

The other obligation of conduct to be discharged to satisfy the obligation to ensure ACHR's rights are not infringed entails acting with due diligence.[265] This implies taking actions in full knowledge of the situation, considering, for example, an individual's or a group's real and immediate risk that could be brought about by third party's actions, and then being conditioned by the reasonable possibilities to avert such risk,[266] following an examination of the circumstances involving each particular case.[267] The IACoHR assumes states' knowledge of a real and imminent risk if complaints and request for protective measures have been awarded by domestic courts, but also if request and awards of IACommHR's precautionary measures and IACoHR's provisional measures are in force.[268] Understood in this way, the obligation to act with due diligence under the ACHR thus assigns a duty to regulate foreign investment activities upon states parties. This coincides with the fact that IACoHR has usually condemned states parties' failure to exercise due diligence in cases where private hospitals have been involved in inappropriate provision of public health services,[269] or foreign corporations impairing local communities' enjoyment of the ACHR's rights.[270]

Moreover, the adoption of legislative and other necessary measure to give effect is another obligation of the ACHR that allocates a duty to regulate foreign

---

[263] *Velásquez-Rodríguez v Honduras* (n 257) para 174; *Case of the Pueblo Bello Massacre v Colombia* (Merits, Reparations and Cost) Judgement, IACoHR Series C No. 40 (31 January 2006) (*Pueblo Bello v Colombia*) para 143.

[264] For a detailed overview of Court's approach in awarding remedies, see Ferrer Mac-Gregor and Pelayo Möller (2019a) pp. 47–48.

[265] *Velásquez-Rodríguez v Honduras* (n 257) para 173.

[266] *Pueblo Bello v Colombia* (n 263) para 123.

[267] *Case of the 19 Merchants v Colombia* (Merits, Reparations and Cost) Judgement, IACoHR Series C (5 July 2004) (*Case of the 19 Merchants v Colombia*) paras 139–141.

[268] *Caso Familia Barrios v Venezuela* (Fondo, Reparaciones y Costas) Sentencia, CIDH Serie C 237 (24 November 2011) para 124.

[269] *Case of Alban Cornejo v Ecuador* (Merits, Reparations and Costs) Judgement Series C No. 171 (22 November 2007) para 119.

[270] *Yakye Axa v Paraguay* (n 15, ch 1) para 162; *Sawhoyamaxa v Paraguay* (n 15, ch 1) para 153. In addition, the Court has also condemned states parties' lack of due diligence with respect to those human rights abuses committed by paramilitary groups. *Case of Godínez-Cruz v Honduras* (Interpretation of the Judgment of Reparations and Costs) Judgement IACoHR Series C Number 3 (20 January 1989) para 172. *Case of Barnaca-Velazquez v Guatemala* (Merits) Judgement, IACoHR Series C Number 70 (25 November 2000) para 210. *Case of the 19 Merchants v Colombia* (n 267) paras 109, 141; *Pueblo Bello v Colombia* (n 263) para 112. See also IACommHR, Indigenous People and Extractive Industries (n 223), 56; Sandri Fuentes (2014), pp. 213, 222–223.

investment activities upon states parties to the ACHR.[271] Despite being considered a restatement of a general legal obligation under international law,[272] specific obligations derive from this commitment that have relevance to establish regulatory duties in the investment context. They include the promulgation of norms and implementation of policies conducive to the effective observance of ACHR's rights[273] and the elimination of norms and practices conducive to the inobservance of the guarantees laid down in the ACHR.[274] Accordingly, this Convention's obligation complementing the obligation to ensure and respect ACHR's rights provides an additional normative basis of a duty to regulate foreign investment activities since they require the enactment of domestic laws and the adoption of specific policies aimed at effectively ensuring that foreign investors observe ACHR's rights. This means to secure that which the Convention provides is actually complied with in its domestic legal framework, and that foreign economic actors investing in states parties to the ACHR adapt their conduct to what the ACHR requires.[275]

Having identified the general basis of states' duty to regulate foreign investment activities under the ACHR, the question of how to establish its scope of application is contingent upon the scope of protection of the ACHR's right affected by investment activities.[276] To this end, one should take into consideration the universalist interpretative approach favoured by Inter-American human rights bodies when defining the scope of application of this regulatory duty. Based on article 29 of the ACHR,[277] these regional bodies interpret ACHR's rights in conformity with the *pro persona* principle that requires an interpretation of the ACHR in a manner most advantageous to the human being.[278] Mandated to follow this interpretative approach, the IACommHR has not restrained itself from applying other international

---

[271]ACHR (n 11, ch 1) art 2.

[272]This latter obligation embodies the general obligation under international law that states parties assume to make its internal legal framework consistent with its international legal commitments when entering into an international treaty, so that state organs apply it and those protected by the treaty invoke it before domestic courts. *Caso Durand y Ugarte v Peru* (Fondo) Sentencia, CIDH Serie C No. 68 (16 Agosto 2000) para 136.

[273]*Caso Cantoral Benavides v Peru* (Fondo) Sentencia, CIDH Serie C No. 69 (18 Agosto de 2000) para 178.

[274]*Case of Castillo Petruzzi et al v Peru* (Merits, Reparations and Cost) Judgement, IACoHR Series C No. 52 (30 May 1999) para 207. *Case of Cesti Hurtado v Peru* (Merits) Judgement Series C No. 56 (29 September 1999) para 166. *Case of the Last Temptation of Christ v Chile* (Merits, Reparations and Cost) Judgement Series C No. 73 (5 February 2001) para 85.

[275]*Caso Garrido y Baigorria v Argentina* (Reparaciones y Costas) Sentencia, CIDH Serie C No. 39 (27 Agosto 1998) paras 68–69.

[276]*Caso Juan Humberto Sanchez v Honduras* (Excepciones preliminares, fondo, reparaciones y costas) Sentencia, CIDH Serie C No. 199 (7 June 2003) para 145.

[277]Pursuant to article 29, an interpretation of the ACHR shall not undermine the enjoyment or exercise of the rights enshrined in other international treaty to which the state concerned is state party. ACHR (n 11, ch 1) art 29 (b.

[278]Fitzmaurice (2013), pp. 765–767.

instruments when formulating their reports and studies,[279] and the IACoHR, from examining violations of the ACHR in light of other universal and regional instruments alike.[280] Therefore, a review of the scope of states parties' duty to regulate foreign investment activities under the ACHR demands integration of other international norms that may be applicable to ensure right-holders affected by investment activities have free and full enjoyment of ACHR's rights.

### 3.2.2 The Duty to Regulate in Furtherance of Indigenous People's Land Rights

#### 3.2.2.1 Legal Basis

3.2.2.1.1 International Treaties and Non-binding Instruments

Pursuant to article 21 of the ACHR, states parties shall ensure indigenous people's free and full enjoyment of the right to use and enjoy property without any discrimination.[281] Like other universal[282] and regional human rights institutions,[283] Inter-American bodies have often resorted to normative standards that specifically deal with the protection of indigenous people's rights to determine the scope of states' obligation to assure their full and free enjoyment of this ACHR's right. Universal instruments to this effect comprise the ILO Convention 169 and the UN Declaration on the Rights of Indigenous Peoples (UNDRIP),[284] in addition to the American

---

[279] ACHR (n 11, ch 1) art 41 lit.c.

[280] De Pauw (2015).

[281] ACHR (n 11, ch 1) arts 1 para and 21 para 1.

[282] In reviewing Guatemala's implementation of article 27 ICCPR (minorities' right to enjoy their own culture, profess and practise their religion and use their own language), the Human Rights Committee demanded from Guatemala to conduct prior and informed consultation with indigenous people about all projects-related decisions that are likely to affect them. See Human Rights Committee, 'Concluding Observations of the Human Rights Committee, Guatemala' (19 April 2012) UN Doc. CCPR/C/GTM/CO/3 para 27. Moreover, the Committee on the Rights of Child commended Myanmar/Burma to overcome the absence of preventive legislation that protects and redresses indigenous communities against the adverse impacts of private and state-owned companies. Committee on the Rights of the Child, 'Considerations of Reports Submitted by States Parties under Art. 44 of the Convention on the Rights of the Child, Myanmar/Burma' (14 March 2012) UN Doc. CRC/C/MMR/CO/3-4 para 21.

[283] The African Commission have urged, inter alia, land restitution and recognition of property rights in benefit of a particular indigenous group, if the state unlawfully expropriated traditional lands and destroyed their possessions. See *Minority Rights Dev. v Kenya*, African Commission on Human Rights and Peoples, No. 276/03 (4 February 2010) para 214 and recommendation no. 1.

[284] United Nations Declaration on the Rights of Indigenous Peoples (adopted 13 September 2007) UNGA Res 61/295 (UNDRIP), Annex.

Declaration on the Rights of Indigenous Peoples (ADRIP).[285] Although these instruments differ in their legal nature and are not human rights treaties per se, they broadly underpin the protection of several human rights of indigenous communities.

Binding upon 15 Latin American countries,[286] the ILO Convention 169 constitutes an international treaty adopted under the aegis of the International Labour Organization (ILO), which codifies a set of social standards facilitating indigenous people's control over their own institutions and ways of living.[287] The human rights of indigenous people reinforced by the ILO Convention 169 cover their right to exercise human rights without hindrance or discrimination, as well as the prohibition to use force and coercion in violation of these rights.[288] The UNDRIP and the ADRIP, on the contrary, are non-binding instruments adopted under the aegis of the UN and the OAS, respectively, which have been conceived to devise a set of minimum standards for indigenous people's survival, dignity and well-being.[289] Prominent among these benchmarks are the provision underscoring indigenous groups' right to the full enjoyment of their human rights, as recognised in the UN charter, UDHR, and human rights law,[290] and the provision reinforcing their right to be free from any kind of discrimination in their exercise.[291] These external

---

[285] American Declaration on the Rights of Indigenous Peoples (adopted 15 June 2016), OEA/Ser.P AG/RES.2888 (XLVI-O/16) (ADRIP) https://www.oas.org/en/sare/documents/DecAmIND.pdf accessed 10 December 2020. The United States of America objected the adoption of the ADRIP, while Canada adopted a 'non-position' towards this act and Colombia made reservations against provisions on FPIC and the prohibition to develop military activities in indigenous people's lands and territories. Ibidem, 183–185. In addition, although Colombia adhered to the ADRIP, this country delivered interpretative notes with respect to different articles laid down in the ADRIP. See Ibidem, Annex I, 187–189.

[286] The ILO Convention 169 has entered into force for 22 States, from which 15 stem from Latin America. These countries are Argentina, Bolivia, Brazil, Chile, Colombia, Costa Rica, Dominica, Ecuador, Guatemala, Honduras, Mexico, Nicaragua, Paraguay, Peru, Venezuela. ILO, Normlex, Ratifications of C169—Indigenous and Tribal Peoples Convention, 1989 (No. 169) http://www.ilo.org/dyn/normlex/en/f?p=NORMLEXPUB:11300:0::NO::P11300_INSTRUMENT_ID:312314 accessed 10 December 2020.

[287] See ILO Convention 169 (n 64, ch 1), preamble. The monitoring of States parties' compliance with the ILO Convention 169 is entrusted to Committee of Experts on the Application of Conventions and Recommendations and made through the following implementation mechanism established in the organization's constitutive treaty: States parties to the ILO Conventions shall submit reports about their implementation in domestic laws and policies for the Committee of Experts' revision, and employers and workers organizations' comments. See Constitution of the International Labour Organization (adopted 1 April 1919, entered into force 28 June 1919) arts 22 and 24.

[288] See ILO Convention 169 (n 64, ch 1) art 3 paras 1 and 2.

[289] See UNDRIP (n 284) art 43; ADRIP (n 285) art XLI.

[290] See UNDRIP (n 284) art 1; ADRIP (n 285) VII para 1.

[291] See UNDRIP (n 284) art 2. Concerning the ADRIP, although this OAS instrument only guarantees a right to enjoy human rights without discrimination in favour of indigenous women, one may presume an implicit recognition of this right in benefit of all indigenous communities'

benchmarks have generally informed Inter-American bodies' determination of who constitute indigenous people, how property should be understood in relation to this social group and which entitlements comprise their right to 'use and enjoy' property.

To determine the 'indigenous' character of a person or group concerned, Inter-American human rights treaty bodies have employed the objective and subjective criteria codified in these external sources. According to one objective standard, indigenous people are those groups descending from populations that inhabited the country or a particular region, during the colonisation or boundaries' establishment, and have maintained their traditional institutions, irrespective of their legal status.[292] In addition, these groups' self-identification comprise the indigenous or tribal features, the subjective benchmark laid down in the ILO Convention 169 and the ADRIP alike, which human rights institutions usually use to qualify a specific group as indigenous.[293]

Additionally, property in relation to indigenous people has been inextricably associated with their traditional lands and territories, which, pursuant to the ILO Convention 169, includes territories covering the total environment of the areas which these communities occupy or use.[294] In connection to this, the land rights recognised by the above-mentioned indigenous people's instruments have played a central role in the determination of which entitlements comprise their right to 'use and enjoy' property under the ACHR. Notwithstanding differences in the scope of protection provided by these non-human rights instruments, they recognise indigenous people's right to own and use lands traditionally occupied by these groups,[295] a right to natural resources pertaining to their natural resources,[296] and a right to be protected against forced removal from their lands.[297]

In addition to the general admissible restrictions and suspensions applicable to all rights enshrined in the ACHR, article 21 allows states parties to constrain indigenous people's exercise of their right to use and enjoy their traditional lands. Thus, as it is

---

members in light of the ADRIP's prohibition to apply its provisions in a way that constraints the rights already acquired by this group. See, ADRIP (n 285) arts VII para 1 and XL, respectively.

[292]See ILO Convention 169 (n 64, ch 1) art 1 para 1, lit. b. The alternative objective criterion laid down in the ILO Convention 169 qualifies as indigenous those tribal groups in independent countries who differ from other social groups with respect to their social, economic, and cultural conditions, and to their own status regulated by their customs or laws. See ILO Convention 169 (n 64, ch 1) art 1 para 1, lit. a.

[293]See ILO Convention 169 (n 64, ch 1) art 1 para 2; ADRIP (n 285) art I para 2.

[294]The ILO Convention 169 uses this definition of lands in connection to indigenous people's right to natural resources pertaining to their lands and to be protected against removal from the lands traditionally occupied by them. See ILO Convention 169 (n 64, ch 1) art 13 para 2.

[295]See ILO Convention 169 (n 64, ch 1) art 14; UNDRIP (n 284) art 26 para 2; ADRIP (n 285) art XXV para 3.

[296]See ILO Convention 169 (n 64, ch 1) art 15 para 1; UNDRIP (n 284) art 26 para 1; ADRIP (n 285) art XXV para 2.

[297]See ILO Convention 169 (n 64, ch 1) art 16 para 1; UNDRIP (n 284) art 10. In contrast, the ADRIP remains silent concerning the protection of indigenous people against displacement.

the case in other regional human rights treaties,[298] the ACHR further specifies under which legal conditions and requirements states parties may subordinate the exercise of these communities' right to use and enjoy property and limit its enjoyment, respectively. As to the conditions, the ACHR stipulates that host states' laws may subordinate the use and enjoyment that indigenous people have over their property, only in favour of the interest of society.[299] With respect to the requirements, the ACHR allows states' deprivation of indigenous people's exercise of the right to use and enjoy property in cases and forms established by law,[300] upon payment of just compensation and on the grounds of public utility and social interest.[301] In similar vein to the ACHR, international instruments protecting indigenous people's rights also anticipate states' deprivation of some land rights by defining the conditions under which states are entitled to exercise this sovereign power. Consultation of indigenous communities and exceptionally the obtainment of their free, prior and informed consent (FPIC) have been the usual requirements that states shall meet to limit communities' enjoyment of land rights. These external benchmarks have served as a reference point for the application of the limitations of indigenous people's enjoyment of their right to use and enjoy property.

Unlike the ADRIP, states' consultation of indigenous people about any legislative and administrative measures likely to affect them constitutes one of the most important standards of general application under the ILO Convention 169 and the UNDRIP.[302] To conduct this process, states are compelled to undertake it in good faith, by resorting to appropriate procedures and through representative institutions,[303] and with the intention to obtain this group's agreement or consent to the measures concerned.[304] States' consultation of indigenous people is required whenever the alienation or transmission of indigenous land rights are at stake,[305] such as when states retain ownership of mineral resources pertaining to indigenous groups' lands,[306] and decide or allow private actors to undertake exploration and/or

---

[298]The African Charter on Human and People's rights guarantees the right to property in general terms and enable restrictions to this right for public need or community's interest in accordance with domestic laws. See African Charter on Human and Peoples' Rights (signed 27 June 1981, entered into force 21 October 1986) OAU Doc. CAB/LEG/67/3 rev. 5, (1982) 21 ILM 58 art 14.

[299]ACHR (n 11, ch 1) art 21 para 1.

[300]ACHR (n 11, ch 1) art 21 para 2.

[301]Ibidem.

[302]The ADRIP certainly attaches great importance to states' consultation of indigenous groups about legislative and administrative measures likely to affect them, but only as the corresponding obligation deriving from their right to fully participate in decision-making ADRIP (n 285) art XXIII para 2.

[303]See ILO Convention 169 (n 64, ch 1) art 6 para 1 lit. a; UNDRIP (n 284) art 19.

[304]See ILO Convention 169 (n 64, ch 1) art 6 para 2; UNDRIP (n 284) art 19.

[305]See ILO Convention 169 (n 64, ch 1) art 17 para 2.

[306]See ILO Convention 169 (n 64, ch 1) art 15 para 2. Another obligation that states shall meet is enabling indigenous groups to participate in benefit-sharing, or providing fair compensation to those concerned. See ILO Convention 169 (n 64, ch 1) art 15 para 2.

extraction activities.[307] Under the UNDRIP and ADRIP, indigenous people's consultation shall aim at obtaining their free, prior and informed consent (FPIC).[308] Finally, another entitlement granted to indigenous people is to not be forcibly removed from their lands.[309]

Although the adoption of ADRIP has been upheld as a normative source for the interpretation of the ADRDM and the ACHR in relation to indigenous people,[310] indigenous people's entitlements under the ILO Convention 169 and the UNDRIP have informed, for the most part, Inter-American bodies' material and personal protection of indigenous people's right to use and enjoy their land rights under article 21 of the ACHR, as well as the permissible limitations upon their enjoyment. Both universal instruments are mutually reinforcing notwithstanding their differences concerning the protection of land rights.[311] Article 29 of the ACHR, a treaty provision fostering an interpretation of article 21 in a manner most advantageous to

---

[307] See ILO Convention 169 (n 64, ch 1) art 15 para 2. The same obligation arises for states under the UNDRIP and the ADRIP, in cases where these types of economic activities limit indigenous people's right to determine and develop strategies for the development or use of their lands and resources. UNDRIP (n 284) art 32 paras 1 and 2; ADRIP (n 285) art XXIX paras 1 and 4. In addition to consultation, states also have the obligation to provide effective remedies to mitigate the impacts of these economic activities over their development strategies.

[308] See, UNDRIP (n 284) art 32 para 3; ADRIP (n 285) art XXIX para 5.

[309] See ILO Convention 169 (n 64, ch 1) art 16 para 2; UNDRIP (n 284) art 10. Despite the above-mentioned contention, the ILO Convention 169 is certainly more deferent to states' regulatory discretion than the UNDRIP in the deprivation of this land right. States parties are allowed to relocate the groups concerned, if their FPIC is not available, in accordance with the legal procedure established in domestic laws and regulations, and to provide either lands of similar quality and legal status or payment of compensation, if indigenous groups are prevented from returning to the lands traditionally occupied by them. See ILO Convention 169 (n 64, ch 1) arts 16 paras 2 and 4. In contrast, FPIC and compensation are mandatory conditions for states' relocation of indigenous people. UNDRIP (n 284) art 10.

[310] IACommHR, 'The IACHR celebrates the adoption of the American Declaration on the Rights of Indigenous Peoples' (Washington, 22 June 2016) http://www.oas.org/en/iachr/media_center/PReleases/2016/082.asp accessed 10 December 2020.

[311] ILO, Equality Team of the International Labour Standards Department, ILO, *ILO standards and the UN Declaration on the Rights of Indigenous Peoples Information note for ILO staff and partners.* Available at: https://view.officeapps.live.com/op/view.aspx?src=http%3A%2F%2Fpro169.org%2Fres%2Fmaterials%2Fen%2Fconvention169%2FInformation%2520Note%2520on%2520ILO%2520standards%2520and%2520UNDRIP.doc. Accessed 10 December 2020. It has been argued that both instruments are the result of a long 'process of 'juridification' underpinned by international treaties and institutions, which have gradually upheld the claims, this specific social group distinctively made as indigenous people These international instruments have ranged from international declarations and treaties governing specifically issues on indigenous peoples, to treaties among States addressing these issues through special provisions, and policy standards formulated by international organizations. For an overview, see Anaya (2004). According to Kingsbury, there are five legal frames invoked by indigenous peoples (as a distinctive group) to bring their claims in international law. They constitute claims made distinctively as indigenous peoples; human rights and non-discrimination claims, historic sovereignty claims; self-determination claims, and claims as a minority or a member of a minority. In detail see Kingsbury (2001).

indigenous people, has certainly enabled the integration and adaptation of these external standards to review the regulatory conduct of states in preventing the real and imminent risks that foreign investment activities may pose upon indigenous people's enjoyment of land rights. Section 3.2.2.2 below explains in detail what consists states' duty to regulate in furtherance of indigenous people's land rights, and whether there is a remaining duty to regulate for states with respect to foreign investment activities, even though granting investors concessions represents in itself an admissible limitation of indigenous groups' enjoyment of these rights.

#### 3.2.2.1.2   Customary International Law

*State Practice*

Increasingly, Latin American countries have codified some of the rights that indigenous people distinctively assert as such within their Constitutions, domestic laws or Executive decrees, in addition to domestic courts' legal recognition. On the one hand, indigenous communities' right to enjoy communal property features as one of the rights commonly proclaimed in these legal instruments in terms of their traditional lands,[312] or their right to conserve inalienable property of communal lands.[313] To a lesser extent, indigenous communities are also entitled to enjoyment of the natural resources available in their traditional lands and territories.[314] On the other hand, widespread recognition can be observed with regard to indigenous people's right to consultation on issues that may affect them, even though divergence exits about the issues subject to consultation, and the mandatory nature of this process.

Some Latin American countries guarantee constitutional protection to indigenous people's right to consultation in general terms,[315] and regulate in detail the conduct of consultation process through domestic laws or executive decrees.[316] In some countries, legislative and administrative measures that may potentially affect indigenous groups are the object of consultation,[317] what, in some cases, are more clearly defined by limiting indigenous people's consultation over the formulation of

---

[312]Constitution of the Republic of Nicaragua (1987, as of September 2010), art 89; Constitution of Paraguay (1992) art 64. *Eben Ezer Indigenous Community v/Province of Salta—Ministry of Labour and Production*, Supreme Court of Justice of the (Argentina) Nation, Amparo, (30 September 2008), C. 2124. XLI, p. 4.

[313]Constitution of the Republic of Ecuador (2008) art 84 lit. 2.

[314]Constitution of the Republic of Nicaragua (1987, as of September 2010), art 180.

[315]See Constitution of the Plurinational State of Bolivia (2009), art 30 (II, numeral 15.

[316]See 3058 Law (2005) (Bolivia) and Executive Decree No. 29033 (2007) Bolivia). See also Decree No. 4633 (2011) (Colombia); Decree No. 1220 (2005) (Colombia); Decree Law No. 200 (2003) (Colombia).

[317]Mexican Constitution, Title I, ch 1, art 2 (b (ix; Indigenous Law No. 19253 (1993) (Chile) art 34; Ley No. 29785 del Derecho a la Consulta Previa a los Pueblos Indigenas y Originarios, Reconocido en el Convenio 169 de la Organizacion Internacional del Trabajo (OIT) (2011) (Peru) art 2; See Nequen Superior Court of Justice, TSJN, Mapuche Catalan Commnity and Neuquina Indigenous

national development plans with the purpose of integrating their special needs,[318] or programs and projects that are likely to affect them.[319]

In connection with the exploitation activities of natural resources pertaining to their traditional lands and territories, the codification of indigenous people's right to consultation is relatively minor.[320] For instance, indigenous people's consultation is compulsory in Bolivia and Venezuela if the state pursues the exploitation of non-renewable natural resources belonging to their traditional territories,[321] whereas, in Ecuador, it is exclusively limited to their observations and their involvement in decision-making on bidding process of exploration and exploitation of oil and gas.[322] For the most part, the major recognition of this indigenous people's entitlement has taken place at the adjudicative level when alluding to the purpose it fulfils with respect to indigenous communities. Some courts have argued that indigenous people's consultation leads to the sustainable use and exploitation of natural resources pertaining to their traditional lands;[323] others, as an instrument to avert impairments upon these groups,[324] or to reconcile their needs of preserving their own way of life with economic measures informed by market economy policies by means of dialogue.[325]

The description provided above exhibits that states' protection of indigenous people's land rights is neither widespread among states, nor consistent regarding the legal entitlements that the states under review endorse as land rights. Notwithstand-

ing the former, consultation of indigenous people, broadly speaking, constitutes a well-established right recognised in favour of this group and thus a states' obligation codified by laws and adjudicated by domestic courts, in those cases where states'

---

Confederation v Province of Neuquen, Action on Unconstitutionality (25 October 2010) (Argentina).

[318] See Constitution of the United Mexican States (2010, as of September 2017) Title I, ch 1, art 2 (b (ix.

[319] See 2011 Law on the right to prior consultation of indigenous and tribal peoples (Peru) art 2.

[320] The participation of indigenous communities' representatives is compulsory in cases involving decision-making process concerning natural resources' exploitation in their territories. See Constitution of Colombia (1991, as last amended on 2005) art 330.

[321] See Constitution of the Plurinational State of Bolivia (2009), art 30 (II, numeral 15; Bolivarian Republic of Venezuela (1999), art 120 and 2005 Organic Law on Indigenous Peoples Communities (Venezuela) art 11.

[322] Decreto No. 1247 que dicta el Reglamento para la Ejecucion de la Consulta Previa Libre e Informada en los Procesos de Licitacion y Asignacion de Areas y Bloques Hidrocarburiferos (Ecuador) (adopted 19 Julio 2012), Registro Oficial No. 759 (Separata) (Decreto No. 1247) arts 1 and 3.

[323] Constitutional Court of Bolivia, Judgement 0045/2006 (2 June 2006) para II.5.3.

[324] See Peruvian Constitutional Court, Case No. 0022-2009-PI/TC, paras 23 and 41.

[325] Constitutional Court of Colombia, Judgement C-169/01, para 5.1.

measures are likely to affect them. Even though states considerably limit the scope of this consultation process when the exploration and/or exploitation of natural resources pertaining to their traditional lands is at stake, the explicit requirement of consultation within the domestic legal orders of some states suggest that there is some consistent and uniform state practice regarding the compulsory nature of consultation.

*Opinio Juris*

The UNDRIP has been the only UNGA resolution that articulates in detail a set of rights in benefit of indigenous people. Certainly, the content and conditions involving its endorsement may certainly reveal whether the community of states regard indigenous people's land rights as a legally binding norm. The content and conditions involving the adoption of the UNDRIP are briefly discussed below.

The UNDRIP underscores the general importance of indigenous people's consultation about the laws and administrative measures likely to affect them,[326] while delineating indigenous people's land rights and the corresponding states' obligations. Indigenous people have a general right to lands, territories and resources that they have traditionally owned, occupied or otherwise used,[327] and right of ownership, use, development or control land, territories and resources possessed on the grounds of traditional ownership, occupation or use.[328] The corresponding states' obligations arising from these rights comprise affording legal recognition and protection to these lands, territories and resources, including to conduct such recognition with due deference to indigenous customs, traditions and land tenure systems.[329]

Another states' obligation under the UNDRIP is the implementation and establishment of a fair, independent, impartial and open process that enables the recognition and adjudication to the above-mentioned rights.[330] Moreover, states are mandated to protect indigenous groups against forcible removal from their lands and territories,[331] by obtaining their FPIC in case of relocation,[332] and reaching an agreement on just and fair compensation.[333] Furthermore, the UNDRIP proclaims a right to determine and develop strategies for the development or use of their lands

---

[326]However, while indigenous people's agreement or consent are the objectives of consultation under the ILO Convention 169, the purpose of consultation within the UNDRIP is only states' obtainment of free, prior, and informed consent. See UNDRIP (n 284) art 19.

[327]UNDRIP (n 284) art 26 para 1.

[328]UNDRIP (n 284) art 26 para 2.

[329]UNDRIP (n 284) art 26 para 3.

[330]UNDRIP (n 284) art 27.

[331]UNDRIP (n 284) art 10.

[332]UNDRIP (n 284) art 10.

[333]Ibidem.

and resources,[334] while the corresponding states' obligation include obtaining FPIC before any exploration or exploitation of extractive activities affecting their lands and resources[335] and providing effective remedies and appropriate measures to address negative impacts of these economic activities.[336] The other indigenous communities' right is a general right to be redressed,[337] by means of restitution, or fair and equitable compensation in favour of those communities for the confiscation, taking, use or damage of the lands, territories or natural resources traditionally owned, occupied or used by them.[338]

As to the conditions involving the adoption of the UNDRIP, one can identify that 144 UN member states endorsed this declaration, a number significantly higher than the number of UN member states adhering to the UNGA resolution 64/292 concerning the protection of the right to water.[339] This outcome suggests that a two-third majority of UN member states accept in principle to observe consultation of indigenous people and their respective rights to lands and territories as a normative standard in their relationship with indigenous groups, despite the fact that its adoption encountered 4 negative votes,[340] and 11 abstentions of UN member states.[341] However, all states voting against the UNDRIP and few abstaining from giving a vote reversed their position and finally endorsed the political commitments achieved in the UNDRIP in subsequent conferences.[342]

The HRC has also contributed to the promotion of the discussion about indigenous people's rights by addressing the hurdles that these groups face in having full and effective protection by means of Special Rapporteurs. The predecessor of the HRC, the United Nations Commission on Human Rights (UNHRC), began with this task by appointing the first Special Rapporteur on the situation of human rights and fundamental freedoms of indigenous people in 2001,[343] and renewing its initial

---

[334]UNDRIP (n 284) art 32 para 1.

[335]UNDRIP (n 284) art 32 para 2.

[336]UNDRIP (n 284) art 32 para 3.

[337]UNDRIP (n 284) art 28 para 1.

[338]Ibidem.

[339]See Sect. 3.1.2.1.2.

[340]Australia, Canada, New Zealand, and the United States favoured against the UNDRIP. See, UN, Department of Economic and Social Affairs, Indigenous People, Historical Overview. Available at: https://www.un.org/development/desa/indigenouspeoples/declaration-on-the-rights-of-indigenous-peoples/historical-overview.html. Accessed 10 December 2020.

[341]Azerbaijan, Bangladesh, Bhutan, Burundi, Colombia, Georgia, Kenya, Nigeria, Russian Federation, Samoa and Ukraine. Ibidem.

[342]UNGA, 'Outcome document of the high-level plenary meeting of the General Assembly known as the World Conference on Indigenous Peoples' (2014) UN Doc. A/RES/69/2 paras 3 and 9.

[343]Through this resolution, Rodolfo Stavenhagen was appointed as Special Rapporteur. See UNHRC, 'Human rights and indigenous issues' (2001) UN Doc. E/CN.4/RES/2001/57 para 1.

mandate in 2007.[344] With the adoption of the UNDRIP, the HRC appointed other two independent experts for subsequent periods.[345]

As part of their mandate, the work of these independent experts have not restricted itself to report on the human rights situation of indigenous people in a particular country. They also promote best practice conducive to the implementation of the UNDRIP, which thus implies working towards the materialization of indigenous people to traditional lands and territories within UN member states' territory. Despite their importance, however, these HRC's efforts cannot be considered as a representative reference of what states believe to be legally mandatory in their relationship with indigenous people's right to traditional lands and territories since the composition of this UN organ entrusting these Independent Experts only represent a minority of UN member states.

In principle, one may conclude that there is a major consensus among states regarding the necessity to protect indigenous people's land rights, including their entitlement to be consulted against any measure that may affect their enjoyment. Recalling the above-mentioned findings of the discussion regarding state practice in indigenous people's rights, one may contend that there might be space for the formation of a customary rule on states' consultation of indigenous people in the near future, if domestic laws and courts upholding this right become widespread. Already, the UNDRIP provides a concrete basis for *opinio juris* that, if coupled with a widespread and consistent state practice, may unequivocally provide the basis for a customary international norm on consultation. Yet, whether this hypothetical customary rule on consultation assigns a duty to regulate upon recipient states of foreign investment will depend on the scope of this obligation, which, however, for the time being, considerably varies in scope.

### 3.2.2.2  Scope of Application

The normative basis of states' duty to regulate in favour of indigenous people's right to traditional lands and territories is the right to property laid down in the ACHR, under which states parties shall ensure *everyone* has the free and full exercise of the right to use and enjoy his or her property.[346] When indigenous people are those right-holders allegedly affected by states' failure to meet this obligation, the

---

[344]HRC, 'Human rights and indigenous peoples: mandate of the Special Rapporteur on the situation of human rights and fundamental freedoms of indigenous people' (2007) UN Doc. A/HRC/RES/6/12 para 1.

[345]HRC, 'Human rights and indigenous peoples: mandate of the Special Rapporteur on the rights of indigenous peoples' (2010) UN Doc. A/HRC/RES/15/14; 'Human rights and indigenous peoples: mandate of the Special Rapporteur on the rights of indigenous peoples' (2013) UN Doc. A/HRC/RES/24/9; 'Human rights and indigenous peoples: mandate of the Special Rapporteur on the rights of indigenous peoples' (2016) UN Doc. A/HRC/RES/33/12.

[346]ACHR (n 11, ch 1) arts 2 and 21.

IACoHR has expanded the personal scope of application of the ACHR, even though only *persons* are entitled to claim the legal protection under the Convention.[347]

The close relationship that indigenous people have with their traditional lands and territories as the basis of their culture, spiritual practice and economic survival has been the main ground to justify the expansion of the personal scope of application of the ACHR.[348] In conformity with the ILO Convention 169[349] and the UNDRIP,[350] the Court has thus understood that concepts such as property and possession concerning indigenous people's relation with lands and territories '[are] not centred on an individual, but rather on the group and its community'.[351] The IACommHR has also referred to this indigenous people's right in similar terms by applying the ILO Convention 169 and corresponding soft-law instruments in some of its thematic reports,[352] and the IACoHR usually applied standards laid down in these instruments to protect effectively ACHR's rights of this social group, even when state concerned is not a state party.[353]

The right to use and enjoy property has been understood as *any* right that may derive from the right-holder's patrimony and the term 'property' in this context has been understood as including all movables and immovable, corporal and incorporeal elements and any other intangible object capable of having cultural value.[354] In this context, the Inter-American human rights system accords legal protection to indigenous people's right to use and enjoy lands and territories in accordance with their

---

[347] ACHR (n 11, ch 1) art 2 para 1. Under the ACHR, every human being is considered person. ACHR (n 11, ch 1) art 2 para 2.

[348] *Awas Tingni Community v Nicaragua* (n 16, ch 1) para 148. For the Court, a collective conception of the right to property with respect of indigenous peoples is essential since their relationship with traditional lands and territories is not merely a matter of possession and production, but also a material and spiritual element that they are entitled to fully enjoy, inclusive for the purpose of preserving their cultural heritage and transmit it to future generations. *Awas Tingni Community v Nicaragua* (n 16, ch 1) para 149.

[349] *Yakye Axa v Paraguay* (n 15, ch 1) paras 127 and 130.

[350] *Saramaka v Suriname* (n 18, ch 1) paras 129–131.

[351] *Sawhoyamaxa v Paraguay* (n 15, ch 1) para 120. This, nevertheless, has proceeded without submitting its protection to stricter criteria as it is the case when shareholders of companies are the right-holders allegedly affected by State's actions. For a detailed comparison, see Gonza (2019), pp. 626–629.

[352] In light of IACommHR's mandate to 'promote respect for and defence of human rights', the Commission has the power to formulate studies or reports it considers necessary for discharging its task. ACHR (n 11, ch 1) art 41 lit. c. In promoting and respect of indigenous peoples' rights, see IACommHR, Indigenous People and Extractive Industries (n 223) paras 152 and 156. Also, IACommHR, 'Indigenous and Tribal People's Rights over their Ancestral Lands and Natural Resources. Norms and Jurisprudence of the Inter-American Human Rights System' OEA/Ser.L/V/II. Doc. 56/09 (30 December 2009) (Indigenous People, Inter-American Jurisprudence) para 4.

[353] *Saramaka v Suriname* (n 18, ch 1) para 93. The proactive interpretative approach of the IACoHR, however, has not come without criticism. See Ruiz-Chiriboga (2013). In the context human rights violations' reparations, see Attanasio (2016).

[354] *Awas Tingni Community v Nicaragua* (n 16, ch 1) para 144.

customs, traditions and land tenure system,[355] but seems more restrictive to provide the same protection to the use and enjoyment of natural resources pertaining thereto.[356] Accordingly, states parties to the ACHR shall regulate foreign investors' activities if they interfere with indigenous people's right to enjoy possession of their traditional lands.

However, it is noteworthy to recall that the above-mentioned right is not absolute since states parties are entitled to restrict it for reasons of society's interest or public utility.[357] To this end, states parties are generally called to prove that its measures are legal, necessary and proportional with a 'legitimate objective in a democratic society'.[358] But, if a state aims at limiting collective property of indigenous people, it shall ensure, in addition, that these restrictions do not deny their survival.[359] To this end, 'survival' has been understood as more than merely physical survival, and requires that indigenous communities may continue living their traditional way of life, and that their distinct cultural identity, social structure, economic system, customs, beliefs and traditions are respected, guaranteed and protected.[360] Therefore, the second situation where states parties to the ACHR shall discharge their duty to regulate foreign investors' exploration and exploitation activities near their traditional lands and territories is when the activities may pose imminent threats upon the survival of indigenous people in a particular case.[361]

The following section discusses which preventive measures states need to adopt to protect these entitlements to assess how the exercise of their duty to regulate in IIL should be understood. They also intend to shed light on whether Latin American countries do exercise their duty to regulate foreign investment activities in favour of indigenous people's survival by means of regulatory measures in a concrete case, and by legislative or other policy instruments aiming at inducing foreign investor's compliance with the ACHR.

---

[355]See *Xákmok Kásek v Paraguay* (n 15, ch 1) para 87; *Saramaka v Surinam* (n 18, ch 1) para 88; *Sawhoyama v Paraguay* (n 15, ch 1) para 118; *Yakye Axa v Paraguay* (n 15, ch 1) para 137.

[356]See Gonza (2019), p. 524.

[357]ACHR (n 11, ch 1) art 21 paras 1 and 2.

[358]*Saramaka v Suriname* (n 18, ch 1) para 127; *Yakye Axa v Paraguay* (n 15, ch 1) para 144.

[359]*Saramaka v Suriname* (n 18, ch 1) para 128.

[360]*Saramaka v Suriname* (n 18, ch 1) para 121.

[361]*Saramaka v Suriname* (n 18, ch 1) para 128. According to the IACoHR, 'survival as a peoples' implies more than merely physical survival and requires 'that they may continue living their traditional way of life, and that their distinct cultural identity, social structure, economic system, customs, beliefs and traditions are respected, guaranteed and protected. Ibidem, para 121.

### 3.2.2.2.1 In the Context of Foreign Property Rights' Interference with Indigenous People's Rights to Possess Traditional Lands and Territories

According to the IACoHR, indigenous people have been those groups stemming from pre-colonial groups, or those having an 'all-encompassing relationship' to their lands and whose conception of ownership is centred on the community as a whole, even though they do not have strong ties with pre-colonial communities.[362]

To protect indigenous people's right to possess their traditional land and territories, states parties to the ACHR shall meet the following basic obligations. They shall recognise that indigenous people have the right to claim the official recognition of their communal property based on their traditional possession;[363] provide official titles over their territories to guarantee the use and enjoyment upon their traditional lands;[364] provide for a clear land demarcation;[365] and land restitution when corresponding.[366]

State practice suggests that some Latin American countries formally recognise indigenous people's right to enjoy communal property in domestic laws.[367] This is nevertheless a states' measure of general character that show that specific actions are required to grant land titles to specific indigenous groups and to demarcate their corresponding lands. Demarcation of traditional lands is vital to provide legal titles of ownership. However, the cases that have appeared before the IACoHR suggest that states usually fail to ensure the enjoyment of this land right to indigenous people.[368]

One specific action through which states would discharge their duty to regulate foreign investment activities include restitution of traditional lands to indigenous people if foreign investors have legal ownership over these lands by means of the expropriation of foreign property. From the perspective of the IIL regime, this sovereign right of the state must be discharged in accordance with the lawfulness conditions laid down in IIAs.[369] However, expropriation of foreign property seems

---

[362]To illustrate, see *Case of the Moiwana Community v Suriname* (Preliminary Objections, Merits, Reparations and Costs) Judgement, IACoHR Series C No. 124 (15 June 2005) para 133.

[363]*Xákmok Kásek v Paraguay* (n 15, ch 1) para 109; *Sawhoyamaxa v Paraguay* (n 15, ch 1) para 128; *Awas Tingni Community v Nicaragua* (n 16, ch 1) para 151.

[364]*Xákmok Kásek v Paraguay* (n 15, ch 1) para 109; *Saramaka v Surinam* (n 18, ch 1) para 115; *Awas Tingni Community v Nicaragua* (n 16, ch 1) para 153.

[365]*Yakye Axa v Paraguay* (n 15, ch 1) para 143.

[366]*Xákmok Kásek v Paraguay* (n 15, ch 1) para 284.

[367]See state practice, Sect. 3.2.2.1.2.

[368]The last case brought on this ground was the Lhaka Honhat case under which the IACoHR recognised for the first time the justiciability of ESC rights, including a right to a healthy environment, as autonomous rights to indigenous people. *Case of the Indigenous Communities of the Lhaka Honhat (Our Land) Association v Argentina*, Judgment (6 February 2020) (*Lhaka Honhat v Argentina*).

[369]See Sect. 2.3.1.1.1, ch 2.

to remain the last resort for the host states to prevent foreign investors' interference with indigenous people's right to possess traditional lands as highlighted in the *Sawhoyamaxa v Paraguay* case.[370] Certainly, this states' stance has been indirectly underpinned by the IACoHR's approach towards the compliance of states with final judgements that generally provide for the restitution of lands to indigenous people with alternative lands, if objective and reasoned grounds are provided.[371]

### 3.2.2.2.2    In Cases Where Natural Resources' Exploration and Exploitation Activities May Pose a Real and Imminent Risk upon Indigenous People's Survival

States parties to the ACHR will not compromise indigenous people's survival by their limitations of their right to use and enjoy traditional lands and territories, if they conduct a prior, free, and informed consultation process,[372] and an environmental and social impact assessment (ESIA) regarding the activities that may interfere with the survival of these communities,[373] informed by the existing international instruments designed to protect indigenous people.[374] Accordingly, both instruments allow states to discharge their duty to regulate foreign investment activities in this particular context.

Indigenous people's consultation embodies the general entitlement in case of limitations of their right to enjoy and use traditional lands,[375] whereas obtaining their consent is essential if 'large-scale' investment or development projects are the third party entities that may pose a real and imminent risk upon their survival.[376] Situations conducive to create such major threats upon their survival include their

---

[370] *Sawhoyamaxa v Paraguay* (n 15, ch 1).

[371] *Xákmok Kásek v Paraguay* (n 15, ch 1) para 286; *Sawhoyamaxa v Paraguay* (n 15, ch 1) para 212; *Yakye Axa v Paraguay* (n 15, ch 1) paras 144-154.

[372] In *Sarayaku v Ecuador*, the IACoHR levelled this requirement as 'free, prior and informed consent' (FPIC). However, the court recently seems to exercise more caution with the use of terminology when defining states' obligation. See, *Sarayaku v Ecuador* (n 17, ch 1) paras 159-164, 177 and *Lhaka Honhat v Argentina* (n 368) paras 327–327, respectively paras 326–327. In other cases, the IACoHR has contended that indigenous peoples' consultation does not only constitute a treaty-based obligation under international instruments, but also reflects a general principle of international law. *Sarayaku v Ecuador* (n 17, ch 1) para 164; *Comunidad Garífuna de Punta Piedra v Honduras* (n 18, ch 1) para 222; *Comunidad Garífuna Triunfo de la Cruz v Honduras* (n 19, ch 1) para 158.

[373] *Saramaka v Suriname* (n 18, ch 1) para 128.

[374] See Sect. 3.2.2.1.1.

[375] *Saramaka v Suriname* (n 18, ch 1) para 134. IACommHR, Indigenous People, Inter-American Jurisprudence (n 352) para 273.

[376] *Saramaka v Suriname* (n 18, ch 1) para 134. The Commission has strongly endorsed this view in its thematic reports. To illustrate, IACommHR, Indigenous People and Extractive Industries (n 223) paras 183–193.

displacement from their traditional lands and territories,[377] or the storage or disposal of hazardous materials.[378]

To discharge their duty to regulate by means of indigenous people's consultation, this process shall be free, prior, and informed about the foreign investment activities planned in their traditional lands and territories. First, indigenous people's consultation shall be free. Consultation of indigenous people shall be adequate, which would imply observing their traditional customs, in particular, ensuring that those delegated observe their social organisation in case of delegation,[379] as well as being made in good faith,[380] with the objective to reach an agreement or their consent on the planned development project.[381] The criterion of good faith requires in particular ensuring that there is no type of coercion against indigenous communities, nor bribery of indigenous leaders to obtain their agreement or consent. Second, states parties to the ACHR are mandated to conduct FPICs and ESIAs prior the commencement of development project's exploration phase,[382] or at the earliest possible period of the execution of development projects.[383] Complying with this temporal requirement thus requires for states parties, as recipient countries of private foreign investment, to carry out consultation with indigenous people regarding a development project that win a bidding process,[384] or prior to granting a mining concession for exploration activities of natural resources.[385] Additionally, states parties are to conduct consultation process by informing indigenous people about the real and imminent threats that proposed investment projects may pose upon their survival, including information about the environmental and health risks inherent to these activities. This latter aspect of consultations process in closely related to ESIAs. These technical studies complement the consultation process because they enhance these communities to be aware of the potential risks that development projects may pose upon their survival.[386]

Similarly to consultation process, ESIAs should apply prior to the operation development projects[387] and serve as conducive instrument to ensure indigenous

---

[377]IACommHR, Indigenous People, Inter-American Jurisprudence (n 352) para 334 numeral 1.

[378]IACommHR, Indigenous People, Inter-American Jurisprudence (n 352) para 334, numeral 2.

[379]*Saramaka v Suriname* (n 18, ch 1) para 133.

[380]Discharging State's duty to regulate in favour of indigenous communities' survival requires conducting a consultation process in good faith demands adopting adequate and accessible means to provide indigenous peoples with relevant information. *Saramaka v Suriname* (n 18, ch 1) para 133.

[381]*Sarayaku v Ecuador* (n 17, ch 1) para 185.

[382]See *Sarayaku v Ecuador* (n 17, ch 1) paras 168-176. In fact, States parties to the ACHR shall induce compliance with this requirement immediately after the design of investment or development plans, or once issued the license for exploration activities pursuant to article 2 of the ACHR. *Kaliña and Lokono Peoples v Suriname* (n 18, ch 1) para 211.

[383]*Comunidad Garifuna de Punta Piedra v Honduras* (n 18, ch 1) paras 216–221.

[384]*Sarayaku v Ecuador* (n 17, ch 1) paras 165–176.

[385]*Kaliña and Lokono Peoples v Suriname* (n 18, ch 1) para 200; *Comunidad Garifuna de Punta Piedra v Honduras* (n 18, ch 1) para 222.

[386]*Sarayaku v Ecuador* (n 17, ch 1) para 180–210.

[387]See *Sarayaku v Ecuador* (n 17, ch 1) para 206.

people's participation in their undertaking.[388] Participation requires involving indigenous people's members in all decisions affecting their traditional land and territories, taking into consideration their special relationship with their lands and natural resources.[389] This implies involving indigenous people 'in the process of design, implementation and evaluation of development projects carried out in their traditional lands and territories'.[390]

Although states parties to the ACHR are the ones mainly responsible in averting imminent and real threats upon indigenous people's survival and therefore in protecting this core right by means of FPIC and ESIAs,[391] delegation of FPIC and ESIAs to third parties is not forbidden provided that they exercise strict control and monitoring over their undertaking.[392] This presupposes for states parties to ensure that third parties meet the normative requirements that they themselves are called to comply with in the undertaking of FPIC and ESIAs.[393]

Against this background, if one assesses the existing state practice of Latin American countries regarding indigenous people's consultation, one may conclude that Latin American countries exceptionally recognise this right with respect to development projects, and if so, they do that very broadly. Taking Ecuador as an example, the executive enacted a decree laying down the requirements governing the consultation process, only after Ecuador was held responsible for violations of Sarayaku communities' right to property under the ACHR.[394] This consultation process delineates different participation mechanisms,[395] which are to be implemented *prior* to the assignment plans or programs of concession blocks or areas.[396] Other states instead prevail ruling consultation process by means of regulatory agencies within investment codes,[397] or broadly provide in their mining laws that their application shall be in accordance with the ILO Convention No. 169.[398] Although these legal measures of general character may give a higher degree of regulatory manoeuvre to host states in aligning investor's activities with the consultation standard during the bidding process of the exploration phase, they remain too broad so as to guarantee that consultation process are made prior the operation of economic activities.

---

[388] *Sarayaku v Ecuador* (n 17, ch 1) para 207.

[389] IACommHR, Indigenous People, Inter-American Jurisprudence (n 352) para 273.

[390] IACommHR, Indigenous People, Inter-American Jurisprudence (n 352) paras 289–290.

[391] *Sarayaku v Ecuador* (n 17, ch 1) paras 187, 189, 203,205, 207.

[392] Ibidem.

[393] Ibidem.

[394] Decreto No. 1247 (n 322).

[395] Decreto No. 1247 (n 322) art 13.

[396] Decreto No. 1247 (n 322) art 4.

[397] Republica Bolivariana de Venezuela, Ley Constitucional de Inversion Extranjera Productiva (2017) art 35 para 4.

[398] *South American Silver v Bolivia* (n 3, ch 1) para 95, citing *Mining Law 1777* (17 March 1997) art 15.

Moreover, it is noteworthy to mention that delegation of indigenous people's consultation and ESIAs to foreign investors is the general rule in the context of exploration and exploitation activities of natural resources.[399] Hence, the host state claiming compliance with its duty to regulate or investor's misconduct when undertaking these tasks in ISDS shall show that it has clearly ensured that the investor consulted these communities without any type of coercion, prior the commencement of its activities and appropriately informed them about the impact of its activities by means of ESIAs. The practice of Latin American countries may likely suggest that this is taking place, albeit not very consistent with Inter-American standards.

Some Latin American countries request private foreign investors to commit in written form that they will respect the uses and traditions of indigenous people inhabiting in the areas directly affected by exploitation activities.[400] Others demand to record the opinions and suggestions of those inhabiting in these areas in public instruments as a requirement of the bidding process,[401] or generally condition the concession of exploration or exploitation license to a holding of public meetings with the purpose of informing those potentially affected about direct or indirect environmental impact of the project concerned.[402] Although these measures constitute initial steps in the recognition of indigenous communities' particular needs, it remains highly doubtful whether they ensure that investors' consultations are made in good faith and its ESIA met the standards as described above-.[403]

Foreign investors undertake 'socialization' process of their development projects via workshops or agreements with the communities potentially affected,[404] or through public media.[405] Socialization, however, is not equivalent to consultation, nor to participation as required within ESIAs, since the objective of these activities seem to be communicating, rather than consulting indigenous people about their economic activities. Evidence suggests that there is a potential correlation between states' omission to guarantee participatory rights to indigenous people through

---

[399]Concerning ESIAs, see *Sarayaku v Ecuador* (n 17, ch 1) para 68 citing *Partnership contract for the exploration of hydrocarbons and exploitation of crude oil in in Block No. 23 of the Amazonian region, between the State Oil Company Ecuador (PETROECUADOR) and the Compania General de Combustibles S.A.*, Clause 5.1.21.6. *Bear creek mining v Peru* (n 3, ch 1) paras 142 and 167.

[400]*Bear creek mining v Peru* (n 3, ch 1) para 105, referring to different instruments containing such commitments in footnote 105.

[401]*Sarayaku v Ecuador* (n 17, ch 1) para 77 citing *Regulations to substitute the Environmental Regulations for Hydrocarbon Operations*, Executive Decree 1215, Official Record 265 (13 February 2001) art 9.

[402]*Sarayaku v Ecuador* (n 17, ch 1) para 76 citing *Promotion of Investment and Citizen Participation Act*, Decree Law 2000-1, Registration number 144 (18 August 2000), footnote 85.

[403]*Sarayaku v Ecuador* (n 17, ch 1) para 205; *Saramaka v Suriname* (n 18, ch 1) para 130.

[404]*Bear Creek v Peru* (n 3, ch 1) para 162 citing *Acta de Primer Taller Participativo*, Linea de Transmision, Huacullani, (10 Septiembre 2010) and *Acta de Primer Taller Participativo*, Linea de Transmision, Pomata (10 Septiembre 2010) in footnote 103. For further examples of informal workshops with different communities, see Ibid paras 163 and 166. See also *Sarayaku v Ecuador* (n 17, ch 1) para 188.

[405]*Bear Creek v Peru* (n 3, ch 1) paras 168–169.

consultation and the radicalization of social protest against foreign development projects.[406]

Accordingly, in cases where foreign corporations socialize their development projects with the approval of the host state, reaching an agreement with indigenous people potentially affected by investor's economic activities, or even their consent is mostly impracticable because these communities are denied from the outset the opportunity to propose alternatives to an extractive model mainly based on natural resource extraction.[407] If states' agencies or Ministries' delegates responsible for the license's conferral attend such meetings and endorse them without objections, they would fail meeting their duty to regulate foreign investment activities.[408] A host state could challenge these socialization activities and thereby strengthen indigenous people's participation in cases where not all communities potentially affected are invited to attend these meetings.[409]

In this context, the radicalization of social protest due to lack of indigenous people's participation may encounter corporate attempts to quell them by recruitment of paramilitary groups. In such circumstances, a host state satisfies its duty to regulate in favour of indigenous people's survival, if it counteracts these corporate actions by all means available, including measures conducive to cease such threats by sanctioning corporations with the nationalization or termination of its exploration or exploitation concession.[410] Additionally, failure to take actions against corporate attempts of bribery of indigenous communities' leaders and of division among indigenous people's members,[411] is indeed contrary to the criterion of good faith that states parties shall ensure that corporations conduct comprehensive consultation process. Lastly, it is very unlikely that impartiality is the rule in relation to the implementation of ESIAs, if foreign companies entrust the conduct of an ESIA to an external technical entity selected by them,[412] or even worse, plan the undertaking of ESIAs by themselves.[413]

### 3.2.3   Interim Conclusion

Under the ACHR, states parties have three general obligations in relation to all rights codified therein. First is an obligation to abstain from taking any direct or indirect

---

[406]For study about this correlation in the mining sector see Jaskoski (2014) and Schilling-Vacaflor and Flemmer (2015).

[407]Altmann (2013).

[408]*Bear Creek v Peru* (n 3, ch 1) para 411.

[409]*Bear Creek v Peru* (n 3, ch 1) para 169. *Sarayaku v Ecuador* (n 17, ch 1) paras 67 and 122.

[410]*Bear Creek v Peru* (n 3, ch 1) para 84.

[411]*South American Silver v Bolivia* (n 3, ch 1) paras 81–82.

[412]*Sarayaku v Ecuador* (n 17, ch 1) para 69.

[413]*Bear Creek v Peru* (n 3, ch 1) para 162.

action conducive to breach ACHR rights. Second is an obligation to ensure free and full enjoyment of their traditional lands and territories, without discrimination of Convention's rights, which implies, on the contrary, to take any action conducive to prevent, investigate, prosecute and remedy breaches of the ACHR. This obligation requires the adoption of measures of general application such as the incorporation of the ACHR in domestic legal framework, and compliance with the following obligations of conduct: acting with due diligence to prevent third party' abuses of the rights codified in the ACHR; sanctioning those responsible for human rights violations, and providing effective remedies to victims.

Against this background, one may conclude that the obligation to act with due diligence is the normative basis of the duty to regulate private foreign investment activities for all states parties to the ACHR. To meet this obligation of conduct, and therefore to discharge their duty to regulate in IIL, states parties shall avert the real and imminent risks that foreign investors' activities may exert over an individual or specific group through all reasonable means determined by the circumstances. Additionally, giving effect to Convention's rights, if their exercise is not already guaranteed within their respective domestic legal framework, is the last general obligation owed by all states parties. Complementarily, this may constitute another source of states' duty to regulate private foreign investors under the circumstance just described, and may entail adoption of any legislative and policy instruments conducive to foster their effective observance and elimination of norms and practices leading to foreign investors' inobservance of these rights. Although the scope of the regulatory duty of states is determined by the scope of protection of the right at stake, one may argue that Inter-American human rights bodies have developed clear standards to guide states in discharging this duty and to substantiate it in ISDS.

Concerning indigenous people's right to their traditional lands and territories, a duty to regulate foreign investment activities arise from article 21 of the ACHR, and arguably from CIL. State practice and the UNGA resolutions on indigenous people suggest that states regard compulsory the consultation of the indigenous people. However, lack of consensus seems to remain over which issues these communities should be consulted.

According to the case law of the IACoHR, states parties to the ACHR should discharge its duty to regulate foreign investment activities to prevent abuses of indigenous people's right to land possession if they, inter alia, restitute traditional lands in hands of foreign investors, what inextricably entails the expropriation of foreign property. Discharging this states' duty does not automatically represent a violation of investor's treaty rights; contrarily, IIL recognises this states' inherent power whose exercise does not breach IIAs provided that expropriation of foreign property is lawful under the conditions established in these latter treaties. In relation to states parties' actual compliance with this duty arising out of the ACHR, one may observe that there is a remarkable tendency to legally recognise indigenous people's right to communal property among Latin American countries; however, expropriation of foreign property rights seems to be the last resort for meeting this states' duty.

Yet, if states restrict indigenous people's right to enjoy traditional lands, for instance, by approving the development of exploration and exploitation activities on the grounds of necessity, legality, and proportionality, they are still required to prevent that these economic activities do not pose a real and imminent risk upon indigenous people's survival. The conduct of a free, prior, informed consultation and an ESIA are the two regulatory actions that would allow states parties to meet their regulatory duty in favour of indigenous people's survival.

On the one hand, indigenous people's consultation of the planned economic activities in their traditional lands and territories shall be undertaken if development projects may lead to their displacement or involve storage of hazardous materials. To this end, the state or the entity in charge of the conduct of process through states' delegation shall ensure that the process is conducted, inter alia, in good faith by observing the political organisation of the community, and without any act of coercion or bribery vis-à-vis potentially affected communities. Moreover, their consultation shall be prior exploration phase in case of extractive industries activities or the execution of development plans, as well as informed in order to allow these communities to know about the risk of proposed investment projects. On the other hand, ESIAs enhance states' fulfilment of the latter criterion of consultation process if this instrument facilitates information about the environmental and health risk inherent to these activities. Notwithstanding the former, the function performed by ESIAs is also securing indigenous people's participation in their design, implementation, and evaluation.

Concerning the questions whether Latin American countries discharge as states parties to the ACHR their duty to regulate foreign investment activities in the terms above described, one may argue that at least the recognition of indigenous people's right to consultation is widespread in Latin American countries regarding the legal and administrative practices that may potentially affect them, while the legal protection of the indigenous people's consultation about development projects is the exception. In fact, few states required the consultation process on the investment projects, but they took up this requirement only after the IACoHR found them responsible for violations of the indigenous people's right to use and enjoy their traditional lands and territories.

If one analyses the facts of investment treaty cases involving the protection of the indigenous people's right that have emerged in Latin America,[414] one may conclude that states parties mostly delegate the undertaking of this task to those foreign investors interested in obtaining approval of their development projects and seem to satisfy their obligation to consult indigenous people. However, from the findings made by arbitral tribunals in determining states' compliance with their duty to regulate claimant investors' undertaking of consultation process, one may observe that some respondent states failed to adequately meet the normative standards governing consultation's process and thus compliance with this regulatory duty.

The practice prevailing in Latin American countries seem to be that of socialization, rather than of consultation about their development projects, and in this vein fail to oversight how foreign investors in the mining sector conduct such process.

---

[414]See Sect. 4.1.1.2, ch 4.

Concerning ESIAs, they usually constitute one of the requirements for Latin American countries' approval of development projects by means of laws or investor-state contracts. Despite this fact, the implementation of these studies is mostly in the hands of companies aiming at developing these economic activities and thereby casting doubts about the impartiality that shall govern them, and the indigenous people's participation is virtually non-existent contrary to the requirement under Inter-American human rights standards.

## 3.3 Conclusion

The analysis undertaken in chapter three shows that universal and Inter-American human rights law allocates a duty to regulate foreign investment activities upon Latin American countries. This finding allows putting forward of the proposition that these countries could re-politicise IIL through an articulation of the 'duty to regulate' paradigm to voice the need to preserve regulatory autonomy in order to prevent foreign investors' abuses of human rights. It could detail how these countries should do that (the claims), on one hand, and also highlight the potential of IIL to inhibit states' protection of human rights in Latin America (the issues of contention), on the other.

Moreover, this assessment also exhibits that IHRL doctrine clearly develops normative standards that IIL could integrate in the review of respondent states' actions impairing investors' treaty rights which they had pursued to avert its human rights abuses, and states could prove the non-arbitrariness of these measures vis-à-vis-foreign investors without articulating it in terms of the so-called 'right to regulate'.

Under UN and Inter-American human rights instruments, states members are to discharge a duty to regulate foreign investment activities. Under the UNGP, this duty derives from the duty to protect, while under the Report on Business and Human Rights, from the obligation to ensure, which arises from the ADRDM and ACHR. In both cases this regulatory task implies adopting legislative and executive measures conducive to avert corporations' abuses that could take place within the framework of their economic activities. However, both instruments exhibit great differences when it comes to defining this regulatory duty. While the UNGP explicitly underscores the fact that their standards do not create new obligations, the report defines the task of regulating in a more comprehensive way, taking into consideration the developments of the universal human rights system. Furthermore, while the UNGP endorses the promotion of 'voluntary' initiatives as a regulatory mechanism available to states to induce corporate social responsible behaviour, the Report on Business and Human Rights condemns the deficiencies of voluntary efforts to protect human rights and thus speaks in less flexible terms when it comes to the regulation of foreign investment activities.

Under universal human rights law, a states' duty to regulate foreign investment activities arises from an obligation of conduct that requires protecting human rights through all appropriate measures.

Under the ICESCR, the states' duty to regulate foreign investment activities derives from the obligation to protect ESC rights that is implicit in the obligation of conduct that is required by article 2 (1) to achieve progressively the full realization of ESC rights, namely, to undertake to take steps and to resort to all appropriate means to satisfy this obligation of result. To discharge this regulatory duty, states shall adopt all executive and legislative measures that are adequate to prevent human rights abuses within the context of foreign investment activities, determined by the scope of protection of the ESC right at stake. According to General Comment No. 24, examples of regulatory measures that would be considered appropriate to discharge this Covenant's obligation include introducing a strict regulation upon public services' providers, or even, in some cases, the revocation of licenses or any privilege awarded to business entities, if they fail to observe ESC rights when developing their economic activities. Hence, the potential of normative frictions with the investment treaty obligations is certainly high because the regulatory demands imposed by the Covenant directly affects foreign investment activities and is likely to give rise to an investment treaty claim. That said, the Covenant's purpose will not be fulfilled if states parties fail to comply with further obligations of conduct such as the obligation to respect and to fulfil ESC rights, which would require in the investment context, abstaining from adopting actions conducive to prevail the protection of foreign investment over ESC rights' protection and guarantee goods or services' provision through the involvement of foreign investment, thus guaranteeing the enjoyment of ESC rights.

Accordingly, the states' duty to regulate foreign investment activities under the above-mentioned human rights treaties consists of the positive actions that states shall take to avert human rights abuses prior and during the operation of private foreign investment activities. This normative paradigm thus denotes states parties' compliance with the obligation to protect ESC rights under the ICESCR and to act with due diligence under the ACHR and, in this vein, its link with IHRL. However, this normative paradigm distinguishes itself from their normative foundations under both treaties since it only involves the preventative measures required to fulfil this obligation, rather than remedial measures to address foreign investor's abuses. Moreover, the 'duty to regulate' paradigm has a connection with IIL to the extent that it reflects the host states' actions directed at averting the human rights abuses of private foreign investors, who may feel their investment treaty rights adversely affected by them and seek damages before an investor-state arbitral tribunal. Yet, this paradigm certainly differs from the notion 'right to regulate' that has been pervasively used in IIL to indicate the states' right to rule and control foreign investment activities to ensure their compliance with domestic laws and regulations.

As far as the states' duty to regulate in relation to the right to water is concerned, this arises out of the right to an adequate standard of living codified in article 11 of the ICESCR, rather than from CIL. According to the General Comment No. 15, states parties to the ICESCR are particularly called upon to discharge their duty to regulate against direct or indirect foreign investor's interferences with the right to water in two specific situations. On the one hand, states parties to the ICESCR shall take actions against foreign corporations in charge of the provision of drinking water services if they limit consumers' access to water and facilities by compromising the affordability of these services through tariff increase. On the other hand, direct corporate interference with the right to water that states are called to prevent include foreign investors' actions conducive to affect the sufficiency and continuity of drinking water supply, or the provision of drinking water that is unfit for human consumption.

As to the means appropriate to discharge this duty to regulate investment activities in both scenarios, one may observe that Latin American countries have already tried to induce foreign investors' observance of the above-mentioned entitlements implicit in the right to water. In the context of provision of drinking water services, many states have developed strict legal framework to regulate corporations' provision of these services and established regulatory agencies in charge of monitoring their compliance.

Additionally, the regulatory entities are expected to supervise concessionaires' fulfilment of their legal obligations under water concession agreements and, where justified, impose penalties and other types of administrative sanctions in case of contractual omissions. To a lesser extent, these states have exercised this duty through more detailed rules and mechanisms.

In relation to corporate activities conducive to polluting water sources, or leading to their depletion by deposit of chemical substances or their unsustainable extraction, the majority of domestic laws have counteracted corporate pollution or depletion of water resources by requesting foreign investors to observe environmental laws, while a minority have even gone as far as to suspend granting of new concessions near these water resources, or prohibiting the use of water sources relating to mining activities.

Accordingly, the regulatory duties to be discharged to protect the right to water thus provide normative elements to advance and review how states should discharge this duty and which regulatory means are appropriate to regulate foreign investors' conduct in conformity with the ICESCR.

Under the ACHR, states' duty to regulate foreign investment activities in favour of indigenous people's right to traditional lands and territories derives from the right to property enshrined in its article 21. In the determination of its scope of protection, Inter-American human rights bodies have favoured a universalist approach, according to which this ACHR's provision is interpreted and applied in a manner most advantageous to the human being (the so-called *pro persona* approach). This practice has led to the integration of all international instruments designed to protect indigenous people and thus to foster a universalist protection of their traditional land rights at the Inter-American level. In addition to the ADRIP, these instruments have included the ILO Convention 169, the UNDRIP. Regarding CIL, this legal source of obligation generally allocates a duty to consult indigenous people upon the community of states; yet, lack of consensus still remains over the issues that states should consult indigenous people.

The original duty of states parties to the ACHR is averting foreign investors interference with indigenous people's right to possess these lands and territories, which they would discharge, inter alia, through the expropriation of investors' property rights and the corresponding provision of official titles to indigenous communities. Yet, the legal basis of this duty to regulate also permits restrictions upon the enjoyment of this legal entitlement on the grounds of society interest or public utility and in accordance with legality, necessity and proportional, which usually relate to the approval of exploration or exploitation activities in these lands and territories. Under these circumstances, states are to adopt two regulatory instruments to comply with this duty: conduct of a prior, free and informed consultation, and an ESIA.

Consultation process shall aim at reaching an agreement with indigenous people, or their consent if these activities are performed at large-scale, follow adequate means, namely, observing indigenous people's traditional customs and political organization, and being made in good faith. Under the latter requirement, there is implicit prohibition of coercion against indigenous communities and bribery of indigenous communities' leaders. Moreover, the informative aspect of consultation process shall be raising awareness about the impact of these economic activities over their traditional way of living, including environmental and health threats. To attain this latter objective, a host state shall carry out ESIAs prior the commencement of these economic activities as the second instrument to discharge its duty to regulate. Its purpose shall be ensuring indigenous people's participation in all decisions relating to the design, implementation, and evaluation of planned development projects.

Therefore, the normative elements guiding the undertaking of a free, prior and informed consultation and the conduct of an ESIA under the ACHR could unequivocally instruct states' deployment and tribunals' review of the effective performance of these regulatory duties in compliance with Inter-American standards in ISDS.

However, if one reviews states' practice of Latin American countries regarding the adoption of above-mentioned regulatory instruments, one may identify that major gaps still exist to prevent investors' interference with indigenous people's survival. On one hand, the enactment of domestic laws recognising the right of indigenous people to be consulted over the implementation of development projects and regulatory frameworks ruling the process of indigenous people's consultation are still precarious in the Latin American region to ensure that these investment projects may not pose real and imminent threats upon these communities' survival. In some cases, domestic laws merely refer to the ILO Convention 169 and broadly provide that this Convention directly applies within its domestic jurisdiction. On this basis, many states generally delegate indigenous people's consultation to foreign investors by requiring some type of socialization of their investment projects, thereby affording a large degree of discretion on how they conduct this consultation process.

Nevertheless, states do not satisfy their duty to regulate in favour of indigenous people's survival by assuming that corporations will undertake consultation process in accordance with the international standards codified in this non-human rights treaty. Contrarily, the exercise of their duty to regulate calls for a close monitoring of corporations' consultation process in order to ensure that they observe indigenous people's traditional customs and do not exert any form of coercion over them as a mechanism to obtain their acceptance of their economic activities in their traditional lands. Concerning ESIAs, one may argue that Latin American countries partially meet their duty to regulate foreign investment activities because they subject their approval of development projects to the undertaking of environmental impact assessment studies, thereby omitting to cover the social aspect that ESIAs are called to fulfil, namely guaranteeing indigenous people's participation in the design and evaluation of the development projects.

# References

Akhmouch A (2002) Water governance in Latin America and the Caribbean: a multi-level approach. OECD Reg Dev Work Pap 4:29–36

Altmann P (2013) Good life as a social movement proposal for natural resource use: the indigenous movement in Ecuador. Consilience: J Sustain Dev 10(1):59–71

Anaya J (2004) Indigenous peoples in international law, 2nd edn. OUP, New York

Arambulo K (1999) Strengthening the supervision of the international covenant on economic, social and cultural rights: theoretical and procedural aspects, 2nd edn. Intersentia, Antwerp

Attanasio D (2016) Extraordinary reparations, legitimacy, and the inter-American court. Univ Pa J Int Law 37:813-871. Available at: https://scholarship.law.upenn.edu/jil/vol37/iss3/1. Accessed 10 Dec 2020

Bernaz N (2013) Enhancing corporate accountability for human rights violations: is extraterritoriality the magic potion? J Bus Ethics 117:493–511

Carrillo-Santarelli N (2020) A regional, multi-level and human-centered approach to business and human rights issues. DPCE Online 43(2):2979–2991

De Pauw M (2015) The Inter-American court of human rights and the interpretive method of external referencing: regional consensus v. universality. In: Haeck Y, Ruiz-Chiriboga O, Burbano Herrera C (eds) The Inter-American Court of human rights: theory and practice, present and future. Intersentia, Cambridge, pp 3–24

De Schutter O (2014) International human rights law, 2nd edn. CUP, Cambridge

De Schutter O (2016) Towards a new treaty on business and human rights. Bus Human Rights J 1 (1):41–67

Eabre C (1998) Constitutionalising social rights. J Polit Philosophy 6(3):263–284

Ferrer Mac-Gregor E, Pelayo Möller C (2019a) Articulo 1. Obligacion de respetar los derechos. In: Steiner C, Fuchs MC (eds) Convencion Americana sobre derechos humanos: Comentario. Nomos, Bogota, pp 31–69

Ferrer Mac-Gregor E, Pelayo Möller C (2019b) Artículo 2. Deber de adoptar disposiciones de derecho interno. In: Steiner C, Fuchs MC (eds) Convencion Americana sobre derechos humanos: Comentario. Nomos, Bogota, pp 73–105

Fitzmaurice M (2013) Interpretation of human rights treaties. In: Shelton D (ed) The oxford handbook of international human rights law. OUP, Oxford, pp 739–771

Gonza A (2019) Articulo 21. Derecho a la propiedad privada. In: Steiner C, Fuchs MC (eds) Convencion Americana sobre derechos humanos: Comentario. Nomos, Bogota, pp 599–694

Hennebel L (2011) The inter-American court of human rights: The ambassador of universalism. Spec Edn Quebec J Int Law 57:87–97

Hepburn J (2016) Analysis: In long-awaited Pac Rim award, tribunal finds that investor held no domestic law rights to ground alleged breaches of investment statute. IA Reporter (16 October). Available at: https://www.iareporter.com/articles/analysis-in-long-awaited-pac-rim-award-

tribunal-finds-that-investor-held-no-domestic-law-rights-to-ground-alleged-breaches-of-invest
    ment-statute/. Accessed 10 Dec 2020
Herencia-Carrasco S (2020) Report of the IACHR on business and human rights: towards the inter-
    americanization of business and human rights. Rights as Usual, 24 February 24. Available at:
    Report of the IACHR on Business and Human Rights: towards the Inter-Americanization of
    Business and Human Rights | Rights as Usual. Accessed 10 Dec 2020
Jaskoski M (2014) Environmental licensing and conflict in Peru's mining sector: a path-dependent
    analysis. World Dev 64: 873–883. : https://doi.org/10.1016/j.worlddev.2014.07.010
Kingsbury B (2001) Reconciling five competing conceptual structures of indigenous peoples'
    claims in international and comparative law. N Y Univ J Int Law Law Polit 34(1):189–250
Koch IE (2005) Dichotomies, trichotomies or waves of duties? Human Rights Law Rev 5
    (1):81–103
Lixinski L (2010) Treaty interpretation by the inter-American court of human rights: expansionism
    at the service of the unity of international law. Eur J Int Law 21:585–604
Lopez C (2017) Struggling to take off?: The second session of intergovernmental negotiations on a
    treaty on business and human rights'. Bus Human Rights J 2(2):365–370. https://doi.org/10.
    1017/bhj.2017.15
McBeth A (2010) International economic actors and human rights. Routledge, New York
McCorquodale R, Simons P (2007) Responsibility beyond borders: state responsibility for extra-
    territorial violations by corporations of international human rights law. Mod Law Rev 70
    (9):598–625
Medellin Urquiaga X (2019) Principio Pro Persona: Una Revision Critica desde el Derecho
    Internacional de los Derechos Humanos. Estudios Constitucionales 17(1):397–440
Reuters Staff (2017) El Salvador congress approves law prohibiting metals mining. Reuters
    (29 March). Available at: https://www.reuters.com/article/us-el-salvador-mining-
    idUSKBN1702YF. Accessed 10 Dec 2020
Rodiles A (2016) The law and politics of the Pro Persona principle in Latin America. In: Aust H,
    Nolte G (eds) The interpretation of international law by domestic courts: uniformity, diversity,
    convergence. OUP, Oxford, pp 168–171
Rodríguez-Pinzón D (2013) Precautionary measures of the Inter-American commission on human
    rights: legal status and importance. Human Rights Brief 20(2):13–18
Ruiz-Chiriboga O (2013) The American convention and the protocol of San Salvador: two
    intertwined treaties: non-enforceability of economic, social and cultural rights in the Inter-
    American System. Neth Q Human Rights 31(2):159–186
Sandri Fuentes A (2014) Negocios y derechos humanos. La responsabilidad de los Estados cuando
    intervienen empresas multinacionales en la violación de derechos humanos. In: Rey SA (ed) Los
    Derechos Humanos en el Derecho Internacional. Ministerio de Justicia y Derechos Humanos de
    la Nación, pp 213–228
Saul B, Kinley D, Mowbray J (2014) The international covenant on economic, social and cultural
    rights. Commentary, cases, and materials. OUP, Oxford
Schilling-Vacaflor A, Flemmer R (2015) Rohstoffabbau in Lateinamerika: Fehlende
    Bürgerbeteiligung schürt Konflikte. GIGA Focus Lateinamerika, 05 August. https://nbn-
    resolving.org/urn:nbn:de:0168-ssoar-441992
Sepúlveda M (2003) The nature of the obligations under the international covenant on economic,
    social and cultural rights. Intersentia, Antwerp
Shue H (1980) Basic rights. Subsistence, affluence, and US foreign policy. Princeton University
    Press, Princeton
Vierdag EW (1978) The legal nature of the rights granted by the international covenant on
    economic, social and cultural rights. Neth Yearb Int Law 9:69–105. https://doi.org/10.1017/
    S0167676800003780
Wolfrum R (2011) Obligation of result versus obligation of conduct: some thoughts about the
    implementation of international obligations. In: Arsanjani MH, Cogan J, Sloane RD, Wiessner S
    (eds) Looking to the future. essays on international law in honor of W. Michael Reisman
    Martinus Nijhoff Publishers, Leiden/Boston, p 363-383

# Chapter 4
# Re-politicisation of IIL by States Through an Articulation of Their Duty to Regulate in IIAs

Regardless of the investment policy approach prevailed at the domestic and regional level, Latin American countries have articulated their 'right to regulate' as a reaction of the policy implications that could derive from an expansive interpretation and application of IIAs provisions by arbitral tribunals[1] While the use of the 'right to regulate' paradigm has not always strictly intended to preserve states' regulatory autonomy in the investment context in Latin America,[2] it is certainly true that it greatly differs from the 'duty to regulate' paradigm that should be used in IIL. While through an articulation of the 'right to regulate' paradigm host states seek to vindicate their right to rule and control foreign investment activities to ensure their compliance with their domestic laws and regulations,[3] through the 'duty to regulate' paradigm, states can articulate their need to preserve regulatory autonomy in IIL to hinder the fact that human rights abuses occur prior and during the undertaking of foreign investment activities by all appropriate regulatory means under IHRL.[4]

Yet, notwithstanding the prevalence of the 'right to regulate' paradigm in the investment policy approaches of Latin American countries, it has been noticeable that, in addition to the frequent deployment of human rights arguments made by Argentina in cases arising from claimant investors' provision of drinking water services,[5] some Latin American countries seem to have invoked human rights arguments in connection with the indigenous people in cases involving claimant

---

[1]See Sect. 2.3.3.1.1, Chap. 2.

[2]The need to preserve states' jurisdiction to rule how they settle investment disputes has been the value informing those Latin American countries that have gradually abandoned the IIL regime or returned to inter-state dispute settlement mechanisms. See Sect. 2.3.3.1.2, Chap. 2.

[3]See Sect. 2.2.1.2, Chap. 2.

[4]See Chap. 3.

[5]See n 1, Chap. 1.

© The Author(s), under exclusive license to Springer Nature Switzerland AG 2021
M. J. Luque Macías, *Re-Politicising International Investment Law in Latin America through the Duty to Regulate Paradigm*, European Yearbook of International Economic Law 14, https://doi.org/10.1007/978-3-030-73272-1_4

investors' exploration and exploitation activities of natural resources.[6] This trend raises the initial question as to what extent these arguments have been directed to request the application of IHRL as applicable law for the interpretation of its investment treaty obligations; and if so, whether they mirror respondent states' recognition of inter-regime frictions in ISDS and/or the articulation of their 'duty to regulate' foreign investment activities. The same questions are raised regarding Latin American countries' defence arguments on questions of their substantive IIA obligations and procedural rights in ISDS.

As corollary of the above-mentioned questions, the inquiries that follow are premised on the need to find out whether tribunals engage in the review of respondent states' need to regulate foreign investment activities in favour of non-investment concerns, when they come to underpin their defence, and if so, which legal techniques they favour to deal with the latter type of arguments. Finding answers to these questions is essential to ascertain whether certain line of investment case law strives for an accommodation of private and public interests, and whether new ways could be explored to integrate states' duty to regulate investment activities in IIAs to those that have been put forward so far.[7]

To provide answers to the above-mentioned questions, Sect. 4.1.1 reviews the argumentative strategies prevailed by Latin American countries to justify IHRL as an applicable law in ISDS. Section 4.1.2 assesses the extent to which these countries have articulated their duty to regulate claimant investors' activities related to the provision of drinking water services and extractive industries on questions of their substantive obligations under the FET standard and indirect expropriation. Each section is accompanied by an analytical and critical review of arbitral tribunals' assessment of these defence arguments. Section 4.1.3, on its part, investigates the extent to which these countries and tribunals respectively articulate and review the duty to regulate foreign investment activities on questions of procedural rights of respondent states.

Based on the findings of the doctrinal analysis undertaken in Sects. 4.1 and 4.2 formulates several proposals that can be applied to reform IIAs with a view to strengthening tribunals' consideration of states parties' duty to regulate in ISDS and thus underpinning the re-politicisation of IIL. These IIAs reforms not only involve an articulation of the 'duty to regulate' in these treaties, but also explore the possibility of using IIAs as another regulatory instrument of foreign investment activities in connection with procedural clauses. Following the great concerns expressed by international human rights bodies and civil society alike about the negative impact for states of having IIAs inconsistent with their human rights

---

[6]See *Bear Creek v Peru* (n 3, Chap. 1); *Copper Mesa v Ecuador* (n 3, Chap. 1); *South American Silver v Bolivia* (n 3, Chap. 1).

[7]Such as the 2005 IISD Model International Agreement on Investment for Sustainable Development that aimed to balance the interest of all participants in the investment process. See Mann et al. (2005). See also, Norway Model BIT (2007); UNCTAD (2015) Investment Policy Framework for Sustainable Development 110.

obligations,[8] Sect. 4.3 briefly discusses the legal obligation that Latin American countries might breach under human rights treaties if they negotiate or maintain IIAs that may restrict their fulfilment in the investment context. Subsequently, this section discusses the normative consequences that may derive from their inobservance of human rights obligations in the formulation of investment policies. Last but not the least, Sect. 4.4 summarises the findings that emerge in this chapter.

## 4.1 Current Deployment of Human Rights Argumentation Before ISDS Tribunals

### 4.1.1 Invoking IHRL as Applicable Law in ISDS?

#### 4.1.1.1 In Cases Arising in the Context of Investors' Provision in the Drinking Water Services

The *Aguas del Tunari v Bolivia* and *Vivendi v Argentina* cases, which were settled under the ICSID Convention, were the first cases that attracted great public attention especially because they highlighted the potential negative implications that IIL may have upon host states' protection of the right to water, more precisely, the affordability and quality of drinking water services provided by foreign corporations.

In *Aguas del Tunari v Bolivia*, the claimant investor challenged the termination of a concession contract for potable water and sewage service's provision in Cochabamba, following widespread social protest against the high tariffs demanded for their access and due to the affectation of private wells, as an expropriation and other breaches of the Netherlands-Bolivia BIT provisions.[9] From all documents relating to this arbitration proceeding, only the decision on jurisdiction was publicly available, revealing that the tribunal upheld its jurisdiction to hear the case, and Bolivia did not articulate its duty to regulate claimant investors' activities to challenge the admissibility of investor's claims.[10] Nevertheless, it is noteworthy to point out that the tribunal rejected an *amicus curiae* submission by alleging that this request was

---

[8]See n 71 and 72, Chap. 1.

[9]*Aguas del Tunari v Bolivia* (n 447, Chap. 2).

[10]*Aguas del Tunari v Bolivia* (n 447, Chap. 2) paras 63–64. Against Bolivian objection to its jurisdiction based on the US and Spanish companies' ownership of the Dutch intermediary running Aguas del Tunari, the Tribunal justified its jurisdiction on the control exercised by the Dutch company over the Bolivian company. In contrast to the *Vivendi v Argentina* tribunal, the choice-of-law clause in the concession agreement providing for dispute settlement before Bolivian courts was no impediment to establish its jurisdiction. *Aguas del Tunari v Bolivia* (n 447, Chap. 2) 264–268. For an analysis of this decision see Onwuamaegbu (2005).

beyond its jurisdictional competence,[11] and that the claimant investor withdrew its claim due to continued massive protests following the increase in water tariffs.[12] Hence, just as Bolivia did not articulate its regulatory duty to protect the right to water, nor did the tribunal engage in reviewing the existence of normative frictions between IIL and IHRL.

An opposite approach is noticeable in investment treaty claims faced by Argentina, evidenced in the first investment treaty case it had to respond to, namely *Vivendi v Argentina I*, which involved the privatization of drinking water and sewages services in the Argentine province of Tucuman. Claimant investors alleged, inter alia, breaches of the FET standard and an expropriation of their investment under the France-Argentina BIT.[13] In their views, Argentina breached these treaty obligations through the provincial authorities' unilateral modifications of tariffs contrary to what concession contract had prescribed,[14] and through their coercion to modify and renegotiate the concession contract in terms that deprived them of their right to cut off their services to non-paying customers.[15]

In addition, investors contended that federal authorities' omission to avert provincial authorities' acts also gave rise to Argentina's international legal responsibility under these BIT provisions. Despite upholding jurisdiction, the *Vivendi v Argentina I* tribunal dismissed, on merits, the investors' claims relating to the concession contract because it was of the view that an adequate evaluation of these claims required the interpretation and application of the contract by Argentinian administrative courts as articulated in its forum selection clause.[16] Yet, the French investors successfully obtained the partial annulment of this award before an annulment committee (annulment committee I) since, in its view, the *Vivendi v Argentina* tribunal had failed to examine the merits of contract-based claims.[17] These investors thus resubmitted their claim (*Vivendi v Argentina II*) under the ICSID Convention and obtained a favourable award,[18] which Argentina, pursuant to the rules laid down in the ICSID Convention to this effect, intended to annul but did not succeed.[19]

---

[11]*Letter from Professor David D. Caron to J Martin Wagner* (Letter to NGO regards Petition to Participate as amici curiae) (29 January 2003) Available via ITA Law at: http://www.italaw.com/cases/57#sthash.wwd6obSl.dpuf accessed 10 December 2020.

[12]Vis-Dunbar and Eric Peterson (2006).

[13]*Vivendi v Argentina I* (n 1, Chap. 1) para 43.

[14]*Vivendi v Argentina I* (n 1, Chap. 1) para 65.

[15]*Vivendi v Argentina I* (n 1, Chap. 1) para 66.

[16]*Vivendi v Argentina I* (n 1, Chap. 1) Award (21 November 2000).

[17]*Vivendi v Argentina I* (n 1, Chap. 1) Decision on Annulment (3 July 2002).

[18]*Vivendi v Argentina II* (n 1, Chap. 1) Award (20 august 2007).

[19]*Vivendi v Argentina II* (n 1, Chap. 1) Decision on Annulment (10 August 2010).

In *Vivendi v Argentina II*, similar claims were advanced by French investors.[20] Nevertheless, Argentina, based on the contractual nature of the dispute[21] and investors' claims on the merits, challenged the tribunal's jurisdiction basing their challenge on following arguments: First, Argentina claimed that the subsidiary doubled the water bills of low-income users without prior notice and without improving the drinking water service; and second, it deepened the increasing frictions with users by supplying unsafe water, which consequently provoked users' refusal to paying the high values required by subsidiary's water bills.[22]

Based on these two allegations of investors' misconduct, Argentina asserted that the role of BITs is neither to protect covered investors and their investment against their own failures, nor to insulate them from any regulatory measure that a host state shall take, especially when it comes to the regulation of corporate provision of public services.[23] In addition, it asserted that, as a result of investors' breaches of the water concession agreement,[24] local authorities had the right and the *responsibility* to take appropriate measures to ensure that affordable and accessible drinking water is availed to its population.[25] Therefore, despite not referring to any legal source imposing such duty, Argentina did articulate its duty to regulate foreign investor activities by emphasising on local authorities' status as a contracting party and as a state, and that under such capacities no breaches of the FET standard nor expropriation of claimant investors' investment should occur.[26] However, the *Vivendi v Argentina II* tribunal did not engage in reviewing Argentina's arguments justifying its regulatory duties and centred on evaluating the impact of that measures upon claimant investors' investment.[27]

After *Vivendi v Argentina II*, Argentina faced further investment treaty claims within the same economic sector[28] and, generally, resorted to different types of human rights argumentation when responding to these claims. However, in the interpretation of IIAs provisions, not all have been directed to request the application of human rights as the applicable law. In some cases, these arguments have been directed to reinforce argument on necessity defence, as presented below.

---

[20]*Vivendi v Argentina II* (n 1, Chap. 1) paras 1.1.1, 3.2.1–3.2.4.

[21]In this connection, Argentina contended that the contract exclusively provided for the settlement of contract-based disputes before its administrative courts. *Vivendi v Argentina II* (n 1, Chap. 1) para 3.3.1.

[22]*Vivendi v Argentina II* (n 1, Chap. 1) para 3.3.2.

[23]*Vivendi v Argentina II* (n 1, Chap. 1) para 3.3.2–3.3.3.

[24]*Vivendi v Argentina II* (n 1, Chap. 1) para 3.3.4.

[25]*Vivendi v Argentina II* (n 1, Chap. 1) para 3.3.5 (emphasis added).

[26]Ibidem.

[27]This approach was noticeable in tribunals' determination of alleged existence of an indirect expropriation. See Sect. 2.3.3.2, Chap. 2.

[28]Two cases were discontinued. See *Aguas Cordobesas and Suez v Argentina* (n 1, Chap. 1) and *Azurix v Argentina II* (n 1, Chap. 1) Other cases have not been public available. See Suez and *Interagua v Argentina* (n 1, Chap. 1).

First, Argentina has advanced an incompatibility between its investment treaty obligations and its obligation to protect the human right to water, coupled with the argument of normative primacy that should be attached to the protection of this human right. In *Azurix v Argentina I*, this country explicitly alluded to an incompatibility between its BIT and human rights treaties protecting users' right to water, and requested to solve inter-regime frictions in favour of the public interest underlying the protection of human rights.[29] Hence, Argentina did acknowledge the potential of inter-regime tensions, however, it failed to articulate how the international obligations were incompatible since the provision of drinking water services were maintained for some months after the termination of water concession contract.[30]

In *Suez and Vivendi v Argentina II*, the protection of the human right to water was one relevant normative argument to justify Argentina's measures on the grounds of necessity.[31] After emphasising on the significance of water to human life and health and the exceptional nature of water as a commodity, Argentina requested the tribunal to give a great margin of discretion when assessing its investment treaty obligation and to make an interpretation of the later in conformity with its human rights obligations.[32] The tribunal dismissed the implicit proposition that human rights obligations triumphed over investment treaty obligations because there is no basis for such primacy in international law and that Argentina shall comply with both obligations equally since there is no inconsistency or contradiction among them.[33]

Cases such as *Azurix v Argentina I* and *Suez and Vivendi v Argentina II* suggest that Argentina intended to deploy normative arguments to underpin the normative primacy of protecting users' right to water (through its regulation of claimant investors' investment in the provision of drinking water) over investment treaty protection. However, deploying such an argument would have success only if human rights constituted peremptory norms in terms of article 53 VCLT, which the international community recognised and accepted as a whole and from whom no derogation is permitted. Yet, international legal doctrine has not hitherto attached such as status to most human rights norms so that states should justify by other means the superior status that they have under international law.[34] Moreover, had Argentina engaged in explaining how the ICESCR, for instance, imposes a duty to regulate investors' provision of water services to ensure the affordability and access to drinking water and thus users' enjoyment of the right to water, the tribunal could

---

[29]*Azurix v Argentina I* (n 1, Chap. 1) para 254.

[30]*Azurix v Argentina I* (n 1, Chap. 1) para 261.

[31]*Suez and Vivendi v Argentina II* (n 1, Chap. 1) Decision on Liability para 252.

[32]Ibidem.

[33]*Suez and Vivendi v Argentina II* (n 1, Chap. 1) Decision on Liability para 262.

[34]Examples of *jus cogens* norms include the prohibition of aggression, slavery and the slave trade, genocide, racial discrimination apartheid and torture, as well as basic rules of international humanitarian law applicable in armed conflict. *Case concerning armed activities on the territory of the Congo* (Democratic Republic of the Congo/Rwanda) (Judgement) [2006] ICJ Rep para 64.

arguably have more elements to recognise the potential of an inter-regime frictions, when assessing its defence arguments.

Second, in addition to the incompatibility and normative primacy arguments, Argentina has also invoked the constitutional rank of human rights norms within its domestic legal order to justify human rights as an applicable law in ISDS. In *SAUR v Argentina*, Argentina clearly stated that BITs do not displace its legal obligations under human rights treaties that particularly enjoy constitutional rank within its domestic legal order.[35] Considering the special status of its human rights obligations, Argentina thus requested an interpretation of its investment treaty obligations in conformity with its human rights obligations, especially with those obligations deriving from the right to water.[36] In connection with this, Argentina further contended that the domestic authorities' intervention in the concessionary company and termination of concession agreement were consistent with its obligation to guarantee water supply, so that it could not be considered as an unfair action nor as an expropriation since it constituted a necessary exercise of policy and regulatory powers.[37] These arguments deployed by Argentina implicitly reflect its understanding that its investment and human rights obligations collide, on one hand, and the articulation of its duty to regulate, albeit in terms of sovereign rights, on the other.

In contrast to the approaches prevailed by tribunals in the above-mentioned cases, the *SAUR v Argentina* tribunal did engage in reviewing Argentina's arguments, holding that human rights treaties should be an interpretative source, in this case, for having a constitutional rank within the respondent state's legal order and for their character as legal principle of international law.[38] Recognising the access to drinking water as a primary public service and fundamental right of consumers, the tribunal conceded that national authorities shall be entitled to have a broad regulatory competence.[39] Yet, in its view, these regulatory prerogatives are consistent with investors' rights under BITs.[40] It held that although the right to water and investors' right to have protection under the BIT operate at different level (arguably intending to mean the domestic and international level), the host state shall exercise these prerogatives in conformity with investors' rights and guarantees under the BIT, so that it shall pay damages to the investor in case of breaches.[41] Hence, the *SAUR v Argentina* tribunal did not recognise any inconsistency between investment treaty obligations and human rights norms. Arguably, the reason for this was tribunal's approach to human rights norms as part of Argentina's domestic law.

---

[35] *SAUR v Argentina*, Decision on Jurisdiction and Liability (6 June 2012) (n 1, Chap. 1) para 328.
[36] Ibidem.
[37] Ibidem.
[38] *SAUR v Argentina*, Decision on Jurisdiction and Liability (6 June 2012) (n 1, Chap. 1) para 330.
[39] Ibidem.
[40] *SAUR v Argentina*, Decision on Jurisdiction and Liability (6 June 2012) (n 1, Chap. 1) para 331.
[41] Ibidem.

In investment case law, tribunals may either favour the concurrent application of international and domestic law or opt for the application of one over the other.[42] In the case concerned, the *SAUR v Argentina* tribunal seemed to favour the concurrent application of international and domestic laws, thereby recognising the monist legal tradition of Argentina. This domestic practice of attaching a constitutional rank to human rights norms is common among many Latin American countries, whose constitutions contain clauses that anchor constitutions' openness to human rights norms, albeit with different ranks of hierarchy.[43]

Finally, in *Urbaser v Argentina*, Argentina abandoned the deployment of the incompatibility and normative primacy arguments in tribunals' determination of the applicable law to review the merits of claimant investors' claims alleging breaches of the FET standard.[44] It initially contended that the BIT provision ruling the applicable law in ISDS requires the application of international law, which entails the application of the BIT and all international law norms that may be applicable to the dispute at stake, since BITs are not rules of self-contained nature.[45] As a consequence of this general application of international law, Argentina called upon a harmonious application of the BIT, its domestic laws and international law in tribunal's review of the merits in a way that 'none of them nullifies the others'.[46] As a response, the tribunal endorsed a broad understanding of the applicable law clause, implying that with its application of the BIT, domestic laws of the respondent state and other sources of international law 'where appropriate'.[47] That said, Argentina's calls for harmonious application of all pertinent international and domestic laws seems to be more inclined to suggest a call for an interpretation of the FET standard in a ways that it does not disregard Argentina's regulatory powers by arguing that 'the freedom of the host State to enact or change its laws and regulations in the furtherance of general or specific policies is basically unaffected by BITs'.[48] Accordingly, relying upon the broad formulation of the applicable law clause, Argentina demanded that the tribunal deal with all applicable legal regimes as a whole and in terms that did not undermine the exercise of its 'right to regulate'. While this might be an implicit recognition of the potential for inter-regime frictions, it is also true that this demand did not entail an articulation of its 'duty to regulate' under IHRL.

---

[42]Kjos (2013).

[43]León Bastos and Wong Meraz (2015); Morales Antoniazzi (2014).

[44]*Urbaser v Argentina* (n 1, Chap. 1) para 555–558.

[45]*Urbaser v Argentina* (n 1, Chap. 1) para 555.

[46]*Urbaser v Argentina* (n 1, Chap. 1) para 557.

[47]*Urbaser v Argentina* (n 1, Chap. 1) para 558.

[48]*Urbaser v Argentina* (n 1, Chap. 1) para 557.

#### 4.1.1.2   In Cases Arising Out of Investors' Exploration and Exploitation Activities of Natural Resources

Like Argentina, Bolivia, Ecuador, and Peru have resorted to human rights arguments relating to indigenous people's protection to respond to investment treaty claims that arose from several regulatory measures introduced against claimant investors' exploration and exploitation of natural resources following local protest against these extractive industries.[49] Yet, except for Bolivia in the *South American Silver* case, neither Ecuador nor Peru attempted to request the application of human rights as applicable law in the interpretation of IIAs provisions in the *Copper Mesa* and *Bear Creek* cases, respectively.[50] The purpose of advancing indigenous people-related arguments was instead to justify the so-called 'unclean hands' of claimant investors in order to challenge tribunals' jurisdiction and/or the admissibility of their claims. According to the 'unclean hands' doctrine, a plaintiff may be prevented from bringing a claim due to its illegal conduct in relation to the claims it makes.[51] The answers to whether indigenous people-related argumentation reflects respondent states' recognition of inter-regime frictions in ISDS or whether the articulation of their 'duty to regulate' foreign investment activities is justifiable and solid, are provided below, together with views of the tribunals on these matters.

The *South American Silver v Bolivia* case arose from British investors' allegations of an indirect expropriation of their investment in mining and quarrying activities through the adoption of an executive decree, ordering the reversion of their concession's ownership to the Bolivian state, and requesting the regulatory mining agency to take management over the concession.[52] Bolivia justified these measures, among others, for the breaches of the Mallku Khota community's rights allegedly committed by claimant investor's subsidiary and called upon the tribunal to apply human rights as applicable law in the settlement of the claim by resorting to two argumentative strategies: (1) the normative primacy of international protection of indigenous people's rights and the call for a consistent interpretation of its investment treaty obligations and its international and domestic obligations demanding to protect indigenous people,[53] and (2) the articulation of its duty to regulate claimant investors conduct vis-à-vis indigenous communities and the relevance of its domestic laws.[54]

As far as the argumentative strategy of the normative primacy of international protection of indigenous people's rights and a harmonious interpretation of investment and non-investment obligations of Bolivia towards indigenous people is

---

[49]*Copper Mesa v Ecuador* (n 3, Chap. 1); *Bear Creek v Peru* (n 3, Chap. 1); *South American Silver v Bolivia* (n 3, Chap. 1).

[50]On the issue of applicable law, see *Bear Creek v Peru* (n 3, Chap. 1) paras 267–269.

[51]The role of the 'unclean hands' doctrine in relation to jurisdictional issues will be addressed in Sect. 4.1.3.1 of this chapter. For a general overview of its scope of application see Moloo (2010).

[52]For a description of investor's claims see Trevino (2015).

[53]*South American Silver v Bolivia* (n 3, Chap. 1) paras 195–196, 199, 203–204.

[54]*South American Silver v Bolivia* (n 3, Chap. 1) paras 197, 198, 202.

concerned, Bolivia requested the tribunal to read the systemic integration principle as an interpretative rule that permits complementing the interpretation of BITs provisions with human rights norms. This strategy requires an interpretation of investment treaty obligation in a way that does not imply breaching its human rights obligations towards indigenous people.[55]

In connection with this, Bolivia contended that if a reconciliation of international investment and non-investment rules is unfeasible during the interpretation of BIT's provisions, it requested to give priority to the protection of indigenous people's rights.[56] Relying upon the statements given by the IACoHR[57] and the findings of the International Law Commission (ILC) Group on the fragmentation of international law,[58] Bolivia further sought to justify the normative primacy of international norms protecting indigenous people by recalling two factors highlighted in the ILC Fragmentation Report: On the one hand, article 103 of the UN Charter provides that member states' obligations arising from this Charter (such as taking action to achieve respect for human rights) override their obligations under other treaty; and on the other hand, the *erga omnes* character of human (and fundamental) rights of indigenous communities.[59] To this end, Bolivia enumerated some international instruments relating to indigenous people and soft-law standards pursuant to which the tribunal had to construct its investment treaty obligations.[60] Accordingly, the arguments provided by Bolivia clearly manifest its recognition of the great potential of normative frictions between its investment and human rights obligations towards indigenous people and its call for resolving inter-regime tensions in favour of human rights.

To complement these argumentative strategies, Bolivia underscored the relevance of its domestic law in the interpretation of investment treaty rights and obligations in cases where IIL and IHRL may not apparently collide.[61] Arguably, this was Bolivia's attempt to highlight the challenges implicit in discharging its duty to

---

[55] *South American Silver v Bolivia* (n 3, Chap. 1) para 195.

[56] *South American Silver v Bolivia* (n 3, Chap. 1) para 196.

[57] Ibidem. In its counter-memorial, Bolivia explicitly endorsed IACoHR's position in the *Sawhoyamaxa v Paraguay* case, where this court held that the application of BITs shall be consistent with human rights obligations. *South American Silver v Bolivia* (n 3, Chap. 1), Respondent Counter-Memorial para 203.

[58] *South American Silver v Bolivia* (n 3, Chap. 1) para 196. In its counter-memorial, Bolivia recalled the conclusion of the ILC Group on the issue of fragmentation of international law, highlighting the fact that despite the absent hierarchical nature of international law, there are some international rules that are more important than other rules and for that reason, they enjoy a special status. *South American Silver v Bolivia* (n 3, Chap. 1) Respondent Counter-Memorial para 204.

[59] *South American Silver v Bolivia* (n 3, Chap. 1) para 196.

[60] The ACHR, the ILO Convention 169 and the UNDRIP featured as some of the international instruments according to which the *South American Silver v Bolivia* tribunal was requested to consider in its interpretation of Bolivia's investment treaty obligations. *South American Silver v Bolivia* (n 3, Chap. 1) para 199. In addition, Bolivia also invoked the UNGP and OECD Guidelines for Multinational Enterprises. *South American Silver v Bolivia* (n 3, Chap. 1) para 200.

[61] *South American Silver v Bolivia* (n 3, Chap. 1) para 197.

regulate foreign investment activities through domestic instruments in compliance with IHRL before an arbitral tribunal. In fact, Bolivia further deployed the constitutional rank of international instruments protecting indigenous people and the binding nature of these constitutional norms over claimant investors and over the state alike,[62] highlighting its legal responsibility 'for reasonably preventing the violation of such rights'. With the latter, Bolivia clearly articulated its duty to regulate foreign investment activities under international instruments governing the protection of indigenous people and the ACHR, and its fulfilment through domestic laws.

As a response, the *South American Silver v Bolivia* tribunal primarily focused on the incompatibility argument and on the alleged normative supremacy of human rights, without addressing, at this stage, Bolivia's articulation of its duty to regulate. In the absence of disputing parties' agreement on the applicable law to the dispute, the *South American Silver v Bolivia* tribunal reaffirmed the application of the BIT as the principal instrument to settling the dispute.[63] Having identified that the rules applicable for the interpretation of the BIT was the subject matter of controversy between disputing parties,[64] the tribunal determined the scope of the customary interpretative rule of systemic integration. To Bolivia's contention that article 31 (3 (c of the VCLT not only allow interpreting the BIT in accordance with rules applicable between the parties, but also those international norms that are necessary to avoid breaching other international norms such as those existing regarding the indigenous people,[65] the tribunal held that the customary rule of systemic integration must be applied in harmony with other interpretative maxims, and cautiously, to avert applying rules to which states parties of the BIT did not consent.[66] The tribunal dismissed the normative primacy argument deployed by Bolivia by pointing out its failure to provide reasons for the application of human rights norms when they are not CIL, and to show that states parties to the BIT concerned are also parties to the human rights treaties invoked.[67] In connection with this, it held that Bolivia 'also fails to explain how [human rights] rules conflict with the [BIT] or why they should prevail over its provisions'.[68] As far as the domestic laws of Bolivia are concerned, including the constitutional rank of human rights treaties and its corresponding horizontal applicability to claimant investors, the tribunal did recognise the relevance of Bolivia's domestic law in the interpretation of the BIT, including the incorporated human rights treaties. However, it dismissed Bolivia's argument that its domestic laws shall prevail over BIT.[69]

---

[62]*South American Silver v Bolivia* (n 3, Chap. 1) para 202.

[63]*South American Silver v Bolivia* (n 3, Chap. 1) para 208.

[64]*South American Silver v Bolivia* (n 3, Chap. 1) para 209.

[65]*South American Silver v Bolivia* (n 3, Chap. 1) para 195.

[66]*South American Silver v Bolivia* (n 3, Chap. 1) para 216.

[67]*South American Silver v Bolivia* (n 3, Chap. 1) para 217.

[68]Ibidem.

[69]*South American Silver v Bolivia* (n 3, Chap. 1) para 218.

In contrast to Bolivia, Ecuador and Peru deployed human rights-related arguments with respect to indigenous people to substantiate the 'unclean hands' of Canadian investors in the *Copper Mesa* and *Bear Creek* cases respectively to challenge the admissibility of their investment treaty claims. It was the case because of the relevance of claimant investors' compliance with indigenous people's consultation for the operation of their mining concessions. In *Copper Mesa v Ecuador*, the Canadian investor alleged breaches of the FET standard and expropriation of its investment out of the local authorities' termination of Junin and Chaucha concessions on the grounds of the lack of compliance with the prior and informed indigenous communities' consultation.[70] The consultation requirement was imposed upon its investment once it was already established in Ecuador, following the 2008 Constituent Assembly's Mining Mandate that ordered the termination of all mining concessions that have not complied with this requirement following proclamation of the exploitation of natural resources' in accordance with the national interest.[71] In *Bear Creek v Peru*, the Canadian investor also alleged an indirect expropriation of its investment as a result of the revocation of its silver mining concession in the Santa Ana silver mine, once it undertook the ESIA and the consultation process instructed by the governmental authorities failed due to massive opposition to its exploration activities in the Puno region.[72]

As to the arguments deployed to object the admissibility of claimant investors' claims, Ecuador alleged the existence of the 'unclean hands' of the Copper Mesa in the Junin concession due to the flagrant breaches of international law, including human rights, committed by its subsidiary following the admission of its investment.[73] Peru, on the other hand, was more explicit in developing its allegations of 'unclean hands' against Bear Creek by alleging that it omitted to observe the standards of the ILO Convention 169 applicable to the consultation process that led to failures to obtain the 'social license', and its responsibility to 'address community concerns'.[74] In this connection, Peru further argued that, although it is the one called to ensure that companies obtain indigenous communities' consent, the company is the one that shall take any step to achieve this result.[75]

In both cases, however, arbitral tribunals dealt with respondent states' arguments as issues of the merits phase, rather than as admissibility issues.[76] In *Copper Mesa v Ecuador*, the tribunal proceeded to review this argument on questions relating to breaches of the FET standard and indirect expropriation because Ecuador did not question Canadian corporation's conduct under international law (including human

---

[70]*Copper Mesa v Ecuador* (n 3, Chap. 1) paras 1.110 and 6.53.

[71]Ibidem.

[72]*Bear Creek v Peru* (n 3, Chap. 1) paras 168, 190–202.

[73]*Copper Mesa v Ecuador* (n 3, Chap. 1) paras 5.42, 5.60–5.63.

[74]*Bear Creek v Peru* (n 3, Chap. 1) para 256.

[75]*Bear Creek v Peru* (n 3, Chap. 1) para 258.

[76]*Copper Mesa v Ecuador* (n 3, Chap. 1) para 5.62.

rights) prior its submission of its investment treaty claim to arbitration.[77] Therefore, had Ecuador discharged its duty to regulate Copper Mesa's activities (that included pre-meditated suppression of anti-mining protesters and subsidiary's recruitment of armed men to quell these protests) as soon as they impaired indigenous people's rights, the tribunal would have to deal with the 'unclean hands' argument at the admissibility phase. In *Bear Creek v Peru*, the tribunal decided to review the 'unclean hands' argument deployed by Peru at the merits phase because it considered that the social license is only relevant at the merits and during the quantification of damages.[78]

At the merits phase, the *Copper Mesa v Ecuador* and *Bear Creek v Peru* tribunals greatly differ in how they dealt with respondent states' allegations of 'unclean hands'. In *Copper Mesa v Ecuador*, the tribunal proceeded to review them once it declared that the termination of the mining concessions by Ecuadorian local authorities amounted to an indirect expropriation, and constituted a violation of the FET standard.[79] The tribunal examined whether claimant investor's conduct was manifestly wilful or negligent in relation to the damages it sought before its jurisdiction,[80] and found that the claimant investor contributed to 30% of its own loss by the above-mentioned abuses of indigenous people's rights.[81] In contrast, the *Bear Creek v Peru* tribunal dealt with the conduct of the claimant investor in obtaining the 'social license' to operate its mining concession as an essential element to assess the character of respondent state's measure allegedly tantamount to an indirect expropriation.[82] To deal with this question, the tribunal discussed whether additional claimant investor's actions were required other than the one undertaken, which in their absence caused social unrest and thus justified the concession's revocation.[83] The tribunal found that governmental authorities were aware of local communities' discontent and unequivocally endorsed investor's outreach actions in this region to move forward with the matter now that these actions were contrary to the ILO Convention 169.[84] Consequently, it upheld investor's claim about the existence of an indirect expropriation.[85]

To sum up, the *Copper Mesa v Ecuador* and *Bear Creek v Peru* cases show that both South American countries advanced weak human rights arguments to show the 'unclean hands' of the claimant investor, rather than to justify their own compliance with its duty to regulate Canadian investors' activities to prevent abuses over indigenous communities.

---

[77]*Copper Mesa v Ecuador* (n 3, Chap. 1) paras 5.63–5.65.

[78]*Bear Creek v Peru* (n 3, Chap. 1) paras 333–335.

[79]*Copper Mesa v Ecuador* (n 3, Chap. 1) para 6.51.

[80]*Copper Mesa v Ecuador* (n 3, Chap. 1) paras 6.90–6.93.

[81]*Copper Mesa v Ecuador* (n 3, Chap. 1) paras 6.99–6.102.

[82]*Bear Creek v Peru* (n 3, Chap. 1) paras 400–404.

[83]*Bear Creek v Peru* (n 3, Chap. 1) paras 403–408.

[84]*Bear Creek v Peru* (n 3, Chap. 1) paras 409–414.

[85]*Bear Creek v Peru* (n 3, Chap. 1) paras 415–416.

## 4.1.2  Articulation of the Duty to Regulate on Questions of Substantive IIA Obligations

### 4.1.2.1  On Questions of the FET Standard

As already highlighted in Chap. 2, the protection of investors' legitimate expectations constitutes one of the elements forming the content of the FET standard.[86] As such, this criterion has received great attention in IIL scholarship for its controversial nature and implications upon the regulatory autonomy of the host states.[87] To avoid considering any state's actions as a source of foreign investors' legitimate expectations, thereby implicating a standstill of their regulatory exercise, tribunals additionally focus on the following: the expectations that the claimant investor had at a particular moment; the investor's reliance on its expectation to its detriment and whether it was legitimately entitled to have such expectations.[88] To assess this legitimacy criterion, tribunals, in turn, analyse the legal and regulatory framework against all circumstances prevailing in the respondent state,[89] and the legality of foreign investors' investment,[90] if explicit in IIAs by means of 'in accordance with law' clauses[91] or as an issue of the merits[92]

---

[86]See Sect. 2.3.2.1, Chap. 2.

[87]To illustrate, Zeyl (2011); Cameron (2010), specially ch 8.

[88]In this sense, see *Parkerings v Lithuania* (n 378, Chap. 2) para 329; *Enron v Argentina* (n 366, Chap. 2) para 262; *Duke Energy v Ecuador* (n 367, Chap. 2) para 347; *Glamis Gold v USA* (n 368, Chap. 2) 766.

[89]*Continental Casualty Company v Argentina*, ICSID Case No. ARB/03/09, Award (5 September 2008) para 260; *Total v Argentina* (n 378, Chap. 2) para 333; *Grand River v USA* (n 411, Chap. 2) paras 140–141.

[90]See *Tokios Tokeles v Ukraine*, ICSID Case No. ARB/02/18, Decision on Jurisdiction (29 April 2004) (Tokios Tokeles v Ukraine) para 84; *Consortium Groapentent L.E.S.I. – DIPENTA v People's Democratic Republic of Algeria*, ICSID Case No. ARB/03/8, Award (10 January 2005) para 244 (iii); *Gas Natural SDG, S.A. v The Argentine Republic*, ICSID Case No. ARB/03/10, Decision on Jurisdiction (14 November 2005) paras 33-34; *Bayandir Insaal Turizm Ticoret Ve Sanayi A.S. v Islamic Republic of Pakistan*, ICSID Case No. ARB/03/09, Decision on Jurisdiction (14 November 2005) paras 109-110; *Inceysa Vallisoletana S.L. v Republic of El Salvador*, ICSID Case No. ARB/03/26, Award (2 August 2006) (*Inceysa v El Salvador*) paras 187–188; *Saipem S.p.A. v The People's Republic of Bangladesh*, ICSID Case No. ARB/05/07, Decision on Jurisdiction (21 March 2007) paras 120–124.

[91]Treaty references to the legality of investment have either come in form of a qualifier of the assets defined as an investment, or as a condition for the admission of foreign investment entitled to investment treaty protection. To illustrate, see Colombia-United Arab Emirates BIT (n 416, Chap. 2) art 1.1 and Colombia-France BIT (n 416, Chap. 2) art 3 para 1, respectively. In some cases, treaty provisions linking investors' compliance with host states' laws for investments' admission are considered equivalent to references to legality within the treaty definition of an investment, if another provision extends investment treaty protection to those investment already admitted prior the entry into force of the treaty. See *Inceysa v El Salvador* (n 90) para 130.

[92]The so-called 'in accordance in law' clauses devise a limited scope of temporal application since they only sanction initial illegality, namely the one occurred at the admission phase of foreign

Regarding the legal and regulatory framework of host states as a benchmark in tribunals' determination of the legitimacy of investors' expectations, some tribunals have showed certain openness to include those objectives that they qualify as legitimate.[93] The shortcoming of this line of reasoning is that it remains at tribunals' discretion which regulatory objectives fall under this category. Other tribunals, instead, address the political, socio-economic, or historical context of respondent states.[94] Under these circumstances, tribunals have recognised states' needs of regulatory flexibility and thus resolved an investment claim in their favour in cases where claimant investors were certainly aware of their level of economic development,[95] or of their emergency situation.[96] Nevertheless, it is very unlikely under both interpretative approaches that tribunals regard states' fulfilment of their duty to regulate foreign investment activities in the provision of drinking water services, or to their prevention of abuses of indigenous people's rights. *Urbaser v Argentina* as well as *South American Silver v Bolivia* may provide answers as to what extent arbitral tribunals could review respondent states' duty to regulate claimant investors' activities on their analysis of the legal and regulatory framework of the states concerned particularly on questions of the legitimacy of claimant investors' expectations and, thus, in their review of breaches of the FET standard.

With respect to tribunals' analysis of the legality of investors' investment to establish the legitimacy of investors' expectations, tribunals relied upon different types of illegalities that may potentially deprive claimant investors from having protection under the FET standard,[97] as well as criteria that facilitate a determination of whether the claimant investor is entitled to the legal protection afforded by the IIA.[98] The illegal conduct of claimant investors is the type of illegality that may be

---

investment. *Fraport AG Frankfurt Airport Worldwide v The Republic of Philippines*, ICSID Case No. ARB/03/25, Award (16 August 2007) (*Fraport v Philippines*) para 344; *Gustav F W Hamester GmbH & Co KG v Republic of Ghana*, ICSID Case No. ARB/07/24, Award (18 June 2010) (*Hamester v Ghana*) para 127. It is for this reason that questions regarding the legality of investment are being addressed as an issue of jurisdiction. *Alasdair Ross Anderson et al v Republic of Costa Rica*, ICSID Case No. ARB(AF)/07/3, Award (19 May 2010) paras 59–60.

[93]For instance, *Saluka v Czech Republic* (n 363, Chap. 2) para 306.

[94]See *Generation Ukraine, Inc v Ukraine*, ICSID No. ARB/00/9, Award (16 September 2003) paras 20.37; *Duke Energy v Ecuador* (n 367, Chap. 2) para 340; *El Paso Energy v Argentina* (n 363, Chap. 2) para 359.

[95]In *Genin v Estonia*, the tribunal rejected to consider the Central Bank's revocation of an operating license of the Estonian financial institution, in which claimant investors were shareholders, as a breach of FET because respondent State's regulatory instability was of public domain. *Genin v Estonia* (n 357, Chap. 2) para 348.

[96]*Eureko BV v Poland*, Partial Award (19 August 2005) paras 232–235.

[97]Illegalities having the effect of depriving investors from investment treaty protection include those business activities performed by the claimant investor or the assets used for this purpose that are forbidden by host State's law. *Tokios Tokeles v Ukraine* (n 90) para 97. Other illegalities relate to the investment made disregarding the legal restrictions that domestic laws impose upon foreign national's ownership in a specific economic sector. *Fraport v Philippines* (n 92) para 349.

[98]Tribunals have generally relied on the severity of investment's illegality or investor's good faith, to determine whether the claimant investor is entitled to the legal protection afforded by the treaty in both cases. *Desert Line Projects LLC v The Republic of Yemen*, ICSID Case No. ARB/05/17,

relevant to identify the extent to which tribunals could deal with respondent states' compliance with their duty to regulate claimant investors' activities,[99] since domestic laws and regulations of respondent states are employed as parameters to assess the legality of claimant investors' conduct, besides providing regulatory instruments to prevent human rights abuses in the investment context.[100]

In addition to domestic laws, tribunals have not excluded international law as a legal basis for reviewing the legality of investors' conduct.[101] The *Plama Consortium v Bulgaria* tribunal, for instance, assessed the legality of claimant investor's investment so as to include all 'applicable rules and principles of international law' by recalling its treaty's mandate to strengthen the rule of law in the energy sector.[102] The rationale behind this approach was to fill the legal void existing in domestic law concerning investors' obligations by means of the applicable law clause that enables the application of other sources of international law.[103]

Hence, the question to be addressed in this connection becomes whether, and if so under which conditions, tribunals employ the domestic and international legal instruments founding respondent states' duty to regulate claimant investors' activities (to prevent both their abuses of the right to water and indigenous people's right) as the sources of the legality of investors' investment in ISDS, whose non-compliance may deprive them from investment treaty protection. The *Copper Mesa v Ecuador* and *Bear Creek v Peru* may provide some answers to these last questions.

In the analysis of alleged breaches of the FET standard, the *Urbaser v Argentina* tribunal did consider the domestic and regulatory framework of respondent states that are vital in reviewing claimant investors' expectations and thus the breaches of the FET standard,[104] while the *South American Silver v Bolivia* explicitly recognised not only the legitimacy of investors' expectations as one the criteria to establish

---

Award (6 February 2008) (*Desert Line Projects v Yemen*) paras 116–117; *Phoenix Action Ltd. v Czech Republic*, ICSID Case No. ARB/06/5, Award (15 April 2009) (*Phoenix v Czech Republic*) paras 106–108. For a discussion, see Diel-Gligor and Hennecke (2015) para 21.

[99]This type of illegality may include misrepresentation or corruption. In *Plama Consortium v Bulgaria*, the claimant investor misrepresented the identity of the participating members in the bidding process for the privatization of a State-owned oil company to win the tender. *Plama Consortium Limited v Republic of Bulgaria*, ICSID Case No. ARB/03/24, Award (27 August 2008) (*Plama Consortium v Bulgaria*) para 133. In this investor-state contracted-based dispute, the claimant investor bribed the Head of State to be awarded with a contract for the construction, maintenance and operation of duty-free complexes in different airports within that State. *World Duty Free Company Limited v The Republic of Kenya*, ICSID Case No. ARB/00/7, Award (4 October 2006) para 136.

[100]*Inceysa v El Salvador* (n 90) paras 230–233.

[101]*Plama Consortium v Bulgaria* (n 99) para 135; *Phoenix v Czech Republic* (n 98) paras 75–80.

[102]*Plama Consortium v Bulgaria* (n 99) Award paras 138–140.

[103]Finding claimant investor's conduct contrary to the good faith and *nemo auditur propriam turpitudinem allegans*, the Tribunal precluded the application of the substantive protection of the Energy Charter Treaty. *Plama Consortium v Bulgaria* (n 99) paras 141–146.

[104]*Urbaser v Argentina* (n 1, Chap. 1) para 619.

breaches of the FET standard[105] but also the fact that this legal standard neither deprives states from exercising their regulatory powers in the public interest nor from adopting legislative changes.[106] That said, the *Urbaser v Argentina* tribunal primarily focused on the provisions of water concession agreement as the legitimate source of investors' expectations,[107] since the contract itself explicitly underscores the regulatory powers of the water regulatory agency and provides that Argentina's laws, as the applicable law under BIT, also governs investors' rights and obligations.[108] In making their assessment, the *South American Silver v Bolivia* tribunal, on the contrary, centred on the legal and business framework governing claimant investor's investment within the respondent state.[109] Hence, one may contend that the domestic instruments through which respondent states had discharged their duty to regulate investors' activities are essential elements in the tribunals' determinations of breaches of the FET.

As far as the *Urbaser v Argentina* case is concerned, the most important aspect of its reasoning was that the legitimate expectation of Argentina to protect the right to water as required by its domestic and international legal obligations was a central element in its assessment of the legitimacy of Urbaser's expectations,[110] acknowledging the potential broad scope of legal rules that may charge such regulatory duties upon Argentina.[111] Thus, since these rules should have informed the expectations of Spanish corporations, the tribunal assimilated corporate interests with the legal framework into which its investment activities operate,[112] which included the rights and powers of local authorities as defined by the concession agreement and other legal obligations that Argentina had to prevail over the contract, such as its constitutional obligation to 'ensure the population's health and access to water and to take all measures required to that effect'.[113] For the tribunal, the latter regulatory objective was 'an important objective of the privatization of the water and sewage services, including [of Spanish corporations'] investment', so that the regulatory measures implemented to achieve that purpose 'cannot hurt the [FET] standard

---

[105] *South American Silver v Bolivia* (n 3, Chap. 1) para 648.

[106] *South American Silver v Bolivia* (n 3, Chap. 1) para 649.

[107] It held that their protection under the BIT is not equivalent to investor's own understanding of its entitlements as they are protected under the contract. *Urbaser v Argentina* (n 1, Chap. 1) paras 616–617. Moreover, host state's legal framework, including its rights and obligations subject to what the BIT provides, represents an essential element in the assessment of investor's expectations, even though this analysis is initially made based on host state's contractual commitments assumed in investor's benefit. *Urbaser v Argentina* (n 1, Chap. 1) para 619.

[108] Ibidem.

[109] *South American Silver v Bolivia* (n 3, Chap. 1) para 652.

[110] *Urbaser v Argentina* (n 1, Chap. 1) para 621.

[111] Ibidem.

[112] *Urbaser v Argentina* (n 1, Chap. 1) para 622.

[113] *Urbaser v Argentina* (n 1, Chap. 1) para 622.

because their occurrence must have been deemed to be accepted by the investor when entering into the investment and the Concession Contract'.[114]

While the *Urbaser v Argentina* tribunal conceded that this reading does not mean that Argentina should adopt measures that are inconsistent with the elements of the FET standard,[115] the meaning attached to host state's regulatory framework by the *Urbaser v Argentina* tribunal reflects an instrumental understanding of investment treaty protection for the realization of the right to water. In fact, the tribunal held that FET standard comprises expectations of legal nature and the social and economic environment of the host state forming investor's expectations when making its investment,[116] and endorsed Argentina's view that the right to water 'constitutes the framework within which Claimants should frame their expectations'.[117] Accordingly, the *Urbaser v Argentina* tribunal initially confirms the proposition that host states' duty to regulate foreign investors' activities to prevent abuses of the enjoyment of human rights, which they are expected to guarantee through their provision of public services, can be considered in the analysis of the legitimacy of claimant investors' expectations. Based on these views, the *Urbaser v Argentina* tribunal dismissed investors' claims alleging violations of the FET standard by emergency measures on the water concession[118] and terminated concession agreement,[119] or did not award damages even when it found breaches of FET due to the worthlessness of their concession.[120]

In *South American Silver v Bolivia*, the tribunal found that there were no breaches of the FET standard because the claimant investors failed to explain not only which expectations were frustrated, but also the alleged changes of the legal and regulatory framework governing its mining activities that should have informed its expectations.[121] The investor only considered the reversion of its mining concession as the only act impairing its legitimate expectations.[122] To motivate its findings, when reviewing the legitimacy of claimant investor's expectation, the tribunal held that it should have assumed that its subsidiary's operation takes place in an area inhabited by indigenous people living under precarious conditions. It also observed that the

---

[114]*Urbaser v Argentina* (n 1, Chap. 1) para 622.

[115]Ibidem.

[116]*Urbaser v Argentina* (n 1, Chap. 1) para 623.

[117]*Urbaser v Argentina* (n 1, Chap. 1) para 624.

[118]The main reasons for tribunal's dismissal of investor's claims were that claimant investor's investment was already struggling prior the adoption of these measures and that Argentina met the criteria to satisfy the defence of necessity under customary international law. *Urbaser v Argentina* (n 1, Chap. 1) paras 634–738.

[119]Tribunal dismissed investor's claims due to its own inobservance of contractual obligations. *Urbaser v Argentina* (n 1, Chap. 1) paras 890–950.

[120]Renegotiation efforts of the contract constituted a breach of the FET standard due to the opaque conduct of local authorities towards investor's investment. *Urbaser v Argentina* (n 1, Chap. 1) paras 812–847.

[121]*South American Silver v Peru* (n 3, Chap. 1) para 653.

[122]Ibidem.

investor's own advisors had warned of this situation and made recommendations that they were to implement as some measures in its development project.[123] In connection with this, the tribunal also emphasised Bolivia's duty to protect and offer oversight in relation to the well-being of the indigenous communities.[124] Further, the tribunal not only recognised its duty to regulate investor's activities because its actions towards the community exacerbate the frictions already existing with communities, but also that the mining concession' reversion did serve to restore the public order and to protect indigenous communities as defined by the reversion decree.[125] Therefore, the *South American Silver v Bolivia* case suggests that a tribunal could acknowledge the respondent state's duty to regulate claimant investor's activities in its review of the legitimacy of foreign investors' expectations, even in cases where their provision of goods or services do not directly serve to guarantee the enjoyment of a specific human right. In the extractive sector, this understanding of the legitimacy of investor's expectation could also underpin state's fulfilment of its duty to regulate foreign investment activities, if their exploration or exploitation activities led to depletion or pollution of water sources and thus impair the enjoyment of the right to water.

As far as the legality of claimant investors' investment is concerned as an element in tribunals' review of the legitimacy of their expectations under the FET standard, cases such as *Copper Mesa v Ecuador* and *Bear Creek v Peru* indicate that respondent states' allegations of investors' inobservance of international instruments protecting indigenous communities come in the form of allegations of 'unclean hands' than as allegations of investment's illegality. Arguably, the main reason for this approach is that respondent states are only able to substantiate the existence of human rights responsibilities for corporate actors with basis on soft-law standards.[126] That said, as Sect. 4.1.1.2 illustrated, to consider this argument requires that the respondent states prove first that they did not deliberately tolerate investors' abuses of indigenous communities' rights, and second, that they did not endorse investors' way of conducting consultation of indigenous communities to be successful on the merits.[127] Accordingly, one may argue that tribunals under this line of reasoning may underpin respondent states' fulfilment of their duty to regulate extractive industries if they were taken prior to the submission of the investment

---

[123] *South American Silver v Peru* (n 3, Chap. 1) para 655.

[124] Ibidem.

[125] *South American Silver v Peru* (n 3, Chap. 1) para 656.

[126] In the *South American Silver* case, Bolivia also requested the application of the 'clean hands' principle and invoke the UNGP and the OECD Guidelines for Multinational Enterprises. See n 64.

[127] To assess this type of illegality, tribunals generally resorted to the estoppel principle under which a state is prevented from alleging the existence of an illegality, if it previously knew about investor's conduct and deliberately tolerate it. *Tecmed v Mexico* (n 375, Chap. 2) para 149; *Tokios Tokeles v Ukraine* (n 90) para 86; *International Thunderbird Gaming Corporation v The United Mexican States*, UNCITRAL (NAFTA), Award (26 January 2006) (*Thunderbird v Mexico*) para 165; *Fraport v Philippines* (n 92) paras 346–347; *Desert Line Projects v Yemen* (n 98) paras 117–118.

treaty claim. The *South American Silver v Bolivia* tribunal confirms that reading as shown above.

### 4.1.2.2  On Questions of Indirect Expropriation

Latin American countries have increasingly defined criteria according to which tribunals assess their regulatory actions challenged by foreign investors as indirect expropriation,[128] to avoid the fact that the 'sole effect' of their measures is sufficient to establish a regulatory taking.[129] Yet, the question arising becomes whether, and if so, according to which criteria, tribunals currently review respondent states' regulatory motivations behind the adoption of measures qualified by claimant investors as (indirect) expropriation, so as to permit the incorporation of states' fulfilment of their duty to regulate claimant investors' activities on their analysis of treaty provisions relating to expropriation. To answer this question, this section uses the *Copper Mesa v Ecuador*, *Urbaser v Argentina* and *South American Silver v Bolivia* as case studies.

In *Copper Mesa v Ecuador*, one of the issues at stake was whether the termination of the Junin concession granted to the Canadian corporation without compensation for investor's lack of compliance with indigenous communities' consultation over the former's project constituted an expropriation.[130] The tribunal departed from the premise that the revocation of this mining concession permanently deprived the investor of its investment,[131] so that after identifying that Ecuadorian authorities did not create legitimate expectations about the stability of the regulatory and legal framework,[132] the tribunal mainly devoted itself to determining the lawfulness of this regulatory act. The *Copper Mesa v Ecuador* tribunal did not engage in reviewing what constituted the public purpose of the measure in its determination of its lawfulness, since, as a regulator, Ecuador is entitled to determine what lies in its national interest and thus in compliance with their domestic and international obligations.[133] Notwithstanding the former, it also added that 'it could not do so unlawfully inconsistently with its obligations under the Treaty'.[134] Therefore, although the tribunal left the definition of 'public purpose' at respondent state's discretion, it foreclosed an accommodation of the state's protection of indigenous groups in the assessment. As result of that stance, the tribunal focused on whether the termination resolution was arbitrary and whether due process guarantee was met.[135] The analysis of the 'due process' requirement was of particular importance because

---

[128]See Sect. 2.3.2.1.1, Chap. 2.

[129]See Sect. 2.3.2.2, Chap. 2.

[130]*Copper Mesa v Ecuador* (n 3, Chap. 1) paras 6.53 and 6.54.

[131]*Copper Mesa v Ecuador* (n 3, Chap. 1) para 6.59.

[132]*Copper Mesa v Ecuador* (n 3, Chap. 1) para 6.61.

[133]*Copper Mesa v Ecuador* (n 3, Chap. 1) para 6.64.

[134]Ibidem.

[135]*Copper Mesa v Ecuador* (n 3, Chap. 1) para 6.66.

the applicable BIT particularly underscores an investor's right to have a prompt review of its claims before the competent authorities of states parties.[136] The tribunal answered this question in the negative because Ecuador did not pay the compensation, nor did it observe the standard governing the payment,[137] and, lastly, it failed to provide effective remedies to appeal the termination resolution.[138]

The findings of the *Copper Mesa v Ecuador* tribunal suggest that exploring the regulatory objectives underlying state's measures challenged as indirect expropriation has not established itself as a general trend in current case law. For instance, the *bona fide* and police powers doctrines were only relevant as elements to determine the lawfulness of an expropriation than as criteria to balance investor and host state's interests in a particular case. Likely, the formulation of provisions on expropriation under the Canada-Ecuador BIT wielded great influence on the outcome of the dispute because Ecuador's observance of its obligation to guarantee due process attracted great attention in the analysis of the merits of this Canadian corporation.

Like in *Copper Mesa v Ecuador*, the *Urbaser v Argentina* and *South American Silver v Bolivia* tribunals initially addressed the lawfulness of respondent states' actions deemed by claimants as indirect expropriation. Yet, in their assessments, both tribunals exhaustively reviewed respondent states' compliance with their regulatory duties. The *Urbaser v Argentina* tribunal examined states' duties on questions relating to the legality of regulatory acts leading to the termination of water concession owned by Spanish investors that were regarded as indirect expropriation, while the *South American Silver* tribunal made a similar analysis regarding the reversion of Canadian investor's mining concession on questions relating to its public purpose and proportionality.

After restating the regulatory acts deemed as indirect expropriation,[139] the *Urbaser v Argentina* tribunal found that the emergency measures did not constitute an indirect expropriation because of the temporal character of the loss suffered by the concessionaire resulting from their implementation and the possibility of shareholders' funding in the absence of external loans.[140] In addition, the tribunal also dismissed investors' allegations of disrupted renegotiation of the concession agreement based on the presumption that concessionaire's participation in this process

---

[136] *Copper Mesa v Ecuador* (n 3, Chap. 1) para 6.68. More precisely, the BIT provides that covered investors 'have a right, under [its] law (…) making the expropriation, to prompt review, by a judicial or other independent authority of that Party, of its case and of the valuation of its investment or returns in accordance with the principles set out in this Article'. Agreement between the Government of Canada and the Government of the Republic of Ecuador for the Promotion and Reciprocal Protection of Investments (signed 29 April 1996, entered into force 6 June 1997) art VIII para 2.

[137] *Copper Mesa v Ecuador* (n 3, Chap. 1) paras 6.60, 6.67.

[138] *Copper Mesa v Ecuador* (n 3, Chap. 1) para 6.69.

[139] They comprised emergency measures (namely, pesification and freezing of water tariffs), disruption of the renegotiation of the concession agreement and executive decree terminating the water concession. *Urbaser v Argentina* (n 1, Chap. 1) para 1001.

[140] *Urbaser v Argentina* (n 1, Chap. 1) para 1002.

implied the perception that local authorities did not aim at depriving it from its rights.[141] Lastly, the tribunal found that shareholders' omission to provide further funding for the expansion of the water network as agreed in the concession agreement clearly justified the termination of the concession so that executive decree was not tantamount of an indirect expropriation.[142]

Accordingly, the *Urbaser v Argentina* tribunal clearly reviewed Argentina's fulfilment with its duty to regulate claimant investor's provision of drinking water services by means of concession agreement's definition of shareholders and concessionaire's obligations on questions relating to allegations of indirect expropriation. Certainly, the lack of substantial activities by the concessionaire in Argentina during the period when Spanish investors alleged that the breaches of the IIA occurred also played a fundamental role,[143] which, in turn, indicates the tribunal's attempt to accommodate the interests of both disputing parties.

In *South American Silver v Bolivia*, the tribunal had to resolve whether the executive decree reverting the mining concession of the Canadian investor amounted to an indirect expropriation. In addressing the public purpose of the decree, the tribunal confirmed that the decree clearly exposed the facts[144] and the motivations underlying the reversion.[145] After upholding the social character behind the decree and the contribution of claimant investor's concessionaire towards the escalation of social conflicts,[146] the tribunal established that the public purpose condition was met.[147] Subsequently, although proportionality was not a requirement under the lawfulness criteria, the tribunal deemed it relevant as alleged by the claimant and found that the reversion decree was a proportional measure. This was because social conflict was not temporary and clearly constituted a major concern for Bolivia, and the development project of the Canadian investor was at the initial stage so as to bear great loss.[148] In reaching to this conclusion, the *South American Silver v Bolivia* tribunal clearly exhibits its intention to integrate the regulatory needs of Bolivia by strongly refusing to merely assimilate the economic benefit pursued by the investor, with social benefit for the community as requested by the claimant investor.[149]

---

[141] *Urbaser v Argentina* (n 1, Chap. 1) para 1004.

[142] *Urbaser v Argentina* (n 1, Chap. 1) para 1007.

[143] *Urbaser v Argentina* (n 1, Chap. 1) para 1008.

[144] They included clear references to the existence of a conflict that escalated and led to acts of violence, shortcomings in the management of community relations, and social conflict even conducive to death of community members. *South American Silver v Bolivia* (n 3, Chap. 1) para 559.

[145] The reasons behind the revocation of the reversion decree included the difficulties arising with the communities during the exploration activities, risk for the life of population and need to preserve peace. *South America Silver v Bolivia* (n 3, Chap. 1) para 660.

[146] *South American Silver v Bolivia* (n 3, Chap. 1) paras 561–563.

[147] *South American Silver v Bolivia* (n 3, Chap. 1) para 567.

[148] *South American Silver v Bolivia* (n 3, Chap. 1) paras 570, 577.

[149] *South American Silver v Bolivia* (n 3, Chap. 1) para 578.

Hence, an arbitral tribunal clearly challenges the proposition that economic development unequivocally entails social development of host state's population.[150]

The *South American Silver v Bolivia* tribunal concluded that the reversion decree was an indirect expropriation because, although the due process requirement was satisfied since the claimant investor failed to seek domestic remedies,[151] the state of necessity and the alleged powers doctrine invoked by Bolivia were not designed to excuse it from the payment of compensation that it had omitted as a result of its reversion of the mining concession.[152]

To sum up, the cases studies under review in this section suggest that some tribunals are willing to recognise the regulatory duties of respondent states in their review of alleged existence of indirect expropriation. Lawfulness criteria such as public purpose and legality of the regulatory measures allegedly amounting to an indirect expropriation may permit this integration. That said, it is important to keep in mind that the formulation of IIAs' provisions plays a key role in the determination of the criteria according to which tribunals frame their analysis. Besides, the circumstance of the case might lead tribunals to engage in this assessment, particularly if affording investment treaty protection under IIAs must be guarantee under conditions that involve social unrest and serious human rights abuses committed within the context of claimant investors' activities.

### 4.1.3  Articulation of the Duty to Regulate on Questions of Procedural IIA Rights

#### 4.1.3.1  On Questions of States' Right to Challenge Tribunals' Jurisdiction and/or the Admissibility of Investors' Claims

Since the purpose of ISDS is affording investment treaty protection only to *bona fide* investment,[153] tribunals have engaged in reviewing the 'unclean hands' of claimant investors. Based on this ground, Ecuador and Peru sought to challenge the admissibility of claimant investors' claims, by alleging abuses of indigenous people's right to be consulted over the development projects that may likely affect their livelihood in *Copper Mesa* and *Bear Creek* cases, respectively.[154]

The 'unclean hands' doctrine is generally considered a principle of international law that may cover any type of wrongdoing and has been distinguished from the legality requirement since the latter only ties investors' entitlement to investment

---

[150]See Sect. 2.3.1.1.1, Chap. 2.

[151]*South American Silver v Bolivia* (n 3, Chap. 1) paras 579–586.

[152]*South American Silver v Bolivia* (n 3, Chap. 1) paras 590, 596, 604, 608, 613, 620, 625–630.

[153]*SAUR v Argentina* (n 1, Chap. 1) Decision on Jurisdiction, para 308.

[154]See Kriebaum (2018b). In relation to tribunals' analysis of the 'unclean hands' of claimant investors on their assessment of the merits of their claims on the FET standard, see Sect. 4.1.2.1.

treaty protection to its compliance with host states' domestic laws.[155] Unlike the legality requirement generally imposed by IIAs that could have the effect of depriving a tribunal from exercising jurisdiction since these treaty provisions embody states' consent to arbitration,[156] the 'unclean hands' doctrine provides a wider range of argumentative manoeuvre to respondent states to challenge any type of wrongdoings at the admissibility phase,[157] if respondent states had questioned investors' acts prior to the submission of an investment treaty claim.[158] Otherwise, this review becomes an issue of the merits. For this reason, the *Bear Creek v Peru* tribunal dealt with defence arguments in its review of the merits of investor's allegations,[159] because Peru only questioned investor's unclean hands based on the ILO Convention 169 as the normative basis of investors' wrongdoings during the conduct of arbitration proceedings.[160]

Against this background, the question to be addressed then touches on conditions under which tribunals review the fulfilment of the states' duty to regulate claimant investors' activities on questions of their procedural rights to challenge the 'unclean hands' of claimant investors. To this end, the analysis followed by the *Bear Creek v Peru* tribunal concerning Peru's allegations of 'unclean hands' on its review of the merits of investor's allegations of an indirect expropriation is discussed below.

In *Bear Creek v Peru*, the tribunal, by evaluating the character of the measure allegedly tantamount to an indirect expropriation,[161] had to decide whether the revocation of Canadian investor's mining license in the wake of social protest amounted to an indirect expropriation.[162] It was under this criterion that the tribunal dealt with Peru's allegations of 'unclean hands' put forward against the investor and in parallel with the corresponding regulatory conduct of the respondent state. After upholding the significant economic impact of this measure with the distinguishable legitimate expectations of the claimant investor, the tribunal engaged in assessing its character by exploring whether the claimant investor had contributed to this social

---

[155]Moloo (2010).

[156]*Saba Fakes v Republic of Turkey*, ICSID Case No. ARB/07/20, Award (14 July 2010) para 114. *Inceysa v El Salvador* (n 90) paras 142–144.

[157]See *Waguih Elie George Siag and Clorinda Vecchi v The Arab Republic of Egypt*, ICSID Case No. ARB/05/15, Award (1 June 2009).

[158]*Copper Mesa v Ecuador* (n 3, Chap. 1).

[159]See Sect. 4.1.2.1.

[160]See n 78.

[161]Pursuant to the Annex 812.1 of the Canada-Peru FTA, both states parties indicate that '[i]ndirect expropriation results from a measure or series of measures of a Party that have an effect equivalent to direct expropriation without formal transfer of title or outright seizure' and that 'the character of the measure or series of measures' shall be one of the factors upon which a tribunal shall rely to determine whether it/they constitute an indirect expropriation. Free Trade Agreement between Canada and Peru (signed 29 May 2008, entered into force 1 August 2009) ch. 8, art 812 and Annex 812.1 para 2, lits. (a) and (b) iii.

[162]See n 76.

unrest, and whether a legal justification underlay respondent state's actions.[163] To deal with this question, the tribunal centred on whether additional actions were required to the claimant investor than the one undertaken, which, in their absence, caused social unrest and thus justified the concession's revocation.[164]

In analysing claimant investor's actions, the tribunal found that they were insufficient and that the investor could have made further efforts to reach all communities potentially affected by its development project,[165] highlighting that the objective of such consultation process, pursuant to international law, is obtaining the consent of the communities concerned.[166] Having said that, the *Bear Creek v Peru* tribunal, nevertheless, reiterated that the relevant question was whether the respondent state demanded from the investor further outreach, so as to justify the revocation of licenses for its inobservance.[167] To solve it, the tribunal applied the *Abengoa test* according to which the respondent state has to prove the omission or fault of the claimant investor and the causal link between this omission and the damages suffered as a result.[168] The tribunal concluded that Peru failed to prove the connection between investor's failure to consult indigenous people inhabiting the environs of its development project and the social protest resulting because of its presence in that area. The tribunal based its conclusion on the fact that local authorities had approved and endorsed the activities conducted by claimant investor's subsidiary.[169] The tacit tolerance of the acts of claimant investor's subsidiary by Peruvian authorities made the *Bear Creek* tribunal presumed that the Canadian corporation took for granted that it was complying with the social license required for its exploration activities.[170] On this basis, the tribunal concluded that the revocation of licenses constituted an indirect expropriation because the respondent state was unable to show its authorities deemed investor's actions as contrary to the ILO Convention 169,[171] as Peru argued to justify the revocation of claimant investor's licenses.[172]

The approach followed by the *Bear Creek v Peru* tribunal is consistent with investment case law that generally reviews the legality of investors' conduct against a varying set of benchmarks,[173] which, in this case, was the estoppel principle under which one disputing party is deterred from presenting one fact as the basis of its legal

---

[163]*Bear Creek v Peru* (n 3, Chap. 1) para 401.

[164]*Bear Creek v Peru* (n 3, Chap. 1) paras 403–408.

[165]*Bear Creek v Peru* (n 3, Chap. 1) paras 403–407.

[166]In this regard the Tribunal alluded to the article 32 of the UNDRIP as the basis of such contention. *Bear Creek v Peru* (n 3, Chap. 1) para 406, footnote 525.

[167]*Bear Creek v Peru* (n 3, Chap. 1) para 408.

[168]*Bear Creek v Peru* (n 3, Chap. 1) para 410.

[169]*Bear Creek v Peru* (n 3, Chap. 1) para 411.

[170]*Bear Creek v Peru* (n 3, Chap. 1) para 412.

[171]Ibidem.

[172]*Bear Creek v Peru* (n 3, Chap. 1) para 413.

[173]These criteria consist in severity of investment's illegality, investor's good faith and the estoppel principle. See Diel-Gligor and Hennecke (2015) paras 8–10 and 20–28.

claim if it did not rely upon the conduct of the other party to its own detriment or to the other's advantage.[174] Under the estoppel principle, it is the claimant investor that generally has a major interest to advance estoppel claims if the respondent state tolerated its illegal conduct and it subsequently reckon with the validity of its acts,[175] or if the state is itself accountable for the illegality of its own conduct.[176] However, since the respondent state is the one who usually invokes the application of the 'unclean hands' doctrine, it is therefore the one called to prove that it did not endorse the conduct of the investor.[177]

Against this background, one may argue that tribunals may review respondent state's fulfilment of its duty to regulate claimant investor's conduct of consultation with the indigenous people's as far as questions relating to the allegations of 'unclean hands' against the investor are concerned. Yet, the 'character' of the mining concessions' revocation was in fact the benchmark that facilitated tribunal's review of Peru's regulatory conduct and of investor's unclean hands on its review of the merits of investor's allegations of an indirect expropriation.

That said, to be successful, the respondent state must show that it prevented *in advance* investor's impairments of local communities' rights and did not tolerate these abuses by any regulatory means. In this case, Peru could have invoked its duty to regulate foreign investment activities deriving from the ACHR that required prevention of the real and imminent risk that investor's activities could have posed upon indigenous communities' survival, despite legal limitations upon their right to traditional lands and territories. This would have initially implied to concede, as it certainly made in relation to the ILO Convention 169, that it is the only one responsible to ensure that the Canadian corporation's mining activities do not impair indigenous groups' survival and that their consultation with the indigenous communities is a process to make them aware of the real and imminent threats of corporate activities.[178] However, since Peru delegated the consultation process to the corporation interested in operating the mining area concerned, it was unable to invoke Inter-American standards as the normative basis of its regulatory duty because it failed to ensure the 'independency' requirement of the consultation process.[179] In addition, Peru failed to ensure that the claimant investor undertakes consultation process without any type of coercion towards indigenous peoples, or bribery of indigenous leaders to obtain their approval.[180]

---

[174]*Temple of Preah Vihear (Cambodia v Thailand)*, Judgement (15 June 1962) ICJ Reports (1962) 52 para 63, Separate Opinion of Sir Gerald Fitzmaurice.

[175]*Tecmed v Mexico* (n 375, Chap. 2) para 149; *Tokios Tokeles v Ukraine* (n 90) para 86; *Thunderbird v Mexico* (n 127) para 165.

[176]*Kardassopoulos v Georgia* (n 371, Chap. 2) paras 183–184.

[177]*Niko Resources (Bangladesh) Ltd. v Bangladesh Petroleum Exploration & Production Company Limited ("Bapex") and Bangladesh Oil Gas and Mineral Corporation ("Petrobangla")*, ICSID Case No. ARB/10/11, Decision on Jurisdiction (19 August 2013).

[178]See Sect. 3.2.2.2.2, Chap. 3.

[179]See Sect. 3.2.2.2.2, Chap. 3.

[180]Ibidem.

To sum up, a successful substantiation of the 'unclean hands' of investors to challenge the merits of its claims presupposes for the respondent state to explain how it meets its duty to regulate corporate activities operating in areas inhabited by indigenous communities. In other words, a respondent state that clearly exhibits which regulatory measures it adopted, to prevent investors from interfering with the indigenous people's right to be consulted over the development projects affecting their survival, may achieve tribunals' dismissal of claimant investor's claims at the merits, if the investor is unable to counteract allegations of 'unclean hands'. From a broader perspective, the 'unclean hands' doctrine provides an entry point for tribunals' consideration of respondent state's regulatory duties under IHRL and thus of inter-regime frictions, provided that the respondent state is willing to disclose how it discharges such a duty.

### 4.1.3.2 On Questions of States' Right to Submit Counterclaims

According to well-established case law, states can bring counterclaims against claimant investors if they substantiate, on one hand, a separate cause of action, namely, the existence of a legal obligation with which the claimant investor failed to comply. On the other hand, states must meet additional procedural requirements that the investor itself must fulfil to bring its claim:[181] First, they must prove that the formulation of the arbitration clause was broad enough to cover the consent of the other disputing party (namely, the investor) for the submission of counterclaims,[182] since they implicitly form the source of claimant investors' consent to the submission of counterclaims.[183] In fact, how disputing parties perfect their consent allows tribunals to draw a *de facto* equivalence between investors' acceptance of the irrevocable offer of consent given by states parties in an IIA for the submission of its claim, and investors' consent to states parties' counterclaims.[184] Second, there

---

[181]The UNCITRAL rules as revised in 2010 broadly provide that a respondent state could bring a counterclaim if the arbitral tribunal has jurisdiction over it. UNCITRAL Arbitration rules, as revised in 2010) art 21 para 3. This presupposes, inter alia, having competence to settle any legal dispute whether contractual or not. To recall, the 1976 UNCITRAL Arbitration Rules are only applicable to 'dispute in relation to [a] contract' and therefore exclusively admit the submission of counterclaims 'arising out of [a] contract'. UNCITRAL Arbitration Rules 1976 (n 297, Chap. 2) art 1 para 1 and art 19 para 3, respectively. Subsequently, the UNCITRAL Arbitration Rules (as revised in 2010) expanded its scope of application to 'disputes between [the parties] in respect of a defined legal relationship, whether contractual or not (. . .)'. UNCITRAL Arbitration Rules, as revised in 2010 (n 330, Chap. 2) art 1 para 1. See Bjorklund (2013), pp. 471–471.

[182]*Spyridon Roussalis v Romania*, ICSID Case No. ARB/06/1, Award (7 December 2011) (*Roussalis v Romania*).

[183]*Saluka v Czech Republic* (n 363, Chap. 2) para 39; *Paushok v Mongolia* (n 372, Chap. 2) para 689; *Hamester v Ghana* (n 92) paras 353–354. See also Bjorklund (2013), pp. 468–470.

[184]*Roussalis v Romania* (n 182) para 866. Under this approach, claimant investors' consent performs a 'double' function so that just as respondent states' consent to arbitration include the settlement of investors' claims and counterclaims, investors' consent 'ipso facto' devise its consent

must be a close connection between the subject matter of respondent states' counterclaim and claimant investors' claim.[185] As an issue of counterclaims' admissibility, tribunals review jurisdictional clauses, together with clauses on applicable law (if laid down in IIAs), since the latter also constitutes part of the arbitration agreement on the set of laws pursuant to which investment disputes must be settled.[186]

Moreover, the subject matter of counterclaims has ranged from investors' breaches of contractual obligations[187] and/or their inobservance of domestic laws.[188] Yet, in *Urbaser v Argentina*, the question addressed by the tribunal was whether the subject matter of Argentina's counterclaim alleging Spanish investors' breaches of human rights, which are a set of obligations that do not strictly relate to the investment, had a connection with the subject matter of Urbaser's claims. The tribunal found that the dispute settlement clause applicable was drafted in neutral terms in relation to the 'identity' of the party entitled to bring a claim,[189] and to the disputes to be arbitrated so as to include the submission of this counterclaim.[190] Yet, to establish the direct connection between both legal claims, the *Urbaser v Argentina* tribunal relied upon a different methodology than the one usually followed by tribunals. To contextualise, tribunals generally explore whether the contract related to the investment covered by the IIA[191] and whether the respondent state is party to the respective contract.[192] Tribunals lack jurisdiction to hear respondent state's counterclaim, if the answer to both questions are in the negative, and/or when the contract under review has its own dispute settlement clause.[193]

The *Urbaser v Argentina* tribunal, however, despite being based on less stringent criteria, found Argentina's counterclaim admissible, on the grounds of a legal link between investment treaty claim of Spanish investors and the human rights-based counterclaim of Argentina since both legal fields belong to international law that is

---

for both claims. *Antoine Goetz and others v Republic of Burundi*, ICSID Case No. ARB/01/2, Award (21 June 2002) paras 278–279. See also *Aven v Costa Rica* (n 66, Chap. 1) paras 732–743.

[185]ICSID Convention (n 162, Chap. 2) art 46.

[186]Schreuer (2014).

[187]The subject matter of Czech Republic's counterclaim was Saluka's parent company breaches of its domestic laws and certain provisions of the Share Purchase Agreement it concluded with a Czech entity. *Saluka v Czech Republic* (n 363, Chap. 2) Decision on Jurisdiction over the Czech Republic Contract-claims paras 47–48. In *Hamester v Ghana*, this state brought a counterclaim due claimant investor's breaches of the joint venture agreement, which provoked losses to Ghana and Ghana Cocoa Board. *Hamester v Ghana* (n 92) paras 1–3, 22, 351.

[188]*Saluka v Czech Republic* (n 363, Chap. 2) para 79; *Paushok v Mongolia* (n 372, Chap. 2) para 694.

[189]*Urbaser v Argentina* (n 1, Chap. 1) paras 1143–1144.

[190]*Urbaser v Argentina* (n 1, Chap. 1) para 1147.

[191]*Paushok v Mongolia* (n 372, Chap. 2).

[192]*Saluka v Czech Republic* (n 363, Chap. 2).

[193]*Saluka v Czech Republic* (n 363, Chap. 2).

applicable in the settlement of the dispute.[194] Furthermore, the admissibility of the counterclaim was also upheld on the basis of a factual link between both legal claims because they related to the same investment in connection with the same concession.[195] In the other two cases, where an assessment on the merits have proceeded so far, namely *Burlington* and *Perenco*, both against Ecuador, compliance with the admissibility requirements was unproblematic due to the arbitration agreement achieved by the disputing parties to submit the counterclaims.[196] Accordingly, at least at the admissibility phase, the *Urbaser v Argentina* tribunal did not deny the interaction between IIL and IHRL on the basis of the applicable law clause allowing the interpretation of the BIT's provisions stipulated in the international law. Yet, the next question becomes whether existing case law permits addressing the regulatory duties of respondent states on questions of tribunals' review of counterclaims' merits.

Most arbitral tribunals admit hearing counterclaims of respondent states if domestic laws inextricably related to claimant investors' obligations arising out of the contract.[197] Otherwise, tribunals generally abstain to rule on counterclaims, where states allege claimant investors' breaches of general domestic law on the grounds that the legal systems of respondent states already provide appropriate procedures to deal with such allegations.[198] Under this line of reasoning, tribunals' consideration of respondent states' regulatory duties imposed by IHRL may proceed indirectly if they review investors' obligations deriving from domestic executive and if the legislative instruments through which the respondent state discharge this international duty was specifically intended to rule claimant investors' provision of good or services that facilitate states' fulfilment of human rights. Domestic laws and concession agreements governing foreign corporations' provision of drinking water

---

[194] *Urbaser v Argentina* (n 1, Chap. 1) para 1154.

[195] *Urbaser v Argentina* (n 1, Chap. 1) paras 1151.

[196] *Burlington v Ecuador* (n 3, Chap. 1) Decision on Counterclaims (7 February 2017) paras 61–62; *Perenco Ecuador Ltd. v The Republic of Ecuador and Empresa Estatal Petróleos del Ecuador (Petroecuador)*, ICSID Case No. ARB/08/6, Interim Decision on the Environmental Counterclaim (11 August 2015) paras 108–114.

[197] *Burlington v Ecuador* (n 3, Chap. 1) para 63. The *Avec v Costa Rica* tribunal drew this link not only from respondent state's environmental laws, but also from treaty provisions as well to admit Costa Rica's counterclaim. *Avec v Costa Rica* (n 66, Chap. 1) paras 737–742.

[198] To illustrate, in *Amco v Indonesia*, Indonesia refuted investor's allegations of Indonesia's seizure of its investment and the cancellation its investment license by founding its counterclaim on claimant investor's tax evasion. By differentiating between general legal obligations and those directly arising out of the investment, the *Amco v Indonesia* tribunal dismissed Indonesia's counterclaim alleging that its jurisdiction only covers disputes directly arising from an investment pursuant to article 25 of the ICSID Convention. It asserted that although its jurisdiction may cover disputes regarding tax issues, tax obligations are obligations of general nature, and thereupon they in fact differ from those rights and obligations related to the investor's agreed investment, which would have made admissible the respondent State's counterclaim. *Amco Asia Corporation and others v Republic of Indonesia*, ICSID Case No. ARB/81/1, Decision on Jurisdiction in Resubmitted Proceeding (10 May 1988), 1 ICSID Reports, vol. 132, 543. Also, *Saluka v Czech Republic* (n 363, Chap. 2) para 79; *Paushok v Mongolia* (n 372, Chap. 2) para 694.

services to guarantee the access and affordability of drinking water clearly exemplifies this interaction.[199] Similarly, tribunals would incidentally deal with respondent states' performance of their regulatory duties if they review claimant investors' conduct against the domestic laws and contracts that are intended to regulate use of water sources by mining companies so as to avoid an abusive use that could lead to their depletion or to their pollution.[200] The same would apply if tribunals have to assess counterclaims against corporations that had won a bidding process for mining or oil exploration and/or exploitation by not having consultation with the indigenous people and/or complying with ESIAs laid down in domestic laws and decrees.

Nevertheless, the question remains whether tribunals may recognise the international states' duty to regulate claimant investors' activities under IHRL when addressing claimant investors' responsibilities to respect human rights. In *Urbaser v Argentina*, the cause of action of Argentina's counterclaims was that Spanish investors had an obligation with respect to the right to water under human rights law, which it failed to fulfil by omitting to make appropriate investment in the water concession in both the Province of Buenos Aires and the area of Greater Buenos Aires. However, this counterclaim was rejected on the merits because business entities, including foreign investors, are not addressees of legal obligations under IHRL. Yet, this case may be instructive of how arbitral tribunals may address the tensions between IIL and another international legal regime and thereby informing states regarding which treaty and institutional reforms are necessary to foster consideration of their duty to regulate.

Failing to identify the source of international investors' obligations within the Spain-Argentina BIT,[201] the *Urbaser v Argentina* tribunal showed, once again, its engagement with the assessment of inter-regime tensions by invoking the dispute settlement and applicable law clauses to assess the alleged existence of investors' obligations laid down in external legal sources.[202] This is based on the premise that foreign investors are subject of international law,[203] and that corporate social responsibility (CSR) has become an important standard governing the operation of business activities.[204] By implicitly referring to the UNGP, the tribunal understood that corporations may not be immune from being considered subjects of international law since this responsibility mandates them to perform their business activities in conformity with human rights.[205] Notwithstanding the former, the tribunal acknowledged that these initiatives do not bind corporations to derive a legal obligation so that it deemed necessary to contextualise corporate activities in connection with the

---

[199]See Sect. 3.1.2.2.1, Chap. 3.

[200]See Sect. 3.1.2.2.2, Chap. 3.

[201]*Urbaser v Argentina* (n 1, Chap. 1) para 1185.

[202]*Urbaser v Argentina* (n 1, Chap. 1) paras 1186–1187.

[203]*Urbaser v Argentina* (n 1, Chap. 1) para 1194.

[204]*Urbaser v Argentina* (n 1, Chap. 1) para 1195.

[205]*Urbaser v Argentina* (n 1, Chap. 1) para 1195.

human right at stake to determine whether corporate obligations derive from it or not.[206]

To explore whether the Spanish investors concerned owed legal obligations with respect to the right to water, the *Urbaser v Argentina* tribunal invoked the UDHR and the ICESCR, and found that both instruments indirectly imposed upon corporations an obligation to contribute to the fulfilment of the right to water,[207] from article 5 of the ICESCR that precludes an interpretation of protected rights in a way that allows states and non-state actors to limit these rights.[208] In light of these provisions, the tribunal concluded that these legal instruments did not only give effect to the right to water, but also imposed upon states and corporations an obligation to abstain from impairing this right.[209]

The *Urbaser v Argentina* tribunal's reasoning reveals that it constructed investors' obligations in negative terms, demanding to abstain from adopting any action conducive to their impairment.[210] However, this reading of the Covenant's provision has been criticised for considering it as misleading since this Covenant's article devises a standard of interpretation, rather than a legal source of obligations under the Covenant.[211] Nevertheless, Argentina's formulation of its counterclaims in terms of investors' obligations of positive nature was questioned by the tribunal since it failed to indicate the legal basis of such alleged obligation,[212] and Argentina only underpinned its counterclaim for the effect that the investors' performance of drinking water services may have had on the enjoyment of its population's right to access drinking water.[213] In this line of ideas, the tribunal clarified that the human right to water only assigns an obligation upon states, and does not establish a corresponding obligation of performance upon corporations providing drinking water services.[214]

Beyond the attention received by the *Urbaser v Argentina* case for tribunal's need to acknowledge the potential subjectivity of corporations considering the ongoing

---

[206]Ibidem.

[207]More precisely, the tribunal found that the UDHR may impose upon corporations an obligation to contribute to the fulfilment of the obligation to guarantee the right to equal access to public service and to a standard of living adequate for health and well-being. *Urbaser v Argentina* (n 1, Chap. 1) para 1196.

[208]*Urbaser v Argentina* (n 1, Chap. 1) para 1197. General Comment No. 15 and UNGA resolution No. 64/292 featured as another international instruments underpinning the views of the *Urbaser v Argentina* tribunal in this award. *Urbaser v Argentina* (n 1, Chap. 1) para 1197.

[209]The tribunal literally held that these treaties impose 'an obligation on all parts, public and private parties, not to engage in activity aimed at destroying such rights'. *Urbaser v Argentina* (n 1, Chap. 1) para 1199.

[210]For a brief discussion of the obligation to respect human rights under the ICESCR, see Sect. 3.1. 1.2, Chap. 3.

[211]Ibidem. See also, Abel (2018).

[212]*Urbaser v Argentina* (n 1, Chap. 1) para 1205.

[213]*Urbaser v Argentina* (n 1, Chap. 1) para 1206.

[214]*Urbaser v Argentina* (n 1, Chap. 1) para 1208.

international efforts to define their human rights responsibilities,[215] the tribunal unequivocally understood Argentina's duty to regulate corporate operation of water facilities to protect the right to water in similar terms as those described in the third chapter of this study.[216] The tribunal held that the Spanish-Argentina BIT does not provide for the conversion of contracts into international obligations, and that, from its reference to international law sources, it cannot found any obligation that does not actually exist in international law.[217] Following these preliminary thoughts and departing from the premise that Argentina had the primary responsibility to ensure that the concessionaire guarantees population's right to water, it found that its counterclaim was unfounded, inter alia, because the legal and regulatory framework in place at the time of the concession's approval was ineffective to ensure investors' compliance with their contractual commitments.[218]

Against this background, one may conclude that tribunals have possibilities to review investors' conduct within the context of counterclaims and based on IHRL, at least by employing the applicable law clause that permits the interpretation of IIAs' provisions in conformity with international law. In doing so, they may incidentally deal with respondent states' duty to regulate investors' conduct to disentangle their own liability for investors' omission, as in cases where they raise allegations of investors' unclean hands.

Moreover, in the absence of an international treaty that defines corporations' legal obligations towards human rights, the *Urbaser v Argentina* case shows the need of anchoring the notion of investors' responsibilities to respect human rights in IIAs, at least based on the existing international soft-law instruments. In fact, there is some support for the proposition that the non-judicial mechanisms established for addressing allegations of what corporations' inobservance of such soft-law standards may contribute to the creation of behavioural human rights-based standards,[219] and thus inform tribunals' assessment of counterclaims challenging corporations' inobservance of their responsibilities that derive from these soft-law standards. This might subsequently result in the use of ISDS as an indirect venue to review corporate abuses of human rights, even though tribunals' review under such conditions might weaken the status of those aggrieved by corporate activities as they may find it hard to demand and defend their own rights because their protection would now be subject to respondent states' discretion to articulate their protection.[220]

---

[215]See n 1 Chap. 3. See also De Brabandere (2018).

[216]*Urbaser v Argentina* (n 1, Chap. 1) para 1211. See Sect. 3.1.2.2.1, Chap. 3.

[217]*Urbaser v Argentina* (n 1, Chap. 1) para 1212.

[218]*Urbaser v Argentina* (n 1, Chap. 1) para 1214.

[219]Krajewski (2019).

[220]Abel (2018).

## 4.1.4  Interim Conclusion

Having elaborated the 'duty to regulate' paradigm as an instrument that allows an articulation of states' need to undertake all appropriate legislative and executive means to prevent that foreign investment activities interference with the enjoyment of the right to water and indigenous people's survival in Chap. 3, this chapter initially explored to what extent Latin American countries invokes IHRL as applicable law and articulate their regulatory duty through the argumentative strategies prevailed in ISDS to justify their regulatory measures. On the other hand, it discussed whether, and if so by which legal techniques, tribunals engage in the review of human right-based argument if deployed, and/or assess the regulatory needs of respondent states when determining breaches of IIAs, more generally.

The findings regarding the first question suggest that the argumentative strategies prevailed by states at times vary depending on the right at stake in the investment context and are not always intended to justify their regulatory duties. Moreover, not all states put forward human rights-related arguments as issues of applicable law, but rather at the merits phase. Except from the *Urbaser v Argentina* tribunal that did review Argentina's treaty obligations in conformity with IHRL relying upon the broad formulation of the applicable law clause, the other tribunals avert to deal with inter-regime overlapping alleged by respondent states.

In cases involving investors' provision of drinking water services, argumentative strategies prevailed by Argentina included the incompatibility between its investment treaty and its obligations regarding the right to water, the normative primacy of human rights that it derives from the public nature behind the protection of this right and its constitutional obligations, and the contention that IIL is not a self-contained regime. Hence, Argentina did perceive that investment treaty protection inhibits its regulatory autonomy to discharge its duty to regulate foreign investment activities, requesting an interpretation where the application of IIAs does not nullify its regulatory duty towards the right to water, even though it referred to domestic law, rather than IHRL, as its legal basis. As the cases involving the alleged protection of indigenous people in claims arising out of extractive industries, the review shows that only Bolivia requested an interpretation of the IIA considering the integration principle, article 103 of the UN Charter, the *erga omnes* character of indigenous people's protection, the constitutional rank of indigenous people's protection and soft-law instruments to review claimant investor's conduct. Peru and Ecuador only invoked external sources to substantiate the 'unclean hands' of investors and challenge the admissibility of their claims, briefly alluding to the ILO Convention 169.

The second question was to what extent Latin American countries and tribunals correspondingly articulate and review their duty to regulate claimant investors' provision of drinking water services and claimant investors' conduct of consultation process in relation to indigenous people on questions of alleged breaches of the FET and allegations of indirect expropriation.

The critical analysis of case law shows that some tribunals not only recognise the regulatory duties of respondent states, but also weigh out investors' claims against these duties in their review of the legitimacy of investors' expectations to determine breaches of the FET standard. If the legal and regulatory framework of the respondent state is the central criterion to determine the legitimacy of investors' expectations, the findings indicate that tribunals may draw an equivalence between contract-based investors' expectation to be legally protected. This is because of their provision of a public service and contracted-based (and domestic and international law-based) states' regulatory expectations to ensure that that service is adequately provided (*Urbaser v Argentina*), or dismissed investors' claims if the respondent states' legal and regulatory framework clearly provided for the protection of a specific group of society, such as indigenous communities, under the assumption that these laws and policies shall have informed that expectations (*South American Silver v Bolivia*).

On questions of indirect expropriation, tribunals acknowledge states' regulatory duties, but this does not always lead to dismissed investors' claims. Criteria such as legality and the character of the measure were entry points for an extensive review of states' regulatory needs. The formulation of the treaty provision, however, did exert an influence on what aspects tribunals centred their analysis. In some cases, if the state complies with the regulatory and legal framework governing claimant investor's investment and did not deviate from that norms, the tribunal did not find an indirect expropriation (*Urbaser v Argentina*), while in other cases, even when the state complies with its own legal and regulatory framework, the tribunal found a violation of the treaty for failure of compensation's payment (*South American Silver v Bolivia*). Others, like the *Copper Mesa v Ecuador* tribunal, required compliance with the treaty despite the public objective behind the contested measure.

Lastly, the third question posed in Sect. 4.1.1 was whether, and if so under which conditions, tribunals proceeded to review states' fulfilment of their duty to regulate foreign investment activities involving abuses of the right to water and indigenous people's survival on questions relating to their procedural right to challenge the 'unclean hands' and the submission of counterclaims. The findings confirm that tribunals may consider the regulatory instruments through which states discharge their duty to regulate foreign investment activities in reviewing the 'unclean hands' of claimant investors. The precondition for that assessment seems to be that the treaty provision invoked by the investor clearly alludes to a criterion requesting issues such as the 'character' of the measure, on one hand, and the state can prove how it perform its regulatory duty to put the burden of proving the 'clean hands' upon the investor. On questions of counterclaims, states' duty to regulate is addressed incidentally, if the legislative and executive instruments adopted to discharge it clearly found an obligation for investors.

## 4.2   Required IIAs Reforms to Strengthen States' Duty to Regulate in IIL

### 4.2.1   Reformed IIAs Substantive Provisions

#### 4.2.1.1   Explicit Reference to States' Duty to Regulate Protected Investment

States underpinning the cause of human rights in ISDS such as Latin American countries may not find it unreasonable to articulate their duty to regulate foreign investment activities under IIAs, particularly when they increasingly seek to invoke human rights norms to justify their regulatory measures. Hence, just as many Latin American states articulate their right to regulate foreign investment activities in the current IIAs,[221] they could refer to this international regulatory duty in these treaties. A general reference to the duty of states parties to regulate in IIAs' preamble, or through an autonomous clause, may permit tribunals to review regulatory instruments introduced by respondent states against the benchmarks developed by international human rights bodies.

On questions of substantive obligations of respondent states in cases alleging the existence of an indirect expropriation, an IIAs' reference to states parties' duty to regulate foreign investment activities could underpin tribunals' analysis of their performance in their review of the lawfulness of regulatory instruments employed to prevent investors' infringement of the right to water or indigenous people's right to be consulted. The *Urbaser v Argentina* case showed that the tribunal exclusively considers the legality of the actions of local authorities' leading to revoke water concession,[222] so that a reference to this international duty may induce that a tribunal following the same line of reasoning also examines legality of the revocation against the ICESCR's standards on the right to water.[223] Moreover, if a tribunal must resolve a case involving the revocation of mining license in a context where a claimant investor's activities may severely affect indigenous people's survival by interfering in their consultation,[224] this treaty reference to the duty to regulate foreign investment activities could facilitate an assessment of to what extent a public purpose motivated the concession of the revocation or even of its proportionality by resorting to Inter-American standards governing the conduct of this process.[225] This may require, for instance, to determine whether the state concerned legally required the undertaking of an ESIA to ensure that indigenous communities were informed of the

---

[221]See Sect. 2.3.3.1.1, Chap. 2.

[222]See Sect. 4.1.2.2.

[223]See Sect. 3.1.2.2.1, Chap. 3.

[224]See Sect. 4.1.2.2.

[225]See Sect. 3.2.2.2.2, Chap. 3.

real and imminent threats posed by the project, but the investor failed to disseminate that findings.[226]

On questions of procedural states' rights to challenge investors' allegations of an indirect expropriation based on their 'unclean hands', an explicit reference to this duty in IIAs could underpin tribunals' interpretation of the IIA provision requesting an assessment of the character and/or scope of the challenged measure to determine the merits of investors' claims.[227] Along the line of the *Bear Creek v Peru* tribunal's reasoning, tribunals could fully grant states' exercise of this procedural right provided that they clearly disclose how they had discharged such duty in advance to put the burden of proving that the facts alleged by the state are not true.[228] According to well-established case law, respondent states' legal and regulatory environment that foreign investors anticipated as applicable to their investment is one of the acts against which the legitimacy of their expectations in cases involving alleged breaches of FET is assessed.

Consistent with the view of some tribunals that claimant investors' own assessment of these legal and policy practices is relevant to establish the legitimacy of their expectations,[229] the *Urbaser v Argentina* tribunal held that Argentina had the legitimate expectation to act 'in furtherance of rules of fundamental character' that derive from its domestic and *international* legal obligations.[230] Through this statement, this tribunal tacitly endorsed the proposition that Argentina's regulatory legitimate expectations should have informed the expectation of claimant investors, thereby drawing an equivalence between both disputing parties' interests, on the grounds that claimants' investment was an instrument to ensure users' health and access to water and the regulatory measures taken to achieve this end are presumed to be accepted by these investors when making their investment under such regulatory conditions.[231]

Following this instrumental understanding of the purpose of investment treaty protection, states parties could further anchor the deference to their legitimate regulatory expectations as another benchmark for tribunals' revision of investors' expectations.[232] This could proceed through the incorporation of a general provision alluding to states parties' regulatory duties under IHRL or by complementing references to investors' expectations as a constitutive element of the FET standard with references to these regulatory duties. Since most formulations to the FET standard remain vague and thus provide wide discretion to tribunals to determine

---

[226]Ibidem.

[227]As it is already the case in recently signed/ratified IIAs in Latin America. See Sect. 2.3.3.1.1, Chap. 2.

[228]See Sect. 4.1.3.1.

[229]*Joseph Charles Lemire v Ukraine*, ICSID Case No. ARB/06/18, Award (28 March 2011) para 70.

[230]*Urbaser v Argentina* (n 1, Chap. 1) para 621 (emphasis added).

[231]See Sect. 4.1.2.1.

[232]Sauvant and Ünüvar (2016).

their scope of application,[233] leaving treaty references to states parties' duty to regulate in broader terms may grant tribunals broader discretion as to which international human rights standard is applicable to define which legitimate regulatory expectations states have and should have informed investors' expectations.

### 4.2.1.2   Imposing Investor Obligations

The idea of placing human rights-related obligations upon protected investors under IIAs has not only gained support among scholars[234] but also states have increasingly devoted efforts in re-balancing their legal relationships with foreign investors through references to non-economic concerns in their recent investment treaty-making practice. Some Latin American countries, for instance, proclaim their commitment to foster foreign investors' observance of CSR standards,[235] while others, instead, directly provide that states parties will promote responsible corporate conduct in accordance with the Organisation for Economic Cooperation and Development (OECD) Guidelines for Multinational Corporations (OECD Guidelines).[236]

African countries, on the contrary, have preferred to use IIAs as the legal instrument through which they regulate investors' human rights obligations. Years after the Economic Community of Western African States (ECOWAS) defined some rules to align the investment policies of its member states (by requesting that investors uphold human rights in the community which they are located and avoid committing acts that may undermine their enjoyment),[237] Morocco and Nigeria placed a similar obligation upon the protected investors under the Morocco-Nigeria BIT,[238] whereas the African Union developed the Draft Pan-African Investment Code (DPAIC) to ensure investors' compliance with business ethics and human rights through the observance of internationally recognised human rights, and their commitment not to be accomplices of human rights violations.[239]

---

[233]See Sect. 2.3.3.1.1, Chap. 2.

[234]Nowrot (2015), p. 1160 1169; Dumberry and Dumas-Aubin (2011–2012).

[235]Colombia-United Arab Emirates BIT (n 416, Chap. 2) art 12.

[236]Protocolo Alianza del Pacifico (n 485, Chap. 2) art 10.30 para 3.

[237]ECOWAS, Supplementary Act A/SA.3/12/08 Adopting Community Rules on Investment and the Modalities for their Implementation with ECOWAS (signed 19 December 2008, entered into force 19 January 2009) art 14 para 2.

[238]See Reciprocal Investment Promotion and Protection Agreement between the Government of the Kingdom of Morocco and the Government of the Federal Republic of Nigeria (signed 3 March 2016) (Morocco-Nigeria BIT) art 18. For an overview of these developments, see Tarcisio Gazzini, 'The 2016 Morocco–Nigeria BIT: An Important Contribution to the Reform of Investment Treaties' (Investment Treaty News 26 September 2016) https://www.iisd.org/itn/2017/09/26/the-2016-morocco-nigeria-bit-an-important-contribution-to-the-reform-of-investment-treaties-tarcisio-gazzini/#_edn1 accessed 10 December 2020.

[239]African Union Commission, Economic Affairs Department, 'Draft Pan- African Investment Code' (DPAIC) (December 2016) https://au.int/sites/default/files/documents/32844-doc-draft_

Notwithstanding the former, the Latin American and African investment treaty-making practices is not free from shortcomings. The Latin American practice, for instance, embodies the intention of states parties to assume best-endeavour obligations, rather than to impose direct legal commitments upon protected investors. Through this practice, states thus underpin and reinforce what some scholars have called the 'elusive investor responsibility' that advocates for corporate self-regulation and voluntary adherence to soft-law standards, rather than the creation of binding norms.[240] Moreover, this type of treaty clauses subjects the review of investors' conduct to an initial assessment of states' compliance with their encouragement obligations in ISDS context.[241] Under the African investment treaty practice, instead, human rights obligations for protected investors under those treaties clearly arise. However, despite references to human rights, it remains undefined which content should be given to investors' obligations since these treaties fail to explain according to which standards investors' conduct shall be reviewed, particularly since states are the main duty-bearers under current IHRL doctrine.[242]

Faced with the disadvantages of merely placing human rights obligations upon investors without providing a normative basis for the assessment of their scope of application, there are those who advocate for establishing investors' obligations under IIAs through the incorporation of the OECD Guidelines as binding norms.[243] The OECD Guidelines oblige OECD member states and adhering countries' recommendations to multinational enterprises operating in or from their territories.[244] The adoption of the OECD Guidelines dates back to 1976, where the OECD developed this instrument with the initial purpose of promoting responsible business conduct in conformity with applicable laws.[245] Yet, following the adoption of the UNGP, the OECD updated the OECD Guidelines in 2011 to maintain consistency between these Guidelines and the UNGP's provisions on the corporate responsibility to respect human rights.[246] Beyond the fact that IIAs would turn these soft-law guidelines into binding standards, their incorporation in IIAs will facilitate tribunals' determination of which actions protected investors are required to take to

---

pan-african_investment_code_december_2016_en.pdf. Accessed 10 December 2020 (Draft Pan-African Investment Code) art 24. See also Mbengue and Schacherer (2017).

[240]Ho (2019), pp. 13–14.

[241]Krajewski (2020), p. 119.

[242]Krajewski (2020), pp. 114–116.

[243]Van der Zee (2013), p. 33.

[244]OECD, OECD Declaration and Decision on International Investment and Multinational Enterprises, para 1. Available via OECD: http://www.oecd.org/investment/mne/oecddeclarationanddecisions.htm. (OECD Declaration) Accessed 10 December 2020.

[245]OECD, Guidelines for Multinational Corporations (1976) 15 ILM 967.

[246]OECD Guidelines for Multinational Enterprises, 2011 Edition, Recommendations for responsible business conduct in a global context. Available via OECD. http://www.oecd.org/daf/inv/mne/48004323.pdf. Accessed 10 December 2020.

fulfil their IIA obligations and against which legal basis tribunals should undertake this review.[247]

The OECD Guidelines provide further recommendations on how multinational enterprises' responsibilities should be understood. To illustrate, multinational companies discharge their responsibility to avoid infringement of third parties' rights, or contribution to adverse human rights impacts,[248] by seeking to identify, prevent, and mitigate the impacts caused in the context of their investment activities[249] or by taking the steps to cease their contribution and use their leverage to mitigate resulting impacts, respectively.[250] Moreover, according to these guidelines, multinational companies' steps towards the fulfilment of their responsibility to respect human rights would include the adoption of a policy commitment to respect human rights at the management level,[251] performance of due diligence in conformity with their size, the context of their operations and the severity of the risks underlying these impacts, as well as the provision of remedies.[252]

Another advantage of the OECD Guidelines resides in the fact that they clearly indicate which human rights norms are applicable to review corporate conduct, ranging from the UDHR, the ICCPR and the ICESCR.[253] They also inform the specific human rights instruments such as those protecting indigenous people's rights, vulnerable groups such as women, children, and persons with disabilities, especially in determining whether those affected by investor's activities belong to any of this group of right-holders.[254] Hence, the incorporation of the OECD Guidelines into IIAs certainly assist arbitral tribunals in determining which human rights norms should be applied in their review of investor's conduct. Additionally, since the OECD Guidelines set up a non-judicial mechanism, the so-called national contact points (NCP), to ensure their effectiveness, by endowing them with the competence of reviewing alleged corporate breaches of the Guidelines within the framework of specific instances.[255] their determination may guide arbitral tribunals in how to review the conformity of investors' conduct with the Guidelines in an ISDS context.

Although some scholars are critical of soft-law initiatives such as the OECD Guidelines to enhance corporate accountability since they are still anchored on a

---

[247]Krajewski (2019).

[248]OECD Guidelines for Multinational Enterprises (n 246) ch. IV paras 1 and 2, respectively.

[249]OECD Guidelines for Multinational Enterprises (n 246) ch. IV, commentary 41.

[250]OECD Guidelines for Multinational Enterprises (n 246) ch. IV, commentary 42.

[251]OECD Guidelines for Multinational Enterprises (n 246) ch. IV, para 4.

[252]OECD Guidelines for Multinational Enterprises (n 246) ch. IV paras 5–6.

[253]OECD Guidelines for Multinational Enterprises, Commentaries para 39. This is in turn consistent with what the UNGP enumerates as the rights to be respected by business entities. UNGP (n 23, Chap. 1) para 12.

[254]OECD Guidelines for Multinational Enterprises (n 246) ch. IV commentary para 40.

[255]OECD Guidelines (n 246) Part II—Implementation Procedures of the OECD Guidelines for Multinational Enterprises, Procedural Guidance No. I.

state-centred paradigm where only states are the main duty-bearers,[256] other scholars reckon that their merits reside in their anchoring on the UNGP that ease their application to concrete cases[257] and embody the international community's normative expectation towards corporations to behave socially responsible.[258] The benefits of this investment treaty-making approach towards investors' obligations should not be overlooked in the Latin American region. Seven Latin American countries have already committed to promote the observance of the OECD Guidelines in their capacity as adhering states. These countries include Argentina, Brazil, Colombia, Costa Rica, and Peru, aside from Chile and Mexico that already assume this commitment in their capacity of being OECD member states.[259]

Another form of addressing protected investors' obligations in IIAs could be made by reinforcing their obligation to observe human rights-related obligations under domestic law.[260] Within the Latin American context, endorsing this investment treaty making approach may not be unfeasible considering the widespread integration of human rights treaties into their domestic legal order through constitutional opening clauses,[261] and the invocation of this constitutional practice by some Latin American countries when justifying their regulatory measures and condemning claimant investors' behaviour.[262] While the normative basis for tribunal's review of investor conduct would be determined by the legislative of respondent states,[263] and thus no greatly differ from treaty clauses that already allude to the legality requirement, if drafted in broader terms and without limiting its application to the admission phase of claimant investors' investment, it would ease states to challenge investors' claims on issues of admissibility.[264]

## 4.2.2 Reformed IIAs Procedural Provisions

### 4.2.2.1 Jurisdictional Clauses

From a procedural standpoint, states parties to IIAs can only strengthen tribunals' review of the regulatory instruments through which they prevent human rights abuses on questions of their procedural rights in ISDS, if tribunals determine

---

[256]Kanalan (2016), pp. 427–437.

[257]In general, see Krajewski (2019).

[258]Krajewski (2020), pp. 117–118.

[259]Indeed, they adhered to the OECD Declaration and Decisions on International Investment and Multinational Enterprises, and thus to the OCED Guideline for Multinational Corporations, then the former includes the later framework. See OECD Declaration (n 244).

[260]Krajewski (2020), pp. 119–120.

[261]Morales Antoniazzi (2014), León Bastos and Wong Meraz (2015)

[262]See Sect. 4.1.1.

[263]Muchlinski (2017), p. 346, 350.

[264]See Sect. 4.1.3.1.

whether the human rights abuses they alleged were committed within the framework of claimant investors' activities,[265] or if responding states bring a separate cause of action with basis on the same ground.[266] In either case, IIAs' substantive provisions laying down investors' obligations under the OECD Guidelines and domestic human rights law would enormously facilitate the tribunals' review of respondent states' defence arguments or counterclaims.

An IIA provision referring to protected investors' human rights-related obligations would enable, for instance, avoidance of limiting the temporal scope of tribunals' jurisdiction to review investors' human rights abuses that only occurred during the admission phase of their investment. Under current treaty-making practice, states refer to the legality of investment in form of a qualifier of the assets defined as an investment,[267] or as a condition for the admission of foreign investment entitled to investment treaty protection.[268] In some cases, treaty provisions linking investors' compliance with states' laws to the admission of their investment are considered equivalent to references to legality within the treaty definition of an investment,[269] if another provision extends investment treaty protection to those investment already admitted prior the entry into force of the treaty.[270] Accordingly, these treaty provisions devise a limited scope of temporal application since they only sanction initial illegality, namely the one that occurred at the admission phase of foreign investment.[271] An IIA provision imposing human rights obligations upon states would revert this effect and permit to challenge adverse human rights impacts that may have occurred prior and during investors' undertaking of their investment activities.

Moreover, a treaty provision defining protected investors' human rights-related obligations would permit states to materially substantiate their allegations of investors' abuses of human rights based on the international and domestic human rights-related standards alluded to in this clause. If the OECD Guidelines were the applicable standard, for instance, a tribunal could review state's defence that its revocation of mining concession was the last resort after a series of measures that sought to prevent, for instance, that claimant's mining activities made an abusive use of water sources, even though it was required to ensure pursuant to this IIA's provision that its activities do not cause impact over communities' access to water sources. On the other hand, this treaty provision would unequivocally expand the material scope of tribunals' jurisdiction to review states' counterclaims based on

---

[265]See Sect. 4.1.3.1.

[266]See Sect. 4.1.3.2.

[267]See Colombia-United Arab Emirates BIT (n 416, Chap. 2) art 1.1.

[268]See Colombia-France BIT (n 416, Chap. 2) art 3 para 1.

[269]Ibidem.

[270]See Acuerdo para la Promocion y Proteccion Reciproca de Inversiones entre El Reino de Espana y la Republica del Salvador (signed 14 February 1992, entered into force 20 February 1996) art 2 paras 1 and 2. See *Inceysa v El Salvador* (n 90) para 130.

[271]See *Fraport v Philippines* (n 92) para 344; *Hamester v Ghana* (n 92) para 127.

claimant investor's inobservance of OECD Guidelines or domestic laws imposing upon them human rights obligations.

Finally, recalling investment case law on the admissibility requirements that a state's counterclaims must meet,[272] a treaty clause imposing direct obligations upon protected investors by attaching to the OECD Guidelines a binding character or by requesting to comply with human rights-related domestic law may indirectly provide a basis for deriving investor's consent to state's submission of counterclaims. If a dispute settlement clause does not limit the type of dispute to be settled in accordance with the IIA and, in addition, codify human rights-related standards, a tribunal could presume that both disputing parties had consented to its review of state and investor's behaviour alike under the same arbitration proceedings.

### 4.2.2.2   Counterclaims

Most IIAs omit to expressly codify states parties' right to submit a counterclaim, thus either by leaving the formulation of dispute settlement clauses in broader terms so as to cover *any* type of dispute or by restricting the type of disputes to be arbitrated under their provisions. Since only the former type of dispute settlement clause might permit states parties to bring a separate cause of action, codifying this procedural right within IIAs seem essential to ensure states parties' exercise of this procedural right. In this regard, the already mentioned investment treaty making practice of some African states in laying down direct obligations upon protected investors under IIAs[273] is also noteworthy for supplementing these clauses with treaty provisions that codify states parties' right to bring counterclaims in different ways.[274] However, their broadly drafted references to human rights, without correspondingly providing a normative basis that guides evaluation of corporate behaviour in human rights terms, may prove difficult for the tribunal to rule on the admissibility and/or merits of counterclaims.

Considering the normative pitfalls of creating human rights obligations for investors by means of IIAs without having a corollary set of standards that assists tribunals and disputing parties to review them, this study primarily focuses on those IIA provisions that guarantee states parties' exercise of their right to submit counterclaims and that make the OECD Guidelines the basis of tribunals' determination. As already mentioned, the OECD Guidelines would guide tribunals in identifying which responsibilities multinational companies have, how they should be

---

[272]See Sect. 4.1.3.2.

[273]See Sect. 4.2.1.2.

[274]The Common Market for Eastern and Southern Africa (COMESA) Investment Agreement clearly grants states parties to bring claims against protected investors for their non-compliance with treaty, contractual and/or domestic obligations. See Investment Agreement for the COMESA Common Investment Area (signed 23 May 2007, not yet in force) art 28.9. The DPAIC provides for member states' right to submit a counterclaim for breaches of investors' obligations established by this instrument and other relevant rules of international law. See DPAIC (n 239) art 43.

understood, and which human rights norms are applicable in the review of the admissibility/merits of a human rights-counterclaims. Yet, NCPs' statements provided in specific instances involving companies' breaches of their responsibility to respect the right to water, or indigenous people's right to be consulted over economic activities likely to affect their livelihood, could certainly inform tribunals' determination of the scope of investors' obligations under the IIAs in relation to both rights.

Specific instances involving mining companies' abuses of the right to water because of their pollution of water sources have developed normative standards to review the scope of corporate behaviour in conformity with ICESCR-based normative content of this right.[275] In addressing allegations of water pollution, an arbitral tribunal may seek to explore which type of measures an NCP expected from these companies to discharge their responsibility to respect the right to water. In some specific instances, such measures have included collection and evaluation of the information relating to health, environmental and safety risks of its development project and an adequate dissemination of this information among those likely affected by corporate activity.[276] In a similar way, a tribunal could proceed in counterclaims where the respondent state alleges claimant investor's abuses of indigenous communities' right to be consulted since NCPs have also developed several normative standards to define measures by which multinational corporations would discharge their responsibility to respect this specific group.[277] An arbitral tribunal could thus examine, for instance, whether the claimant investor employed the language of the communities affected by its activities to communicate their environmental impact in order to establish whether it performed due diligence.[278]

Finally, tribunals' review of the scope of claimant investors' obligation under IIAs that makes human rights-related domestic law the normative basis of such determination may be certainly instructed by domestic courts understanding of the horizontal effect that constitutional opening clauses towards human rights may have upon claimant investors.[279] As already addressed in this chapter, many South American countries have relied upon these domestic clauses to additionally justify their regulation of claimant investors' activities and indicate the horizontal effect that constitutional rights have over them in ISDS.[280] A tribunal might thus engage in the task of distinguishing the impact of these opening clauses on the domestic laws informing investors' treaty obligations, and then on the more difficult issue of

---

[275]Krajewski (2017), pp. 178–184.

[276]*Complaint from The Future in Our Hands (FIOH) against Intex Resources ASA and the Mindoro Nickel Project*, The Norwegian National Contact Point for the OECD Guidelines for Multinational Enterprises, Final Statement (30 November 2011) paras 38–43.

[277]Morgera (2015), pp. 45–57.

[278]*Complaint from Survival International against Vedanta Resources plc*, Final Statement by the UK National Contact Point for the OECD Guidelines for Multinational Enterprises (25 September 2009) paras 44–46.

[279]Gardbaum (2003).

[280]See Sect. 4.1.1.

ascertaining the horizontal effect of constitutional or domestic laws that aim at protecting human rights.

## 4.2.3    Interim Conclusion

Having established that the formulation of treaty provisions plays certain role on whether tribunals consider the regulatory needs of respondent states on their review of investment treaty obligations, this section proposes the following substantive and procedural reforms to reinforce this perceptible development in investment case law.

On one hand, this section proposes states to clearly articulate their IHRL-based duty to regulate protected investment under the IIA in its preamble or through an autonomous provision. This treaty provision may serve as an entry point to assess the legality of states' measures against the standards developed by IHRL to review, for instance, whether they are lawful exercise of their regulatory duties on questions of alleged (indirect) expropriation, or the legitimacy of protected investors' expectations. This is largely because the international human rights obligations to protect assumed by states parties to IIAs should have informed protected investors which human rights their investment serve to fulfil or which right-holders require more protection through regulation if their investment activities affect them.

A treaty provision referring to their duty to regulate protected investment would also have the advantage to underpin states parties in challenging investors' unclean hands if these treaties clearly place human rights obligations upon protected investors. Disclosing how the states parties comply with their regulatory duties under IHRL in the investment context may allow them to put the burden of proving 'clean hands' upon investors. To this end, this section recommends the use of IIAs as regulatory instruments of the conduct of protected investors, by establishing the OECD Guidelines as one of the legal bases of such obligations under IIAs because they not only define which conduct are expected from them in conformity with the UNGP, but also which human rights they shall observe in the performance of their investment activities. The other legal source of investors' obligations to which IIAs could refer is states parties' domestic laws. While they may not greatly refer to the existing obligation of states to make their investment in accordance with the laws of states parties, if drafted in broad terms, they will not only allow assessment of investors' conduct based on legal norms that are not strictly related to their investment activities but also ensure that their temporal scope of application is not strictly limited to illegalities that are made at the admission phase of investments.

From a jurisdictional perspective, treaty provisions placing direct obligations upon protected investors may ease states to challenge tribunals' jurisdiction from the outset and review investors' conduct in the pre- and post-establishment of their investment, beyond expanding the material scope of tribunals' jurisdiction to dismiss investors' claims. The same reasoning would apply to questions of counterclaims, and even this reference to material source of investors' obligation may provide their implicit consent to tribunals' review of their conduct in this specific procedural setting. The other advantage of incorporating the OECD Guidelines and domestic laws relating to human rights as the basis of protected investors resides in the fact that the original application of these (legal) instruments by the external bodies may assist tribunals in reviewing investors' conduct. These external bodies may develop normative standards that tribunals could borrow to assess investors' conduct in an investment treaty claim.

## 4.3   Legal Consequences Faced by States for Abstaining from Articulating Their Duty to Regulate in IIAs

The review undertaken in Sect. 4.1.2 suggests that some Latin American countries advance their duty to regulate foreign investment activities as an argumentative strategy to respond to investment treaty claims. However, their investment treaty-making practice is only directed to safeguard regulatory autonomy to exercise their 'right to regulate' foreign investment activities with the aim of inducing them to comply with their national domestic laws and policies.[281] Therefore, the question arising in this respect is whether having IIAs that do not conform with their duty to regulate foreign investment constitutes a violation of the ICESCR and the ACHR, and, if so, which legal consequences may derive from such omission.

Pursuant to the Articles on Responsibility of States for Internationally Wrongful Acts (ARSIWA), only an internationally wrongful act engages the international responsibility of a state.[282] To determine the existence of such wrongful act, it shall be established that this wrongful act is attributable to the state and that it constitutes a breach of an international obligation.[283] One may initially argue that the executive branch of the state is the one competent for the negotiation of IIAs, and the legislative expresses state's consent to be bound to these international treaties. Accordingly, it is not particularly difficult to establish the existence of the first element since the negotiation and ratification process of IIAs constitutes an act attributable to a state. Moreover, it shall be determined whether the ICESCR and the ACHR impose upon Latin American countries an obligation to avoid infringements of the rights correspondingly codified therein, for whose non-compliance by means of the negotiation and ratification of IIAs, they would incur as a result of a breach of an international obligation in general terms.[284] The answers to this latter question seem to be clear. As already discussed in Chap. 2, Latin American states parties to the ICESCR are not only compelled to adopt measures to avoid investors' abuses of ESC rights, but also to avoid benefitting foreign investors through actions

---

[281] See Sect. 2.3.2.1.1, Chap. 2.

[282] ILC 'Draft Articles on Responsibility of States for Internationally Wrongful Acts' (2001) Supplement No. 10 (A/56/10), chp.IV.E.1 (ARSIWA) art 1.

[283] ARSIWA (n 282) art 2.

[284] ARSIWA (n 282) art 12.

conducive to impairment of the enjoyment of these rights.[285] One may argue that the latter obligation, known in human rights doctrine as the duty to respect, provides the legal basis for the obligation to avoid IIAs inconsistent with ESC rights under the ICESCR. In fact, the CESCR has qualified the abstention/refraining from entering into IIAs that may potentially conflict with Covenant's obligations as one appropriate means to discharge the duty to respect ESC rights.[286] The same can be argued with respect to the ACHR since this Convention explicitly stipulates that states parties shall respect the rights herein codified,[287] which implies avoidance of any action that may directly or indirectly lead to breaches of Convention's rights.[288]

That said, one should also add that a determination of breaches of these universal and Inter-American human rights treaty obligations primarily takes place in accordance with the terms laid down in the ICESCR and the ACHR. Under the ICESCR, the CESCR would be competent to make this assessment within the framework of a communication submitted by individuals claiming to be victims of breaches of their ESC rights.[289] Arguably, those allegedly affected could resort to this forum to challenge IIAs that are not consistent with one of their ESC rights.[290] Under the ACHR, however, the only forum available to those potentially aggrieved by an IIA non-consistent with the ACHR would be the IACommHR. This treaty body is the only one mandated within the Inter-American human rights system to receive individual petitions alleging breaches of the ACHR.[291] Hypothetically, an individual who may allege that a particular IIA breaches his rights may have the recourse to claim the same before the IACommHR, which may refer the case to the ACHR in order to proceed on the merits if it regarded this sovereign act as a breach of the Convention.[292] Therefore, if one of these human rights treaty bodies finds a violation of the respective human rights by state's negotiation and/or ratification of an IIA, one of the legal consequences that could derive from this breach could be 'to cease that act, if its continued'.[293] This would imply that the state concerned could terminate the IIA, or renegotiate to make it consistent with its human rights obligations. In this regard, the reform proposals advanced in part II of this chapter may contribute to the attainment of this end.

---

[285]See Sect. 3.1.1.2, Chap. 3.

[286]CESCR, General Comment No. 24 (n 55, Chap. 3) para 13.

[287]ACHR (n 11, Chap. 1) art 1 para 1.

[288]*Velásquez-Rodríguez v Honduras* (n 257, Chap. 3) para 165.

[289]Optional Protocol to the ICESCR (n 42) art 2.

[290]See Sect. 3.1.1.2, Chap. 3.

[291]ACHR (n 11, Chap. 1) art 45.

[292]See Sect. 3.2.1.2, Chap. 3.

[293]ARSIWA (n 282) art.

## 4.4 Conclusion

Having established that IHRL provides normative standards that may permit states and tribunals to advance and review states' duty to regulate foreign investment activities to hinder investors' abuses of the right to water and indigenous people's survival in ISDS, Chap. 5 has demonstrated that some Latin American countries have indeed articulated their regulatory duties as a defence against allegations of breaches of the FET standard and of indirect expropriation, albeit not always with an explicit reference to human rights treaties.

Arguments have ranged from the incompatibility argument (between IHRL and IIL) in connection with the normative primacy of human rights, the constitutional rank of human rights treaties within domestic legal orders, to even claims requesting to not consider IIL as self-contained regime. However, on questions of their procedural rights to challenge admissibility and/or the merits claimant investors' claims and to submit counterclaims, human rights argumentation has been deployed to condemn the 'unclean hands' of investors, rather than justify regulatory duties.

Regarding arbitral tribunals, only the *Urbaser v Argentina* tribunal has engaged in reviewing human rights norms by relying upon the applicable law clause that permitted to interpret the BIT concerned with basis on international law. Notwithstanding the former, case studies suggest that tribunals are acknowledging states' needs when making their determinations. In claims relating to FET, tribunals dismissed claims when reviewing the legitimacy of investors' expectations by either making an equivalence between their expectations and the legitimate regulatory expectations of states to ensure investors' adequate provision of public services (*Urbaser v Argentina*), or by considering that if the legal framework clearly provides for the protection of a specific group of society, this should have informed investors' expectations of the regulatory measures that could have being potentially taken to attain that aim (*South American Silver v Bolivia*). In cases relating to indirect expropriation, tribunals such as *Urbaser v Argentina* and *South American Silver v Bolivia* respectively focused on the legality and character of the alleged measures, reaching, however, to different outcomes. This is because the former investors' claims had no merits due to Argentina's compliance with legal and regulatory framework governing its investment, while for the latter, despite the legality of mining concession's revocation, failure to pay compensation amounted to an indirect expropriation.

On questions of respondent states' procedural rights, some of the cases studies indicate that tribunals would admit states' allegations of 'unclean hands' against the investor if they disclose first how they perform their regulatory duties to hinder investors' misbehaviour (*Bear Creek v Peru*). However, on issues of counterclaims, the regulatory duties play an incidental role since the regulatory instruments are used as the basis of tribunals' review of investors' conduct only in cases where the claims of both disputing parties are interconnected, and domestic courts are not competent under investor-state contracts to resolve them.

Against the backdrop of the findings, Chap. 5 has proposed different substantive and procedural reforms to underpin states' articulation of their regulatory duties in IIAs and induced tribunals to deal with normative inter-regime interplay. Concerning substantive reforms, this study encourages the articulation of states parties' duty to regulate protected investment under IIAs since these may foster arbitral tribunals to review states' conduct under 'external' legality criteria that are usually relevant for the review of legitimacy of investors' expectation and the legality of states' measures allegedly tantamount to an indirect expropriation. This type of provision would also strengthen states' allegations of 'unclean hands' since they may allow states to normatively justify how they performed their regulatory duty (if that was case) and to advance that despite that fact investors' abuses were still committed.

The other substantive reform that has been proposed by this research is placing direct obligations upon investors by using IIAs as the regulatory instruments of investors' behaviour. This should proceed by incorporating the OECD Guidelines and states parties' domestic law as the legal basis of review of investors' conduct. The advantage that these reforms have over IIAs that merely allude to these obligations is that these clauses would clearly define which instruments and consequently which standards of conduct should be applicable in the review of investors' conduct. The determination of the scope of these standards by the competent bodies under those external standards may inform tribunals' assessment. In addition to material jurisdiction, the formulation of investors' obligations under IIAs would unequivocally facilitate the submission of counterclaims against investors, because they would provide arbitral tribunals with temporal jurisdiction, inducing to limit its review to initial illegality, as well as with consent, since these clauses may be understood as embodying the consent of protected investors.

Otherwise, if states fail to align their IIAs with the regulatory duties that they shall perform under IHRL in the investment context, they may breach their obligation to respect human rights.

# References

Abel P (2018) Counterclaims based on international human rights obligations of investors in international investment arbitration. falacies and potentials of the 2016 ICSID Urbaser v Argentina Award. Brill Open Law 1(1):61–90. https://doi.org/10.1163/23527072-00101003

Bjorklund AK (2013) The role of counterclaims in rebalancing investment law. Lewis Clark Law Rev 17(2):461–480

Cameron P (2010) International energy investment law: the pursuit of stability. OUP, Oxford

De Brabandere E (2018) Human rights counterclaims in investment treaty arbitration (October 8). Grotius Centre Working Paper 078-IEL. https://ssrn.com/abstract=3264167. Accessed 10 Dec 2020

Diel-Gligor K, Hennecke R (2015) Investment in accordance with the law. In: Bungenberg M, Griebel J, Hobe S, Reinisch A (eds) International investment law: a handbook. C.H. Beck, Nomos and Hart, Baden-Baden/München/Oxford, pp 566–576

Dumberry P, Dumas-Aubin D (2011–2012) How to impose human rights obligations on corporations under investment treaties? Yearb Int Invest Law Policy 4:569–600

Gardbaum S (2003) The "horizontal effect" of constitutional rights. Mich Law Rev 102(3):387–459

Ho J (2019) The creation of elusive investor responsibility. AJIL Unbound 113:10–15. https://doi.org/10.1017/aju.2018.91

Kanalan I (2016) Horizontal effect of human rights in the era of transnational constellations: on the accountability of private actors for human rights violations. Eur Yearb Int Econ Law 7:423–460

Kjos H (2013) Applicable law in investor-state arbitration. The interplay between national and international law. OUP, Oxford

Krajewski M (2017) Protecting the human right to water through the regulation of multinational enterprises. In: Chaisse J (ed) The regulation of the global water services market. CUP, Cambridge, pp 167–195

Krajewski M (2019) Human rights in international investment law: recent trends in arbitration and treaty-making practice. Yearb Int Invest Law Policy 2017:177–193

Krajewski M (2020) A nightmare or a noble dream? Establishing investor obligations through treaty-making and treaty-application. Bus Human Rights J 5:105–129

Kriebaum U (2018b) Human rights and international investment law. In: Radi Y (ed) Research handbook on human rights and investment: Research handbooks in international law series. Research handbooks in international law. Edward Elgar Publishing, Cheltenham/Northampton, pp 13–40

León Bastos C, Wong Meraz VA (2015) Clausulas de apertura al derecho internacional de los derechos humanos: constituciones iberoamericanas. FORO. Revista de Ciencias Jurídicas y Sociales, Nueva Época 18 (2):93–125. https://doi.org/10.5209/rev_FORO.2015.v18.n2.51784

Letter from Professor David D. Caron to J Martin Wagner (Letter to NGO regards Petition to Participate as amici curiae) (29 January 2003). Available via ITA Law. http://www.italaw.com/cases/57#sthash.wwd6obSl.dpuf. Accessed 10 Dec 2020

Mann H, von Moltke K, Peterson L, Cosbey A (2005) international institute for sustainable development (2005) IISD model international agreement on investment for sustainable development. IISD (26 April). Available at: https://www.iisd.org/publications/iisd-model-international-agreement-investment-sustainable-development. Accessed 10 Dec 2020

Mbengue MM, Schacherer S (2017) The 'Africanization' of international investment law: the pan-African investment code and the reform of the international investment regime. JWIT 18 (3):414–448

Moloo R (2010) A comment on the clean hands doctrine in international law. Available via SSRN. https://ssrn.com/abstract=2358229. Accessed 10 Dec 2020

Morales Antoniazzi M (2014) El nuevo paradigma de la apertura de los órdenes constitucionales: una perspectiva Sudamericana. In: Von Bogdandy A, Serna de la Garza JM (eds) Soberanía y Estado abierto en América Latina y Europa, Instituto de Investigaciones Juridicas: Instituto Iberoamericano de Derecho Constitucional and Max Planck Institut Für Ausländisches Öffentliches Recht und Völkerrecht, Mexico D.F., pp 233–282

Morgera E (2015) Benefit-sharing as a bridge between the environmental and human rights accountability of multinational corporations. In: Boer B (ed) Environmental law dimensions of human rights. OUP, Oxford, pp 37–68

Muchlinski P (2017) The impact of a business and human rights treaty on investment law and arbitration. In: Deva S, Bilchitz D (eds) Building a treaty on business and human rights. CUP, Cambridge, pp 346–374

Nowrot K (2015) Obligations of investors. In: Bungenberg M, Griebel J, Hobe S, Reinisch A (eds) International investment law: a handbook. C.H. Beck, Nomos and Hart, Baden-Baden/München/Oxford, pp 1154–1185

Onwuamaegbu U (2005) Aguas del Tunari SA. v. Republic of Bolivia (ICSID Case No. ARB/03/2), Introductory Note. ICSID Rev Foreign Invest Law J 20(2):445–449. https://doi.org/10.1093/icsidreview/20.2.445

Sauvant KP, Ünüvar G (2016) Can host countries have legitimate expectations?. Columbia FDI
    Perspectives 183. Available at SSRN: https://ssrn.com/abstract=2844432
Schreuer C (2014) Jurisdiction and applicable law in investment treaty arbitration. McGill J Disp
    Resol 1(1):2–25
Trevino C (2015) South American Silver lays out $385 million case against Bolivia; government
    counters that UK treaty should not protect "Canadian Investment". IA Reporter (14 June).
    https://www.iareporter.com/articles/23275/. Accessed 10 Dec 2020
Van der Zee E (2013) Incorporating the OECD guidelines in international investment agreements:
    turning a soft law obligation into hard law?. Legal Iss Econ Integr 40(1):33–72. Available at
    SSRN: https://ssrn.com/abstract=2725836
Vis-Dunbar D, Peterson L (2006) Bolivian water dispute settled, bechtel forgoes compensation.
    Investment Treaty News (20 January). https://www.iisd.org/itn/wp-content/uploads/2010/10/
    itn_jan20_2006.pdf. Accessed 10 Dec 2020
Zeyl T (2011) Charting the wrong course: The doctrine of legitimate expectations in investment
    treaty law. Alberta Law Rev 49(1):203–235

# Chapter 5
# Re-politicisation of IIL by a Regional ISDS Tribunal Through Its Engagement with Inter-Regime Tensions

Although IIAs inform and steer IIL and thus could likely drive it towards its re-politicisation, IIAs can only partially counteract arbitral tribunals' expansive interpretation and application of IIAs and their narrow consideration given to host states' duty to regulate foreign investment activities under IHRL when responding to investment treaty claims. This is so because this process requires that investor-state tribunals also engage with a review of inter-regime tensions in which host states may be probably involved in the investment context. Considering that South American countries took initial steps to establish the UNASUR Centre under UNASUR's framework due to their perception that the existing ISDS regime disregards their needs of preserving regulatory autonomy,[1] the chapter analyses various mechanisms that may facilitate a *regional* ISDS tribunal to deal with inter-regime tensions and thus contribute to the re-politicisation of IIL, acknowledging that normative (or even an institutional) interplay might not only lead to inter-regime frictions, but also provides an opportunity for the re-politicisation of IIL.

Based on the potential for an indirect inter-regime interplay, this chapter begins expanding the overview of potential scenarios where inter-regime tensions could arise and thus provide a venue for re-politicisation of IIL during the conduct of legal proceedings. In this context, special attention will be given to the function of provisional measures in an ISDS context considering the striking role played by these procedural instruments in the *Chevron v Ecuador II* case[2] and the place of Latin America features among the regions where respondent states usually are the addressees of these interim measures.[3] Further, this chapter sketches out different legal strategies already available in ISDS to which this regional tribunal could resort to address these inter-regime tensions either by itself or with international human

---

[1] See Sect. 2.3.3.2.2, Chap. 2.

[2] The terms provisional measures and interim measures are used interchangeably.

[3] See Goldberg et al. (2019), p. 6.

© The Author(s), under exclusive license to Springer Nature Switzerland AG 2021
M. J. Luque Macías, *Re-Politicising International Investment Law in Latin America through the Duty to Regulate Paradigm*, European Yearbook of International Economic Law 14, https://doi.org/10.1007/978-3-030-73272-1_5

rights bodies' assistance. Finally, the chapter highlights further mechanisms at hand to Latin American countries to underpin the regional ISDS tribunal's engagement with the resolution of inter-regime normative discrepancies.


## 5.1  Hypothetical Scenarios Likely to Cause Inter-Regime Tensions During the Conduct of Arbitration Proceedings

### 5.1.1  ISDS Tribunal's Review of States' Measure Adopted in Compliance with a Human Rights Body's Interim Measure

The IACommHR is the human rights body within the Inter-American system that promotes and protects human rights implicit in the ADRDM as an OAs organ, and those rights are enshrined in the ACHR as a treaty body.[4] In both capacities, the Commission has issued a great number of precautionary measures to prevent corporate logging, oil, or mining activities from inflicting serious and irreparable harms to indigenous communities' rights and petitioners' right to health that derive from corporate activities.[5] In many of them, the suspension of investment activities has been one of the most common precautionary measures taken in Latin American countries, which, if adopted by the states concerned, is highly likely to culminate in the submission of an investment treaty claim, since the investor affected by this regulatory measure may consider it as an indirect expropriation.

In *Maya Indigenous Communities*, the Commission advised Belize to suspend any permit, licenses and concessions that allowed SOLCARSA to continue with its oil drilling activities in the traditional Maya communities' lands.[6] In *Communities of the Maya People*, the Commission also required the suspension of mining activities, but in addition subjected their resumption to the adoption of concrete measures conducive for the prevention of environmental pollution and the decontamination of water sources.[7] In *Indigenous Communities of Cuenca del Rio Xingu*, the IACommHR required from Brazil the immediate suspension of the licensing procedure of an hydroelectric plant's construction until its compliance with indigenous peoples' consultation.[8] However, there is broad consensus that the adoption of precautionary measures is not mandatory since these measures are considered

---

[4]See Sects. 3.2.1.1 and 3.2.1.2, Chap. 3.

[5]See Anicama (2008).

[6]See *Maya Indigenous Communities* (n 221, Chap. 3).

[7]See n 13, Chap. 1.

[8]*Indigenous Communities of Cuenca del Rio Xingu, Para, Brazil* (Precautionary Measures) IACommHR PM 382-10 (1 April 2011).

mere recommendations of the IACommHR.[9] However, if followed, these measures could have an important evidentiary value to justify states' duty to regulate foreign investment activities before an ISDS tribunal.

According to well-established IACoHR's case law, a state party to the ACHR meets its duty to regulate foreign investment activities if it adopts positive actions in knowledge of the real and imminent risk for right-holders.[10] Since the IACoHR presupposes the existence of such state's knowledge based on the existence of precautionary measures issued by the IACommHR,[11] their adoption by a respondent state could inform tribunal's review of the character of state's suspension of a mining concession that a claimant investor may allege as amounting to an indirect expropriation.

### 5.1.2   A Provisional Measure Issued by an Investor-State Tribunal Encounters a Human Rights Body's Interim Measure

An indirect interplay between ISDS tribunals' interim measures and the precautionary measures issued by the IACommHR may also create inter-regime tensions during the former's resolution of an investment treaty-based dispute. In practice, this inter-institutional encounter would occur if an arbitral tribunal issues a provisional measure following claimant investor's request, and the IACommHR goes ahead to request the state to address that interim measure, thus complying with it, because it may pose an irreparable damage to third parties' rights. The *Chevron v Ecuador II* effectively exhibits the chances of this type of scenario. The *Chevron v Ecuador II* tribunal requested Ecuador to suspend the enforcement of a domestic court's decision ordering Chevron to pay damages to the Lago Agrio plaintiffs affected by the oil operation of Texaco, its former parent company, within and outside its domestic jurisdiction.[12] Indeed, a stay of parallel proceedings in respondent states is one of the most common types of provisional measures requested by claimant investors[13] and granted by arbitral tribunals if the legal criteria laid down in their constitutive treaties are met.[14] The problematic issue was, from a human rights perspective, that the *Chevron v Ecuador* II tribunal dismissed Ecuador's submission requesting it to abstain from exercising jurisdiction over the dispute based on the

---

[9]See Sect. 3.2.1, Chap. 3.

[10]See n 266, 267, Chap. 3.

[11]See n 268, Chap. 3.

[12]See n 38, Chap. 1.

[13]See Goldberg et al. (2019), p. 12.

[14]Provisional measures are issued pursuant to a set of criteria such as, inter alia, urgency, necessity to avoid risk or harm, existence of extreme circumstance. For a comprehensive discussion, see Goldberg et al. (2019), pp. 15–25.

'monetary gold principle', pursuant to which an international tribunal should exercise self-restrain if the subject matter of its judgement would determine third parties' rights or obligations (in this case, those of the Lago Agrio plaintiffs).[15]

Among the justifications provided by the tribunal was its lack of jurisdiction over Lago Agrio plaintiffs and the fact that they are not indispensable third parties to solve the investment treaty-based claims dealt in arbitration proceedings.[16] In fact, this tribunal held that '[i]f there were an inconsistency between [the investment treaty obligations of Ecuador] and [third parties'] rights as determined by [domestic] [c]ourts, it would be for the Respondent to decide how to resolve that inconsistency'.[17] Transferring this tension to the international legal realm,[18] had Ecuador decided to comply with these interim measures issued by *Chevron v Ecuador II* tribunal, could have led to encountering a precautionary measure of the IACommHR to preserve Lago Agrio plaintiffs' right to judicial protection laid down in the ACHR and thus derived in an indirect institutional encounter.[19]

Cases such as *Chevron v Ecuador II* and *Renco v Peru* highlight that ISDS might considerably undermine Latin American countries' fulfilment of their human rights obligation to protect and ensure the enjoyment of human rights through the provision of legal remedies and lead to problematic inter-institutional encounters.[20] In fact, the approach favoured by the *Chevron v Ecuador II* tribunal in requesting the suspension of the Lago Agrio judgement through provisional measures has been criticised for its lack of comity to Ecuadorian courts' jurisdiction and sensitivity to domestic legal concerns.[21] Yet, not all interim measures aim at staying legal proceedings,[22] as some seek the implementation of specific measures[23] or the adoption of a specific

---

[15]*Chevron v Ecuador II* (n 36, Chap. 1) Third interim award, paras 4.59–4.71.

[16]*Chevron v Ecuador II* (n 36, Chap. 1) Third interim award, para 4.67.

[17]Ibidem.

[18]On the contrary, Ecuador did not follow any of these interim measures and thus preferred to protect the legal interests of those affected by Texaco's activities domestically. *Chevron v Ecuador II* (n 36, Chap. 1) para 10.18.

[19]See n 39, Chap. 1.

[20]To recall, the states' duty to regulate under IHRL differs from states obligation to protect and ensure the enjoyment of human rights under the ICESCR and ACHR, respectively. The *duty to regulate* is one of the appropriate *means of preventive nature* to discharge this obligation to protect and ensure. However, this regulatory duty diverges from this international obligation since compliance with it also requires *measures of remedial nature* such as the prosecution of corporation's manager and the award of remedies to those affected by their corporate activities. For the discussion of the differences among these concepts, see Sects. 3.1.1.2 and 3.2.1.2, Chap. 3.

[21]See Kalderimis (2016), p. 549.

[22]See Sinclair and Repousis (2017), p. 431.

[23]*Biwater Gauff (Tanzania) Ltd v United Republic of Tanzania*, ICSID Case No. ARB/05/22, Procedural Order No. 3 (29 September 2006) para 135; *Vigotop Limited v Hungary*, ICSID Case No. ARB/11/22, Award (1 October 2014) para 60; *Churchill Mining and Planet Mining Pty Ltd v Republic of Indonesia*, ICSID Case No. ARB/12/14 and 12/40, Procedural Order No. 14 (22 December 2014) para 71.

performance.[24] This implies that not only host states' fulfilment of their human rights obligation to provide effective domestic legal remedies may be at stake by means of these procedural instruments, but also that provisional measures may equally constrain respondent states' fulfilment of their duty to regulate. To illustrate this, a foreign investor may institute arbitration proceedings for considering that the termination of its mining license operating near a river violates the international legal treatment to which it is entitled under IIAs, and the tribunal could request the respondent state, by means of provisional measures, to refrain from imposing the undertaking of clean-up activities of water sources allegedly polluted through its mining activities upon the claimant[25] or the cleaning up of the surrounding mining area, where indigenous communities live.[26]

Inter-regime tensions could be exacerbated if the state's suspension of the mining license initially targeted by the claimant investor was taken in compliance with a IACommHR's precautionary measure in cases of urgency, or when an arbitral tribunal's interim relief orders the respondent state to suspend the execution of complementary remediation measures, thus encounters a precautionary measure by the IACommHR. In fact, if the IACommHR requested the adoption of provisional measures to the IACoHR because the state concerned failed to follow its precautionary measure by complying with tribunal's interim relief, this would constitute another factor conducive for exacerbating inter-regime tensions.[27]

Against the background of this troubling inter-regime interplay, how best can these inter-regime tensions be addressed and re-politicisation of IIL promoted by an ISDS tribunal? In principle, an ISDS tribunal could address inter-regime tensions, and thus promote this re-politicisation, particularly by applying the IACoHR's standard of review on its assessment of state's defence arguments to justify regulatory measures to discharge its duty to regulate foreign investment activities in an investment dispute. Yet, as highlighted in the *Chevron v Ecuador II* case, a tribunal can exercise its competence to issue provisional measures in a way that might lead to unreasonable restriction of the respondent states' regulatory autonomy. To counteract this, a refinement of the requirements to be met to grant these procedural measures may be required.

---

[24] *Occidental v Ecuador* (n 373, Chap. 2) Decision on Provisional Measures (17 August 2007) paras 72–76.

[25] See Sect. 3.1.2.2.2, Chap. 3.

[26] See Sect. 3.2.2.2.2, Chap. 3.

[27] To recall, provisional measures are required to the IACoHR in a situation of gravity and urgency of irreparable damage and upon the condition that the state concerned did not comply with a previous precautionary measure. See, Sect. 3.2.1, Chap. 3.

## 5.2  Legal Strategies Available to a Regional ISDS Tribunal for Settling Inter-Regime Tensions

Different judicial techniques have been developed so far in international dispute settlement to address normative frictions that may arise between international legal systems and regimes.[28] Along this line, a regional ISDS tribunal has, at its disposal, different legal strategies to deal with normative tensions that may arise in the context of a specific investment dispute.[29] However, arbitral tribunals have generally acted with caution when it comes to the integration of international legal norms that do not underpin its functional purpose.[30] Yet, although few investment treaty-based cases may not represent a significant sample of a new trend, they are still indicative of the possibility of being engaged in the review of inter-regime discrepancies in ISDS. The following sections briefly describes the legal strategies to which a regional ISDS tribunal could resort to address inter-regime discrepancies.

### 5.2.1  Tribunal's Settlement of Inter-Regime Tensions by Itself

Broadly drafted IIAs provisions stipulating that general international law is also the applicable law to investment disputes could serve as a 'gateway' for the integration of IHRL,[31] based on the presumption that an arbitral tribunal could have general jurisdiction to apply any rule in the settlement of international investment disputes.[32] In *Urbaser v Argentina*, this was the legal technique applied by the tribunal. The Spanish-Argentina BIT provision on applicable law was employed as an entry point for the application of internationally recognised human rights instruments protecting the right to water[33] On this basis, the *Urbaser v Argentina* tribunal dealt with the matter related to Argentina's duty to regulate claimants' provision of drinking water services in relation to the right to water in its determination of alleged breaches of the FET standard[34] and the merits of Argentina's counterclaims.[35]

References to human rights in IIAs could complement the so-called 'gateway' strategy. As already discussed in Chap. 4, these references could be made through

---

[28] See Peters (2017), pp. 682–698; Crawford and Nevill (2012), p. 235.

[29] See Shany (2012), p. 14.

[30] See Sect. 1.1.2, Chap. 1.

[31] See Crawford and Nevill (2012), p. 835.

[32] Ibidem.

[33] *Urbaser v Argentina* (n 1, Chap. 1) para 1192.

[34] See Sect. 4.1.2.1, Chap. 4.

[35] See Sect. 4.1.3.2, Chap. 4.

states parties' articulation of their 'duty to regulate' foreign investment activities,[36] and by indicating that investors under IIAs have a responsibility to respect human rights.[37] The purpose of these treaty proposals is anchoring the human rights-based duty to regulate foreign investment activities in IIL. More precisely, they seek to reinforce the notion that host states' regulation of foreign investment activities is conducive to prevent their adverse impacts over third parties' full enjoyment of human rights. This implies that regulation of foreign investment activities is not always arbitrary since it must be adopted in accordance with a well-established set of normative standards under IHRL. These types of references would unequivocally ensure that tribunals resort to IHRL when reviewing respondent states and claimant investors' conduct alike.

### 5.2.2 Tribunal's Settlement of Inter-Regime Tensions with the Assistance of Human Rights Bodies

Dealing with inter-regime tensions in ISDS requires certain domain of the exogenous legal field to be incorporated in tribunal's review of an investment dispute. However, this might not always be the case. This scenario then raises the question of whether international human rights bodies could participate as *amici curiae*, as friends of the regional ISDS tribunal, to provide their knowledge or perspectives on matters over which this tribunal shall resolve in a particular case.[38] The answer to this question is of particular importance because, although the ICSID Convention permits *amici curiae* submissions,[39] and increasing efforts have been devoted to reinforce their participation within UNCITRAL's framework,[40] submissions brought by the civil society have had, so far, limited success.[41]

The *Philip Morris v Uruguay* case provides a good example of how non-economic international organizations could assist ISDS tribunals in the resolution of investment disputes. The dispute arose from the claim by Swiss tobacco companies that Uruguay breached several standards of treatment granted to it in the

---

[36]See Sect. 4.2.1.1, Chap. 4.

[37]See Sect. 4.2.1.2, Chap. 4.

[38]See Bastin (2012), p. 208; Fach Gómez (2012), p. 510.

[39]ICSID, Rules of Procedure for Arbitration Proceedings, Rule 37 para 2.

[40]In those investor-state arbitration proceedings conducted pursuant to the UNCITRAL Arbitration Rules as revised in 2010, amici curiae submissions are allowed in cases commenced pursuant IIAs concluded on or after the 1st of April 2014. Otherwise, for disputes brought before that date, UNCITRAL adopted the Mauritius Convention to extend the application of these transparency rules to these treaties. In that order, see UNCITRAL, UNCITRAL Rules on Transparency in Treaty-based Investor-State Arbitration (effective as of 1 April 2014) art 4 and United Nations Convention on Transparency in Treaty-Based Investor State Arbitration (The "Mauritius Convention on Transparency") (signed 10 December 2014, entered into force 18 October 2017).

[41]See n 111, Chap. 4.

Switzerland-Uruguay BIT through the implementation of several restrictive tobacco packaging and marketing regulations.[42] The ICSID tribunal allowed the participation of the World Health Organization (WHO) as an *amicus curiae* to explain the relation between health warnings and labelling of cigarettes' packets and how this contributes to the protection of public health, and on tobacco control globally.[43] It found that WHO satisfied the three requirements laid down in ICSID arbitration rules to make its written submission: (1) WHO appeared to have a specific knowledge on the matters at stake in the investment dispute different from that of disputing parties; (2) its submission dealt with matters relating to it, and (3) it seemed to have a significant interest in the proceeding.[44] Additionally, the tribunal accepted the written submission of the Pan American Health Organization (PAHO) on the same grounds.[45]

A regional ISDS tribunal could allow, for instance, that the IACommHR participates as an *amicus curiae* in cases where an investment treaty claim is brought against a regulatory measure that was taken in conformity with its precautionary measure, or when the respondent state abstains to follow a provisional measure rendered by it during the conduct of proceedings for being requested by the IACommHR by means of precautionary measures. In the scenarios just described, the IACommHR could smoothly meet the above-mentioned requirements to determine the participation of the IACommHR as an *amicus curiae* of the regional ISDS tribunal.

## 5.3   Additional Legal Strategies Conducive to Underpin Tribunal's Engagement with Inter-Regime Tensions

Finally, another option to promote the regional ISDS tribunal's participation in dealing with inter-regime tensions, with the IACommHR's assistance, would be to establish it within the umbrella of the OAS, particularly when the regional organization initially underpinning its creation is now likely to be extinct.[46] From a historical and functional perspective, this proposition is not totally unreasonable. Nothing hinders Latin American countries from advocating that the OAS re-assumes its role as the successor of the PAU to engage in critical discussions about the

---

[42]*Philip Morris Brands Sàrl, Philip Morris Products S.A. and Abal Hermanos S.A. v Oriental Republic of Uruguay*, ICSID Case No. ARB/10/7, Award (8 July 2016) (*Philip Morris v Uruguay*).

[43]In relation to tribunal's acceptance of the WHO's submission, see *Philip Morris v Uruguay* (n 42) Procedural Order No. 3 (17 February 2015).

[44]Ibidem.

[45]In relation to tribunal's acceptance of the PAHO's submission, see *Philip Morris v Uruguay* (n 42) Procedural Order No. 4 (24 March 2015).

[46]See Sect. 2.3.3.2.2, Chap. 2.

negative impacts of IIL.[47] The OAS is designed to contribute to the search of political and legal problems that may arise among their member states.[48] In addition, the operation of a regional ISDS tribunal within the OAS might arguably facilitate the participation of the IACommHR in ISDS because the Commission is already endowed with the competence to provide consultation to OAS organs on issues relating to human rights.[49]

The downside of creating a regional ISDS tribunal under the OAS framework, however, resides in the limited reach that the regional ISDS tribunal would have since only investment disputes arising out of the IIAs concluded among OAS member states would fall within its jurisdiction. Moreover, attempts relating to the establishment of common regional rules on investment have been discussed outside the framework of the OAS, as exhibited in relation to the FTAA within the framework of the Summit of the Americas.[50] Considering the latter development, it is thus also feasible to establish a regional ISDS tribunal that operates autonomously without being under the umbrella of a regional organization that is already in existence. The inclusion of provisions ruling the submission of amicus curiae brief is the adequate path to allow the assistance of the IACommHR in the settlement of inter-norms tensions.

## 5.4  Conclusions

Inspired by the UNASUR's initiative to establish the UNASUR Centre, its creation may not be out of question to promote its engagement with inter-regime tensions and thus with a re-politicisation of IIL. Two scenarios might arise that could exacerbate inter-regime discrepancies during the conduct of legal proceedings. On one hand, the ISDS tribunal reviews a respondent state's measure that was adopted in compliance with the precautionary measure issued by the IACommHR; on the other hand, the regional ISDS tribunal issues a provisional measure ordering the adoption of a specific behaviour, and the IACommHR issues a precautionary measure to avert the respondent state's compliance with the former. Against the background of these challenges, the regional ISDS tribunal could resort to adopting some of few legal strategies applied in ISDS that may facilitate dealing with inter-regime discrepancies: the first, a resolution of an inter-regime collision by itself resorting to the applicable law provision in IIAs (following the example of the *Urbaser v Argentina* case), complemented by IIAs provisions referring to human rights; the second, with

---

[47]For a discussion of the role of the PAU as a forum for the contestation of capital-exporting countries' attempts to ensure greater legal protection in favour of their nationals, see Sect. 2.1.1.2, Chap. 2.

[48]OAS Charter (n 216, Chap. 3) art 2 lit. e.

[49]OAS Charter (n 216, Chap. 3) art 106 para 1.

[50]See Sect. 2.3.1.2.2, Chap. 2.

the assistance of the IACommHR allowing its participation as an *amicus curiae* (following the example of the *Philipp Morris v Uruguay* case). In addition to these steps, Latin American countries could look back to existing regional organisations to underpin these re-politicising endeavours envisaged by the regional ISDS tribunal.

## References

Anicama C (2008) State responsibilities to regulate and adjudicate corporate activities under the inter-American human rights system, report on the American convention on human rights. Available at: https://media.business-humanrights.org/media/documents/ef3d3a9990b249cfb7850eae75e8e88762fd2789.pdf. Accessed 10 Dec 2020

Bastin L (2012) The *Amicus Curiae* in investor-state arbitration. Cambridge J Int Comp Law 1 (3):208–234. https://doi.org/10.7574/cjicl.01.03.57

Crawford J, Nevill P (2012) Relations between international courts and tribunals: the regime problem. In: Young MA (ed) Regime interaction in international law, facing fragmentation. CUP, Cambridge, pp 235–260

Fach Gómez K (2012) Rethinking the role of amicus curiae in international investment arbitration: how to draw the line favorably for the public interest. Fordham Int Law J 35(2):510–564

Goldberg D, Kryvoi Y, Philippov I (2019) Empirical Study: Provisional Measures in Investor-State Arbitration. British Institute of International and Comparative Law/White & Case. https://www.biicl.org/projects/2019-empirical-study-provisional-measures-in-investorstate-arbitration. Accessed 10 Dec 2020

Kalderimis D (2016) The authority of investment treaty tribunals to issue orders restraining domestic court proceedings. ICSID Rev Foreign Invest Law J 31(3):549–575

Peters A (2017) The refinement of international law: from fragmentation to regime interaction and politicization. I•CON 15(3):671–704

Shany Y (2012) One law to rule them all: should international courts be viewed as guardians of procedural order and legal uniformity? In: Fauchald OK, Nollkaemper A (eds) The practice of international and national courts and the (de-)fragmentation of international law. Hart, Oxford, pp 15–34

Sinclair AC, Repousis OG (2017) An overview of provisional measures in ICSID proceedings. ICSID Rev-Foreign Invest Law J 32(2):431–446

# Chapter 6
# Conclusions and Outlook

Chapter 1 of this study has outlined two of the main issues of contention regarding the operation of the IIL regime in Latin America that should be addressed from a human rights perspective. Beyond the so-called regulatory chill effect of ISDS, the first issue of debate should be the overly expansive interpretation and application of IIAs' provisions by arbitral tribunals that do clash with their protection of human rights and the potential of provisional measures that may be put in place to inhibit this protection in pursuit of preserving the integrity of arbitration proceedings. The second issue of contention should be the lack of engagement of arbitral tribunals to address inter-regime clashes in ISDS, arguably, on the grounds that the IIL has been mainly designed to guarantee effective legal protection, thereby denying other legitimate concerns that may also be affected within the context of investor-state relations.

Informed by critical views about the IIL regime that highlight the anchoring of a de-politicisation narrative that induce denial of other concerns than those affecting the legal protection of foreign investment, the study thus argues that re-politicisation could be an initial step to recognise and discuss the issues of contention highlighted above. To this end, the study departs from Peters' understanding of the term 'politicisation as a contestatory process where certain issues are subject of debate' to further question (1) to what extent the critical stand of Latin American countries towards international legal instruments of investment protection can be categorised as such, exploring the issues of contention and the claims raised by these states; and (2) whether the forms prevailed to politicise these international legal instruments so far are adequate to frame the concerns highlighted above, and if not, whether IHRL provides basis to develop, from a human rights perspective, a paradigm that assists in this politicisation process.

The study argues that Latin American critical stand towards international legal instruments of investment protection can be characterised as a politicisation process, whose basis has been the articulation of sovereign rights. However, it also maintains that these paradigms of politicisation are inadequate from a human rights perspective

M. J. Luque Macías, *Re-Politicising International Investment Law in Latin America through the Duty to Regulate Paradigm*, European Yearbook of International Economic Law 14, https://doi.org/10.1007/978-3-030-73272-1_6

and that an appropriate politicisation initially requires from Latin American countries to reconceptualize how they articulate their need of regulatory autonomy. Based on this need, the study further asserts that the duty to regulate paradigm is appropriate to re-politicise IIL since it embodies the regulatory need of these states to maintain regulatory space to adopt all preventative measures required to prevent foreign investors' abuses of human rights. After this discussion, the study outlines the structure of the project to discuss these hypotheses and the specific methodology employed to address them.

Chapter 2 has demonstrated that, throughout the last two centuries, politicisation of international legal instruments protecting foreign investment has been a constant in Latin America and that this contestation has been always articulated in terms of sovereign rights. Nevertheless, the paradigms prevailed to articulate this critical stand have varied over time depending not only on the issues of contention but also the values informing their claims. The prevailing paradigms have ranged from idea of states' right to freely determine how they protect foreign property rights (informed by ideas of state jurisdiction) and right to expropriate foreign property (informed by the principle of permanent sovereignty of natural resources) to the so-called 'right to regulate'. The latter paradigm currently prevails in Latin American countries and it embodies states' right to supervise foreign investment activities' compliance with their regulatory needs and policies based on their national law and policies.

Moreover, Chap. 2 has also revealed that the consolidation of investment treaty protection did not lead to a de-politicisation of the IIL regime in Latin America. On the contrary, the overly expansive interpretation and application of the FET standard and provisions ruling on the lawful exercise of states' right to expropriate by arbitral tribunals raised great concerns in this region, leading to a renewed politicisation of international legal instruments for the protection of foreign investment through the articulation of the 'right to regulate' paradigm. Nevertheless, this articulation has not always entailed a departure from the investment treaty protection paradigm prevailing in IIL in Latin America. On the contrary, many states keep negotiating IIAs and some even still endorse broadly-drafted formulation of IIAs' standards pursuant to which their regulatory conduct shall be reviewed in investment disputes.

On the other side of the spectrum, there have been some countries that have engaged in politicising the IIL regime that is in place, expressed through withdrawal from these international legal instruments and design of new ones that clearly exclude protection of foreign investment in similar terms as IIAs. In this regard, although the articulation of the 'right to regulate' has been the prevailing paradigm applied to politicise the IIL regime in place, the values informing these sovereign claims date back to claims deployed prior to the consolidation of the investment treaty regime in Latin America. The latter means that although the need of preserving regulatory space has been one of the claims currently voiced against the IIL regime, ideas of preserving jurisdiction to rule how they legally protect foreign investment seem to have primarily inform this politicisation.

The findings of Chap. 2 thus initially confirm the hypothesis of this study about the inadequacy of maintaining the 'right to regulate' paradigm pervasively used in

Latin America to politicise the IIL regime, considering its great potential to frustrate states' protection of human rights in the investment context, on the one hand, and about the need of re-politicising the IIL regime with its basis on a new paradigm informed by IHRL, on the other.

Chapter 3 has supported the second hypothesis of this study that IHRL provides sufficient normative basis to develop the 'duty to regulate' paradigm to re-politicise the IIL regime in conformity with IHRL, while it applies terms already familiar in IIL to express states' need of preserving regulatory autonomy to address the two issues of concern mentioned above.

Universal and Inter-American human rights law assigns upon Latin American countries a duty to regulate foreign investment activities in the investment context. Both treaty-based and non-treaty-based UN human rights bodies have recognised the obligation to protect as the legal basis for such duty, while the IACommHR and IACoHR have derived this duty from the obligations to ensure and give legal effect to human rights. In both systems, this duty is understood as an obligation of conduct that requires adopting all appropriate legislative and executive measures to prevent foreign investment activities' interference with the full enjoyment of human rights. Which executive and legislative measures are appropriate in a particular case then depends on the scope of protection of the right at stake developed by human rights bodies. Understanding the states' duty to regulate foreign investment activities in this way exhibits how it relates to IHRL. However, this regulatory duty distinguishes itself from the obligations to protect and ensure since the latter also requires states' provision of legal remedies once abuses of human rights have been committed by foreign investors. In addition, the conceptualisation of regulation as a duty shows how it relates to IIL because it embodies the states' actions that are usually taken in the investment context and lead to the submission of investment treaty claims. Nevertheless, it differs from IIL because the 'right to regulate' paradigm embodies states' sovereign right to rule and control foreign investment activities to ensure their compliance with basis on their domestic laws and regulations.

As the duty to regulate foreign investment activities to prevent their abuses of the right to water, the legal basis of such duty resides on article 11 of the ICESCR, rather than on CIL. In two situations, Latin American countries are called to comply with this duty as states parties to the Covenant. The first situation is in case of foreign investors' provision of drinking water services, and appropriate means to discharge this regulatory duty include controlling tariff increase, supervise investors' observance of contractual agreements and even the imposition of sanctions to prevent that users have no access to water facilities, the affordability of services is compromised, or drinking water is not delivered in unfit conditions for human consumption. The second situation relates to depletion or pollution of water sources that may be induced by corporate mining activities and that may interfere with the access to water sources.

As far as the duty to regulate foreign investment activities to prevent abuses of indigenous people's right to traditional lands is concerned, the legal basis of such duty arises from article 21 of the ACHR. CIL only recognises consultation of indigenous people's land rights as a norm, but its content remains vague. Pursuant to the ACHR, this right allows states' restriction to indigenous people's right to use and enjoy their right to traditional lands upon compliance with a set of requirements. Typical ground for this restriction is the approval of development projects in their traditional lands. Yet, even in these cases, the ACHR requires that states discharge a duty to regulate foreign investment activities by demanding undertaking of consultation processes and ESIAs in knowledge of the real and imminent risk that claimant investors' activities pose upon survival of the indigenous communities. To make the enjoyment of these safeguards effective, both safeguards shall guarantee, inter alia, respect of the social organization of the community, prohibition of coercion to achieve projects' approval and ensuring the participation of these stakeholders in decisions relating to the design, implementation, and evaluation of the projects.

Chapter 4 has shown that several Latin American countries are engaging in a process of re-politicisation of the IIL regime through several argumentative strategies to articulate their duty to regulate investors' activities in ISDS. Cases studies include *Urbaser v Argentina*, *South American Silver v Bolivia*, *Bear Creek v Peru*, and *Copper Mesa v Ecuador*. In some cases, they clearly alluded to their duty to regulate private foreign investment activities as in the terms defined in Chap. 3. Arguments deployed to justify the application of IHRL indicate that they clearly recognise an inter-regime overlapping as problematic. They have ranged from the incompatibility argument of IIL and IHRL obligations, the primacy of human rights norms, the constitutional rank of these international norms and the argument that IIL is not a self-contained regime.

Except from the *Urbaser* tribunal, other tribunals have not averted to address inter-regime frictions that may arise in the context of a particular dispute. Notwithstanding the former, they are weighing out under certain circumstances investors' claims against states' regulatory needs, so that Latin American countries could use as reference point to develop reforms that induce the re-politicisation of IIL among arbitral tribunals. Informed by the *Urbaser* tribunal's approach that employ the applicable law clause as the legal basis to proceed with its assessment of inter-regime interplay, the reforms of IIAs seem to be the initial step to foster this re-politicisation.

Concerning FET, the factor enhancing tribunals' review of the regulatory duties of states relates to the legitimacy of investors' expectations. Regarding issues of expropriation, the character of measure, in addition to the legality requirement, constitutes an entry point. Moreover, the 'unclean hands' of the investor may provide another benchmark to incorporate the regulatory needs and thus its non-liability under IIAs provided that states disclose first how they discharge their regulatory duties to clearly show that their behaviour was not arbitrary. However, counterclaims are not yet an instrument through which states could challenge investors' misconduct towards the human rights they intend to protect through regulatory measures. There is no legal basis yet in current international law that obliges investors to respect and ensure human rights.

Faced with this gap, Latin American countries can foster inter-regime convergence as far as the performance of their duty to regulate investment activities is concerned by means of IIAs. There is not only certain support for the adoption of this investment policy approach in investment case law but IHRL also has already appealed to foster certain degree of convergence with IIL. Treaty reform is the principal means to achieve this aim. The following substantive and procedural reforms could be implemented: (1) An explicit articulation of their duty to regulate protected investment in the preamble or through an autonomous provision. This may facilitate an integration of states parties' regulatory duties on questions relating to the above-mentioned factors with respect to FET, expropriation, and unclean hands of investors. (2) Using the IIA as another regulatory instrument of investors' conduct. Establishing direct obligations under IIAs by incorporating the OECD Guidelines or states parties' laws relating to human rights as the legal basis of that obligations. They clearly determine which conduct investors should adopt and which human rights should be observed during their activities. The advantage of these instruments is that states could borrow the standards already developed by external bodies to assess investors' conduct within the context of an investment dispute. (3) Using IIAs as the source of investors' obligations will not only enhance states that comply with their duty to regulate to challenge tribunals' jurisdiction when they have to respond an investment treaty claim, but also to adequately justify their counterclaims.

If states, otherwise, maintain IIAs with broadly drafted provisions that may thus enhance tribunals to assess their regulatory conduct without any consideration of their duty to regulate protected investment they may be held liable for disregarding their obligation to respect human rights under the ICESCR and ACHR.

Considering that reformed IIAs only foster re-politicisation of IIL regime if the competent tribunal do engage with inter-regime normative interplay, the Chap. 6 has outlined which options a regional ISDS tribunal would have at their disposal to achieve this aim, based on the already existing techniques employed in ISDS this far. This might proceed by resolving inter-regime interplay by itself via the applicable law clause or assisted by IIAs provisions that directly allude to states parties' duty to regulate protected investment and that establish investors' obligations, and with the assistance of human rights bodies such as the IACommHR in its capacity as *amicus curiae*. Alternatively, placing an ISDS tribunal within the framework of a regional organization that commits to the observance of human rights may also underpin the re-politicisation of IIL regime.

The present study, however, has left unaddressed the potential negative impact that provisional measures may have upon states' protection of human rights that may be at stake in a specific dispute, and the impact of the IIL regime over states' provision of legal remedies for investors' abuses of human rights. From a Latin American perspective, the discussion of the latter topic is essential considering the increasing investment treaty claims that increasingly challenge domestic courts' protection of the environment and thereby the protection of the environmental dimension of human rights.

# Table of Cases

## International Court of Justice

*Asylum case* (Colombia v Peru) Judgement [1950] ICJ Rep 266

*Case concerning armed activities on the territory of the Congo* (Democratic Republic of the Congo/Rwanda) (Judgement) (2006) ICJ Rep

*Case concerning the Barcelona Traction, Light and Power Co Ltd* [New Application: 1962] (Belgium v Spain) (Second Phase) ICJ Rep X

*Legal Consequences for States of Continued Presence of South Africa in Namibia (South West Africa) notwithstanding Security Council Resolution 276 (1970)* (Advisory Opinion) ICJ Rep X

*Legality of the Threat or Use of Nuclear Weapons* (Advisory Opinion) (1996) ICJ Rep 226

*Mavromatis Palestinian Concession Case* (Greece v United Kingdom) PICJ Serie A No. 2

*Military and Paramilitary Activities in and against Nicaragua* (Nicaragua v United States of America) (Merits) [1986] ICJ Rep 14 (referring to the use of force)

*North Sea Continental Shelf cases* (Federal Republic of Germany v Denmark and the Netherlands) (Judgement) [1969] ICJ Rep 3

*Pannevesys-Saldutikis Railway Case* (Estonia v Latvia) PCIJ Serie A/B No. 76

*Temple of Preah Vihear* (Cambodia v Thailand), Judgement (15 June 1962) ICJ Reports (1962)

© The Author(s), under exclusive license to Springer Nature Switzerland AG 2021    237
M. J. Luque Macías, *Re-Politicising International Investment Law in Latin America through the Duty to Regulate Paradigm*, European Yearbook of International Economic Law 14, https://doi.org/10.1007/978-3-030-73272-1

# Mixed Claims Commissions

Award of the Tribunal of Arbitration Constituted in Virtue of the Protocols signed at
Washington on 7 May 1903 between Germany, Great Britain, and Italy on the
One Hand and Venezuela on the Other Hand, done at the Hague, In the Perma-
nent Court of Arbitration, 22 February 1904, RIAA IX 107

*Douglas G. Collie Mac Neill (Great Britain) v United Mexican States* (Decision
No. 27, April 10, 1931), Decisions of Claims Commissions Great-Britain-Mexico, France-Mexico, and Germany-Mexico, RIAA V 135

*El Oro Mining and Railway Company (Limited) (Great Britain) v United Mexican
States* (Decision No. 55, June 18, 1931), Decisions of Claims Commissions
Great-Britain-Mexico, France-Mexico, and Germany-Mexico, RIAA V 191

*International Fisheries Company (USA) v the United Mexican States* (July 1931,
concerning Opinion by Presiding Commissioner, July 1931, dissenting opinion
by American Commissioner, Decisions of Claims Commissions Mexico-United
States, RIAA IV 691

*LFH Neer and Pauline Neer v Mexico* (US v Mexico) (1926) 4 RIAA 60

*Mexican Union Railway (Limited) (Great Britain) v United Mexican States* (Decision No. 21, 21 February 1930), Decisions of Claims Commissions Great-Britain-
Mexico, France-Mexico, and Germany-Mexico, RIAA V 115

*North American Dredging Company of Texas (USA) v United Mexican States*
(31 March 1926) Decisions of Claims Commissions Mexico-United States,
RIAA) IV

*The Interoceanic Railway of Mexico (Acapulco to Veracruz) (Limited), and the
Mexican Eastern Railway Company (Limited), and the Mexican Southern Railway (Limited) (Great Britain) v United Mexican States* (Decision No. 53, June
18, 1931), Decisions of Claims Commissions Great-Britain-Mexico, France-
Mexico, and Germany-Mexico, RIAA V 178

*Veracruz Railways (Mexico) Railways (limited) (Great Britain) v United Mexican
States* (Decision No. 72, July 7, 1931), Decisions of Claims Commissions Great-
Britain-Mexico, France-Mexico, and Germany-Mexico, RIAA V 221

# Investor-State Arbitral Tribunals

*ADC Affiliate Limited and ADC & ADMC Management Limited v Hungary*, ICSID
Case No. ARB/03/16, Award (2 October 2006)

*ADF Group Inc. v United States of America*, ICSID Case No. ARB (AF)/00/1,
Award (9 January 2003)

*Aguas Cordobesas, S.A., Suez, and Sociedad General de Aguas de Barcelona, S.A. v
Argentine Republic*, ICSID Case No. ARB/03/18, Order Taking Note of the
Discontinuance of the Proceeding (24 January 2007) (no public available)

*Aguas del Tunari S.A. v Bolivia*, ICSID Case No. ARB/02/3, Decision on Respondent's Objections to Jurisdiction (21 October 2005)

*Alasdair Ross Anderson et al v Republic of Costa Rica*, ICSID Case No. ARB(AF)/07/3, Award (19 May 2010)

*Alex Genin, Eastern Credit Limited, Inc and AS Baltoil (US) v Estonia*, ICSID Case No. ARB/99/2, Award (25 June 2001)

*Álvarez y Marín Corporación S.A. and others v Republic of Panama*, ICSID Case No. ARB/15/14, Reasoning of the Decision on Respondent's Preliminary Objections pursuant to ICSID Arbitration Rule 41(5) (4 April 2016)

*AMCO Asia Co. v Indonesia*, Decision (16 May 1986) (1986) 25 ILM 1441

*Amco Asia Corporation and others v Republic of Indonesia*, ICSID Case No. ARB/81/1, Decision on Jurisdiction in Resubmitted Proceeding (10 May 1988), 1 ICSID Reports, vol. 132, 543

*Antoine Goetz and others v Republic of Burundi*, ICSID Case No. ARB/01/2, Award (21 June 2002)

*Archer Daniels Midland Company and Tate & Lyle Ingredients Americas, Inc v The United Mexican States*, ICSID Case No. ARB(AF)/04/5, Award (21 November 2007)

*Azurix Corp. v Argentine Republic*, ICSID Case No. ARB/03/30 (data no available)

*Azurix Corp. v Argentine Republic*, ICSID Case No. ARB/01/12, Award (14 July 2006)

*Bayandir Insaal Turizm Ticoret Ve Sanayi A.S. v Islamic Republic of Pakistan*, ICSID Case No. ARB/03/09, Decision on Jurisdiction (14 November 2005)

*Bear Creek Mining Corporation v Republic of Peru*, ICSID Case No. ARB/14/2, Award (30 November 2017)

*Biwater Gauff (Tanzania) Ltd v United Republic of Tanzania*, ICSID Case No. ARB/05/22, Procedural Order No. 3 (29 September 2006)

*Burlington Resources Inc. v Republic of Ecuador (formerly Burlington Resources Inc. and others v Republic of Ecuador and Empresa Estatal Petróleos del Ecuador (PetroEcuador)*, ICSID Case No. ARB/08/5, Decision on Reconsideration and Award (7 February 2017)

*Burlington Resources Inc. v Republic of Ecuador (formerly Burlington Resources Inc. and others v Republic of Ecuador and Empresa Estatal Petróleos del Ecuador (PetroEcuador)*, ICSID Case No. ARB/08/5, Decision on Liability (14 December 2012)

*Chevron Corporation and Texaco Petroleum Company v The Republic of Ecuador (II)*, PCA Case No. 2009-23, Second Partial Award on Track II (30 August 2018)

*Chevron Corporation and Texaco Petroleum Company v The Republic of Ecuador (II)*, PCA Case No. 2009-23, First Interim Award on Interim Measures (25 January 2012)

*Chevron Corporation and Texaco Petroleum Company v The Republic of Ecuador (II)*, PCA Case No. 2009-23, Second Interim Award on Interim Measures (16 February 2012)

*Chevron Corporation and Texaco Petroleum Company v The Republic of Ecuador* (II), PCA Case No. 2009-23, First Interim Award on Interim Measures (25 January 2012)

*Chevron Corporation and Texaco Petroleum Company v The Republic of Ecuador* (II), PCA Case No. 2009-23, Second Interim Award on Interim Measures (16 February 2012)

*Chevron Corporation and Texaco Petroleum Company v The Republic of Ecuador* (II), PCA Case No. 2009-23, Second Partial Award on Track II (30 August 2018)

*Churchill Mining and Planet Mining Pty Ltd v Republic of Indonesia*, ICSID Case No. ARB/12/14 and 12/40, Procedural Order No. 14 (22 December 2014) para 71

*CMS Gas Transmission Company v The Republic of Argentina*, ICSID Case No. ARB/01/8, Award (12 May 2005)

*CMS Gas Transmission Company v The Republic of Argentina*, ICSID, Case No. ARB/01/8, Decision on Annulment (25 September 2007)

*Compañiá de Aguas del Aconquija S.A. and Vivendi Universal S.A. v Argentine Republic (formerly Compañía de Aguas del Aconquija, S.A. and Compagnie Générale des Eaux v Argentine Republic)* ICSID Case No. ARB/97/3, Award (20 August 2007)

*Compañía de Aguas del Aconquija, S.A. & Compagnie Générale des Eaux, Claimants v Argentine Republic*, ICSID Case No. ARB/97/3, Award (21 November 2000)

*Compañía del Desarrollo de Santa Elena, S.A v Republic of Costa Rica*, ICSID Case No. ARB/96/1, Award (17 February 2000) 5 ICSID Rep. 153

*Consortium Groapentent L.E.S.I. – DIPENTA v People's Democratic Republic of Algeria*, ICSID Case No. ARB/03/8, Award (10 January 2005)

*Continental Casualty Company v Argentina*, ICSID Case No. ARB/03/09, Award (5 September 2008)

*Copper Mesa Mining Corporation v Republic of Ecuador*, PCA No. 2012-2, Award (15 March 2016)

*Desert Line Projects LLC v The Republic of Yemen*, ICSID Case No. ARB/05/17, Award (6 February 2008)

*Duke Energy Electroquil Partners & Electroquil SA v Ecuador*, ICSID Case No. ARB/04/19, Award (18 August 2008)

*Eco Oro Minerals Corp. v Republic of Colombia*, ICSID Case No. ARB/16/41, Request for Arbitration (8 December 2016)

*EcoDevelopment in Europe AB & others v United Republic of Tanzania*, ICSID Case No. ARB/17/33 (documents are not public available)

*EDF (Services) Limited v Romania*, ICSID Case No. ARB/05/13, Award (8 October 2009)

*El Paso Energy International Company v The Argentine Republic*, ICSID Case No. ARB/03/15, Award (31 October 2011)

*Empresas Lucchetti, S.A. and Lucchetti Peru, S.A. v The Republic of Peru*, ICSID Case No. ARB/03/4, Award (7 February 2005)

*Enron Corporation and Ponderosa Assets, L.P. v Argentine Republic (also known as: Enron Creditors Recovery Corp. and Ponderosa Assets, L.P. v The Argentine Republic)*, ICSID Case No. ARB/01/3, Award (22 May 207)

*Eureko BV v Poland*, Partial Award (19 August 2005)

*Fraport AG Frankfurt Airport Worldwide v The Republic of Philippines*, ICSID Case No. ARB/03/25, Award (16 August 2007)

*Galway Gold Inc. v Republic of Colombia* (ICSID Case No. ARB/18/13) Request for Arbitration (Spanish) (21 March 2018)

*Gami Investments, Inc. v The Government of the United Mexican States*, UNCITRAL (NAFTA), Final Award (15 November 2004)

*Gas Natural SGD, S.A. v The Argentine Republic*, ICSID Case No. ARB/03/10, Decision on Jurisdiction (14 November 2005)

*Generation Ukraine, Inc v Ukraine*, ICSID No. ARB/00/9, Award (16 September 2003)

*Glamis Gold, Ltd v The United States of America*, UNCITRAL (NAFTA), Award (8 June 2009)

*Grand River Enterprises Six Nations Ltd. Et al. v USA*, UNCITRAL (NAFTA), Award (12 January 2011)

*Gustav F W Hamester GmbH & Co KG v Republic of Ghana*, ICSID Case No. ARB/07/24, Award (18 June 2010)

*Impregilo S.p.A. v Argentine Republic*, ICSID Case No. ARB/07/17, Award (21 June 2011)

*Inceysa Vallisoletana S.L. v Republic of El Salvador*, ICSID Case No. ARB/03/26, Award (2 August 2006)

*International Thunderbird Gaming Corporation v The United Mexican States*, UNCITRAL (NAFTA), Award (26 January 2006)

*Ioannis Kardassopoulos v The Republic of Georgia*, ICSID Case ARB/05/18, Award (10 March 2010)

*Italian Republic v Republic of Cuba*, ad hoc state-state arbitration (Final Award) (1 January 2008)

*Jan de Nul NV and Dredging International N.V. v Arab Republic of Egypt*, ICSID Case No. ARB/04/13, Award (6 November 2008)

*Joseph Charles Lemire v Ukraine*, ICSID Case No. ARB/06/18, Award (28 March 2011)

*Klöckner v Cameroon*, Award (21 October 1983) 2 ICSID Reports, pp. 13–18

*Klöckner v Cameroon*, Decision (3 May 1985) 9 Foreign Investment Law Journal 89

*LG &E Energy Corp., LG&E Capital Corp., LG&E International Inc. v Argentina*, ICSID Case No. ARB/02/1, Decision on Liability (3 October 2006)

*LG&E v Argentina*, Decision on Liability (3 October 2006) (2007) 46 ILM 36

*Liberian Eastern Timber Co. (Letco) v Liberia*, Award (31 March 1986) (1987) 26 ILM 647

*Libyan Arab Republic*, Award (19 January 1977) (1978) 17 ILM 1

*Loewen Group, Inc. and Raymond L. Loewen v United States of America*, ICSID Case No. ARB(AF)/98/3, Award (26 June 2003)

*Marvin Roy Feldman Karpa v The United Mexican States*, ICSID Case No. ARB (AF)/99/1, Award (16 December 2002) 7 ICSID Report 341

*Metalclad Corporation v The United Mexican States*, ICSID Case No. ARB(AF)/97/ 1, Award (30 August 2000)

*Metalpar S.A. and Buen Aire S.A. v The Argentine Republic*, ICSID Case No. ARB/03/5, Award on the Merits (6 June 2008)

*Methanex Corp v United States of America*, UNCITRAL (NAFTA), Award, 3 August 2005, (2005) 44 ILM 1343

*Methanex Corporation v United States of America*, UNCITRAL (NAFTA), Final Award (3 August 2005)

*Middle East Cemen shipping and Handling Co SA v Arab Republic of Egypt*, ICSID Case No. ARB/99/6, Award (12 April 2002)

*Mondev International Ltd v United States of America*, ICSID Case No. ARB(AF)/ 99/2, Award (11 October 2002)

*MTD Equity Sdn. Bhd. and MTD Chile S.A. v Republic of Chile*, ICSID Case No. ARB/01/7, Decision on Annulment (21 March 2007)

*Niko Resources (Bangladesh) Ltd. v Bangladesh Petroleum Exploration & Production Company Limited ("Bapex") and Bangladesh Oil Gas and Mineral Corporation ("Petrobangla")*, ICSID Case No. ARB/10/11, Decision on Jurisdiction (19 August 2013)

*Occidental Exploration and Production Co v Ecuador*, LCIA Case No. UN3467, Award (1 July 2004)

*Pac Rim Cayman LLC v Republic of El Salvador*, ICSID Case No. ARB/09/12 Award (14 October 2016)

*Parkerings-Compagniet AS v Lithuania*, ICSID Case No. ARB/05/8, Award (11 September 2007)

*Perenco Ecuador Ltd. v The Republic of Ecuador and Empresa Estatal Petróleos del Ecuador (Petroecuador)*, ICSID Case No. ARB/08/6, Interim Decision on the Environmental Counterclaim (11 August 2015)

*Phelps Dodge International Corp v Islamic Republic of Iran*, Award No. 217-99-2 (19 March 1986) 10 Iran-US CTR 121

*Philip Morris Brands Sàrl, Philip Morris Products S.A. and Abal Hermanos S.A. v Oriental Republic of Uruguay*, ICSID Case No. ARB/10/7, Award (8 July 2016)

*Phoenix Action Ltd. v Czech Republic*, ICSID Case No. ARB/06/5, Award (15 April 2009)

*Plama Consortium Limited v Republic of Bulgaria*, ICSID Case No. ARB/03/24, Award (27 August 2008)

*Plama Consortium Limited v Republic of Bulgaria*, ICSID Case No. ARB/03/24, Decision on Jurisdiction (8 February 2005)

*Pope & Talbot Inc. v The Government of Canada*, UNCITRAL (NAFTA), Award in Respect of Damages (31 May 2002)

*Pope & Talbot Inc. v The Government of Canada*, UNCITRAL (NAFTA), Award on the Merits of Phase 2 (10 April 2001)

*PSEG Global et al. v Republic of Turkey*, ICSID Case No. ARB/02/5, Award (19 January 2007)

*Red Eagle Exploration Limited v Republic of Colombia* (ICSID Case No. ARB/18/12) Notice of Intent (14 September 2017)

*Republic of Ecuador v United States of America* (PCA Case No. 2012-5)) Award (29 September 2012)

S.A.C (4 April 2011)

*Saba Fakes v Republic of Turkey*, ICSID Case No. ARB/07/20, Award (14 July 2010)

*Saipem S.p.A. v The People's Republic of Bangladesh*, ICSID Case No. ARB/05/07, Decision on Jurisdiction (21 March 2007)

*Saluka Investments B.V. v The Czech Republic*, UNCITRAL, Decision on Jurisdiction over the Czech Republic Contract-claims (7 May 2004)

*Saluka Investments B.V. v The Czech Republic*, UNCITRAL, Partial Award (17 March 2006)

*SAUR International v Argentine Republic*, ICSID Case No. ARB/04/4, Award (22 May 2014)

*Sergei Paushok, CJSG Golden East Company and CJSC Vostokneftegaz Company v The Government of Mongolia*, UNCITRAL, Award on Jurisdiction and Liability (28 April 2011)

*Siemens A.g. v The Republic Argentine Republic*, ICSID Case No. ARB/02/08, Award (17 January 2007)

*South American Silver Limited (Bermuda) v The Plurinational State of Bolivia*, PCA Case No. 2013-15, Award (22 November 2018)

*South American Silver Limited (Bermuda) v The Plurinational State of Bolivia*, PCA Case No. 2013-15, Repondent Counter-Memorial (31 March 2015)

*Spyridon Roussalis v Romania*, ICSID Case No. ARB/06/1, Award (7 December 2011)

*Suez, Sociedad General de Aguas de Barcelona, S.A. and Interagua Servicios Integrales de Agua, S.A. v Argentine Republic*, ICSID Case No. ARB/03/17, Decision on Liability (30 July 2010)

*Suez, Sociedad General de Aguas de Barcelona, S.A. and Vivendi Universal, S.A. (formerly Aguas Argentinas, S.A., Suez, Sociedad General de Aguas de Barcelona, S.A. and Vivendi Universal, S.A.) v Argentine Republic*, ICSID Case No. ARB/03/19, Award (9 April 2015)

*Suez, Sociedad General de Aguas de Barcelona, S.A. and Vivendi Universal, S.A. (formerly Aguas Argentinas, S.A., Suez, Sociedad General de Aguas de Barcelona, S.A. and Vivendi Universal, S.A.) v Argentine Republic*, ICSID Case No. ARB/03/19, Decision on Liability (30 July 2010)

*Técnicas Medioambientales Tecmed, S.A. v The United Mexican States*, ICSID Case No. ARB (AF)/00/2, Award (29 May 2003)

*Texaco Overseas Petroleum Company and California Asiatic Oil Company v Government of the Libyan Arab Republic*, Award (19 January 1977) (1978) 17 ILM 1

*The Renco Group, Inc. v The Republic of Peru*, ICSID Case No. UNCT/13/1, Final Award (9 November 2016)

*Tokios Tokeles v Ukraine*, ICSID Case No. ARB/02/18, Decision on Jurisdiction (29 April 2004)

*Total S.A. v The Argentine Republic*, ICSID Case No. ARB/04/01, Decision on Liability (27 December 2011)

*Toto Construzioni Generali S.p.A v The Republic of Lebanon*, ICSID Case No. ARB/02/8, Award (7 June 2012)

*United Parcel Service of America Inc. v Canada*, ICSID Case No. UNCT/02/1, Award on the Merits (24 May 2007)

*United Parcel Service of America Inc. v Canada*, ICSID Case No. UNCT/02/1, Award on the Merits (24 May 2007)

*Urbaser S.A. and Consorcio de Aguas Bilbao Bizkaia, Bilbao Biskaia Ur Partzuergoa v The Argentine Republic*, ICSID Case No. ARB/07/26, Award (8 December 2016)

*Vigotop Limited v Hungary*, ICSID Case No. ARB/11/22, Award (1 October 2014)

*Waguih Elie George Siag and Clorinda Vecchi v The Arab Republic of Egypt*, ICSID Case No. ARB/05/15, Award (1 June 2009)

*Waste Management Inc. v United Mexican States*, ICSID Case No. ARB(AF)/00/3, Award (30 April 2004)

*Wena Hotels Limited v Arab Republic of Egypt*, ICSID Case No. ARB/98/4, Award (8 December 2000)

*World Duty Free Company Limited v The Republic of Kenya*, ICSID Case No. ARB/00/7, Award (4 October 2006)

# International Committee on Economic, Social and Cultural Rights

*Mohamed Ben Djazia and Naouel Bellili v Spain* (20 June 2017) Communication No. 5/2015, CESCR/E/C.12/61/D/5/2015

# Inter-American Court of Human Rights

*Case of Alban Cornejo v Ecuador* (Merits, Reparations and Costs) Judgement Series C No. 171 (22 November 2007)

*Case of Barnaca-Velazquez v Guatemala* (Merits) Judgement, IACoHR Series C Number 70 (25 November 2000)

*Case of Castillo Petruzzi et al v Peru* (Merits, Reparations and Cost) Judgement, IACoHR Series C No. 52 (30 May 1999)

*Case of Cesti Hurtado v Peru* (Merits) Judgement Series C No. 56 (29 September 1999)

*Case of Godínez-Cruz v Honduras* ((Interpretation of the Judgment of Reparations and Costs) Judgement IACoHR Series C Number 3 (20 January 1989)

*Case of the "Five Pensioners" v Peru* (Merits, Reparations and Costs) Judgment, IACoHR Series C No. 98 (28 February 2003)

*Case of the "Juvenile Re-education Institute" v Paraguay* (Preliminary Objections, Merits, Reparations and Costs) IACHR Case (Sr. C) No. 63 (2 September 2004)

*Case of the 19 Merchants v Colombia* (Merits, Reparations and Cost) Judgement, IACoHR Series C (5 July 2004)

*Case of the Indigenous Communities of the Lhaka Honhat (Our Land) Association v Argentina*, Judgment (6 February 2020)

*Case of the Ittuango Masacres v Colombia* (Preliminary Objections, Merits, Reparations and Costs) Judgement, IACoHR Series C No. (1 July 2006)

*Case of the Kaliña and Lokono Peoples v Suriname*, (Merits, Reparations and Costs) Judgement IACoHR, Series C No. 309 (25 November 2015)

*Case of the Last Temptation of Christ v Chile* (Merits, Reparations and Cost) Judgement, IACoHR Series C No. 73 (5 February 2001)

*Case of the Mayagna (Sumo) Awas Tingni Community v Nicaragua*, (Merits, Reparations and Costs) Judgement, IACoHR Series C No. 79 (31 August 2001)

*Case of the Moiwana Community v Suriname* (Preliminary Objections, Merits, Reparations and Costs) Judgement, IACoHR Series C No. 124 (15 June 2005)

*Case of the Pueblo Bello Massacre v Colombia* (Merits, Reparations and Cost) Judgement, IACoHR Series C No. 40 (31 January 2006)

*Case of the Saramaka People v Suriname*, (Preliminary Objections, Merits, Reparations, and Costs) Judgement, IACoHR Series C No. 172 (28 November 2007)

*Case of the Xákmok Kásek Indigenous Community v Paraguay*, (Merits, Reparations, and Costs) IACoHR Series 214 (24 August 2010)

*Case of Velásquez-Rodríguez v Honduras (*Merits) Judgement, IACoHR Serie C No. 4(29 July 1980)

*Case of Velásquez-Rodríguez v Honduras* (Merits) Judgement, IACoHR Series C No. 4 (29 July 1980)

*Caso Cantoral Benavides v Peru* (Fondo) Sentencia, CIDH Serie C No. 69 (18 de Agosto de 2000)

*Caso Comunidad Garifuna de Punta Piedra v Honduras* (Excepciones Preliminares, Fondo, Reparaciones, y Costas) Sentencia, CIDH Serie C No. 304 (8 de Octubre 2015)

*Caso Comunidad Garifuna Triunfo de la Cruz y sus Miembros v Honduras* (Fondo, Reparaciones, Costas) Sentencia, CIDH Serie C No. 305 (8 de Octubre 2015)

*Caso del Pueblo Indigena de Sarayacu* (Medidas Provisionales) CIDH Resolucion (17 June 2005)

*Caso Durand y Ugarte v Peru* (Fondo) Sentencia, CIDH Serie C No. 68 (16 Agosto 2000)

*Caso Familia Barrios v Venezuela* (Fondo, Reparaciones y Costas) Sentencia, CIDH Serie C 237 (24 Noviembre 2011)

*Caso Garrido y Baigorria v Argentina* (Reparaciones y Costas) Sentencia, CIDH Serie C No. 39 (27 Agosto 1998)

*Caso Juan Humberto Sanchez v Honduras* (Excepciones preliminares, fondo, reparaciones y costas) Sentencia, CIDH Serie C No. 199 (7 June 2003)

*Caso Lago del Campo v Peru* (Excepciones Preliminares, Fondo, Reparaciones y Costas) Sentencia, CIDH Serie C No. 340 (31 Agosto de 2017)

*Caso Lago del Campo v Peru* (Excepciones Preliminares, Fondo, Reparaciones y Costas) Sentencia, CIDH Serie C No. 340 (31 Agosto de 2017)

*International Responsibility for the Promulgation and Enforcement of Laws in Violation of the Convention (Arts. 1 and 2 of the American Convention on Human Rights*, Advisory Opinion OC-14/94, IACoHR Series A No. 14 (9 December 1994)

*Interpretation of the American Declaration of the Rights and Duties of Man with the Framework of Article 64 of the American Convention on Human Rights*, Advisory Opinion OC-10/89, IACoHR Series A, No. 10 (14 July 1989)

*Juridical Condition and Human Rights of the Child*, Advisory Opinion OC-17/02, IACoHR (28 August 2002)

*Kichwa Indigenous People of Sarayaku v Ecuador*, (Merits and Reparations) Judgement, IACoHR Series C No. 245 (27 June 2012)

*Obligaciones Estatales en Relación con el Medio Ambiente en el Marco de la Protección y Garantía de los Derechos a la Vida y a la Integridad Personal - Interpretación y Alcance de los Artículos 4.1 y 5.1, En Relación con los Artículos 1.1 Y 2 de la Convención Americana Sobre Derechos Humanos Solicitada por la República de Colombia*, Opinión Consultiva OC-23/17 Serie A No. 23 (15 November 2017).

*Provisional Measure regarding Colombia Matter Peace Community of San Jose de Apartado*, IACoHR Order (21 November 2000)

*Provisional Measure regarding Panama Matter of Four Ngöbe Indigenous Communities and Their Members*, IACoHR Order (28 May 2010)

*Provisional Measures ordered by the Court in the Ivcher Bronstein case*, IACoHR Order (23 November 2000)

*Provisional Measures regarding Brazil Matter Socio-educational Internment Unit (UNIS)*, IACoHR Order (25 February 2011)

*Provisional Measures regarding Ecuador Matter of Pueblo Indígena Sarayaku*, IACoHR Order (6 July 2004)

*Provisional Measures with regard to the Republic of Argentina, Matter of the Mendoza Prisons*, IACoHR Order (1 July 2011)

*Provisional Measures with regard to Venezuela, Matters Capital El Rodeo I and El Rodeo II Judicial Confinment Center* IACoHR order (8 February 2008)

*Sawhoyamaxa Indigenous Community v Paraguay*, (Merits, Reparations and Costs) Judgement, IACoHR Series C No. 146 (29 March 2006)

*The Environment and Human Rights (State Obligations in Relation to the Environment in the Context of the Protection and Guarantee of the Rights to Life and to Personal Integrity – Interpretation and Scope of Articles 4(1) and 5(1) of the American Convention on Human Rights)*, Advisory Opinion OC-23/18, IACoHR Series A No. 23 (15 November 2017)

*Yakye Axa Indigenous Community v Paraguay*, (Merits, Reparations and Costs) Judgement, IACoHR Series C No. 125 (17 June 2005)

# Inter-American Commission on Human Rights

*Caso del Pueblo Indigena de Sarayacu* (Medidas Provisionales) CIDH Resolucion (17 June 2005)

IACommHR (Resolution) 2009, *National Association of Ex-Employees of the Peruvian Social Security Institute et al. v Peru*, Case 12.670, Report No. 38/09, OEA/Serv.L/V/II, Doc. 51 corr. 1

IACommHR, 'Case of Mayagna (Sumo) Awas Tingni v Nicaragua' (3 March 1998) Report 27/98

IACommHR, 'Case of Yanomani Indigenous Peoples v Brazil' (5 March 1985) Res 12/85, Case 7615

IACommHR, 'Garza v United States', Case 12.243, IACommHR, Report No. 1255, OEA/ser.L/V/II/111, doc. 20 rev (2001)

IACommHR, 'Indigenous and Tribal People's Rights over their Ancestral Lands and Natural Resources. Norms and Jurisprudence of the Inter-American Human Rights System' OEA/Ser.L/V/II. Doc. 56/09 (30 December 2009)

IACommHR, 'Jessica Lenahan (Gonzales) and others (United States)' Report 80/11, Case No, 12.626 (21 July 2011)

IACommHR, 'Maya Indigenous Communities of the Toledo District v Belize', Report No. 40/04, Case 12.053 (12 October 2004)

IACommHR, 'Murdered and Missing Indigenous Women in British Columbia, Canada' OEA/Ser.L/V/II, Doc. 30/14 (21 December 2014)

IACommHR, 'Report on the Situation of Human Rights in Ecuador' OAS/Serv/V/II.96 Doc. Rev 1 (24 April 1997)

IACommHR, 158 Extraordinary Period of Sessions 'States, Corporations, and Human Rights in South America' (7 June 2016)

IACommHR, 159 Period of Sessions 'Human Rights Situation in the Context of the Implementation of the Trans-Pacific Partnership (TPP) in the Americas', (7 December 2016)

IACommHR, 160 Extraordinary Period of Sessions 'Human Rights Situation of Indigenous Persons in the Context of Projects and Extractive Industries in the United States', (9 December 2016)

IACommHR, *Communities of the Maya People (Sipakepense and Mam) of the Sipacapa and San Miguel Ixtahuacán Municipalities in the Department of San Marcos, Guatemala*, Precautionary Measures 260-07, (7 December 2007)

IACommHR, *Community of La Oroya, Peru*, Precautionary measures (31 August 2007)

*Indigenous Communities of Cuenca del Rio Xingu, Para, Brazil* (Precautionary Measures) IACommHR PM 382-10 (1 April 2011)

## OECD National Contact Points

*Complaint from The Future in Our Hands (FIOH) against Intex Resources ASA and the Mindoro Nickel Project*, The Norwegian National Contact Point for the OECD Guidelines for Multinational Enterprises, Final Statement (30 November 2011)      http://www.responsiblebusiness.no/files/2013/12/intex_fivh_final.pdf. Accessed 10 December 2020

*Complaint from Survival International against Vedanta Resources plc*, Final Statement by the UK National Contact Point for the OECD Guidelines for Multinational Enterprises (25 September 2009) http://www.oecd.org/investment/mne/43884129.pdf. Accessed 10 December 2020

## Other Case Law

*Minority Rights Dev. v Kenya*, African Commission on Human Rights and Peoples, No. 276/03 (4 February 2010)

*The Social and Economic Rights Action Center, and the Center for Economic and Social Rights v Nigeria*, African Commission on Human and Peoples' Rights Comm. No. 155/96 (2001) A.H.R.L.R. 60 (ACHPR 2001)

# Table of Legal Instruments

## International Investment Agreements

Acordo de Cooperação e Facilitação de Investimentos entre a República Federativa do Brasil e a República do Colômbia (signed 9 October 2015)

Acordo de Cooperação e Facilitação de Investimentos entre o Governo da República Federativa do Brasil e o Governo da República de Moçambique (signed 30 March 2015)

Acuerdo de Cooperación y de Facilitación de las Inversiones entre la República Federativa del Brasil y los Estados Unidos Mexicanos (signed 26 May 2015)

Acuerdo de Cooperación y Facilitación de Inversiones entre la República Federativa del Brasil y la República de Chile (signed 24 November 2015)

Acuerdo entre el Gobierno de la Republica de Colombia y el Gobierno de la Republica Francesa Sobre El Fomento y Proteccion Reciprocos de Inversiones (signed 10 July 2014)

Acuerdo entre el Gobierno de la Republica del Peru y el Gobierno de la Republica de Colombia sobre Promocion y Proteccion Reciproca de Inversiones (signed 11 December 2007, entered into force 30 Decmeber 2010) Annex A

Acuerdo para la Promocion y Proteccion Reciproca de Inversiones entre El Reino de Espana y la Republica del Salvador (signed 14 February 1992, entered into force 20 February 1996)

Additional Protocol to the Framework Agreement of the Pacific Alliance (signed 10 February 2014, entered into force 1 May 2016)

African Union Commission, Economic Affairs Department, 'Draft Pan- African Investment Code' (December 2016) https://au.int/sites/default/files/documents/32844-doc-draft_pan-african_investment_code_december_2016_en.pdf accessed 10 December 2020

© The Author(s), under exclusive license to Springer Nature Switzerland AG 2021      249
M. J. Luque Macías, *Re-Politicising International Investment Law in Latin America through the Duty to Regulate Paradigm*, European Yearbook of International Economic Law 14, https://doi.org/10.1007/978-3-030-73272-1

Agreement between Japan and the Oriental Republic of Uruguay for the Liberalization, Promotion and Protection of Investment (signed 26 January 2015; entered into force 14 April 2017)

Agreement between the Government of Canada and the Government of the Republic of Ecuador for the Promotion and Reciprocal Protection of Investments (signed 29 April 1996, entered into force 6 June 1997)

Agreement between the Government of the Kingdom of the Netherlands and the Government of the Republic of Indonesia on Promotion and Protection of Investment (7 July 1968) 11386 UNTS 14

Agreement between the Government of the Republic of Chile and the Government of the Kingdom of Denmark concerning the Promotion and Reciprocal Protection of Investments (signed 28 May 1993, entered into force 3 November 1995)

Agreement between the Government of the Republic of Colombia and the Government of the Republic of Turkey Concerning the Reciprocal Promotion and Protection of Investment (signed 28 July 2014)

Agreement between the Government of the Republic of Indonesia and the Government of the Republic of Cuba concerning the Promotion and Protection of Investment (signed 19 September 1997, entered into force 29 September 1999)

Agreement between the Government of the Republic of Korea and the Government of the Republic of Bolivia on the Reciprocal Promotion and Protection of Investments (signed 1 April 1996, entered into force 4 June 1997)

Agreement between the Government of the United Kingdom of Great Britain and Northern Ireland and the Government of the Republic of Argentina for the Promotion and Protection of Investments (signed 11 December 1990, entered into force 19 February 1993)

Agreement between the Government of the United Kingdom of Great Britain and Northern Ireland and the Government of the Oriental Republic of Uruguay (signed 21 October 1991, entered into force 1 August 1997)

Agreement between the Republic of Guatemala and the Republic of Trinidad and Tobago on the Reciprocal Promotion and Protection of Investments (signed 13 August 2013)

Agreement between the Swiss Confederation and the Republic of Peru on the Promotion and Reciprocal Protection of Investment (signed 22 November 1991, entered into force 23 November 1993)

Bilateral Agreement for the Promotion and Protection of Investments between the Government of the Republic of Colombia and the Government of the United Arab Emirates (signed 13 November 2017)

Convenio entre el Gobierno de la Republica del Ecuador y el Gobierno de la Republica Popular de China para el Fomento y Protección Reciprocos de Inversiones (signed 21 March 1994, terminated)

Convenio entre la Republica de Panama y Ucrania sobre la Promoción y Protección Reciproca de Inversiones (signed 4 November 2003)

Convenio para la Promocion y la Proteccion Reciproca de las Inversiones suscrito con la Union Economica Belgo-Luxemburguesa (signed 28 June 1990, entered into force 20 May 1994).

Cooperation and Investment Facilitation Agreement between the Federative Republic of Brazil and the Co-Operative Republic of Guyana (signed 13 December 2018)

ECOWAS, Supplementary Act A/SA.3/12/08 Adopting Community Rules on Investment and the Modalities for their Implementation with ECOWAS (signed 19 December 2008, entered into force 19 January 2009)

Free Trade Agreement between Canada and Peru (signed 29 May 2008, entered into force 1 August 2009)

FTAA - Trade Negotiations Committee Costa Rica, El Salvador, Guatemala, Honduras, Nicaragua, Canada, Mexico, Chile, Dominican Republic, Panama, Colombia, Peru and Bolivia, Vision of the FTAA, Public FTAA.TNC/w/219 October 4, 2003 (Original: Spanish, Translation: FTAA Secretaria)

FTAA - Trade Negotiations Committee, Uruguay, Vision of the FTAA, Public FTAA.TNC/w/221October 4, 2003 (Original: Spanish Translation: FTAA Secretaria)

FTAA, Second Draft Agreement, Chapter on Investment (Derestricted FTAA.TNC/w/133/Rev.2 November 1, 2002) Foreign Trade Information System, Trade Policy Developments, Free Trade Agreement of the Americas (FTAA), Draft texts of the FTAA Agreement. Available via SICE: http://www.sice.oas.org/tpd/ftaa/ftaa_e.asp#DraftTexts. Accessed 10 December 2020

FTAA, Third Draft Agreement, Chapter XVII Investment (Derestricted FTAA.TNC/w/133/Rev.3 November 21, 2003) Foreign Trade Information System, Trade Policy Developments, Free Trade Agreement of the Americas (FTAA), Draft texts of the FTAA Agreement. Available via SICE: http://www.sice.oas.org/tpd/ftaa/ftaa_e.asp#DraftTexts. Accessed 10 December 2020

Investment Agreement between the Government of the Hong Kong Special Administrative Region of the People's Republic of China and the Government of the Republic of Chile (signed 18 November 2016)

Investment Agreement for the COMESA Common Investment Area (signed 23 May 2007, not yet in force)

Investment Cooperation and Facilitation Agreement between the Federative Republic of Brazil and the Republic of Malawi (signed 26 June 2015)

North American Free Trade Agreement between the Government of the United States of America, the Government of Canada and the Government of the United Mexican States (signed 17 December 1992, entered into force 1 January 1994) (1993) 32 ILM 289

Norway Model BIT (2007)

Notes of Interpretation of Certain Chapter 11 Provisions (NAFTA Free Trade Commission, 31 July 2001)

Protocolo de Cooperación y Facilitación de Inversiones Intra-Mercosur (signed 7 April 2017) Available at: https://www.mercosur.int/documento/protocolo-de-cooperacion-y-facilitacion-de-inversiones-intra-mercosur/.                Accessed 10 December 2020.

Reciprocal Investment Promotion and Protection Agreement between the Government of the Kingdom of Morocco and the Government of the Federal Republic of Nigeria (signed 3 March 2016)

The Reciprocal Promotion and Protection of Investment between the Argentine Republic and the State of Qatar (signed 6 November 2016)

Tratado de Libre Comercio entre Argentina y Chile (signed 2 November 2017)

Tratado de Libre Comercio entre los Estados Unidos Mexicanos y la Republica de Panama (signed 3 April 2014)

Tratado de Libre Comercio entre Panama y Peru (signed 25 May 2011, entered into force 1 May 2012)

Tratado entre la Republica Federal de Alemania y la Republica del Paraguay sobre Fomento y Reciproca Proteccion de Inversiones de Capital (signed 11 August 1993, entered into force 3 July 1998)

Treaty for the Promotion and Protection of Investments (with Protocol and exchange of notes) Germany-Pakistan (signed 25 November 1959, entered into force 26 March 1963) 457 UNTS 24

## Universal Human Rights Instruments

Convention on the Elimination of All Forms of Discrimination against Women (adopted 18 December 1979, entered into force 3 September 1981) 1249 UNTS 13

Convention on the Rights of Persons with Disabilities (adopted 13 December 2006, entered into force 3 May 2008) 2515 UNTS 3

Convention on the Rights of the Child (adopted 20 November 1989, entered into force 2 September 1990) 1577 UNTS 3

International Covenant on Civil and Political Rights (adopted 16 December 1966, entered into force 23 March 1976) 999 UNTS 171

International Covenant on Economic, Social and Cultural Rights (adopted 16 December 1966, entered into force 3 January 1976) 993 UNTS 3

Optional Protocol to the International Covenant on Economic. Social and Cultural Rights (adopted on 10 December 2008) UNGA Res A/RES/63/117

United Nations Declaration on the Rights of Indigenous Peoples (adopted 13 September 2007) UNGA Res 61/295

Universal Declaration of Human Rights (adopted 10 December 1948) UNGA Resolution Res 217 A (III)

## Inter-American Human Rights Instruments

Additional Protocol to the American Convention on Human Rights in the Area of
Economic, Social and Cultural Rights "Protocol of San Salvador" (signed on
17 November 1988, entered into force on 16 November 1999) (1989) 28 ILM 156
American Convention on Human Rights (adopted 22 November 1969, entered into
force 18 July 1978) 1144 UNTS 123
American Declaration of the Rights and Duties of Man (adopted 2 May 2008) OAS
Res XXX adopted by the Ninth International Conference of American States
(1948), AJIL Vol. 43 Supp. 133
American Declaration on the Rights of Indigenous Peoples (adopted 15 June 2016),
OEA/Ser.P AG/RES.2888 (XLVI-O/16) https://www.oas.org/en/sare/docu
ments/DecAmIND.pdf. Accessed 10 December 2020
IACommHR, Resolution No. 1/05 (8 March 2005)
IACommHR, Rules of Procedure of the Inter-American Commission on Human
Rights. Available at: http://www.oas.org/en/iachr/mandate/basics/rulesiachr.asp.
Accessed 10 December 2020
IACommHR, Special Rapporteurship on Economic, Social, Cultural an Environ-
mental Rights, 'Informe sobre Empresas y Derechos Humanos: Estándares
Interamericanos' (1 November 2019) OEA/Ser.L/V/II
Rules of Procedure of the Inter-American Court of Human Rights, as amended
approved by the Court during its LXXXV Regular Period of Sessions, held
from November 16 to 28, 2009.2 (originally approved by the Tribunal in its III
Regular Period of Sessions, held from June 30 to August 9, 1980)
Statute of the Inter-American Commission on Human Rights, Res. No. 447 adopted
by the OAS General Assembly during its ninth period of sessions (1979).
Available at: http://www.oas.org/xxxiiga/english/docs_en/cidh_statute_files/
basic15.htm. Accessed 10 December 2020

## United Nations

Economic and Social Council 'Guiding Principles on Internal Displacement'
E/CN.4/1998/53/Add.2 (11 February 1998) Annex
UNCHR (Commission), Resolution on Adverse effects of the illicit movement and
dumping of toxic and dangerous products and wastes on the enjoyment of human
rights (14 April 2005) UN Doc. E/CN.4/RES/2005/15
'Programme of Action of the International Conference on Population and Develop-
ment, Cairo'(5-13 September 1994) UN Doc. A/CONF.171/13
'Report of the United Nations Conference on Environment and Development
'Agenda 21' (3-14 June 1992) UN Doc. A/CONF.151/26, Vol. II chap 18.47
'Report of the United Nations Water Conference, Mar del Plata Action Plan' (14-25
March 1977) UN Doc. E/Conf.70/29

'Study on the right to adequate food as a human right: report prepared by Asbjorn Eide' (1987) UN Doc E/CN.4/Sub.2/1987/23

High Commissioner of Human Rights of the United Nations, The Corporate Responsibility to Respect Human Rights, An Interpretative Guide (2012)

Report of the Special Representative of the Secretary-General on the issue of human rights and transnational corporations and other business enterprises, John Ruggie, 'Protect, Respect and Remedy: A Framework for Business and Human Rights' (2008) UN Doc. A/HRC/8/5

Report of the United Nations Conference on Human Settlements (Habitat II), Istanbul, 3–14 June 1996, UN. Doc. A/CONF.165/14)

See Open-ended Intergovernmental Working Group on transnational corporations and other business enterprises with respect to human rights, OEIGWG Chairmanship Second Revised Draft 06.08.2020, Legally Binding Instrument to Regulate, in International Human Rights Law, the Activities of Transnational Corporations and Other Business Enterprises. Available at: https://www.ohchr. org/Documents/HRBodies/HRCouncil/WGTransCorp/Session6/OEIGWG_ Chair-Rapporteur_second_revised_draft_LBI_on_TNCs_and_OBEs_with_ respect_to_Human_Rights.pdf. Accessed 10 December 2020

The Maastricht Guidelines on Violations of Economic, Social and Cultural Rights (1997) (adopted by a group of academic experts meeting in Maastricht 22-26 January 1997, later reissued as UN Doc. E/C.12/2000/13)

UNCHR, 'Preliminary Report of the Special Rapporteur on the Right to Education, Ms Katarina Tomasevski, submitted in accordance with Commission on Human Rights Resolution 1998/33' (1999), UN Doc. E/CN/.4/1999/49

UNGA 'Summary of the 18th plenary meeting of the 64th General Assembly' UN Doc. A/64/PV.108, (2010) (Statement by the Bolivian representative, or Statement of the Colombian representative)

UNGA 'The human right to water and sanitation' (2010) UN Doc. A/RES/64/292

UNGA Res 799 (VIII), Request for the Codification of the Principles of International Law Governing State Responsibility (7 December 1953) 52

UNGA, 'Outcome document of the high-level plenary meeting of the General Assembly known as the World Conference on Indigenous Peoples' (2014) UN Doc. A/RES/69/2

UNGA, 'Report of the Special Rapporteur on extreme poverty and human rights' (26 September 2018) UN Doc A/73/396

UNGA, 'The human right to safe drinking water and sanitation' (18 December 2013) UN Doc. A/RES/68/1567

UNGA, 'The human rights to safe drinking water and sanitation' (17 December 2015) UN Doc. A/RES/70/169

UNGA, Report of the Economic and Social Council, Permanent Sovereignty over Natural Resources, Report of the Secretary General, Supplement to the report of the Secretary-General, Document A/9716 (20 September 1974)

UNGA, Report of the Special Rapporteur of the Human Rights Council on the rights of indigenous peoples on the impact of international investment and free trade on the human rights of indigenous peoples, A/70/301 (7 August 2015)

UNHRC, 'Human rights and indigenous issues' (2001) UN Doc. E/CN.4/RES/2001/57

UN-Sub-Commission on Prevention of Discrimination and Protection of Minorities 'Study on the right to adequate food as a human right: preliminary report/ by Asbjorn Eide, Special Rapporteur' (1983) UN Doc. E/CN.4/Sub.2/1983/25

UNHRC, 'Resolution 33/10 on the human rights to safe drinking water and sanitation' (29 September 2016) UN Doc. A/HRC/RES/33/10

Charter of the United Nations (24 October 1945) 1 UNTS XVI

UNGA Res 523 (VI) (12 January 1952) GAOR 6th Session Supp. 20, 20 (on integrated economic development and commercial agreements)

UNGA Res 626 (VII) (21 December 1952) GAOR, 7th Session Supp. 20, 18

UNGA Res 1314 (XIII) (12 December 1958), GAOR, 13th Session Supp. 18, 27

UNGA Res 1514 (XV) (14 December 1960)

UNGA Res 1803 (XVII) (14 December 1962) GAOR 17th Session Supp. 17, (Declaration on Permanent Sovereignty over Natural Resources)

UNGA Res 3201 (S-VI) (1 May 1974) UN Doc A/Res/S-6/3201 (Declaration on the Establishment of a New International Economic Order)

UNGA Res 3281 (XXIX) (12 December 1974) GAOR, 29th Session, Supp. 31 (1), 50

UNGA 'The Right to Development' Res. 54/175 (15 February 2000)

UNHRC, Resolution 16/2 on the human right to safe drinking water and sanitation' (8 April 2011) UN Doc. A/HRC/RES/16/2

UNHRC, 'Resolution 21/2 on the human right to safe drinking water and sanitation' (9 October 2012) UN Doc. A/HRC/RES/21/2

UNHRC, 'Resolution 7/22 on human rights and access to safe drinking water and sanitation' (28 March 2008) UN Doc. A/HRC/RES/7/22

UNHRC, 'Resolution 27/7 on the human right to safe drinking water and sanitation' (2 October 2014) UN Doc. A/HRC/RES/27/7

## International Law Commission

ILC, 'Report of the Study Group of the International Law Commission on the Fragmentation of International Law: Difficulties Arising from the Diversification and Expansion of International Law' (18 July 2006) UN Doc. A/CN.4/L.702

ILC, 'Report of the International Law Commission on the work of its fifteenth session' (6 May – 12 July 1963) UN Doc A/5509

ILC, First Report on State responsibility by Mr. Roberto Ago. Special Rapporteur - Review of previous work on codification of the topic of the international responsibility of States (7 May 1969 and 20 January 1970), Document A/CN.4/217 and Corr.1 and Add.1, citing Principles of international law that govern the responsibility of the State in the opinion of Latin American countries, prepared by the Inter-American Juridical Committee in 1962, Annex XIV

ILC 'Draft Articles on Responsibility of States for Internationally Wrongful Acts' (2001) Supplement No. 10 (A/56/10), chp.IV.E.1

# Economic Commission for Latin America and the Caribbean ECLAC

ECLAC (Department of Economic Affairs) 'The Economic Development of Latin America and its Principal Problems' (27 April 1950) E/CN.12/89/Rev. 1

ECLAC, 'A Contribution to the Economic Policy in Latin America' (3 June 1965) E/CN.12/728

ECLAC, 'The Latin American Common Market' (July 1959) E/CN.12/531

# United Nations Conference on Trade and Development

Joint Declaration of the Seventy-Seven Developing Countries Made at the Conclusion of the United Nations Conference on Trade and Development (15 June 1964)

UNCTAD, Bilateral Investment Treaties 1959-1999, UNCTAD/ITE/IIA/2

UNCTAD, *Bilateral Investment Treaties in 1995-2006: Trends in Investment Rulemaking* (2007)

UNCTAD, Investment Policy Framework for Sustainable Development (2015)

UNCTAD, *Investor-State dispute Settlement: Review of Developments in 2019* (2020) 2 IIA Issues Note

UNCTAD, *Latest Developments in Investor–State Dispute Settlement* (2010) (1) IIA Issues Note

# League of Nations

'Letter from the Chairman of the Committee of Experts for the Progressive Codification of International Law to the Secretary-General of the League of Nations, Communication to the Later, For Transmission to Governments, the Questionnaires and Reports adopted by the Committee at its Second Session Held in January 1926' (1926) 20 AJIL (Special Supplement)

Committee of Experts for the Progressive Codification of International Law, Questionnaire No. 4 adopted by the Committee as its Second Session, held in January 1926 (Responsibility of States for Damage done in their Territories to the Person or Property of Foreigners)' (1926) 20 AJIL (Special Supplement)

Committee of Experts for the Progressive Codification of International Law, Report to the Council of the League of Nations on the Questions which Appear Ripe for

International Regulation (1928) 22 AJIL (Special Supplement) 4–5, and Annex
    III, Analyses of Replies Received from Governments to Questionnaires Submit-
    ted by Members of the Committee (1928) 22 AJIL (Special Supplement)
Council Resolution (1924) LNOJ, Special Supplement No. 21 10
Covenant of the League of Nations, *International Law Documents* (8th edn OUP
    2007) 1-7
Draft Convention on the Treatment of Foreigners, (1930) LNOJ Doc. C. 97, M. 23,
    13-22
Economic Committee of the League of Nations, Draft Convention on the Treatment
    of Foreigners (1928) C.174.M.53.1928. II
League of Nations, Resolutions and Recommendations Adopted by the Assembly,
    September 27, 1927, (1928) 22 AJIL (Special Supplement)
Work of the Committee of Experts for the Progressive Codification of International
    Law during its first Session (1925) LNOJ (Annex, List of Subject of Study,
    adopted by the Committee on April 6th and 8th, 1925), Doc. C.275.1925.V, 843

# MERCOSUR

Additional Protocol to the Treaty of Asuncion on the Institutional Structure of
    MERCOSUR ('Protocol of Ouro Preto') (signed 17 December 1994) (1995)
    34 ILM 1244
Colonia Protocol on Reciprocal Promotion and Protection of Investments within
    MERCOSUR (signed 17 January 1994)
Protocol on the Promotion and Protection of Investments coming from states
    non-Parties of MERCOSUR (signed 5 August 1994)

# Andean Common Market

Agreement on Andean Subregional Integration (signed 26 May 1969, entered into
    force 16 October 1969) (1969) 8 (5) ILM (Cartagena Agreement) 910
Andean Group: Commission, 'Decision 291 – Common code for the Treatment of
    Foreign Capital and on Trademarks, Patents, Licenses and Royalties' (adopted
    21 March 1991) (1991) 30 ILM 1283
Treaty of Ouro Preto. Treaty establishing a Common Market (signed 26 March
    1991) 30 ILM 1041

## International Labour Organization

Committee of Experts, 73rd Session, 2002, Observation, Peru, published 2003
Committee of Experts, 76th Session, 2005, Observation, Guatemala, published 2006
Constitution of the International Labour Organization (adopted 1 April 1919, entered into force 28 June 1919)
Governing Body, 289th Session, March 2004, Representation under article 24 of the ILO Constitution, Mexico, GB.289/17/3
ILO Governing Body (282nd Session) 'Second Supplementary Report: Representation alleging non-observance by Ecuador of the Indigenous and Tribal Peoples Convention, 1989 (No. 169), made under article 24 of the ILO Constitution by the Ecuadorian Confederation of Free Trade Union Organizations (CESOSL)' November 2001, GB.282/14/2
Convention concerning Indigenous and Tribal Peoples in Independent Countries (adopted 27 June 1989, entered into force 5 September 1991) XXX
ILO, Equality Team of the International Labour Standards Department, ILO, ILO standards and the UN Declaration on the Rights of Indigenous Peoples Information note for ILO staff and partners. Available at: https://view.officeapps.live.com/op/view.aspx?src=http%3A%2F%2Fpro169.org%2Fres%2Fmaterials%2Fen%2Fconvention169%2FInformation%2520Note%2520on%2520ILO%2520standards%2520and%2520UNDRIP.doc. Accessed 10 December 2020.

## Organization for Economic Co-operation and Development

OECD Guidelines for Multinational Enterprises 2011 Edition, Recommendations for responsible business conduct in a global context. Available via OECD. http://www.oecd.org/daf/inv/mne/48004323.pdf. Accessed 10 December 2020
OECD, 'Guidelines for Multinational Corporations' (1976) 15 ILM 967
OECD Guidelines for Multinational Enterprises ,2011 Edition, Recommendations for responsible business conduct in a global context. Available via OECD. http://www.oecd.org/daf/inv/mne/48004323.pdf. Accessed 10 December 2020

## Organization of American States

Charter of the Organization of American States (adopted 30 April 1948, entered into force 13 December 1951)
OAS, 'Conferencia Especializada InterAmericana sobre Derechos Humanos', reprinted in Buergenthal T, Norris R (eds) (1984) Human Rights: The Inter-American System, Ocean Publication, New York

OAS, 'Promotion and Protection of Human Rights in Business' General Assembly Res AG/Res 2840 (XLIV-O/14) (Washington DC 4 June 2014)

OAS, 'Promotion and Protection of Human Rights' General Assembly Res AG/Res 2887 (XLVI-O/16) (Washington DC 14 June 2016)

OAS, Res. VIII, Fifth Meeting of Consultation of Ministers of Foreign Affairs, Final Act, Santiago, Chile (12–18 Aug. 1959)

# Pan American Union

'Protocol on Adherence to the Convention of the Hague' reprinted in *The International Conferences of American States 1889-1928, Scott Collection*

'Proposed Treaty Presented by the Delegation of Costa Rica Regarding the Creation of the Permanent Court of American Justice', reprinted in *The International Conferences of American States 1889-1928, Scott Collection*

'Recommendation, Claims and Diplomatic Intervention' (adopted April 8, 1890), reprinted in *The International Conferences of American States 1889-1928, Scott Collection*

'Convention Relative to the Rights of Aliens' reprinted in *The International Conferences of American States 1889-1928, Scott Collection*

'Convention on the Status of Aliens' (signed on 20 February 1928) reprinted in *The International Conferences of American States 1889-1928, Scott Collection*

'Resolution Consideration of the Rights of Aliens Resident within the Jurisdiction of Any of the American Republics' (adopted May 3, 1923) reprinted in *The International Conferences of American States 1889-1928, Scott Collection*

'Invitation to the (First) Conference of American States, Circular Instruction of the Secretary of State of the United States to the American Diplomatic Representations accredited to the Governments of Mexico, Central and South America, Haiti and Santo Domingo' (July 13, 1888), reprinted in *The International Conferences of American States 1889-1928, Scott Collection*

'Plan of Arbitration' (signed 24 April 1890), reprinted in *The International Conferences of American States 1889-1928, Scott Collection*

'Invitation to the (Second) Conference, The Minister of Foreign Relations of Mexico to the Ministers Plenipotentiary of the Republics of North, Central and South America' (August 15, 1900), reprinted in *The International Conferences of American States 1889-1928, Scott Collection*

'Treaty on Compulsory Arbitration' (signed 29 January 1902), reprinted in *The International Conferences of American States 1889-1928, Scott Collection.*

Convention Pecuniary Claims (adopted 11 August 1910), reprinted in *The International Conferences of American States 1889-1928, Scott Collection.*

'Resolution Consideration of the Best Means to Give Wider Application to the Principle of the Judicial or Arbitral Settlement of Disputes that may arise between the Republics of the American Continent', reprinted in *The International Conferences of American States 1889-1928, Scott Collection.*

Resolution Arbitration and Conciliation Conference (adopted 18 February 1928), reprinted in *The International Conferences of American States 1889-1928, Scott Collection.*

Treaty to Avoid or Prevent Conflicts Between the American States, reprinted in *The International Conferences of American States 1889-1928, Scott Collection.*

General Treaty of Inter-American Arbitration, reprinted in *The International Conferences of American States 1889-1928, Scott Collection.*

## Human Rights Council

HRC, 'Concluding Observations of the Human Rights Committee, Guatemala' (19 April 2012) UN Doc. CCPR/C/GTM/CO/3

HRC, 'Elaboration of an international legally binding instrument on transnational corporations and other business enterprises with respect to human rights' (2014) UN Doc. A/HRC/RES/26/9

HRC, 'Human rights and indigenous peoples: mandate of the Special Rapporteur on the situation of human rights and fundamental freedoms of indigenous people' (2007) UN Doc. A/HRC/RES/6/12

HRC, 'Human rights and indigenous peoples: mandate of the Special Rapporteur on the rights of indigenous peoples' (2010) UN Doc. A/HRC/RES/15/14

HRC, 'Human rights and indigenous peoples: mandate of the Special Rapporteur on the rights of indigenous peoples' (2013) UN Doc. A/HRC/RES/24/9

HRC, 'Human rights and transnational corporations and other business enterprises' (2011) UN Doc. A/HRC/17/4

HRC, 'Mandate of the Special Representative of the Secretary General on the issue of human rights and transnational corporations and other business enterprises' (2008) UN Doc. A/HRC/8/7

HRC, 'Report of the Special Rapporteur on the Right to Food, Olivier De Schutter, Guiding Principles on Human Rights Impact Assessments of Trade and Investment Agreements' (2011) Un Doc. A/HRC/19/59/Add.5

HRC, 'Report of the Special Representative of the Secretary-General on the issue of human rights and transnational corporations and other business enterprises, John Ruggie, Guiding Principles on Business and Human Rights: Implementing the United Nations "Protect, Respect and Remedy" Framework' (2011) UN Doc. A/HRC/17/31

HRC, 'Report of the Working Group on the Issue of Human Rights and Transnational Corporations and other Business Enterprises' (2013) UN Doc. A/HRC/23/32

HRC, 'Report of the Working Group on the Issue of Human Rights and Transnational Corporations and other Business Enterprises' (2013) UN Doc. A/HRC/23/32

HRC, Res. 26/9 Elaboration of an international legally binding instrument on transnational corporations and other business enterprises with respect to human rights (2014), UN Doc A/HRC/RES/26/9 (14 July 2014)

Human rights and indigenous peoples: mandate of the Special Rapporteur on the rights of indigenous peoples' (2016) UN Doc. A/HRC/RES/33/12

# International Committee on Economic, Social and Cultural Rights

CESCR General Comment No. 9: The domestic application of the Covenant (3 December 1996) UN Doc. E/C.12/1998/24

CESCR, Concluding observations on the second to fourth periodic reports of Viet Nam (15 December 2014) UN Doc. E/C.12/VNM/CO/2-4

CESCR, Concluding observations on the sixth periodic report of Canada (23 March 2016) UN Doc. E/C.12/CAN/CO/6

CESCR, General Comment No. 12 on the Right to Adequate Food (Art. 11)' (12 May 1999) UN Doc. E/C.12/1999/5

CESCR, General Comment No. 13: The Right to Education (Art. 13) (8 December 1999) UN Doc. E/C.12/1999/10

CESCR, General Comment No. 14: The Right to the Highest Attainable Standard of Health (Art. 12) (11 August 2000) UN Doc. E/C.12/2000/4

CESCR, General Comment No. 15: The Right to Water (Arts. 11 and 12 of the Covenant) (20 January 2003) UN Doc. E/C.12/2002/11

CESCR, General Comment No. 18: The Right to Work (Art. 6)' (6 February 2006) UN Doc. E/C.12/GC/18

CESCR, General Comment No. 24 on State obligations under the International Covenant on Economic, Social and Cultural Rights in the context of business activities (10 August 2017)

CESCR, General Comment No. 3: The Nature of States Parties Obligations (Art. 2, par.1 of the Covenant)' (14 December 1990) UN Doc. E/1991/23

CESCR, General Comment No. 4: The Right to Adequate Housing (Art. 11 (1) of the Covenant (13 December 1991), UN Doc. E/1992/23

CESCR, Statement on the Obligations of States Parties regarding the Corporate Sector and Economic. Social and Cultural Rights, (2011) UN Doc E/C.12/2011/1

# Constitutive Treaties of Mixed Claims Commissions

Convention between Great Britain and the United Mexican States (signed November 19, 1926, entered into force March 8, 1928), Decisions of Claims Commissions Great-Britain-Mexico, France-Mexico, and Germany-Mexico, RIAA No. V 7

General Claims Convention of September 8. 1923 (entered into force for the USA on 4 February 1924, and for Mexico on 16 February 1924), Decisions of Claims Commissions Mexico-United States, RIAA IV

Protocol between Germany and Venezuela for the Reference of Certain Questions to the Permanent Court of Arbitration at the Hague, signed at Washington, May 7, 1903, The Venezuelan Preferential Case (Germany, Great Britain, Italy, Venezuela et al) RIAA IX 105

Protocol of an Agreement of 17 February 1903 between the Secretary of State of the United States of America and the Plenipotentiary of the Republic of Venezuela for Submission to Arbitration of All Unsettled Claims if Citizens of the United States of America against the Republic of Venezuela, Mixed Claims Commission United States-Venezuela, RIAA IX 115

Protocol of February 13, 1903, Mixed Claims Commission (Germany-Venezuela) RIAA X 359

Protocol of February 13, 1903, Mixed Claims Commission (Italy-Venezuela) RIAA X 479

Protocol of February 13, 1903, Mixed Claims Commission Great Britain-Venezuela, RIAA IX 351

# Other Conventions, International Instruments, and Related Links

'Address by World Bank President Eugene Black to the Annual Meeting of the Board of Governors' (19 September 1961), *International Centre for the Settlement of Investment Disputes (ICSID), History of the ICSID Convention,* Vol. 2 (1) ICSID History 3

'Cartagena Communique on Foreign Debt and Economic Development' (adopted by Argentina, Bolivia, Brazil, Chile, Colombia, Dominican Republic, Ecuador, Mexico, Peru, Uruguay, and Venezuela) (1984) 23 ILM 5

'Circular Instruction of the Netherland Minister of Foreign Affairs to the diplomatic representatives of the Netherlands of 7 April 1899', reprinted in *The Hague Conventions and Declarations of 1899 and 1907.*

'Convention on the Rights and Duties of States' (signed 26 December 1933, entered into force 26 December 1934) (1934) 28 (2) AJIL (Supplement: Official Documents) 75-78. At the end, 16 American countries ratified the Convention

'Convention on the Settlement of Investment Disputes between States and Nationals of Other States, Documents Concerning the Origin and the Formulation of the Convention', *International Centre for the Settlement of Investment Disputes (ICSID), History of the ICSID Convention* Vol. II, Part 1

'Convention Respecting the Limitation of the Employment of Force for the Recovery of Contract Debts' (signed 18 October 1907) reprinted in *The Hague Conventions and Declarations of 1899 and 1907.*

'Final Acts of the First and Second Hague Peace Conferences', together with the 'Draft Convention on a Judicial Court', reprinted in *The Hague Conventions and Declarations of 1899 and 1907.*

'Mexico-United States: Expropriation by Mexico of Agrarian Properties Owned by American Citizens' (1938) 32 (4) AJIL (Supplement: Official Documents 193)

'Paper Prepared by the General Counsel of the World Bank and Transmitted to the Members of the Committee of the Whole' SID/63-2 (18 February 1963) *Inter-*

© The Author(s), under exclusive license to Springer Nature Switzerland AG 2021    263
M. J. Luque Macías, *Re-Politicising International Investment Law in Latin America through the Duty to Regulate Paradigm,* European Yearbook of International Economic Law 14, https://doi.org/10.1007/978-3-030-73272-1

*national Centre for the Settlement of Investment Disputes (ICSID), History of the ICSID Convention* (1968) II-2

'Press Release No. 57 (September 9, 1964, Tokyo), Excerpt from the statement by Felix Ruiz, Governor for Chile', *International Centre for the Settlement of Investment Disputes (ICSID), History of the ICSID Convention* (1968) II-1 2

'Resolution 214 'Settlement of Investment Disputes' of the Board of Governors' (adopted 10 September 1964), *International Centre for the Settlement of Investment Disputes (ICSID), History of the ICSID Convention* (1968) II-1 2 (footnote 2)

'Resolution 214 "Settlement of Investment Disputes" of the Board of Governors' (adopted 10 September 1964), *International Centre for the Settlement of Investment Disputes (ICSID), History of the ICSID Convention* (1968) II-1

'Resolution No. 174 Study of Settlement of Investment Disputes' (adopted 18 September 1962), *International Centre for the Settlement of Investment Disputes (ICSID), History of the ICSID Convention* (1968) II-1 2

'Russian Circular Note Proposing the First Peace Conference of 24. Aug. 1898', reprinted in *The Hague Conventions and Declarations of 1899 and 1907*

'Russian Circular Note proposing the programme of the first conference of 30 December 1898', reprinted in *The Hague Conventions and Declarations of 1899 and 1907*

'U.S. Department of State Report on Nationalization, Expropriation, and Other Takings of U.S. and Certain Foreign Property since 1960' (1972) ILM 11 84

African Charter on Human and Peoples' Rights (signed 27 June 1981, entered into force 21 October 1986) OAU Doc. CAB/LEG/67/3 rev. 5 (1982) 21 ILM 58

African Charter on Human and Peoples' Rights on the Rights of Women in Africa Africa (signed 11 June 2003, entered into force 25 November 2005) Available at: https://www.reproductiverights.org/sites/default/files/documents/pub_bp_africa. pdf#:~:text=On%20November%2025%2C%202005%2C%20the%20Protocol %20on%20the,on%20Human%20and%20Peoples%E2%80%99%20Rights% 20%28the%20African%20Charter%29. Accessed 10 December 2020.

African Charter on the Rights and Welfare of the Child (adopted 1 July 1990, entered into force 29 November 1999) OAU Doc. CAB/LEG/24.9/49 (1990). Available at: https://www.refworld.org/docid/3ae6b38c18.html. Accessed 10 December 2020

Agreement of the International Bank for Reconstruction and Development (signed 22 July 1944, entered into force 27 December 1945) 2 UNTS 134

Agreement of the International Monetary Fund (signed 22 July 1944, entered into force 27 December 1945) 2 UNTS 39

Atlantic Charter (signed 14 August 1941)

Committee on the Rights of the Child, 'Considerations of Reports Submitted by States Parties under Art. 44 of the Convention on the Rights of the Child, Myanmar/Burma' (14 March 2012) UN Doc. CRC/C/MMR/CO/3-4

Convention concerning Indigenous and Tribal Peoples in Independent Countries (adopted 27 June 1989, entered into force 5 September 1991) 1650 UNTS 383

Convention for the Pacific Settlement of International Disputes 1899 (signed 29 July 1899, entered into force 4 September 1900) reprinted in *The Hague Conventions and Declarations of 1899 and 1907*

Dublin Statement on Water and Sustainable Development (1992)

Final Document of the 14th Summit Conference of Heads of State or Government of the Non-Aligned Movement, Havana, Cuba, 11-16 September 2006

General Agreement on Tariffs and Trade of 1947 (signed 30 October 1947, entered into force 1 Januar 1948) 55 UNTS 187

ICSID, Rules of Procedure for Arbitration Proceedings

ILO, Normlex, Ratifications of C169 - Indigenous and Tribal Peoples Convention, 1989 (No. 169). Available at: http://www.ilo.org/dyn/normlex/en/f?p=NORMLEXPUB:11300:0::NO::P11300_INSTRUMENT_ID:312314. Accessed 10 December 2020

Office of the High Commissioner on Human Rights (OHCHR), Status of Ratification Interactive Dashboard, International Covenant on Economic, Social and Cultural Rights, Countries <http://indicators.ohchr.org/> accessed 10 December 2020

See Instrument Establishing the Latin American Integration Association (ALADI) (August 1980). Available via SICE: http://www.sice.oas.org/trade/Montev_tr/Montev1e.asp. Accessed 10 December 2020

South American Union of Nations Constitutive Treaty (signed 23 May 2008, entered into force 11 March 2011)

Statute of the International Court of Justice UKTS 67 (1946)

The Convention on the Settlement of Investment Disputes between States and Nationals of Other States (signed 18 March 1965, entered into force 14 October 1966) 575 UNTS 159

Treaties and other international Agreements of the United States of America 257

Treaty of Amity and Commerce between Brazil and Great Britain (signed 17 August 1827) (1826-1827) 77 CTS 375

Treaty of Friendship, Commerce and Navigation between Paraguay and the Zollverein (signed 1 August 1860) (1860) 122 CTS 283

Treaty of Friendship, commerce and Navigation between the Hanseatic Cities (Bremen, Hanover, Lubeck) and Venezuela (signed 31 March 1860) (1860) 122 CTS 53

Treaty of Friendship, Navigation and Commerce between Brazil and France (signed 8, January 1826) (1825-1826) 76 CTS 59

Treaty of Peace, Amity Navigation and Commerce between Colombia and the United States (signed 3 October 1824) (1824) 74 CTS 455

Treaty of Peace, Friendship, Commerce and Navigation between the Peru-Bolivian Confederation and the United States (signed 30 November 1836) (1776-1949)

Treaty of Peace, Friendship, Navigation and Commerce between the United States and Venezuela (signed 30 January 1826) (1826-1827) 77 CTS 1

UN, Department of Economic and Social Affairs, Indigenous People, Historical Overview. Available at: https://www.un.org/development/desa/

indigenouspeoples/declaration-on-the-rights-of-indigenous-peoples/historical-overview.html. Accessed 10 December 2020.

UNCITRAL Rules on Transparency in Treaty-based Investor-State Arbitration (effective as of 1 April 2014)

United Nations Convention on Transparency in Treaty-Based Investor State Arbitration (The "Mauritius Convention on Transparency") (signed 10 December 2014, entered into force 18 October 2017)

United Nations, General Assembly, Member States (List) <http://www.un.org/en/member-states/index.html> accessed 10 December 2020

Vienna Convention on the Law of Treaties (signed 26 May 1969, entered into force 27 January 1980) 1155 UNTS 331

# Table of State Practice

## Constitutions, Laws and Others

Asamblea Nacional de la Republica del Ecuador, Comisión Especializada Permanente No. 5 de Soberanía, Integración, Relaciones Internacionales y Seguridad Integral, Informe de la Comisión sobre el "Convenio entre el Gobierno de la Republica del Ecuador y el Gobierno de la Republica de Finlandia sobre la promoción y Protección de las Inversiones", DM (18 October 2010) (Ecuador)

Constitution of Afghanistan (2003)

Constitution of Angola (2010)

Constitution of Colombia (1991, as last amended on 2005)

Constitution of Kenya (2010)

Constitution of Paraguay (1992)

Constitution of the Argentine Nation (1994)

Constitution of the Bolivarian Republic of Venezuela (1999)

Constitution of the Democratic Republic of the Congo (2006)

Constitution of the Dominican Republic (2010)

Constitution of the Kyrgyz Republic (2010)

Constitution of the Oriental Republic of Uruguay (1967, as last amended 31 October 2004)

Constitution of the Plurinational State of Bolivia (2009)

Constitution of the Republic of Ecuador (2008)

Constitution of the Republic of Guatemala (1985, as amended in 1993)

Constitution of the Republic of Nicaragua (1987, as of September 2010)

Constitution of the Republic of Panamá (1972, as last amended on 15 November 2004)

Constitution of the Seventh Republic of Niger (2010)

Constitution of the United Mexican States (2010, as of September 2017)

M. J. Luque Macías, *Re-Politicising International Investment Law in Latin America through the Duty to Regulate Paradigm*, European Yearbook of International Economic Law 14, https://doi.org/10.1007/978-3-030-73272-1

Decree 18880 (2003): Further regulating issues covered by Law 1614 (2000)
Decree Law No. 200 (2003) (Colombia)
Decree No. 118-2003, Framework Law for the Drinking Water and Sanitation Sector (Honduras)
Decree No. 1220 (2005) (Colombia)
Decree No. 4633 (2011) (Colombia)
Decree No. 955, Health Code (1988, as last amended 2008)
Decreto Legislativo 662 for the Promotion of Foreign Investment (Ley de Promoción de las Inversión Extranjera, 29 August 1991) (Peru)
Decreto No. 1247 que dicta el Reglamento para la Ejecucion de la Consulta Previa Libre e Informada en los Procesos de Licitacion y Asignacion de Areas y Bloques Hidrocarburiferos (Ecuador) (adopted 19 Julio 2012), Registro Oficial No. 759 (Separata)
Drinking Water Law (2009) (Netherlands)
Environment Canterbury (Temporary Commissioners and Improved Water Management) Act 2010 (New Zealand)
Executive Decree No. 29033 (2007) Bolivia)
Executive Decree No. 30480-MINAE Principles governing the national policy in the field of water resources management (2002) (Costa Rica)
Fiji Constitution (2013)
Flood and Water Management Act (2010) (United Kingdom)
Fundamental Law of Hungary (2011, as last amended 11 March 2013)
General Health Law 5395 (1973, as amended by Law 7600 of 2 May 1996)
General law 1614 governing the regulatory and tariff framework for the public drinking water and sanitation services for the Republic of Paraguay (2000)
General law 297 on drinking water and sanitation services (1998)
Indigenous Law No. 19253 (1993) (Chile)
Indigenous Law, Law No. 19.253 (1993) (Chile)
Law 1182 (1990) (Bolivia)
Law 142 establishing the regime for public household services (1994) (Colombia)
Law 18778, establishing a Subsidy for Payment for the Use of Drinking Water and Sewerage Services (1989, last modified 17 October 1994)
Law 3058 (2005) (Bolivia)
Law 3239 on Water Resources (2007)
Law 440 governing the suspension of concessions for the use of water (2003)
Law 7593 on the Regulating Authority for Public Services (1996, as amended on 27 December 2002) (Costa Rica)
Law 7593 on the Regulating Authority for Public Services (1996, as amended 27 December 2002)
Law governing the suspension of concession for the use of water, Law 440 (11 August 2003) (Nicaragua)
Law No. 2066 on Water and Sanitation (2000)
Law No. 49 "Ley de Promoción y Garantía de Inversiones" (1997) (Ecuador)
Law on Environmental Water Management, City of Buenos Aires (Law No. 3295) (2010) (Argentina)

Law on the right to prior consultation of indigenous and tribal peoples (2011) (Peru)
Law on Water Resources (2012) (Vietnam)
Law on Water Resources Law 3239 (2007) (Paraguay)
Law on Water Resources Management of the Kingdom of Cambodia (2007)
Ley de Prohibicion de la Mineria Metalica, Decreto No. 639 (29 March 2017) (El Salvador)
Ley de Promocion y Garantia de Inversiones (1997) (Ecuador)
Ley de Promoción y Protección de Inversiones (1999) (Venezuela)
Ley Marco para el Crecimiento de la Inversión Privada (Peru)
Ley No. 29785 del Derecho a la Consulta Previa a los Pueblos Indigenas y Originarios, Reconocido en el Convenio 169 de la Organizacion Internacional del Trabajo (OIT) (2011) (Peru)
Organic Law on Indigenous Peoples Communities (2005) (Venezuela)
Organic Law on the Provision of Potable Water (2001) (Venezuela)
Presidencia de la Republica, Decreto 1506, Registro Official No. 958 (21 May 2013) (Ecuador)
Quebec - Bill 27: An Act to Affirm the Collective Nature of Water Resources and Provide for Increased Water Resource Protection (2009) (Canada)
Republica Bolivariana de Venezuela, Ley Constitucional de Inversion Extranjera Productiva (2017) (Venezuela)
Water Act (2013) (Bangladesh)
Water Law (2009) (Afghanistan)
Water Law (January 2007) (Venezuela)
Water Law of the Distrito Federal (2003) (Mexico)
Water Resources Act (2009) (Peru)
Water Resources Act No. 29338 (2009) (Peru)
Water Resources Management Act (2009) (Tanzania)
Water Services Industry Act (Act 655) (2006) (Malaysia)
Water Supply and Sanitation Act (2009) (Tanzania)


# Domestic Courts

*Abadallah Abu Massad and others v Water Commissioner and Israel Lands Administration* (2011) (Israel)
*Beja and Others v Premier of the Western Cape and Others* (2011) (South Africa)
*City of Cape Town v Strümpher* (2012), Supreme Court of Appeal 104/2011, [2012] ZASCA 54 (South Africa)
*Comité Pro-No Construcción de la Urbanización Linda Vista, San Juan Sur de Poás c/ Ministerio de Ambiente y Energía y Otros* (2004), Corte Suprema de Justicia, Corte Suprema de Justicia 2004-01923 (Costa Rica)
*Dagoberto Bohórquez Forero c/ EAAB Empresa de Acueducto y Alcantarillado de Bogotá y Otros*, Tribunal Administrativo (Cundinamarca) (3 May 2012) 11001-33-31-003-2007-00186-01 (Colombia)

*Defensor del Pueblo de la Nación c/ Estado Nacional y Provincia del Chaco* (2007), Suprema Corte D.587.XLIII (Argentina)

*Environment & Consumer Protection Foundation v Delhi Administration and Others* (2012), Supreme Court WP (Civil) no 631 (India)

*Federation for Sustainable Environment and Others v Minister of Water Affairs and Others* (2012), High Court (North Gauteng, Pretoria) 35672/12, [2012] ZAGPPHC 128 (South Africa)

*Government of the Republic of South Africa and Others v Grootboom and Others*, Constitutional Court, 4 October 2009 (South Africa)

*Habeas Corpus Colectivo presentado por Víctor Atencio c/ el Ministerio de Gobierno y Justicia, Director General del Sistema Penitenciario* (2011), Corte Suprema de Justicia 928-09 (Panama)

*Halalt First Nation v British Columbia* (Environment) (2011) (Canada)

*Highveldridge Residents Concerned Party v Highveldridge Transitional Local Council and Others* [2002], High Court (Transvaal Provincial Division) 28521, (2002) (6) SA 66

*Ibrahim Sangor Osman v Minister of State for Provincial Administration & Internal Security eKLR* (2011) (Kenya)

*Ileana Vives Luque c/ Empresa de Servicios Públicos de Heredia* [2003], Corte Suprema de Justicia 2003-04654 (Costa Rica)

*Matsipane Mosetlhanyane and Gakenyatsiwe Matsipane v The Attorney General* (2011) (Botswana)

*Mazibuko and Others v City of Johannesburg and Others (Centre on Housing Rights and Evictions, Amicus Curiae)*, Constitutional Court of South Africa (CCT 39/09) [2009] South Africa)

*Eben Ezer Indigenous Community v/ Province of Salta – Ministry of Labor and Production*, Amparo, (30 September 2008), C. 2124. XLI

*Alejandro Papic Domínguez con Comunidad Indígena Aimara Chusmiza y Usmagama*, Supreme Court of Justice of the (Argentina) Nation, Corte Suprema (25 November 2009) (Chile)

*Asociación Civil por la Igualdad y la Justicia c/ Gobierno de la Ciudad de Buenos Aires*, Cámara de Apelaciones en lo Contencioso Administrativo y Tributario (Ciudad Autónoma de Buenos Aires) (18 July 2007) (Argentina) 70-72 <www.acij.org.ar/blog/2011/12/13/sentencia-por-aguaen-la-villa-31-bis/> accessed 10 December 2020

*Carolina Murcia Otálora c/ Empresas Públicas de Neiva ESP*, Corte Constitucional T-546/09 (6 August 2009) (Colombia) <http://www.corteconstitucional.gov.co/relatoria/2009/t-546-09.htm> accessed 10 December 2020

*Caso no 0006-10-EE* [2010] Corte Constitucional 0010-10-SEE-CC (Ecuador)

Constitutional Court of Bolivia, Judgement 0045/2006 (2 June 2006) (Bolivia)

Constitutional Court of Colombia, Judgement C-169/01 (Colombia)

*Government of the Republic of South Africa and Others v Grootboom and Others* [2000] Constitutional Court CCT11/00, [2000] ZACC 19 (South Africa)

*Hernán Galeano Díaz c/ Empresas Públicas de Medellín ESP, y Marco Gómez Otero y Otros c/ Hidropacífico SA ESP y Otros*, Corte Constitucional T-616/10,

Quinta Camara de Revision (5 August 2010) (Colombia) 107-111 <http://www.corteconstitucional.gov.co/relatoria/2010/T-616-10.htm> accessed 10 December 2020

*Jorge Hernán Gómez Ángel c/ Alcalde Municipal de Versalles – Valle del Cauca y el Gerente de la Empresa de Servicios Públicos de Versalles*, Corte Constitucional, Cuarta Camara de Revision, T-410/03 (22 May 2003) (Colombia) <http://www.corteconstitucional.gov.co/relatoria/2003/T-410-03.htm> accessed 10 December 2020

*Nequen Superior Court of Justice, TSJN, Mapuche Catalan Community and Neuquina Indigenous Confederation v Province of Neuquen*, Action on Unconstitutionality (25 October 2010) (Argentina)

Peruvian Constitutional Court, Case No. 0022-2009-PI/TC

*Quevedo, Miguel Ángel y Otros c/Aguas Cordobesas SA*, Juez Sustituta de Primera Instancia Civil y Comercial (Ciudad de Córdoba) considerando séptimo (8 de Abril 2002) (Argentina) <http://www.cedha.org.ar/docs/doc220-spa.doc> accessed 10 December 2020)

*Red de Vigilancia y Exigibilidad de los Derechos Económicos, Sociales y Culturales Región Junín c/ Municipalidad Provincial de Huancayo*, Corte Superior de Justicia1230-2005 (Junín, Peru) (2 September 2005)

# References

Abel P (2018) Counterclaims based on international human rights obligations of investors in international investment arbitration. falacies and potentials of the 2016 ICSID Urbaser v Argentina Award. Brill Open Law 1(1):61–90. https://doi.org/10.1163/23527072-00101003

Adede AO (1986) The minimum standards in a world of disparities. In: Macdonald R St J, Johnston DM (eds) The structure and process of international law: essays in legal philosophy doctrine and theory. The Hague, Martinus Nijhoff, p 1001

Akhmouch A (2002) Water governance in Latin America and the Caribbean: a multi-level approach. OECD Reg Dev Work Pap 4:29–36

Altmann P (2013) Good life as a social movement proposal for natural resource use: the indigenous movement in Ecuador. Consilience: J Sustain Dev 10(1):59–71

Anaya J (2004) Indigenous peoples in international law, 2nd edn. OUP, New York

Anaya J (2009) International human rights law and indigenous peoples. Aspen Publishers, New York

Anicama C (2008) State responsibilities to regulate and adjudicate corporate activities under the inter-American human rights system, report on the American convention on human rights. Available at: https://media.business-humanrights.org/media/documents/ef3d3a9990b249cfb7850eae75e8e88762fd2789.pdf. Accessed 10 Dec 2020

Arambulo K (1999) Strengthening the supervision of the international covenant on economic, social and cultural rights: theoretical and procedural aspects, 2nd edn. Intersentia, Antwerp

Attanasio D (2016) Extraordinary reparations, legitimacy, and the inter-American court. Univ Pa J Int Law 37:813-871. Available at: https://scholarship.law.upenn.edu/jil/vol37/iss3/1. Accessed 10 Dec 2020

Avendano Valdés J, García Belaunde D (1971) Perù. In: Lowenfeld A F (ed) Expropriation in the Americas, A comparative law study. Dunellen, New York

Avila Martel A, Salvat Maguillot M (1971) Chile. In: Lowenfeld AF (ed) Expropriation in the Americas, A comparative law study. Dunellen, New York

Bastin L (2012) The *Amicus Curiae* in investor-state arbitration. Cambridge J Int Comp Law 1 (3):208–234. https://doi.org/10.7574/cjicl.01.03.57

Benvenisti E, Downs G (2007) The empire's new clothes: political economy and the fragmentation of international law. Standford Law Rev 60:595–631

Bernaz N (2013) Enhancing corporate accountability for human rights violations: is extraterritoriality the magic potion? J Bus Ethics 117:493–511

Bértola L, Ocampo JA (2012) The economic development of Latin America since independence. OUP

Binder C (2015) Einheit oder Fragmentierung des Völkerrechts am Beispiel der Rechtsprechung des Europäischen Menschenrechtsgerichtshofs und der Investitionsschiedsgerichte. ZöR 4:737–778

Binder C (2018) The UNDRIP and interactions with international investment law. In: Hohmann J, Weller M (eds) The UN declaration on the rights of indigenous peoples: a commentary. OUP, Oxford, pp 87–114

Binder C, Hofbauer J (2016) Case study: Burlington Resources Inc. v Ecuador/Kichwa Indigenous People of Sarayaku v Ecuador (July 15, 2016). Available at: https://doi.org/10.2139/ssrn. 2810062. Accessed 10 Dec 2020

Bjorklund AK (2013) The role of counterclaims in rebalancing investment law. Lewis Clark Law Rev 17(2):461–480

Bochard EM (1915) The diplomatic protection of citizens abroad: or the law of international claims. The Banks Law Publishing, New York

Bochard E (1940) The "minimum standards" of the treatment of aliens. Mich Law Rev 38(40):445–461

Bonnitcha J (2014) Substantive protection under investment treaties: a legal and economic analysis. CUP, Cambridge

Bowett DW (1958) Estoppel before international tribunals and its relation to acquiescence. BYIL 33:176–194

Boyle FA (1999) Foundations of world order. The legalist approach to international relations, 1898–1922. Duke University Press, Durham

Brauch M. (2014) Yukos v. Russia: issues and legal reasoning behind US $50 billion awards. Investment Treaty News, September. Available at: https://www.iisd.org/itn/wp-content/ uploads/2014/09/iisd_itn_yukos_sept_2014_1.pdf. Accessed 10 Dec 2020

Burke-White W (2008) The Argentine financial crisis: state liability under BITs and the legitimacy of the ICSID system. Univ Pa Law School Inst Law Econ 8(1):199–234

Cameron P (2010) International energy investment law: the pursuit of stability. OUP, Oxford

Carrillo-Santarelli N (2020) A regional, multi-level and human-centered approach to business and human rights issues. DPCE Online 43(2):2979–2991

Centre on Housing Rights and Evictions, The Significance of Human Rights in MDG-based Policy Making on Water and Sanitation: An Application to Kenya, South Africa, Ghana, Sri Lanka and Laos (Geneva, 2009)

Centro de Informacion Judicial (2019) La Corte Suprema convalidó la constitucionalidad de la ley de preservación de los glaciares rechazando el pedido de Barrick Gold, Minera Argentina Gold y provincia de San Juan, 4 June. Available at: https://www.cij.gov.ar/nota-34763-La-Corte-Suprema-convalid%2D%2Dla-constitucionalidad-de-la-ley-de-preservaci-n-de-los-glaciares-rechazando-el-pedido-de-Barrick-Gold%2D%2DMinera-Argentina-Gold-y-provincia-de-San-Juan.html. Accessed 10 Dec 2020

Claimant's Notice of Arbitration and Statement of Claim from the Renco Group, Inc. and Doe Run Peru S.R.LTDA, to the Republic of Peru and Activos Mineros S.A.C (4 April 2011). Available via ITA Law. https://www.italaw.com/sites/default/files/case-documents/italaw3264.pdf. Accessed 10 Dec 2020

Colectivo sobre Financiamiento e Inversiones Chinas, Derechos Humanos y Ambiente (CICDHA). Evaluación de las Obligaciones Extraterritoriales de la República Popular de China desde Sociedad Civil: Casos de Argentina, Bolivia, Brasil, Ecuador y Perú. Available at: http:// chinaambienteyderechos.lat/informe-regional/. Accessed 10 Dec 2020

Cotula L, Vermeulen S, Leonard R, Keeley J (2009) Land grab or development opportunity? Agricultural investment and international land deals in africa. IIED/ FAO/ IFAD, London/ Rome. http://www.fao.org/3/a-ak241e.pdf. Accessed 10 Dec 2020

Crawford J, Nevill P (2012) Relations between international courts and tribunals: the regime problem. In: Young MA (ed) Regime interaction in international law, facing fragmentation. CUP, Cambridge, pp 235–260

Cueto-Rua J (1957) Administrative, civil and commercial contracts in Latin-American law. Fordham Law Rev 26(1):15–49

Damien C, Peterson L (2017) Analysis: In new Mercosur investment protocol, Brazil, Uruguay, Paraguay and Argentina radically pare back protections, and exclude investor-state arbitration. IIA Reporter, 4 May. Available at: https://www.iareporter.com/articles/analysis-in-new-mercosur-investment-pro-tocol-brazil-uruguay-paraguay-and-argentina-radically-pare-back-protections-and-exclude-investor-sta-te-arbitration/. Accessed 10 Dec 2020

Davison W (2016) Karuturi Challenges Ethiopia Decision to Cancel Farm Project. Bloomberg (11 January). Available at: https://www.bloomberg.com/news/articles/2016-01-11/karuturi-challenges-ethiopian-decision-to-cancel-farming-project. Accessed 10 Dec 2020

Davitti D (2012) On the meanings of international investment law and international human rights law: the alternative narrative of due diligence. Human Rights Law Rev 12 (3):421–453

Davitti D (2019) Investment and human rights in armed conflict. charting an elusive intersection. Hart, Oxford

Dawson FG (1990) The first Latin American debt crisis: the city of London and the 1822-25 Loan Bubble. Yale University Press, New Haven

De Brabandere E (2018) Human rights counterclaims in investment treaty arbitration (October 8). Grotius Centre Working Paper 078-IEL. https://ssrn.com/abstract=3264167. Accessed 10 Dec 2020

De Pauw M (2015) The Inter-American court of human rights and the interpretive method of external referencing: regional consensus v. universality. In: Haeck Y, Ruiz-Chiriboga O, Burbano Herrera C (eds) The Inter-American Court of human rights: theory and practice, present and future. Intersentia, Cambridge, pp 3–24

De Schutter O (2014) International human rights law, 2nd edn. CUP, Cambridge

De Schutter O (2016) Towards a new treaty on business and human rights. Bus Human Rights J 1 (1):41–67

Delaume GR (1986) ICSID and the transnational financial community. ICSID Rev Foreign Invest Law J 1(2):237–256

Desierto D (2018) 'From the Indigenous Peoples' Environmental Catastrophe in the Amazon to the Investors' Dispute on Denial of Justice: The Chevron v. Ecuador August 2018 PCA Arbitral Award and the Dearth of International Environmental Remedies for Private Victims' EJIL:Talk! (13 September). Available at: https://www.ejiltalk.org/from-indigenous-peoples-environmental-catastrophe-in-the-amazon-to-investors-dispute-on-denial-of-justice-the-chevron-v-ecuador-2018-pca-arbitral-award/. Accessed 10 Dec 2020

Diel-Gligor K, Hennecke R (2015) Investment in accordance with the law. In: Bungenberg M, Griebel J, Hobe S, Reinisch A (eds) International investment law: a handbook. C.H. Beck, Nomos and Hart, Baden-Baden/München/Oxford, pp 566–576

Dolzer R (2005) Fair and equitable treatment: a key standard in investment treaties. Int Lawyer 39 (1):87–106

DPLF Staff (2018) IACHR – Inputs to the questionnaire for the thematic report on business and human rights: Inter-American standards. DPLF (8 August). Available at: http://www.dplf.org/en/resources/iachr-inputs-questionnaire-thematic-report-business-and-human-rights-inter-american. Accessed 10 Dec 2020

Drago LM (1907) State loans in their relation to international policy. AJIL 1(3):692–726

Dumberry P, Dumas-Aubin D (2011–2012) How to impose human rights obligations on corporations under investment treaties? Yearb Int Invest Law Policy 4:569–600

Dupuy P, Viñuales J (2015) Human rights and investment disciplines: integration in progress. In: Bungenberg M, Griebel J, Hobe S, Reinisch A (eds) International investment law: a handbook. C.H. Beck, Nomos and Hart, Baden-Baden/München/Oxford, pp 1739–1767

Duve T (2017) In: Global legal history: a methodological approach. Oxford Handbooks Online, History of Law. https://doi.org/10.1093/oxfordhb/9780199935352.013.25

Eabre C (1998) Constitutionalising social rights. J Polit Philosophy 6(3):263–284

Errico S (2017) The American declaration on the rights of indigenous peoples. ASIL Insights (22 June). Available at: https://www.asil.org/insights/volume/21/issue/7/american-declaration-rights-indigenous-peoples#_edn17. Accessed 10 Dec 2020

Fach Gómez K (2012) Rethinking the role of amicus curiae in international investment arbitration: how to draw the line favorably for the public interest. Fordham Int Law J 35(2):510–564

Fach Gómez K (2019) Latin America. In: Krajewski M, Hoffmann R (eds) Research handbook on foreign direct investment. Edward Elgar Publishing, Cheltenham/Northampton, pp 494–522

Fach Gómez K, Titi C (2016a) UNASUR centre for the settlement of investment disputes: comments on the draft constitutive agreement. Investment Treaty News (10 August). Available at: https://www.iisd.org/itn/2016/08/10/unasur-centre-for-the-settlement-of-investment-dis putes-comments-on-the-draft-constitutive-agreement-katia-fach-gomez-catharine-titi/. Accessed 10 Dec 2020

Fach Gómez K, Titi C (eds) (2016b) Special Issue: the Latin American challenge to the current system of investor-state dispute settlement. JWIT 17(4):511–699

Fawcett P, Flinders M, Hay C, Wood M (2017) Anti-politics, depoliticization, and governance. In: Fawcett P, Flinders M, Hay C, Wood M (eds) Anti-politics, depoliticization, and governance. OUP, Oxford, pp 3–27

Feller AH (1935) The Mexican claims commissions, 1823-34: a study in the law and procedure of international tribunals. The MacMillan Company, New York

Ferrer Mac-Gregor E, Pelayo Möller C (2019a) Articulo 1. Obligacion de respetar los derechos. In: Steiner C, Fuchs MC (eds) Convencion Americana sobre derechos humanos: Comentario. Nomos, Bogota, pp 31–69

Ferrer Mac-Gregor E, Pelayo Möller C (2019b) Artículo 2. Deber de adoptar disposiciones de derecho interno. In: Steiner C, Fuchs MC (eds) Convencion Americana sobre derechos humanos: Comentario. Nomos, Bogota, pp 73–105

Fitzgibbon R (1948) The constitutions of the Americas. University of Chicago Press, Chicago

Fitzmaurice M (2013) Interpretation of human rights treaties. In: Shelton D (ed) The oxford handbook of international human rights law. OUP, Oxford, pp 739–771

Franck SD (2005) The legitimacy crisis in investment treaty arbitration: privatizing public international law through inconsistent decisions. Fordham Law Rev 73(4):1521–1625

Fry JD (2007) International human rights law in investment arbitration: evidence of international law's unity. Duke J Comp Int Law 18:77–150

Gantz DA (2003) The evolution of FTA investment provisions: from NAFTA to the United States – Chile Free Trade Agreement. Am Univ Int Law Rev 19(4):679–767

Garcia-Amador FV (1980) The proposed new international economic order: a new approach to the law governing nationalization and compensation. Univ Miami Inter-Am Law Rev 12(1):1–58

Gardbaum S (2003) The "horizontal effect" of constitutional rights. Mich Law Rev 102(3):387–459

Gaukrodger, D, Gordon K (2012) Investor-state dispute settlement: a scoping paper for the investment policy community. OECD Working Papers on International Investment. https://doi.org/10.1787/5k46b1r85j6f-en

Gazzini T (2016) The 2016 Morocco–Nigeria BIT: an important contribution to the reform of investment treaties. Investment Treaty News. 26 September. Available at: https://www.iisd.org/itn/2017/09/26/the-2016-morocco-nigeria-bit-an-important-contribution-to-the-reform-of-investment-treaties-tarcisio-gazzini/#_edn1. Accessed 10 Dec 2020

Gazzini T, Radi Y (2012) Foreign investment with a human face, with special reference to indigenous peoples' rights. In: Hofmann R, Tams C (eds) International investment law and its others. Nomos, Baden-Baden, pp 87–111

Gertz G, Janddhyala S, Poulsen L (2018) Legalization, diplomacy, and development: do investment treaties de-politicize investment disputes? World Dev 107:239–252

Giustini A (1986) Compulsory adjudication in international law: the past, the present, and prospects for the future. Fordham Int Law J 9(2):213–256

Goldberg D, Kryvoi Y, Philippov I (2019) Empirical Study: Provisional Measures in Investor-State Arbitration. British Institute of International and Comparative Law/White & Case. https://www.biicl.org/projects/2019-empirical-study-provisional-measures-in-investorstate-arbitration. Accessed 10 Dec 2020

Gonza A (2019) Articulo 21. Derecho a la propiedad privada. In: Steiner C, Fuchs MC (eds) Convencion Americana sobre derechos humanos: Comentario. Nomos, Bogota, pp 599–694

Gordillo AA (1971) Argentina. In: Lowenfeld AF (ed) Expropriation in the Americas: a comparative law study. Dunellen, New York

Grigera Naón HA (1991) Arbitration in Latin America: overcoming traditional hostility (an update). Univ Miami Int Am Law Rev 22(2/3):203–257

Gross S (2003) Inordinate chill: BITS, Non-NAFTA MITS, and host-state regulatory freedom: an Indonesian case study. Mich J Int Law 24(3):893–960

Guntrip E (2018) Private actors, public goods and responsibility for the right to water in international investment law: an analysis of Urbaser v. Argentina. Brill Open Law 1(1):37–60

Guthrie BK (2013) Beyond investment protection: an examination of the potential influence of investment treaties on domestic rule of law. N Y Univ J Int Law Law Polit 45:1151–1200

Hennebel L (2009) The Inter-American system for human rights: operation and achievements. In: de Feyter K, Gómez Isa F (eds) International human rights law in global context. University of Deusto, Bilbao, pp 805–852

Hennebel L (2011) The inter-American court of human rights: The ambassador of universalism. Spec Edn Quebec J Int Law 57:87–97

Hepburn J (2012) Analysis: Interim Measures Granted by Inter-American Commission Have Featured in Several Recent Investment Controversies. IA Reporter (14 March). Available at: https://www.iareporter.com/articles/analysis-interim-measures-granted-by-inter-american-commission-have-featured-in-several-recent-investment-controversies/. Accessed 10 Dec 2020

Hepburn J (2016) Analysis: In long-awaited Pac Rim award, tribunal finds that investor held no domestic law rights to ground alleged breaches of investment statute. IA Reporter (16 October). Available at: https://www.iareporter.com/articles/analysis-in-long-awaited-pac-rim-award-tribunal-finds-that-investor-held-no-domestic-law-rights-to-ground-alleged-breaches-of-investment-statute/. Accessed 10 Dec 2020

Hepburn J (2019) Pakistan faces hefty loss in newly-rendered ICSID award in Tethyan copper mining case; core damages exceed $4 billion, and pre-award interest adds another $1.75 billion. IA Reporter, 14 July. Available at: https://www.iareporter.com/articles/pakistan-faces-hefty-loss-in-newly-rendered-icsid-award-in-tethyan-copper-mining-case-core-damages-exceed-4-billion-and-pre-award-interest-adds-another-1-75-billion/. Accessed 10 Dec 2020

Herencia-Carrasco S (2020) Report of the IACHR on business and human rights: towards the inter-americanization of business and human rights. Rights as Usual, 24 February 24. Available at: Report of the IACHR on Business and Human Rights: towards the Inter-Americanization of Business and Human Rights | Rights as Usual. Accessed 10 Dec 2020

Hershey A (1907) The Calvo and Drago doctrines. AJIL 26(1):26–45

Hill D (2016) Colombian court bans oil, gas and mining operations in paramos. The Guardian, (21 February). Available at: https://www.theguardian.com/environment/andes-to-the-amazon/2016/feb/21/colombia-bans-oil-gas-mining-paramos. Accessed 10 Dec 2020

Hindelang S, Krajewski M (eds) (2016) Shifting paradigms in international investment law. More balanced, less isolated, increasingly diversified. OUP, Oxford

Hirsch M (2008) Interactions between investment and non-investment obligations. In: Muchlinski P, Ortino F, Schreuer C (eds) The Oxford handbook of international investment law. OUP, Oxford, pp 154–181

Ho J (2019) The creation of elusive investor responsibility. AJIL Unbound 113:10–15. https://doi.org/10.1017/aju.2018.91

Hummel W (2009) Investment rules in regional integration agreements in Latin America: the case of the Andean pact/Andean community. In: Binder C, Kriebaum U, Reinisch A, Wittich S (eds) International investment law for the 21st century: essays in honour of Christoph Schreuer. OUP, Oxford, pp 561–592

ICSID Staff (2007) Bolivia Submits a Notice under Article 71 of the ICSID Convention. ICSID Press Releases (16 May). Available at: http://icsidfiles.worldbank.org/icsid/icsid/staticfiles/Announcement3.html. Accessed 10 Dec 2020

ICSID Staff (2009) Denunciation of the ICSID Convention by Ecuador. ICSID Press Releases (9 July). Available at: https://icsid.worldbank.org/news-and-events/news-releases/denunciation-icsid-convention-ecuador. Accessed 10 Dec 2020

ICSID Staff (2012) Venezuela Submits a Notice under Article 71 of the ICSID Convention. ICSID Press Release (26 January). Available at: https://icsid.worldbank.org/news-and-events/news-releases/venezuela-submits-notice-under-article-71-icsid-convention. Accessed 10 Dec 2020

ICSID Staff (2018) Mexico Ratifies the ICSID Convention. ICSID News Release (27 July). Available at: https://icsid.worldbank.org/en/Pages/News.aspx?CID=285. Accessed 10 Dec 2020

Indlekofer M (2013) International arbitration and the permanent court of arbitration. Kluwer Law International, Augsburg

Jaskoski M (2014) Environmental licensing and conflict in Peru's mining sector: a path-dependent analysis. World Dev 64: 873–883. : https://doi.org/10.1016/j.worlddev.2014.07.010

Joseph S (2013) Law and investment law: intersections with human rights issues (August 13, 2012). In: Shelton D (ed) The Oxford handbook of human rights law. OUP, Oxford, pp 841–870

Justo J, Bohoslavsky JP (2018) Control de convencionalidad y derecho económico internacional. Fines y medios. MPIL Research Papers 31. Available at: https://poseidon01.ssrn.com/delivery. p h p ?
I D
=14506501711911902510011402507400302700807800207404005012508007403102702511106700409904302704203202270320540691210170050140311180400870590200450890811030070670050900760190730800650700810191121231161200681251160181011240030881240971010821070190970080070086&EXT=pdf&INDEX=TRUE. Accessed 10 Dec 2020

Justo JB, Boloslavsky JP (2018) Control de convencionalidad y derecho económico internacional. Fines y medios

Kalderimis D (2016) The authority of investment treaty tribunals to issue orders restraining domestic court proceedings. ICSID Rev Foreign Invest Law J 31(3):549–575

Kammerhofer J (2017) The challenges of history in international investment law: a view from legal theory. In: Schill S, Tams C, Hofmann R (eds) International investment law and history. Edward Elgar Publishing, Cheltenham/Northampton, pp 164–176

Kanalan I (2016) Horizontal effect of human rights in the era of transnational constellations: on the accountability of private actors for human rights violations. Eur Yearb Int Econ Law 7:423–460

Kaushal A (2009) Revisiting history: how the past matters for the present backlash against the foreign investment regime. Harv Int Law J 50(2):491–534

Kay C (2009) Latin American structuralist school. In: Kitchin R, Thrift N (eds) International encyclopedia of human geography, vol 6. Elsevier, Amsterdam, pp 159–164

Kingsbury B (2001) Reconciling five competing conceptual structures of indigenous peoples' claims in international and comparative law. N Y Univ J Int Law Law Polit 34(1):189–250

Kjos H (2013) Applicable law in investor-state arbitration. The interplay between national and international law. OUP, Oxford

Koch IE (2005) Dichotomies, trichotomies or waves of duties? Human Rights Law Rev 5 (1):81–103

Krajewski M (2012) International investment law and human rights: beyond general observations, towards greater differentiation. In: Hofmann R, Tams C (eds) International investment law and its others. Nomos, Baden-Baden, pp 71–78

Krajewski M (2017) Protecting the human right to water through the regulation of multinational enterprises. In: Chaisse J (ed) The regulation of the global water services market. CUP, Cambridge, pp 167–195

Krajewski M (2019) Human rights in international investment law: recent trends in arbitration and treaty-making practice. Yearb Int Invest Law Policy 2017:177–193

Krajewski M (2020) A nightmare or a noble dream? Establishing investor obligations through treaty-making and treaty-application. Bus Human Rights J 5:105–129

Kriebaum U (2007) Regulatory takings: balancing the interests of the investor and the state. JWIT 8 (5):717–744

Kriebaum U (2009) Human rights and the population of the host state in international investment arbitration. JWIT 10:653–677

Kriebaum U (2015) Expropriation. In: Bungenberg M, Griebel J, Hobe S, Reinisch A (eds) International investment law: a handbook. C.H. Beck, Nomos and Hart, Baden-Baden/München/Oxford, pp 959–1030

Kriebaum U (2018a) Evaluating social benefits and costs of investment treaties: depoliticization of investment disputes. ICSID Rev Foreign Invest Law J 33(1):14–28

Kriebaum U (2018b) Human rights and international investment law. In: Radi Y (ed) Research handbook on human rights and investment: Research handbooks in international law series. Research handbooks in international law. Edward Elgar Publishing, Cheltenham/Northampton, pp 13–40

León Bastos C, Wong Meraz VA (2015) Clausulas de apertura al derecho internacional de los derechos humanos: constituciones iberoamericanas. FORO. Revista de Ciencias Jurídicas y Sociales, Nueva Época 18 (2):93–125. https://doi.org/10.5209/rev_FORO.2015.v18.n2.51784

Lerner F (2010) The protection of foreign investment in MERCOSUR. In: Franca Filho MT, Lixinski L, Olmos Giupponi MB (eds) The law of Mercosur. Hart, Portland, pp 277–290

*Letter from Andrea J. Menaker and Rafael Llano to Acisclo Valladares Urruela and Alexander Salvador Cutz Calderón* (Notice of Intent Pursuant to the Free Trade Agreement between the Dominican Republic, Central America and the United States) (16 May 2018) Available via ITA Law. https://www.italaw.com/sites/default/files/case-documents/italaw9713.pdf. Accessed 10 Dec 2020

Letter from Pablo Fajardo, Julio Prieto and Juan Pablo Saenz (Plaintiffs' Legal Representatives Aguinda v Chevron Corp.) and Aaron Marr Page (Counsel) to Santiago Canton (Executive Secretary, Inter-American Commission on Human Rights) (9 February 2012). Available via Slide Share Net. https://www.slideshare.net/EmbajadaUsaEcu/ex-114. Accessed 10 Dec 2020

Letter from Professor David D. Caron to J Martin Wagner (Letter to NGO regards Petition to Participate as amici curiae) (29 January 2003). Available via ITA Law. http://www.italaw.com/cases/57#sthash.wwd6obSl.dpuf. Accessed 10 Dec 2020

Lévesque C (2007) Influences on the Canadian FIPA model and the US model BIT: NAFTA chapter 11 and beyond. Canadian Yearb Int Law/Annuaire canadien de droit international 44:249–298

Lipstein K (2014) The place of the calvo clause in international law. In: Feuerstein P, Heinz-Peter M (eds) Collection of essays by K Lipstein. Mohr Siebeck, Tübingen

Lixinski L (2010) Treaty interpretation by the inter-American court of human rights: expansionism at the service of the unity of international law. Eur J Int Law 21:585–604

Lopez C (2017) Struggling to take off?: The second session of intergovernmental negotiations on a treaty on business and human rights'. Bus Human Rights J 2(2):365–370. https://doi.org/10.1017/bhj.2017.15

Lopez Valdez A (1972) The Andean foreign investment code: an analysis. Georgia J Int Comp Law 7:656–668

Luque Macías MJ (2014) Current approaches to the international investment law regime in South America. Eur Yearb Int Econ Law 5:285–308

Luque Macías MJ (2016a) Inter-State investment dispute settlement in Latin America: is there space for transparency? JWIT 17:634–657

Luque Macías MJ (2016b) Reliance on alternative methods for investment protection through national laws, investment contracts, and regional institutions in Latin America. In: Hindelang S, Krajewski M (eds) Shifting paradigms in international investment law, more balanced, less isolated, increasingly diversified. OUP, Oxford, pp 291–315

Luque Macías MJ (2020) In: Framework Agreement of the Pacific Alliance, 6th June 2012, OXIO 496: Oxford International Organizations (OXIO). Available at: https://opil.ouplaw.com/view/

10.1093/law-oxio/e496.013.1/law-oxio-e496?rskey=rICTWl&result=1&prd=OXIO. Accessed 10 Dec 2020

Maggeti M, Choer Moraes H (2018) The policy-making of investment treaties in Brazil: policy learning in the context of late adoption. Learn Public Policy, 295–316

Mann FA (1981) British treaties for the promotion and protection of investments. Br Yearb Int Law 52(1):241–254

Mann H (2005) The IISD model international agreement on investment for sustainable development: an introductory note. ICSID Rev Foreign Invest Law J 20(1):85–90

Mann H, von Moltke K, Peterson L, Cosbey A (2005) international institute for sustainable development (2005) IISD model international agreement on investment for sustainable development. IISD (26 April). Available at: https://www.iisd.org/publications/iisd-model-international-agreement-investment-sustainable-development. Accessed 10 Dec 2020

Maxwell L (2014) Contestation. In: Gibbons M, Coole D, Ellis E, Ferguson K (eds) The encyclopedia of political thought. Wiley Online Library. https://doi.org/10.1002/9781118474396.wbept0207

Mbengue MM, Schacherer S (2017) The 'Africanization' of international investment law: the pan-African investment code and the reform of the international investment regime. JWIT 18 (3):414–448

McBeth A (2010) International economic actors and human rights. Routledge, New York

McCorquodale R, Simons P (2007) Responsibility beyond borders: state responsibility for extraterritorial violations by corporations of international human rights law. Mod Law Rev 70 (9):598–625

Medellin Urquiaga X (2019) Principio Pro Persona: Una Revision Critica desde el Derecho Internacional de los Derechos Humanos. Estudios Constitucionales 17(1):397–440

Meessen KM (1986) IMF Conditionality and state sovereignty. In: Dicke DD (ed) Foreign debts in the present and a new international economic order, in cooperation with the International Law Association's Committee on legal aspects of a new International Economic Order. Fribourg University Press, Fribourg, pp 117–129

Melish TJ (2008) The Inter-American commission on human rights: defending social rights through case-based petitions. In: Langford M (ed) Social rights jurisprudence: emerging trends in comparative and international law. CUP, New York, pp 339–371

Mijares V, Nolte D (2018) Regionalismo posthegemónico en crisis. ¿Por qué la Unasur se desintegra? Foreign Affairs Latinoamérica 18(3):105–112

Miles K (2013) The origins of international investment law: empire, environment and the safeguarding of capital. CUP, New York

Moloo R (2010) A comment on the clean hands doctrine in international law. Available via SSRN. https://ssrn.com/abstract=2358229. Accessed 10 Dec 2020

Montt S (2012) State liability in investment treaty arbitration. Global constitutional and administrative law in the bit generation. Hart, Oxford

Morales Antoniazzi M (2014) El nuevo paradigma de la apertura de los órdenes constitucionales: una perspectiva Sudamericana. In: Von Bogdandy A, Serna de la Garza JM (eds) Soberanía y Estado abierto en América Latina y Europa, Instituto de Investigaciones Juridicas: Instituto Iberoamericano de Derecho Constitucional and Max Planck Institut Für Ausländisches Öffentliches Recht und Völkerrecht, Mexico D.F., pp 233–282

Morgera E (2015) Benefit-sharing as a bridge between the environmental and human rights accountability of multinational corporations. In: Boer B (ed) Environmental law dimensions of human rights. OUP, Oxford, pp 37–68

Mouyal L (2018) International investment law and the right to regulate. A human rights perspective. Routledge

Muchlinski P (2017) The impact of a business and human rights treaty on investment law and arbitration. In: Deva S, Bilchitz D (eds) Building a treaty on business and human rights. CUP, Cambridge, pp 346–374

Myers DP (1914) The origin of the Hague arbitral courts. Am J Int Law 8(4):769–801

Naim M (2000) Fads and fashion in economic reforms: Washington consensus or Washington confusion? Third World Quart 21(3):505–528

Navarrete JE (1987) La deuda externa. Una perspectiva Latinoamericana. Biblioteca Joven, Fondo de Cultura Economica.

Newcombe A (2011) General exceptions in international investment agreements. In: Cordonier Segger MC, Gehring M, Newcombe A (eds) Sustainable development in world investment law. Kluwer Law International, Alphen aan den Rijn, pp 351–370

Nowrot K (2015) Obligations of investors. In: Bungenberg M, Griebel J, Hobe S, Reinisch A (eds) International investment law: a handbook. C.H. Beck, Nomos and Hart, Baden-Baden/ München/Oxford, pp 1154–1185

O'Leary T (1984) The Andean common market and the importance of effective dispute resolution procedures. Int Tax Bus Lawyer 2:101–128

Ocran TM (1988) International investment guarantee agreements and related administrative schemes. Univ Pa J Int Law 10(3):341–370

Ononaiwu C (2016) Regional investment treaty arrangements in the Caribbean: developments and implications. In: Tanzi A, Asteriti A, Polanco Lazo R, Turrini P (eds) International investment law in Latin America/Derecho internacional de las inversiones en América Latina. Problems and prospects/Problemas y perspectivas. Brill Nijhoff, Leiden/Boston, pp 468–496

Onwuamaegbu U (2005) Aguas del Tunari SA. v. Republic of Bolivia (ICSID Case No. ARB/03/2), Introductory Note. ICSID Rev Foreign Invest Law J 20(2):445–449. https://doi.org/10.1093/icsidreview/20.2.445

Pasqualucci JM (2012) The practice and procedure of the inter-American court of human rights, 2nd edn. CUP, New York

Penfield WL (1903) The Anglo-German intervention in Venezuela. N Am Law Rev 177:86–96

Pérez Olivares E, Brewer-Carias AR, Rondón de Sansó H, Polanco Martínez T (1971) Venezuela. In: Lowenfeld AF (ed) Expropriation in the Americas. A comparative law study. Dunellen, New York, pp 199–240

Perrone N, Schneiderman D (2019) International economic law's wreckage: depoliticization, inequality, precarity. In: Christodoulidis E, Dukes R, Goldoni M (eds) Research handbook on critical legal theory. Edward Elgar Publishing, Cheltenham/Northhampton, pp 446–472

Peters A (2017) The refinement of international law: from fragmentation to regime interaction and politicization. I•CON 15(3):671–704

Petersmann E, Kube V (2016) Human rights law in international investment arbitration. Asian J WTO Int Health Law Policy 11(1):65–114

Peterson E (2019) Updated: Conoco is awarded over $8.3 billion plus interest in battle with venezuela. IA Reporter, 8 March. Available at: https://www.iareporter.com/articles/breaking-conoco-is-awarded-over-15-billion-inclusive-of-interest-for-venezuela-losses/. Accessed 10 Dec 2020

Peterson L (2008) Venezuela surprises the Netherlands with termination notice for bit; this been used by many investors to "route" investments into Venezuela. IA Reporter (16 May). Available at: www.iareporter.com/articles/20091001_93. Accessed 10 Dec 2020

Polanco Lazo R, Mella R (2018) Investment arbitration and human rights cases in Latin America. In: Radi Y(ed) Research handbook on human rights and investment: research handbooks in international law series. Research handbooks in international law. Edward Elgar Publishing, Cheltenham/Northampton, pp 41–92

Pollock F (1922) The league of nations, 2nd edn. Stevens & Sons, London

Potesta M (2013) Legitimate expectations in investment treaty law: understanding the roots and limits of a controversial concept. ICSID Rev 28(1):88–122

Poulsen L (2015) Bounded rationality and economic diplomacy: the politics of investment. CUP, Cambridge

Preziosi A (1989) The Andean pact's foreign investment code decision 220: an agreement to disagree. Univ Miami Int-Am Law Rev 20(3):649–677

Radovi Ć (2018) Inherently unneutral investment treaty arbitration: the formation of decisive arguments in jurisdictional determinations. J Disp Resol 1:143–183

Ratton Sanchez M, Morosini F (2017) Navigating between resistance and conformity with the international investment regime: The Brazilian agreements on cooperation and facilitation of investments (acfis). In: Morosini F, Ratton Sanchez M (eds) Reconceptualizing international investment law from the global south. CUP, New York, pp 1–46

Reinalda B (2009) Routledge history of international organizations. From 1815 to the present day. Routledge, Abingdon

Reus-Smit C (2004) The politics of international law. In: Reus-Smit C (ed) The politics of international law. CUP, Cambridge, pp 14–44

Reuters Staff (2017) El Salvador congress approves law prohibiting metals mining. Reuters (29 March). Available at: https://www.reuters.com/article/us-el-salvador-mining-idUSKBN1702YF. Accessed 10 Dec 2020

Rivera-Pérez W (2012) What's the constitution got to do with It? Expanding the scope of constitutional rights into the private sphere. Creighton Int Comp Law J 1(3):189–214

Rodiles A (2016) The law and politics of the Pro Persona principle in Latin America. In: Aust H, Nolte G (eds) The interpretation of international law by domestic courts: uniformity, diversity, convergence. OUP, Oxford, pp 168–171

Rodríguez-Pinzón D (2013) Precautionary measures of the Inter-American commission on human rights: legal status and importance. Human Rights Brief 20(2):13–18

Rosenfeld F (2014) The trend from standards to rules in international investment law and its impact upon the interpretive power of arbitral tribunals. Proc ASIL Annual Meeting 108:191–193. https://doi.org/10.5305/procannmeetasil.108.0191

Rosenne S (2007) Counter-claims in the international court of justice revisited. In: Essays on international law and practice. Martinus Nijhoff Publishers, Leiden/Boston, pp 267–293

Ruiz-Chiriboga O (2013) The American convention and the protocol of San Salvador: two intertwined treaties: non-enforceability of economic, social and cultural rights in the Inter-American System. Neth Q Human Rights 31(2):159–186

Salacuse J (2015) The law of investment treaties, 2nd edn. OUP, Oxford

Sandri Fuentes A (2014) Negocios y derechos humanos. La responsabilidad de los Estados cuando intervienen empresas multinacionales en la violación de derechos humanos. In: Rey SA (ed) Los Derechos Humanos en el Derecho Internacional. Ministerio de Justicia y Derechos Humanos de la Nación, pp 213–228

Sarcevic P (1987) Two approaches of the debt problem: (a) Adjustment of loan agreements (De Lege Lata) (b) Strengthening of international monetary soft law (De Lege Ferenda). In: Dicke DD (ed) Foreign debts in the present and a new international economic order. Fribourg University Press, Fribourg, pp 130–156

Sarmiento MG (2016) The UNASUR centre for the settlement of investment disputes and Venezuela: will both ever see the light at the end of the tunnel? JWIT 17(4):658–680

Sattorova M (2018) The impact of investment treaty law on host states: enabling good governance? Hart, Oxford

Saul B, Kinley D, Mowbray J (2014) The international covenant on economic, social and cultural rights. Commentary, cases, and materials. OUP, Oxford

Sauvant KP, Ünüvar G (2016) Can host countries have legitimate expectations?. Columbia FDI Perspectives 183. Available at SSRN: https://ssrn.com/abstract=2844432

Schilling-Vacaflor A, Flemmer R (2015) Rohstoffabbau in Lateinamerika: Fehlende Bürgerbeteiligung schürt Konflikte. GIGA Focus Lateinamerika, 05 August. https://nbn-resolving.org/urn:nbn:de:0168-ssoar-441992

Schreuer C (2005) Calvo's grandchildren: the return of local remedies in investment arbitration. Law Pract Int Courts Tribunals 4:1–17

Schreuer C (2007) Investment protection and international relations. In: Reinisch A, Kriebaum U (eds) The law of international relations – Liber Amicorum Hanspeter Neuhold. Eleven International Publisher, Utrecht, pp 345–358

Schreuer C (2014) Jurisdiction and applicable law in investment treaty arbitration. McGill J Disp Resol 1(1):2–25

Scott GW (1908) Hague convention restricting the use of force to recover on contract claims. Am J Int Law 2(1):78–94

Scott JB (ed) (1915) The Hague conventions and declarations of 1899 and 1907. OUP, New York

Scott JB (ed) (1931) The international conferences of American States 1889–1928; A collection of the conventions, recommendations, resolutions, reports, and motions adopted by the first six international conferences of the American States, and documents relating to the organization of the conferences. OUP, New York

Seabra Fagundes M (1971) Brazil. In: Lowenfeld AF (ed) Expropriation in the Americas. A comparative law study. Dunellen, New York

Seidl-Hohenveldern I (1975) Chilean nationalization cases before German courts. Am J Int Lax 69:110–119

Sepúlveda M (2003) The nature of the obligations under the international covenant on economic, social and cultural rights. Intersentia, Antwerp

Shany Y (2012) One law to rule them all: should international courts be viewed as guardians of procedural order and legal uniformity? In: Fauchald OK, Nollkaemper A (eds) The practice of international and national courts and the (de-)fragmentation of international law. Hart, Oxford, pp 15–34

Shea DR (1955) The Calvo clause: a problem of inter-american and international law and diplomacy. University of Minnesota, Minneapolis

Shue H (1980) Basic rights. Subsistence, affluence, and US foreign policy. Princeton University Press, Princeton

Simma B (2011) Foreign investment arbitration: A place for human rights? Int Comp Law Q 60 (3):573–596

Sinclair AC, Repousis OG (2017) An overview of provisional measures in ICSID proceedings. ICSID Rev-Foreign Invest Law J 32(2):431–446

Sornarajah M (1986) The pursuit of nationalized property. Martinus Nijhoff, Dordrecht

Sornarajah M (2010) The international law on foreign investment, 3rd edn. CUP, Cambridge

Steiner HJ, Vagts DF (1986) Transnational legal problems: materials and text, 3rd edn. Foundation Press, Mineola/New York

Steininger S (2018) What's human rights got to do with it? An empirical analysis of human rights references in investment arbitration. Leiden J Int Law 31(1):33–58

Subhash CJ (1983) Nationalization of foreign property: a study in North-South dialogue. Deep & Deep Publications, New Delhi

Taillant J, Bonnitcha J (2011) International investment law and human rights. In: Cordonier Segger M, Gehring M, Newcombe A (eds) Sustainable development in world investment law. Kluwer Law International, The Hague, pp 53–80

Tamada D (2015) Provisional measures in investor-state dispute settlement: reappearance of community of investment interests? In: Hamamoto S, Sakai H, Shibata A (eds) "L'être situé". Effectiveness and purposes of international law. Essays in honour of Professor Ryuichi Ida. Brill Nijhoff, Leiden/Boston, pp 144–164

Tan C (2015) Reviving the emperor's old clothes: the good governance agenda, development and international investment law. In: Schill S, Tams C, Hofmann R (eds) International investment law and development: bridging the gap. Edward Elgar Publishing, Cheltenham/Northampton, pp 147–179

The IACHR celebrates the adoption of the American Declaration on the Rights of Indigenous Peoples (22 June 2016). Available via IACHR Press Releases. Available at: http://www.oas.org/en/iachr/media_center/PReleases/2016/082.asp. Accessed 10 Dec 2020

Thornberry P (2002) Indigenous peoples and human rights. Manchester University Press/Juris Publishing Inc, Manchester

Tienhaara K (2011) Regulatory chill and the threat of arbitration: a view from political science. In: Brown C, Miles K (eds) Evolution in investment treaty law and arbitration. CUP, Cambridge, pp 606–628

Tienhaara K (2018) Regulatory chill in a warming world: the threat to climate policy posed by investor-state dispute settlement. Transnatl Environ Law 7(2):229–250

Titi C (2014) The right to regulate in international investment law. Nomos/Hart Publishing, Baden-Baden

Trevino C (2015) South American Silver lays out $385 million case against Bolivia; government counters that UK treaty should not protect "Canadian Investment". IA Reporter (14 June). https://www.iareporter.com/articles/23275/. Accessed 10 Dec 2020

Treviño JC (1971) Mexico. In: Lowenfeld AF (ed) Expropriation in the Americas. A comparative law study. Dunellen, New York

Urueña R (2018) Después de la fragmentación: ICCAL, derechos humanos y arbitraje de inversiones (After Fragmentation: ICCAL, human rights and investment arbitration) Max Planck Institute for Comparative Public Law & International Law (MPIL) Research Paper 30. Available at: https://poseidon01.ssrn.com/delivery.php?ID=1090640311011230740260130720681070760990570860000170350670901061031120170911070091000560570250021101210521240251090850831170190220730380440320070970300640720750050660840770541040220710240920710211100980280041120980791020871010070721270222076086073004110&EXT=pdf&INDEX=TRUE. Accessed 10 Dec 2020

Van der Zee E (2013) Incorporating the OECD guidelines in international investment agreements: turning a soft law obligation into hard law?. Legal Iss Econ Integr 40(1):33–72. Available at SSRN: https://ssrn.com/abstract=2725836

Vandevelde KJ (2005) A brief history of international investment agreements. UC Davis J Int Law Policy 12(1):157–194

Vernon R (1967) Long-run trends in concession contracts. In: Proceedings of the American Society of International Law at its annual meeting (1921–1969) 61:81–89

Vierdag EW (1978) The legal nature of the rights granted by the international covenant on economic, social and cultural rights. Neth Yearb Int Law 9:69–105. https://doi.org/10.1017/S0167676800003780

Vis-Dunbar D, Peterson L (2006) Bolivian water dispute settled, bechtel forgoes compensation. Investment Treaty News (20 January). https://www.iisd.org/itn/wp-content/uploads/2010/10/itn_jan20_2006.pdf. Accessed 10 Dec 2020

von Bogdandy A, Ferrer Mac Gregor E, Morales Antoniazzi M, Piovesan F, Soley X (2017) Ius constitutionale commune en América Latina: A regional approach to transformative constitutionalism. In: von Bogdandy A, Ferrer Mac Gregor E, Morales Antoniazzi M, Piovesan F (eds) Transformative constitutionalism in Latin America. OUP, New York, pp 3–23

von Bogdandy A, Salazar Ugarte P, Morales Antoniazzi M, Ebert FC (eds) (2018) El constitucionalismo transformador en América Latina y el derecho económico internacional: de la tensión al diálogo. Universidad Nacional Autónoma de México, Instituto de Investigaciones Jurídicas; Instituto Max Planck de Derecho Público Comparado y Derecho Internacional Público, México; Heidelberg

Webb Yackee J (2014) Political risk and international investment law. Duke J Comp Int Law 24:477–500

Weiler T (2005) Methanex Corp. v. U.S.A: turning the page on NAFTA chapter eleven? JWIT 6:903–921

Williamson J (1990) Latin American adjustment. How much has happened? Institute for International Economics, Washington, DC

Williamson J (1993) Democracy and the "Washington consensus". World Dev 21(8):1329–1336

Wolfrum R (2010) General international law (Principles, Rules and Standards). In: Max Planck Encyclopedia of Public International Law (MPEPIL). Available at: https://opil.ouplaw.com/view/10.1093/law:epil/9780199231690/law-9780199231690-e1408?rskey=NWovJq&result=20&prd=MPIL

Wolfrum R (2011) Obligation of result versus obligation of conduct: some thoughts about the implementation of international obligations. In: Arsanjani MH, Cogan J, Sloane RD, Wiessner S (eds) Looking to the future. essays on international law in honor of W. Michael Reisman Martinus Nijhoff Publishers, Leiden/Boston, p 363–383

Zeyl T (2011) Charting the wrong course: The doctrine of legitimate expectations in investment treaty law. Alberta Law Rev 49(1):203–235

Printed by Printforce, the Netherlands